Sacred Communities

Studies in Central European Histories

Sacred Communities

Jewish and Christian Identities in Fifteenth-Century Germany

Dean Phillip Bell

BRILL ACADEMIC PUBLISHERS, INC.
BOSTON • LEIDEN
2001

Brill Academic Publishers, Inc.
112 Water Street, Suite 400, Boston, MA 02109 U.S.A.
Toll free: 800–962–4406
Tel: 617–263–2323
Fax: 617–263–2324
E-mail: cs@brillusa.com

©2001 by Brill Academic Publishers, Inc.

Library of Congress Cataloging-in-Publication Data

Bell, Dean Phillip, 1967–
    Sacred communities: Jewish and Christian identities in fifteenth-century Germany/
Dean Phillip Bell.
        p. cm.—(Studies in Central European histories)
    Includes bibliographical references and index.
    ISBN 0–391–04102–9
    1. Jews—Germany—History—1096–1800. 2. Germany—Ethnic relations.
3. Germany—Social conditions. 4. Christianity and culture—Germany.
5. Social history—Medieval, 500–1500. I. Title. II. Series.
DS135.G31 B45 2001
943'.004924—dc21   2001024080

Printed in the United States of America

for
Juli
*For every wondrous moment that our life together has
brought and continues to bring*

Contents

Glossary, Appendices, Bibliographies, Index

Foreword

This book has evolved over nearly a decade. As with all academic works, this one is certainly the product of numerous scholarly influences and personal events and outlooks. I must note that although my primary conclusions have not changed substantially they have gained added clarity, particularly since July 2, 1999. On that date I was shot five times by a racist and antisemitic gunman as I walked home from Shabbat services in Chicago. The event itself, traumatic as it was, as well as the subsequent reactions, forced me to realize that Jewish and Christian relations, like relations between many groups, are exceedingly complex. They involve timeless, universal elements, individual perspectives and perversions, and local contexts. The incident also forced me to see how complex the idea of community really is. I saw clearly for the first time that each individual belongs to a myriad of communities, some chosen, some assigned by others; some overlapping, others never in concert; some friendly, some built upon and expressed with enmity; some supportive in certain ways, others in very different ways. In the end, I hope that my personal record both intrudes upon the history presented and allows that history to speak for itself, to have its own life. I recognize that the very questions I ask and the arrangement that I present inherently form an individual problem, but I hope that I have not unfairly treated the subject in question.

* * *

Some material in chapters 5–7 appeared previously in Dean Phillip Bell, "Gemeinschaft, Konflikt und Wandel: Jüdische Gemeindestrukturen im Deutschland des 15. Jahrhunderts." Translated by Melanie Brunner. In *Landjudentum im deutschen Südwesten während der Frühen Neuzeit*, edited by Rolf Kießling and Sabine Ullmann. Colloquia Augustana, vol. 10 (Berlin, 1999): 157–191.

Acknowledgments

I am indebted to many individuals and organizations for the preparation and publication of this volume. I would like to recognize the assistance of the library staff at the University of California, Berkeley, University of Chicago, Northwestern University, DePaul University, and Spertus Institute of Jewish Studies. A special debt of gratitude goes to the Mellon Foundation, the Center for German and European Studies, the German Historical Institute, the History Department and Committee on Medieval Studies at the University of California, Berkeley, and to Rosaline Cohn for their support of this project. I must also acknowledge the support and engaging environment of the Institut für Europäische Kulturgeschichte in Augsburg and the Arye Maimon-Institut für Geschichte der Juden at the Universität Trier.

This work owes a great deal to many people. While it is not possible to recognize everyone who has contributed to this work and to my thinking on this subject, I would like, at the very least, to thank the following individuals. Doug Murphy, Russ Rogers, and Miriam Ben-Yoseph at DePaul University all read and commented on early drafts of the manuscript. Thanks to Byron Sherwin, Howard Sulkin, and Herman Spertus for their support and encouragement. A number of colleagues from a variety of my communities in Chicago, who I have been fortunate to call both teachers and friends, offered immeasurable assistance over the years, including Constantin Fasolt, Nathaniel Stampfer, and Yaakov Morgulis. I must thank my colleagues in late medieval and early modern German and Jewish history who have offered comments and encouragement throughout the process of creating this book: David Biale, Rolf Kießling, Alfred Haverkamp, and Michael Toch.

To Elaine Tennant and Thomas A. Brady, Jr., I owe special gratitude for the many lessons that they taught me both about history and life, the active roles they have played in the development of my family, and the care with which they have nourished me over the years. Thomas Brady poured a great deal of his expertise and time into the manuscript and continued both to encourage me and hold me accountable for creating a scholarly and accessible book. Any success that I have in that regard I owe very much to him; any faults in this work remain my own.

In the end, this work would never have been possible without the love, support, and understanding of my children, Malkaya, Chanan, and Ronia, and my wife Juli, who has stood by me in every endeavor. Juli's friendship, love, and faith make every day special. This work is dedicated to her.

Landscape View of Primary Cities Referenced

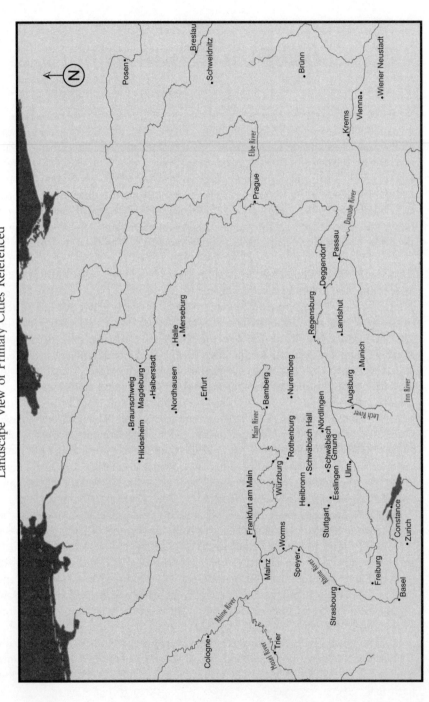

Introduction

The focus of most work on Jewish and Christian relations in the Middle Ages
has been on conflict. For Germany, much has been written about late medieval
anti-Judaism, about the great massacres of the thirteenth and fourteenth centuries, as well as the mass of expulsions, both from the cities and territories,
in the fifteenth century. Many theories, incorporating a variety of sources and
interpretative and methodological constructs, have been advanced to explain
the increasing marginalization of the Jews in late medieval Germany. Such theories and interpretations are typically rather one-sided and often anachronistic.
This book, therefore, seeks to recontextualize the world of Jewish and Christian
relations by focusing on both Jewish and Christian interaction as well as Jewish
and Christian forms of communal organization and identity. Such an emphasis
on community seems appropriate given that much of late medieval discourse
produced by both Jews and Christians revolved around and involved definitions
of community. A broader examination of community also makes it easier to
compare more general transformations that affected Jews and Christians as residents of both shared German society and their own separate communities.

The structure of this work proceeds in three phases. The first two parts offer
somewhat parallel investigations, focusing on the nature of community, the
structure of community, the role and location of authority within community,
communal conflict, as well as self-representation and the representation of the
"other," for both Christian and Jewish communities. Throughout, the "communities" discussed here are located primarily in south and central German urban
areas. The third part, or conclusion, attempts to synthesize some of the more
salient conclusions drawn in the first two parts, but also suggests further analysis, particularly through the comparison of exclusion and communal identity in
late medieval Spain and in the radical Reformation. Some of the central issues
raised throughout the book include: the question of whether and/or to what
extent changes within one religious community affected changes in the other;
the ways in which the notion of "community" may have shifted and/or remained
consistent between the middle of the fourteenth and the middle of the sixteenth centuries; and the use of representation to define authority and ones
own community. I will argue that both Jewish and Christian communities suffered something of a communal identity crisis in the later Middle Ages, but
also that the resolution of those crises by the end of the sixteenth century had
significant implications for the development of European Jewry. An obvious
consequence of this project is the questioning of traditional periodization within
both Jewish and Christian European history.

This book takes advantage of the renewed interest in Jewish history in Germany, and particularly the fruits of that interest in works such as *Germania Judaica*. This work also benefits from recent and important discussions about late medieval German history, the idea of crisis as an historical concept, and Jewish and Christian relations. Little work has appeared in English that deals extensively or systematically with the Hebrew sources, and so, in many ways, this project is also an attempt at a larger historical synthesis.

In short, in this book I argue that: Jews and Christians interacted in a variety of ways, in numerous settings, and at a multitude of levels that defy simple categorization; that there were substantial shifts in communal identity amongst both Jews and Christians in the later Middle Ages; that parallel shifts in both Jewish and Christian communities affected one another but also evolved independently and uniquely; that the Jews and the idea of the Jews were a central consideration in redefinitions within Christian and urban culture in late medieval Germany; that the categorization of late medieval Germany as a period of crisis is too simplistic; and that the "Reformation" should not be viewed as the central development in the shift between medieval and early modern times.

*   *   *

The growing interest in Jewish Studies, particularly Jewish and Christian relations, in Germany and the methodological innovations and careful sourcework in late medieval and early modern history more generally, have combined to make the study of Jewish history in late medieval and early modern Germany a burgeoning and important field. The research of a very diverse and distinguished group of scholars of varying national, historiographical, and methodological perspectives has informed this work. Recent research reveals not only the great amount of knowledge that has been gleaned and the very promising questions that have been asked in the past few years, but it also betrays the tremendous gaps in, and one-sidedness of, our current understanding and research agendas.[1]

As R. Po-chia Hsia has aptly put it, recent work in the history of Jewish and Christian relations in late medieval and early modern Germany falls into two categories. One group focuses on Hebrew and Jewish sources, emphasizing internal Jewish development; a second group works largely with German and Latin sources, focusing primarily on the theme of Christian views and treatment of Jews.

The vast majority of recent work has centered on Jewish and Christian relations, and although there are some worthwhile studies about internal Jewish developments, it has been rare to find studies that combine significant analysis of both subjects. Recent studies have, therefore, focused on one aspect of Jewish

---

[1] See *In and Out of the Ghetto: Jewish-Gentile Relations in Late Medieval and Early Modern Germany*, edited by R. Po-chia Hsia and Hartmut Lehmann, and *Judengemeinden in Schwaben im Kontext des Alten Reiches*, edited by Rolf Kießling.

and Christian relations, viz., anti-Judaism, and could therefore be grouped into two schools of thought. According to the first school, which is transhistorical, the Christian hatred of Jews and vice versa is continuous since the origins of Christianity. Christian and Jewish relations are, in essence, basically antagonistic and abnormal. Periods of relative harmony, of normal or natural relations, between the groups could and did exist, but underneath such a facade of peace there always persisted a fundamental tension—tension that could manifest itself in numerous variations—of mutual religious difference and corresponding hostility.[2]

A second school focuses more particularly on specific cultural transformations evident in religious, political or economic changes. The advantage of this line of thought is that it attempts to offer an historical context and it acknowledges a variety of historical forces. Of course, focusing on one specific theme limits the scope and overall usefulness of the interpretation.

While acknowledging the role of political and socio-economic factors, Jeremy Cohen, for example, tries to frame Jewish and Christian relations in terms of changing theological conceptions. For Cohen, the church was involved in all aspects of medieval existence and proved unwilling to oppose the anti-Jewish activity and mentality that existed in Europe—worse yet, the church fostered such antagonism and somehow veered from earlier Augustinian teaching that emphasized the continued toleration of the Jews, who would serve as witnesses to the final coming of Jesus Christ.[3] While working largely from theological sources Cohen wants to draw a broader picture of Christian perceptions of Jews. What, in part, allows Cohen to carry out this project is the very nature of the theologians whom he examines—that is, the Mendicants, those orders who had a foot in both the ecclesiastical and the secular worlds. Even so, however, Cohen has not firmly fixed the friars' perception as one that is valid for all strata of the population and in all areas of Europe. Instead, he relies too heavily on a notion of theology as the primary transforming factor in medieval history.[4] Cohen's work does, however, raise an important question to which I will turn again in the course of this investigation: to what extent did the pressure of the external, non-Jewish, environment—in theological but also social, cultural, economic, and political conditions and relations—affect the character, structure, and identity of the Jewish community itself? Conversely, one might ask how the image of the Jew fit into the self-identification and the notion of community that developed within Christian society.

R. Po-chia Hsia contends that the legends, or "social discourses," produced about Jews during the ritual murder trials of the late fifteenth and early sixteenth centuries were merely rhetorical frameworks for deeper political concerns, particularly the development of the central state. Hsia's Jews, like other

---

[2] Jacob Katz, *Exclusiveness and Tolerance*, p. 7.
[3] Jeremy Cohen, *The Friars and the Jews*, p. 14.
[4] Ibid., p. 7.

marginal groups, were simply instrumental scapegoats in an escalating confrontation between townsfolk and their noble lords.[5] The German city, in this interpretation, was a "communal Christian politic" that exploited the status of the Jews
as an alien and minority group in order to protect its freedoms and to loosen
itself from the tight grip of the landed nobility, which protected the Jews. The
entire process of anti-Jewish activity was then sanctioned by imperial privilege
allowing burghers the right to deny readmission to the Jews. In this interpretation a variety of interested political forces utilized the Jews and manipulated
trials against the Jews for grander purposes.[6]

František Graus offers an analysis along similar lines. Graus, who is concerned primarily with the pogroms in the wake of the Black Death, focuses on
what he claims is the real late medieval tension—the tension between "Stadt
und Land," between the city and the land surrounding it.[7] For Graus, as for
Hsia, authority over the Jews typically rested with the landed nobility, with its
base of authority beyond the city walls. The city council was not free to exploit
the Jews as a resource in whatever way it saw fit, but could, in the end, manip-
ulate its policies towards the Jews in order to press the landed nobility in other
matters. For Graus, attacks on Jews were directed by this central tension between
the cities and the landed nobility.[8] Graus also concedes that many different developments contributed to the increasing marginalization of the Jews. He notes,
for example, the importance of increased attacks on the taking of interest on
loans after 1350 and the religious motivations behind actions against foreigners spawned by the Hussite revolt. Graus rejects the notion of an eternal and
purely religious bias posited by the transhistorical school, maintaining instead
that the animosity toward Jews included a combination of economic, theological or structural transformations which were played out in the battle between
lords and the cities.

The observations of both Graus and Hsia raise some important questions about
the relation of the Jews to the city rulers and the landed nobility, and they
demonstrate that Jewish and Christian relations were in no way a simple matter. Particularly after the Black Death, perhaps as the role of the Jews within
the cities became less essential, and the tensions between centers of authority
more heated, the Jews found themselves in an increasingly hostile and easily
compromised position.

Both schools of thought, that I have only briefly explained, have advantages
and disadvantages. It is clear, however, that any serious study of Jewish and
Christian relations must reckon with each, because representations that Jews
and Christians use for one another are at once timeless[9] and contingent upon

---

[5] R. Po-chia Hsia, *The Myth of Ritual Murder*, p. 34.
[6] Ibid., p. 36.
[7] František Graus, *Pest-Geisler-Judenmorde*, pp. 373 and 521–523.
[8] Ibid., p. 226.
[9] Based on concepts which see, for example, Jews as the murderers of Jesus, or culled
from tractates of the Talmud against idol worshippers.

the real historical events confronted by a particular group of people.[10] Both elements, the timeless and the historical, appear together in something of a conceptual stew—at once general and specific. That some of the structure, that is the older stock representations, remains in the stew should not surprise us, for as the Italian microhistorians have worked hard to demonstrate, certain ideas have been through the European mill for a long time, even before the advent of Christianity.[11]

* * *

In the fifteenth century, numerous German territories and cities expelled their Jews,[12] though typically without physical violence. Yet these expulsions of Jews in the late fourteenth and throughout the fifteenth centuries were in many important respects quite different from the pogroms and massacres of the late thirteenth century through the Black Death.[13] Shifts in the way of dealing with Jews and new ways of conceptualizing both Jews and Christians tell us that important changes were brewing in both Christian and Jewish communities of late medieval Germany. The question of what these changes were and how they manifested themselves in Jewish and Christian representations of themselves and of each other will be the primary focus of this work.

Of all the general issues that may have affected Christian treatment of, and interaction with, Jews and which are reflected in those interactions and the discourse created about Jews, the role of religious reform and change,[14] and the significance of the elusiveness of central authority, particularly in south Germany—that is to say the power struggles for authority—have received the most attention in recent literature.

The emphasis on religious reform and central authority is in fact evident in the cases of Augsburg and Nuremberg. These two south German cities possessed different systems of government—Augsburg run by the guilds and Nuremberg by a non-guild patriciate—yet they shared similar concerns as the south German urban league to which they both belonged was shattered by the princes of Bavaria between 1449 and 1453. The urban oligarchs of these cities sought refuge from the imperial monarchy against their lordly predators. Indeed,

---

[10] For example, the new rhetoric of the Jews as enemies of the community or reinterpretations of particular Mishnaic rulings in light of recent situations.

[11] See for example Edward Muir and Guido Ruggiero, eds., *Microhistory and the Lost Peoples of Europe*.

[12] See Gerd Mentgen, *Studien zur Geschichte der Juden in mittelalterlichen Elsaß*, p. 72, regarding the increasing displacement of the Jews form the Alsatian imperial cities in the last fifth of the fifteenth century.

[13] Franz-Josef Ziwes notes that in the middle Rhine region expulsion of the Jews by the ruling authorities replaced the massacres of the Jews prevalent at the time of the Black Death. See his *Studien zur Geschichte der Juden in mittleren Rheingebiet während des hohen Mittelalters*, p. 250.

[14] See Jonathan Israel, "Germany and Its Jews: A Changing Relationship (1300–1800)."

the monarchy did eventually triumph over the princes, and yet the monarchy failed to provide good government for the south German cities.[15]

In the midst of such external political turmoil, these cities experienced significant internal upheavals and struggles for authority and communal definition in the later Middle Ages. A rabid anti-clericalism was increasingly enunciated, as clerical rights and exemptions and clerical abuses were seen as posing a threat to the commune's "moral security and reduced the sustenance that religion was obliged to lend to good government."[16] In south Germany, where bishops were not civic patriarchs, as in Italy, but rather great feudal magnates and, often, former rulers of the cities, a deepening fissure between different notions of community—religious, civic, regional, and imperial—was developing. The result, as we will see, was the restructuring of community along both civic and religious lines which redefined the relationship of religion and commune—the development of a mini "corpus Christianum," a "sacred society," which made no differentiation between material welfare and eternal salvation. Burghers came to believe that every civil institution was directly responsible for spiritual as well as merely ecclesiastical matters.[17] Some scholars have gone so far as to speak of a communalization of the church during the south German urban reform of the sixteenth century.[18] Such transformations, however, had deep and significant roots in the fifteenth century.

The German burghers' expansion and consolidation of their identity was accomplished at the expense of groups such as the Jews and the clergy, who were seen as somehow outside the community. Important shifts in late medieval theology and religion, for example, allowed urban Christians to confront questions of community and identity and in the end to turn from an emphasis on a community defined through sacraments to one revolving around a concept of moral law. In the cities the administration of the sacraments was minimized and the space occupied by clergy was being taken over by Christian burghers who began to conceive of themselves as something of a priesthood of all Christians. While all Christians became priests and the uniqueness of the clergy was stripped, the biblical heritage of the Jews was also appropriated in the formation of a new religious and communal identity.

Throughout this study I will draw together disparate threads of Christian and Jewish communal development in an effort to give a deeper understanding to the complex tapestry of Jewish and Christian interaction. Neither Jews nor Christians are shapeless substances simply molded by the other: each has an ability to shape itself and the other, each has a voice and it is necessary to listen to both. Both groups are significant even if Christianity is the religion of

---

[15] Thomas A. Brady, Jr., "In Search of the Godly City: The Domestication of Religion in the German Urban Reformation," pp. 18–21.

[16] Ibid., p. 19.

[17] Bernd Moeller, *Imperial Cities and the Reformation*, p. 46.

[18] Brady, "In Search of the Godly City," p. 20.

the majority and Judaism that of the minority. As Jacob Katz has asserted, Jewish and Christian relations are at all times multi-directional: "the relationship between Jews and Gentiles is at all times a reciprocal one. The behaviour of the former towards their neighbours is conditioned by the behaviour of the latter towards them, and vice versa."[19]

It could be argued that Jews and Christians were treated in a certain way because they were Jewish or Christian. This, however, would be only a half truth. In reality, any culture's methods of defining, talking about, and thinking through its relations with any "outsider" pivot on that culture's own preoccupations, anxieties, systems of belief, rationalizations, and needs. The representation of Jews and Christians, therefore, affords an important portal into a larger cultural universe that both affects and is affected by the way that Christians and Jews came to terms with themselves and their "others."

The marginalization and separation of Jews from Christians in German cities progressed along lines that had a long history and certainly transcended purely religious biases, political motives, or economic concerns. Many different elements came together in a fundamental late medieval attempt to create or at least to define more clearly who was to be included in and who excluded from the "community." What were the results, how did community become defined?

Community itself was a vague concept in the later Middle Ages. "Common" could refer to the "public" at the same time that it could be appropriated "to cover more abstract notions of collectivity, revealing that it was not inimical to, indeed was rather useful for, hierarchy and lordship."[20] Similarly, the boundaries separating Jews and Christians were not always clear: indeed, the very identity of people was frequently called into question—Jews were forced to wear yellow badges or other distinguishing marks, notes one city statute, in order that they might be recognized as Jews and not mistaken for pious Christians. Even the caricatures of physical form, dress, or language that were often employed to mark off the Jews could not always distinguish Jews from other marginal groups such as women, foreigners, peasants, prostitutes, criminals, lepers, priests, Turks, or particular guilds that had fallen out of favor with the municipal government or the local town chronicler. In the self-understanding constructed by burghers and patricians and the polemic they forged against one another, the same terminology that was employed to marginalize Jews and other groups was used to alienate opposing urban factions.[21] Any force that upset the attempt to craft an ordered society, in the midst of the chaos of feuds and wars, had to be expelled from the city—literally and physically.

The late medieval German city was at all times a complex entity that combined elements of Christianity, whether religious or secular, and economic and

---

[19] Katz, *Exclusiveness and Tolerance*, p. 3.

[20] Bob Scribner, "Communities and the Nature of Power," p. 292.

[21] See Reinhard Barth, *Argumentation und Selbstverständnis der Bürgeropposition der Spätmittelalters*, passim.

political associations that worked within and extended beyond the borders of
the city walls. The language of community, of "gemein" (*Gemeinde*), that is so
variable in city chronicles or almost formulaic in city legal codes of the later
Middle Ages, began to take on more solid form by the beginning of the sixteenth century and particularly during the course of the early radical Reformation,
when civic and theological ideals meshed. Attitudes towards Jews must be
understood within this changing context of community.

It is clear that Jews were both unique and yet no different from other marginal, even central groups, in German society. Hartmut Lehmann argues that
Jews were not the only ones who were discriminated against. R. Po-chia Hsia
also notes that the discourse used against Jews reflected broader problems and
could be a hidden form of political subversion, that had little to do with Jews
as Jews. Similarly, Nicoline Hortzitz argues that anti-Semitism could be a form
of social protest. Although very meaningful, such observations, if not combined
with internal Jewish history, may very easily marginalize the Jews even in the
history of *Jewish* and Christian relations.

Significant transformations within the Jewish communities—because of both
external conditions and internal forces—also affected Jewish self-definition and
Jewish interaction with Christians. After the middle of the fifteenth century,
with its widespread expulsion of Jews from a multitude of German cities, Jews
increasingly moved into small towns and villages. Given this apparent rural shift,
combined with increased geographical movement as well as lower densities of
Jewish population, Jewish self-identity was greatly transformed. Authority within,
and identification of, the community became more and more a regional phenomenon in the early modern period. J. Friedrich Battenberg asserts that the
special structures of ecclesiastical territories did have "a stabilizing effect on the
communal institutions of the Jews."[22] The territorial rabbi was even allowed
authority to decide intra-Jewish quarrels "on behalf of the territorial ruler."[23]
The practical effect of such stabilization, however, was that the Jewish communities were more closely bound to each other and more submissive to the
rule and intervention of the territorial ruler. Although not fully explicated,
the "corporate" and institutional Jewish structure was strengthened and more
closely connected to evolving absolutist authorities. Stefan Rohrbacher argues
that Swabian Jewry came to be defined during the course of the late sixteenth
and seventeenth centuries not only by a physical territory but by an organiza-
tional structure with particular customs, autonomy, and self-identity. The importance of the rural shift and the attempts to clarify and define community were
very much pressing issues even in the fifteenth century, a period of transition
between two types of Jewish communal existence, as I will discuss below.

---

[22] J. Friedrich Battenberg, "Jews in Ecclesiastical Territories of the Holy Roman Empire,"
pp. 267–268.
[23] Ibid., p. 269.

A second major transformation within the Jewish communities, the professionalization of the rabbinate, mirrored changes within the Christian urban communities. As with the increasing role of contracted preachers within the Christian cities, the professionalization of the rabbinate simultaneously standardized and weakened the authority of the chief religious figure, the rabbi. Increasingly in the fifteenth century lay leaders appropriated authority and duties that had previously fallen under the purview of the rabbis. The internal struggles within the Jewish communities between lay and rabbinic leaders and between rabbis themselves were indicative of this important change in communal structure and identity.

The internal constitution of the Jewish communities was also correspondingly complex, and an entirely new group of Jews has been uncovered and offered for research. Michael Toch[24] writes that although Jews were very much involved in money-lending, the typical stereotype of Jews as money-handlers and wealthy is not at all typical or reflective of the range and diversity of Jewish social stratification and professional occupation. Toch notes the increasing marginalization of Jewish money-lending throughout the fourteenth century. Toch tried to show that only a handful of Jews were very wealthy and privileged, but instead he discovered a large number of middling and poorer Jews with an extensive list of diverse professions. This new emphasis on the varying social and economic levels within the Jewish communities allows a number of scholars to focus on the polarization of Jewish society and internal class structure, particularly during times of internal conflict. Given the professional diversity he outlines, Toch argues that the numerous internal conflicts in the Jewish communities, particularly over taxation and symbols of social status, leave unanswered questions about the "internal Jewish solidarity in an increasingly hostile environment."

Jewish communal structure, conflict, and identity were shaped as much by external developments as were Jewish relations with the Christian world. Recent scholarship suggests that Jews and Christians interacted much more frequently, at more diverse levels, and more productively than was once thought. Jewish culture was not a culture of the ghetto: rather, Jews took part in the ruling cultural norms and gave external ideas a Jewish meaning. Jews may also have played an important part in the overall urban political system. Jewish and Christian political relationships at times transcended mere toleration, exclusion, and autonomy. Interaction between Jews and Christians was, therefore, not only economic but also theological in nature.

METHOD AND SOURCES
The range of sources employed here is very broad and covers a period in which Jews were slowly and increasingly being squeezed out of the urban community.

---

[24] Michael Toch, "Zur wirtschaftlichen Lage und Tätigkeit der Juden im deutschen Sprachraum des Spätmittelalters."

In many cities a few Jews were readmitted soon after the great massacres of 1348 and 1349. Many Jewish communities experienced new growth, though suffering some decline during the period of great imperial taxation, particularly the special taxes levied on the Jews, during the last three decades of the fourteenth century. Throughout the fifteenth century, however, the Jewish population in many German cities began to decrease. The fourth decade of the fifteenth century, particularly in the wake of the decisions rendered at the Council of Basel in 1434, renewed and intensified legislation which set Jews apart from the civic commune, for example, by requiring Jews to wear distinguishing marks on their clothing. By the middle of the century many Jewish communities in Germany had been expelled from the cities. Of course, there may have been internal reasons as well for the decline within the Jewish communities.

Given the complex nature of Jewish and Christian history during the later Middle Ages as well as the broad range of sources available for understanding this history, my historical method throughout this book has been very consciously comparative and synthetic. At the same time I have made efforts to focus on the language used in the (primary) sources, and the relations between what are typically viewed as "cause" and "effect." After all, history is in many ways a construct, depending on the word choice and compartmentalization of the historian. Not only are our words important, so is the language that contemporaries used, whether consciously or unconsciously. What was meant by certain expressions in the later Middle Ages? Do we find shifts in meaning, clarification, or obfuscation in the same works or in the products of different authors? On the other hand, I have tried to remember that we often find causation where we look for it, and that causation, particularly when comparing two cultures that share geographical boundaries—and to some extent certain cultural, social, and religious traditions as well—in many ways begs a question that leads us down irrelevant roads. Of course causation makes it easier for us to understand, but such "understanding" is largely illusory, disappearing after serious investigation. As Jonathan Culler has noted in his work *On Deconstruction: Theory and Criticism after Structuralism*:

> Causality is a basic principle of our universe. We could not live or think as we do without taking for granted that one event causes another, that causes produce effects. The principle of causality asserts the logical and temporal priority of cause to effect. But, Nietzsche argues in the fragments of *The Will to Power*, this concept of causal structure is not something given as such but rather the product of a precise tropological or rhetorical operation, a *chronologische Umdrehung* or chronological reversal. Suppose one feels a pain. This causes one to look for a cause and spying, perhaps, a pin, one posits the link and reverses the perceptual or phenomenal order, *pain . . . pin*, to produce a causal sequence, *pin . . . pain*. 'The fragment of the outside world of which we become conscious comes after the effect that has been produced on us and is projected *a posteriori* as its 'cause.' In the phenomenalism of the 'inner world' we invert the chronology of cause and effect. The basic

fact of 'inner experience' is that the cause gets imagined after the effect has occurred.' The causal scheme is produced by a metonymy or metalepsis (substitution of cause for effect); it is not an indubitable foundation but the product of a tropological operation.[25]

I do not completely agree with this interpretation. Causation has a significant role even in the scenario outlined; however, that we do not always know the relation of cause and effect, and that we try to find cause where we see "effect" is suggestive, particularly as we begin to explore Jewish and Christian communal identities. Can Jews and Jewish developments "cause" changes within Christian society, even though the Jews represent a very small minority within Europe? On the other hand, is it conceivable that transformations within Judaism or Jewish community are the result of a single cause, that is, the influence of an increasingly hostile environment?

The sources that I have employed to explore Jewish and Christian relations and representations and to understand the struggle to define community in the later Middle Ages run the gamut from Christian theology to the rather more local accounts of city chronicles, lawbooks, and statutes, and include the major German rabbinic responsa of the fifteenth century. Such a wide range of sources is necessary because communities were multifaceted: in this case not only Christian or Jewish, but also German, urban, local and regional.

The accounts presented in this book are drawn from a number of different genres, including the main chronicles of two south German cities—Augsburg and Nuremberg. There are also comparisons with other town chronicles, for example those of Strasbourg. In Augsburg, the earliest chronicle is an anonymous account that covers the period from 1368 until 1406. It is culled largely from city documents and presents its information in rather juristic terminology.[26] The next chronicle is that of Erhard Wahraus[27] (b. before 1409), whose family members, originally from Eichstädt, became important merchants in Augsburg. The *Chronicle from the Founding of the City Augsburg until the Year 1469*[28] was written sometime after 1469 by an unknown author, but it borrows heavily from Sigmund Meisterlin's *Chronographia Augustensium* of 1456, although it is more local in nature, and it shares a number of similarities with the account of Hektor Mülich (b. 1410–20, d. 1489/90), especially regarding Augsburg politics.[29] Hektor Mülich himself offers a detailed account from fifteenth-century Augsburg. Mülich was from a very prominent Augsburg family and he served on the city council and spent time in particularly important civic positions,

---

[25] Jonathan Culler, *On Deconstruction*, pp. 86–87.

[26] *Chronik von 1368 bis 1406 (1447)*, in *Die Chroniken der deutsche Städte* (CdS from here on), vol. 4, here at pp. 5–6. I will refer to this chronicle elsewhere as *Chronicle from 1368 until 1406*.

[27] *Chronik der Erhard Wahraus 1126–1445 (1462)*, in CdS, vol. 4.

[28] *Chronik von der Gründung der Stadt Augsburg bis zum Jahre 1469*, in CdS, vol. 4.

[29] *Chronik des Hektor Mülich 1348–1487*, in CdS, vol. 22.

attaining at one point the position of Baumeister, a position of importance just below that of burgomaster. Mülich was particularly expert in politics and he weathered difficult relations between the emperor and the city as well as the disturbance following the exile of the Augsburg burgomaster Ulrich Schwartz in 1478. First married to Ottilia Könzelmann, a member of one of the oldest and most respected Augsburg families, Mülich later wed Anna Fugger, a sister of the famous Jakob Fugger. The most detailed chronicle for Augsburg and for the history of the Jews in the city is that of the merchant Burkhard Zink[30] (b. 1396/97). Zink's chronicle differs from the early Augsburg chronicles, which do not even mention the expulsion of the Jews, and the later chronicles, which reproduce passages of his chronicle, or offer only concise reports. Clemens Sender[31] (1475-ca. 1536) is the last of the Augsburg chroniclers referred to in this study. Not only is Sender chronologically separated from the others, but his perspective also differed. A monk, Sender spent much of his life in the old and renowned Benedictine monastery St. Ulrich and Afra in Augsburg, although he maintained friendly relations with the Fuggers, one of the chief ruling families in the city.

In Nuremberg the chronicler Ulman Stromer (1329–1407) was from one of the most powerful merchant families in the city.[32] Indeed, his mother was the daughter of the Schultheiß Heinrich Geusmid. Sigmund Meisterlin (1400/10-ca. 1489) is distinguished as the first chronicler in Nuremberg to present a history of that city from its earliest times.[33] Meisterlin had spent sixteen years in the Benedictine monastery in Augsburg, where he gained his theological training and a familiarity with the Latin classics. The rest of his life was spent in clerical positions—in 1476 he was the preacher at the cathedral church in Würzburg, and by 1481 he was a priest in the diocese of Würzburg.

The Strasbourg chronicler Fritsche (Friedrich) Closener (fl. 1360s) was a priest from a noble family, and his chronicle, which dates from 1362, is perhaps the oldest chronicle in German focusing on a specific town.[34] Jacob Twinger von Königshofen (1346–1420), also a priest, was the author of the best known and perhaps most important of the Strasbourg chronicles.[35]

All of the known chroniclers in this study were guild or council leaders or clerics with connections to the important mercantile families in their respective cities. Most were wealthy and were often personally associated with one another. Many of the chronicles employed here were written some time after

---

[30] *Chronik des Burkhard Zinks 1368–1468*, in CdS, vol. 5.
[31] *Die Chronik von Clemens Sender von den ältesten Zeiten der Stadt bis zum Jahre 1536*, in CdS, vol. 23.
[32] *Ulman Stromer's 'puchel von meim geslechet und von abentewr,' 1349 bis 1407*, in CdS, vol. 10.
[33] *Sigmund Meisterlin's Chronik der Reichstadt Nürnberg. 1488*; Latin text, *Nieronbergensis cronica*, both in CdS, vol. 3.
[34] *Fritsche (Friedrich) Closener's Chronik. 1362*, in CdS, vol. 8.
[35] *Chronik des Jacob Twinger von Königshofen*, in CdS, vols. 8 and 9.

the Jews were expelled from the cities. Certainly the chroniclers could have had first-hand experience of the expulsions, but the subject of the Jews was for them largely an historical construction: a manipulation of a world-view that had very little to do with Jews themselves.

I also examine a number of *Fastnachtspiele*, Shrovetide plays, for example, those written by Hans Rosenplüt (ca. 1400–1460) and Hans Folz (ca. 1440–1513), two important Nuremberg playwrights. Rosenplüt almost certainly was not originally from Nuremberg, but he lived there from at least 1426, when his name is first recorded in city documents as a master artisan. Rosenplüt probably lived in a suburb of Nuremberg as a day laborer until he was able to pay for the rights of a burgher.[36] Folz was most likely born in Worms, but by 1459 he also had assumed the privileges of a burgher in Nuremberg. By 1498 he was listed as a master artisan. Folz had ties to members of the ruling oligarchy in Nuremberg, but he was also able to offer his works to a wide spectrum of the urban community.[37]

The political climate in Nuremberg in the later Middle Ages was different than that in many other south German cities. Unlike in Augsburg, for example, the great guild movement was crushed in Nuremberg by a swift patrician city council before it got off the ground. From the middle of the fourteenth century on, guilds were forbidden in Nuremberg. With a number of small concessions, the ruling oligarchy in the city was able to construct and control the crafts workers[38] through an elaborate system of offices, servants, and ordinances.[39] The *Fastnachtspiele* that I examine here reflect the political tensions in the city, and the roles ascribed to, as well as the portrayals of, the Jews by these authors and will help us better to understand the late medieval commune in Germany. In addition to the *Fastnachtspiele*, I also refer to a number of anonymous *Volkslieder*, folksongs, in order to contextualize and deepen our understanding of the representations in the *Fastnachtspiele*.

The *Fastnachtspiele* examined here fall into three major categories regarding the Jews. First is the group of plays that treat the Jews primarily theologically. These plays often take the form of debates between Jews and Christians or between the Synagogue and the Church, and they tend to focus on such topics as the Messiah, baptism, the prefiguration of the New Testament in the Old, or the alleged anti-Christian and heretical contents of the Jewish Talmud. These plays represent the Jews as being in league with the Devil or the Antichrist. In these types of plays Jews are preached against and to. Often in fact the entire discussion proceeds from "Jewish sources"—the Old Testament or the prophets accepted in the Jewish canon. Jews are variously described in the plays as blind,

---

[36] Jörn Reichel, *Der Spruchdichter Hans Rosenplüt*, p. 125.
[37] Edith Wenzel, *"Do worden die Judden alle geschant:" Rolle und Funktion der Juden in spätmittelalterlichen Spielen*, pp. 264–265.
[38] Reichel, *Der Spruchdichter Hans Rosenplüt*, p. 108.
[39] Ibid., p. 111.

false, blasphemous, or heretical, or they are compared to or lumped with pagans. A second category of plays focuses primarily on the role of the Jew as money-lender and usurer. Hans Folz's play *Die jüdische Wucher* is a particularly vivid and energetic attack on the Jews. Such accounts dwell on the wealth of the Jews, who are contrasted with the poor Christians whom they continually suck dry, on the supposed laziness of the Jews, and on the destruction of the city economy and morale brought on by the Jews' business. The playwrights are quick to point out that the interest-mongering of the Jews affects all levels of society: rich and poor, lay and spiritual. An additional category of literature revolves around evil or devious acts supposedly committed by the Jews: host desecration, murder, and ritual murder. Here the carnival plays are sometimes supplemented by folksongs that record the massacre of the Jews in Deggendorf, the murder of Simon of Trent, and the reasons for the expulsions of the Jews from Rothenburg ob der Tauber, Passau, and Regensburg. The language used to describe Jews in these types of plays varies from that of the first group. Here Jews are typically labeled as evil or criminal, or they are portrayed as thieves, poisoners, or bloodthirsty hounds.

Yet all three of the categories within this literature contribute to a common thread of discourse and a common image of the Jew as the subverter of the commune and the common good. In most plays the Jews are directly opposed to the "common city" (*gemeine Stadt*). Jews are described as enemies of Christians and in league with people or practices foreign to the city. Jewish activities, beliefs, and space are separate from the urban community. The Jewish quarter, synagogue, cemetery, and houses are all presented as places of secret Jewish meetings and plots. For their alleged machinations against the community, Jews in these plays are imprisoned, expelled from the city, or burned. In order to gain a better sense of the characterization of the Jews presented in the *Fastnachtspiele* and *Volkslieder* I also compare the treatment of Jews with the treatment of other groups vilified in these works.

How should such plays be interpreted? According to one line of thought, certain civic fears were projected onto particular outsider groups through the plays,[40] but the plays also have a rather more creative power. By combining images and terms, the authors and performers of these plays established connections between different "outsider" groups in ways that reflect the community's unconscious concern with particular forms of behavior and ways of defining itself. Not only who is excluded, but the ways in which they are excluded tell us a great deal about how a society attempts to define itself: "What is socially peripheral is often symbolically central, and if we ignore or minimize inversion and other forms of cultural negation, we often fail to understand the dynamics of symbolic processes generally."[41] What is filthy or disgusting or asymmet-

---

[40] F.R.H. DuBoulay, *Germany in the Late Middle Ages*, p. 156.
[41] Peter Stallybrass and Allon White, *The Politics and Poetics of Transgression*, p. 20.

rical with "clean" society, the ideal imagined community, is separated out. However, such filth also reveals that to which the community is most sensitive and by what it is most challenged. The attempt to bring the outsider into conformity with the community is an attempt to convince the members of that community that, on whatever level, the ideals of the imagined community are the highest and should be the most sought after. The Other must be transformed into the Same, it must be converted and "civilized." The grotesque body of the outsider is contrasted with the classical body of the community ideal, or, I should say, the ideal of a particular part in the community—it must be absorbed and healed. According to one recent interpretation of carnival which also applies to the *Fastnachtspiele*:

> Repugnance and fascination are the twin poles of the process in which political imperative to reject and eliminate the debasing 'low' conflicts powerfully and unpredictably with a desire for this other.[42]

What exactly is meant by "desire" here is not entirely clear, but it does have echoes in recent "political" work on theories of nationalism and the relationship of the community to the Other. According to Ernst Gellner, for example, it is in the interest of the ruling body, or state, to protect the minority outsider groups: it is precisely these groups that are easy to victimize. However, as nationalism takes root, ruling authorities have more interest in depriving minorities of their economic monopolies. The visibility of the minorities and their possessions makes their dispossession and persecution an important means of buying off discontent in the wider population. According to Gellner "the national 'development' requires precisely that everyone should move in the direction which was once open only to a minority and stigmatized group."[43] If this is the case, in our examination of the fifteenth-century German cities we can say that the issues particularly relevant to Jewish and Christian relations were undergoing serious change: the lending of money, for example, was becoming a more widely Christian practice, and many scholars have argued that the Jews were quickly being squeezed out of the last profession that had been open to them. One might even argue that the religious space that Jews, as well as clergy, had occupied was more and more being taken over by the Christian burghers as they shaped their own communal and religious identities. Such inversions were surely significant in preparing the way for the sweeping changes that were ushered in by the Reformation only a half-century later.

Peter Stallybrass and Allon White have argued along very literary lines that the patterns evident in carnival discourse demonstrate psychological and symbolic interdependencies between central and marginal groups:

> A recurrent pattern emerges: the 'top' attempts to reject and eliminate the 'bottom' for reasons of prestige and status, only to discover, not only that it

---

[42] Ibid., pp. 4–5.
[43] Ernst Gellner, *Nations and Nationalism*, p. 106.

is in some way frequently dependent upon that low-Other . . ., but also that
the top *includes* that low symbolically, as a primary eroticized constituent of
its own fantasy life. The result is a mobile, conflictual fusion of power, fear
and desire in the construction of subjectivity: a psychological dependence upon
precisely those Others which are being rigorously opposed and excluded at
the social level. It is for this reason that what is *socially* peripheral is so frequently *symbolically* central . . .[44]

And yet the interrelationship between these groups extends beyond a merely
formulaic mental interface: real, day-to-day dependencies, desires, and concerns can be seen in these types of discourse as well. Significantly, however,
the "low-Other" plays a very significant role in the formation of the identity
and culture of the "top" or dominant culture.

In addition to chronicles and plays, I have also considered a number of theological works, starting with three major theologians, Augustine, Isidore of
Seville, and Hugh of St. Victor. Much of the early medieval thought regarding
the distinctions between circumcision and baptism, and between the Old and
the New Testaments is summarized and revised by Peter Lombard. After giving an account of the first three distinctions of Book IV of his *Sentences* I
examine the shifting assessments of the two Laws, particularly in the exegesis
of the scholastics and later nominalists. I focus primarily on their discussions
and reassessments of circumcision and baptism, and consider how these reassessments affected the Jews in the German cities. The discussion of these sacraments, that is the inter-penetration of Jewish and Christian religious culture
and the supposed evolution from the former to the latter, reveals the significant
place that Judaism, and by extrapolation Jews, both historical and contemporary, played within Christian theological developments.

On the other hand, I also examine Jewish notions of community and representations of Christians, particularly in rabbinic responsa, disputations, and
other legal writings. Many of these writings are based on particular decisions
and discussions in the Talmud, on the decisions of later rabbis, or larger, and
more systematic legal collections such as Maimonides' (1135–1204) *Mishneh Torah*
or the *Arba'ah Turim* of the Tur (Rabbi Jacob Baal HaTurim, 1275–1340).

Responsa were written answers by particularly learned scholars to written questions regarding legal (and so also religious) issues.[45] Often the inquirer as well
as the respondent "do not know" the answer to the question posed. Instead,
the respondent brings forth a number of various interpretations of issues relevant to the particular problem. The respondent then either gives a ruling on
the issue or leaves the information in front of the inquirer for his final evaluation.

While responsa could treat nearly any topic, and they present interesting por-
tals into German Jewish life of the time, their impact depended on the promi-

---

[44] Stallybrass and White, *Politics and Poetics of Transgression*, p. 5.
[45] A recent treatment of the responsa literature can be found in Peter J. Haas,
Responsa: Literary History of a Rabbinic Genre.

nence of the respondent, and, generally speaking, they could not be enforced on the community, outside of the sway held by the rabbi. The responsa were merely opinions and not court decisions. We must be careful, therefore, in assuming that all Jews thought in the same way, or that the responsa represent a more general attitude towards community or Christians and relations with them. Most historians hold that the Jews of five centuries ago were much more religiously observant and unified in community than could ever be the case today. Still, it is worth keeping in mind that, even in the responsa, there exist many cases of conversion, of people going to Christian courts, of disputes among Jews, as well as external pressures from the outside world upon the community. With these precautions in mind, however, we may still learn a great deal from the chief Jewish voices that remain from that period. Anyone who reads through the rabbinic responsa, certainly, cannot help but feel the great excitement that Irving Agus notes in his introduction to the responsa of one of the most important German rabbis of the Middle Ages, Rabbi Meir of Rothenburg (ca. 1215–1293). Agus writes:

> The Responsa of R. Meir, therefore, being so closely linked with his own activities and bound up with the struggles of many individuals and communities, constitute an invaluable source of information on the cultural, social, economic, and political life of the Jews of Germany immediately before their complete subjugation. The Responsa of a great Rabbi, a leader of his generation, however, do not form merely a collection of highly valuable historical documents, or a mine of various bits of information of greater or lesser importance, but are rather the very embodiment of the spirit of the age, the product of the interplay of dynamic forces—social, religious, cultural, and economic—which mold and fashion the group-life of a people. A Responsum, therefore, is not merely a mirror of life; it is also an integral part of life itself, and cannot be fully comprehended and correctly evaluated without a clear understanding of the life that created it.[46]

Responsa do not only reflect contemporary developments, nor do they merely dig up old answers to new questions, they can also transform existing notions, existing relations, and existing frameworks of behavior. Peter Haas has recently argued that responsa, through their very language and literary structure, can create a world of meaning and control the production of community norms of behavior. Significantly for the arguments of this book, Haas asserts that there is an important shift in the responsa of the late medieval and early modern period. He notes further that such a shift has serious implications for community as well:

> Responsa are not written in the vernacular of the addressee, but in the arcane, academic, and holy language of the rabbis. This choice of language

---

[46] Irving A. Agus, *Rabbi Meir of Rothenburg: His Life and his Works as Sources for the Religious, Legal, and Social History of the Jews of Germany in the Thirteenth Century,* pp. xi–xii.

not only stresses the communal nature of the generic responsa readership, but turns the legal and moral discourse of responsa into a technical exercise in which only certain people—basically the educated elite—are able truly to engage.

This choice of language has a complementary effect. While it restricts readership on the synchronic plane, it increases readership on the diachronic plane. It ensures that rabbis at all times and in all places will have access to the literature. At the same time, the language links the discourse of responsa linguistically to all other rabbinic literature, and to Torah itself. This in turn further defines in a certain way the writer/reader relationship. The responsum emerges as a kind of revelation given by holy men in the holy language of Scripture. For these reasons, as I shall point out in due course, the shift to vernacular languages in modern responsa is of major consequence.[47]

The rabbinic responsa from which I draw most heavily are those of Rabbi Jacob Weil. Weil was a student of the Maharil, Rabbi Jacob Molin, in Mainz. Weil, born in Mainz between 1380 and 1390, was the son of a rabbi.[48] He lived for a time in Nuremberg, where he was given permission to establish a yeshivah, or talmudic academy, although one already existed in the city.[49] In Nuremberg he seems to have married, but we next find him as the leading rabbi in Augsburg.[50] When the Jews were expelled from that city (the official expulsion decree was issued in 1438 for two years later, in 1440), he made his way to Bamberg, and finally by 1443 to Erfurt, the seat of a large and thriving Jewish community. There he remained until his death in 1456, just two years before the Jews were expelled from that city as well. In both Augsburg and Erfurt, Weil taught a number of students who then became important rabbis themselves, including Rabbi Joseph ben Moses, author of Leket Yosher, Rabbi Abraham of Katzenellenbogen, Rabbi Moses Mintz, and Rabbi Isaac Segal.[51]

To a selection of Weil's responsa I will compare the writings of other contemporary scholars as well as the decisions handed down by earlier and even more well known authorities such as Maimonides (Rambam), Meir of Rothenburg (215–1293), and Hayyim Eliezer ben Isaac Or Zarua (fl. fourteenth century). I will also examine the issues raised by the responsa of Rabbi Jacob Molin, Maharil (1365–1427), Rabbi Joseph Colon (1410 or 1420–1480), Rabbi Israel Bruna of Regensburg (1400–1480), Rabbi Moses Mintz (c. 1415–c. 1485), and Rabbi Israel Isserlein (c. 1390–1460).

---

[47] Haas, *Responsa*, pp. 59–60.

[48] See Israel Yuval, *Scholars in Their Time: The Religious Leadership of German Jewry in the Late Middle Ages* [Hebrew].

[49] He chose not to start one, as he explains in his decision concerning a similar issue in Regensburg; see his responsum number 131.

[50] Where he replaced a relative of the Maharil. Bernard Rosensweig claims that he arrived in Augsburg in 1412, though, as Israel Yuval has shown, it seems more likely that he did not arrive until the early 1420s.

[51] Bernard Rosensweig, *Ashkenazic Jewry in Transition*, here at pp. 15–16.

Rabbi Joseph Colon was born in Chambery, France, and could trace his lineage back to the great Jewish exegete Rashi. Colon was one of the most outstanding rabbis of his age, the foremost Italian talmudist and one of the legal authorities most often consulted by the Jews of southern Germany and northern Italy. Colon was something of a wanderer, living in Mainz, where he may have studied with the Maharil, and serving as rabbi in Mantua, Pieve di Sacco, Mestre, and Bologna. He died in Padua around 1480.

Rabbi Israel Bruna was born in Germany and studied under Weil, Isserlein, Rabbi David Schweidnitz, Rabbi Meir Kohen and Rabbi Zalman Katz of Nuremberg. He served as rabbi in Brünn, Moravia until around 1446. He next traveled to Regensburg, where he was involved in a heated battle with Rabbi Anshel. His difficulties were not limited to relations with other rabbis. He was also imprisoned in 1456 for thirteen days by Emperor Frederick III, because he refused to excommunicate correligionists who would not give a third of their wealth as a coronation tax. He was again imprisoned in 1474 and sentenced to death on accusations of ritual murder, until a Christian confessed to the crime of murder. Still, Bruna was only freed after he agreed to renounce claims to compensation for the injustice that had been done to him. After this last episode he moved to Prague, where he later died.

Rabbi Moses Mintz, a cousin of Rabbi Judah Mintz of Padua, was a student of Rabbi Zalman Katz, the rabbi of Nuremberg famous for his work on the laws of divorce, between 1430 and 1431 and 1441 and 1442. He learned with Rabbi David Tevel Sprinz, Rabbi Yonah, author of *HaIssur veHeter*, and Rabbi Israel Bruna amongst others at the yeshivah of Jacob Weil. He also studied with Rabbi Israel Isserlein (between 1456 and 1457 and 1459 and 1460), and Rabbi Zalman Yaant of Italy, though we do not know when he crossed over into Italy. Mintz served as rabbi in Würzburg, Mainz, Landau, Ulm, and Bamberg. Mintz left Würzburg after the expulsion of the Jews from that city in 1450, after which he moved on to Mainz. He left Mainz in 1462 after persecutions against the Jews and made his way to Landau, then Ulm (1464), Bamberg (1469), Nuremberg (1473) and finally to Posen (1474), one of the first great rabbis to settle there. It is unclear whether or not he died on the way to Israel, but certainly he had entertained the notion of moving there. His best known pupil was Joseph ben Moses.

Rabbi Israel Isserlein studied under his uncle, Rabbi Aaron Blümlein (c. 1360–1421) of Wiener Neustadt. After the 1421 massacre of the Jews there, which took the lives of his mother and uncle, he moved first to Italy and then to Marburg. In 1445 he returned to Wiener Neustadt and established a yeshivah. His main work, *Terumas HaDeshen*, contains 354 parts, almost halakhic essays, based on actual questions and recast into responsa form.

There are other forms of Jewish "literature" available as well, such as polemical literature and Hebrew chronicles. In this book I refer to the polemical *Sefer Nizzahon* (book of polemic). There are actually three works by the name *Sefer Nizzahon*. The first is *Sefer Nizzachon Yoshon* (or *Nizzahon Vetus* [NV from here on] according to David Berger's rendering). This anonymous work has been dated to the late thirteenth or early fourteenth century[52] and seems to draw largely from two earlier sources. In many cases, however, the NV was drawn from a stock of polemical traditions.[53]

The *Sefer Nizzahon* of Rabbi Yom Tov Lipman Mühlhausen was composed shortly after the beginning of the fifteenth century in Prague.[54] Both Mühlhausen's and the earlier work were first published in the seventeenth century. Both works cover many of the same topics, though the order of presentation is different. In addition, Mühlhausen's approach is rather more direct and at times less rationalistic than a later *Nizzahon* of Isaac Troki. Mühlhausen was an important rabbinic scholar, originally from Alsace, who made his way to Prague, certainly in time for the great Edict of 1389. In 1407 he was appointed "Judex Judaeorum," judge of the Jews in Prague. Mühlhausen traveled throughout Bavaria, Austria, Bohemia, and Poland, and between 1440 and 1450 he headed the council at Erfurt. He was a student of Rabbi Meir ben Barukh ha-Levi, Rabbi Sar Shalom of Neustadt, Rabbi Samson ben Eleazer, and of the brothers Rabbis Menahem and Avigdor Kara. Mühlhausen was a great authority on law and a kabbalist. He corresponded at length with Jacob Molin and Jacob Weil.

Both polemical works that I examine here go through biblical quotations (Old and New Testaments), picking passages that Christians generally interpret to prefigure the coming of Jesus or Christian rituals. They give the Christian argument and then show, based on a clear reading of the context or through juxtaposing statements in the Old and the New Testaments, that Christian comments are not tenable. Naturally, both works spend a great deal of time on the Trinity, the conception of Jesus, the alleged abrogation of the Old Law in the New Law, and the Christian sacraments. Both works aim to give the Jew an armory of information with which to fight off Christian polemic.

Finally, I refer to a number of Hebrew chronicles, but most notably the work of Joseph ben Gershon of Rosheim (ca. 1478–1554). Joseph, better known as Josel or Joselmann of Rosheim, has been much studied for over a century. In the late nineteenth century his story was portrayed in a semi-fictionalized rendering of his life[55] and the scope of his actions was detailed in an important study that carefully scoured the archives in France and Germany[56] and in a number of articles that appeared in the *Revue des Études Juives* and the *Zeitschrift*

---

[52] David Berger, *The Jewish-Christian Debate in the High Middle Ages*, here at p. 33.

[53] Ibid., p. 37.

[54] In 1400, according to J.D. Eisenstein, *Ozar Wikuhim*, here at p. 236; in 1390, according to *Encyclopedia Judaica*, under the article "Muehlhausen," col. 501; and in 1410, according to Hayyim Hillel Ben-Sasson (*Trial and Achievement*, p. 273).

[55] Markus Lehmann. *Rabbi Joselmann von Rosheim: Eine historische Erzählung aus der Zeit der Reformation.*

[56] Ludwid, Feilchenfeld. *Rabbi Josel von Rosheim: Ein Beitrag zur Geschichte der Juden in Deutschland im Reformationszeitalter.*

für die Geschichte der Juden in Deutschland.[57] In the late 1950s the impressive image of Joseph was reinforced by Selma Stern who described Joseph as the "commander of Jewry in the Holy Roman Empire of the German nation."[58] Stern saw in Joseph an important reformer of German Jewry in the period of transition between medieval and modern culture, noting that "Josel led his brethren back to the wellsprings of their history so that they might gain a new awareness of their origins and of the Covenant which God had made with His people."[59] For Stern, writing in the after years of the Shoah and the birth of Israel, Joseph's life and experiences truly represented a modern Jewish hero—one who was critical of the moral and social norms of his people at the same time that he battled for their rights among their Christian neighbors. Stern concluded that, "it may be said also of Josel's political life-work that it was destroyed by forces which are present today, even as they were in the past."[60] More recent studies of Joseph have continued to emphasize the diversity, extent, and import of Joseph's activities, though in no particularly systematic ways, with essentially no new information, and little analysis of his writings.

Little is known about Joseph's place of birth (perhaps Hagenau), though we do know that he spent his adolescence in Mittelbergheim. Mittelbergheim was a village 32 km southwest of Strasbourg that belonged to the bishops of Strasbourg and the lords of Andlau. A number of difficult episodes haunted the Jews of Mittelbergheim in the early sixteenth century. During the course of the war for the Landshut succession the Jewish homes in Mittelbergheim were plundered, and in 1514 eight Jews were held in prison for six weeks on charges having to do either with finances or accusations of host desecration. The Jews were released after their innocence was proven, but by the end of that same year Bishop Wilhelm III von Hohenstein (1506–1541) and the lords of Andlau secured an imperial privilege to have the Jews expelled from the village by the end of May, 1515. Probably as a consequence of the ever increasingly hostile environment, Joseph moved, in 1514, to the nearby imperial city of Rosheim, a member of the Decapolis.[61] In Rosheim Joseph would fight against frequent attempts by the Rosheim city council to expel the Jews. Even before his move to Rosheim, however, Joseph became involved in communal politics and around 1510 was elected the "caretaker in the service of the communities" by the Jews of Lower Alsace. Throughout his career he was involved in matters on an imperial scale and particularly engaged in events in and around

---

[57] Isadore Kracauer, "Rabbi Joselmann de Rosheim," and "Proces der R. Joselmann contre la ville de Colmar;" Elie Scheid, "Joselmann de Rosheim;" Moritz Stern, "Joselmann von Rosheim und seine Nachkommen."

[58] Selma Stern, *Josel of Rosheim: Commander of Jewry in the Holy Roman Empire of the German Nation.*

[59] Ibid., p. xviii.

[60] Ibid., p. xx.

[61] *Germania Judaica* (GJ, hereafter), vol. 3 (1350–1519), pt. 2, pp. 876–877.

Strasbourg. According to a recent study of his *Chronicle*, Joseph addressed six main concerns throughout his career: securing privileges for Jews; preventing expulsions from territories, cities, and villages; preventing the prohibition against Jews taking interest on loans; defending Jews against false accusations of ritual murder, trafficking in stolen goods, and charging excessive interest; opposing leaders of the Reformation and particularly vehement Jewish apostates such as Johannes Pfefferkorn and Anthonius Margaritha; and offering aid to Jews in times of crisis, such as the Peasants' Revolt and the Schmalkaldic War.[62] Indeed, Joseph was not merely a witness, but he and his family experienced many of the tribulations of his age that befell the Jews. He himself debated Margaritha; he fought against the expulsion of the Jews from a number of the places in which he lived;[63] and his father was forced to flee Endingen because of the blood libel accusations that took the lives of three of his father's brothers. But his actions had a deeper communal aspect as well and he frequently chastised the Jews themselves in an effort to lead them to better conduct.[64]

Little is known about Joseph's educational background, though he seems to have come from a distinguished line of scholars. He was the grandson of Eliyahu Ba'al-Shem, rabbi of Worms and author of a commentary on the *Zohar* and a relative of Jacob Jehiel Loanz, the personal physician to Emperor Frederick III.[65] It is likely that he studied with the scholar Johanan Luria[66] (to whom he may have been related), who directed a yeshivah in Alsace (Hagenau).[67]

Joseph's writings can be divided into four major categories. Foremost is his *Sefer ha-Miknah*, which was edited for a modern edition in 1970. The *Sefer ha-Miknah* is an incomplete fragment, the first book of which recounts the travesties facing the Jewish communities in Germany. The second book of the *Sefer ha-Miknah* is a collection of disparate comments woven together with a nearly word for word copying of large portions of the fifteenth-century Spanish philosopher Abraham ben Shem Tov Bibago's work *Derekh Emunah*.[68] Joseph also authored a *Chronicle*, consisting of 29 sections; a "Letter of Consolation" to the Jews of Hesse against the anti-Jewish writings of Martin Bucer; as well as a number of shorter documents available in the archives. The bulk of these last documents have been published by Ludwig Feilchenfeld.

[62] See the lengthy introduction in Joseph of Rosheim, *Sefer ha-Miknah*, edited by Hava Fraenkel-Goldschmidt.
[63] For Rosheim, for example, see sections 2 and 9 of *Joseph of Rosheim: Historical Writings* [Hebrew], edited by Hava Fraenkel-Goldschmidt.
[64] See, for example, his letter of promises to the Strasbourg city council in Ibid.
[65] Stern, *Josel of Rosheim*, p. 2.
[66] Ibid., p. 11.
[67] Ibid., p. 18; GJ, vol. 3, pt. 2, p. 1250. Fritz Reuter suggests the yeshivah existed for about three and a half years in the middle of the 1470s before the Swiss attack in Alsace (GJ, vol. 3, pt. 2, p. 1680). Luria seems to have ended his life in poverty in or near Worms.
[68] See Fraenkel-Goldschmidt, *Sefer ha-Miknah*; and *Encyclopedia Judaica* (EJ, hereafter), vol. 4, cc. 811–812.

Throughout this book I have brought together very divergent sources not often taken together, with the hope that these very different, but equally important, sources will inform one another and offer a fuller picture of Jewish and Christian notions of each other and themselves than has been possible to this point.

1

Between Community and Crisis: The Late Medieval Urban Landscape in Germany

COMMUNITY

The subject of this chapter is the transformation of communal identity in the later Middle Ages, but more specifically of urban communal identities. But community, at any level, is a complex concept, and it is difficult to discuss "community" as an overarching entity to which individuals belong.[1] Perhaps it is better to suggest that individuals belong to a number of communities simultaneously, some which overlap—at times leading to conflict—and others which appear never to intersect; in either case, however, the combination of individual communal relations and identities forms unique individual and group identities and relations. Community even in this context, therefore, is difficult to maintain as a strictly urban phenomenon. Instead, what interests us here is how various communal associations and relations were played out in what was largely an urban arena. The notion of community developed in the eighteenth and nineteenth centuries, predicated upon the opposition of country and city, is no longer tenable.[2] The foci of this chapter are, accordingly, the notions of community, the development of urban areas, and the transformation of both in the later Middle Ages.

In a recent and provocative book, David Nirenberg discusses the persecution of minorities in the fourteenth-century Crown of Aragon, and argues that there was a constructive, indeed necessary, relationship between conflict and

---

[1] Similar assessments have been offered for England. See Sheila Lindenbaum, "Ceremony and Oligarchy: The London Midsummer Watch," in *City and Spectacle in Medieval Europe*, edited by Barbara A. Hanawalt and Kathryn L. Reyerson (Minneapolis, 1994 (second printing, 1999)): 171–188, here at p. 172.

[2] C.J. Calhoun, "Community: Toward a Variable Conceptualization for Comparative Research," pp. 105–106. See also Miri Rubin, "Small Groups: Identity and Solidarity in the Late Middle Ages," pp. 132–134.

coexistence, between violence and tolerance, and that everyday violence maintained minority-majority relations. Nirenberg further notes that violence draws
meaning from coexistence and is not in opposition to it.[3] In describing violent
rituals against Jews, Nirenberg asserts that such rituals functioned to reiterate
a discourse legitimating the presence of Jews in Christian society, even as they
challenged it.[4] Nirenberg's assessment is intriguing for what it says about violence and ritual and for its contextual reading of Jewish and Christian relations. It is also intriguing for what it seems to presuppose, viz., that community
is a broad canvas upon which very different images and colors interact. Though
Jews were a persecuted minority in western Europe, and Christians the majority, both formed part of a larger community, and both were defined, included,
and excluded, through a certain shared discourse. This is not to suggest that
Jews and Christians shared communal discourse at every level and in every aspect
of life; nonetheless, the discourse that they did share, the areas in which they
overlapped, indicate that community is a mosaic of relationships and the description of such relationships.

Otto Brunner had previously taken a rather different view of the question
of enmity in relations between groups or individuals. For Brunner, peace or friendship was a central sociological category. Brunner noted that in the Middle
Ages, the concept of "Friede" (peace) was related to the concepts of "Freund"
(friend) and "frei" (free).[5] For Brunner, therefore, disturbance of the peace—
the feud was central in his analysis—represented enmity (to either individuals
or the collectivity). Medieval legislation required the burgher to swear an oath
of fidelity; that is, membership required an obligation to be friendly to the
community. In exchange, the burgher was "free" as a member of the commune
of the town corporation.[6] Although the axis of distinction for Brunner was
friendship/enmity, he did recognize that the discourse of community in the
Middle Ages took into account both. In a certain sense, then, Brunner's concept also assumed that acts of enmity also helped to crystallize communal identity; though in this case through exclusion, not inclusion.

There has been a long history to the discussion of medieval community,[7] especially since the 1960s. One thing that is clear is that community is a multivalent concept. Lyndal Roper has noted in regard to the Augsburg chronicles
of the Reformation period that "community" is not simply a concept which can
be generalized, rather it is a term which different speakers appropriate in different ways.[8] For Bob Scribner, as for Roper, community was a complex entity.

---

[3] David Nirenberg, *Communities of Violence*, pp. 7–11 and 242–243.
[4] Ibid., p. 15.
[5] Otto Brunner, *Land and Lordship*, p. 18.
[6] Ibid., pp. 288f.
[7] See the informative discussion in Otto Gerhard Oexle, "Kulturwissenschaftliche
Reflexionen über soziale Gruppen in der mittelalterlichen Gesellschaft: Tönnies, Simmel,
Durkheim und Max Weber."
[8] See Lyndal Roper, "'The common man,' 'the common good,' 'common women':
Gender and Meaning in the German Reformation Commune."

In both the villages and towns, Scribner argues, the idea of community could represent a wide range of concepts from the "public" to more narrowly defined groups such as the assembly or council. While reshaping or redefining community might challenge existing structures and relationships, community itself could be utilized to exclude particular groups, such as the clergy, particular guilds, or the Jews, and so simultaneously reinforce hierarchy and lordship.

The idea of community was not simply religious, social, or political. The convergence of many different elements helped to give rise to unique combinations and manifestations of community at different times and in different forms. Community was, of course, not created or defined, even at multiple levels, as a collection of members alone: rather, community was a dynamic entity composed of various and changing relationships. According to recent social anthropology there are essentially "three orders of communal bonds: those based on familiarity, specific obligations and diffuse obligations."[9] For David Sabean community is a matter of mediation and reciprocities that cannot be analyzed apart from "Herrschaft." Sabean notes that "in some respects there are as many communities as there are mediated relationships."[10] For Sabean, then, community is multi-layered and structured over time; it changes in time and can only be understood within the context of historical process. For Sabean, community is more about shared discourse, "in which alternative strategies, misunderstandings, conflicting goals and values are threshed out," more than it is about any shared values or common understanding.[11] For our purposes, one further observation by Sabean is of significance, viz., that relations between individuals within and beyond a given community affect the dynamics and processes within the given community itself: "in so far as the individuals in a community may all be caught up in different webs of connection to the outside, no one is bounded in his relations by the community, and boundedness is not helpful in describing what community is."[12]

To add a deeper dimension to the discussion, let me posit these observations about community within a more theoretical framework. In any given construct, or community, the interaction between two or more agents takes place within a particular context or *habitus*, to borrow the language of Pierre Bourdieu; yet such interaction is not entirely formed by the *habitus* itself. That is to say, that a complete description of any communal transaction must account for a broader relation between the *habitus*, as a socially constituted system of cognitive and motivating structures, as well as the socially structured situation in which the agents' interests are defined. Although *habitus* is itself in part the product of history, it can also produce individual and collective practices, and hence produce history. Further, through the interaction of agents, who presumably

---

[9] Calhoun, "Community," p. 117.
[10] David Sabean, *Power in the Blood*, p. 28.
[11] Ibid., p. 29.
[12] Ibid.

incorporate different levels and combinations of communal affiliations, the *habitus*, or community, can itself be reshaped.[13] Simply stated, communal interaction makes sense and is informed by the confluence of a variety of particular conditions and individual or multiple historical contexts. In fact, one might argue that *habitus* is itself recreated in each unique exchange of interaction between agents. The nature of community changes, in this scheme, with each incident.

CITY

Historians frequently speak of the urbanization and commercialization of Europe in the high Middle Ages. Throughout Europe the number of towns increased dramatically much as the role of existing towns expanded. The number of town foundations in central Europe increased steadily after the beginning of the thirteenth century, hitting a high water mark around 1300 (well over 200 new foundings) and then leveling off until the beginning of the fifteenth century, when the number fell off more perceptibly.[14] According to DuBoulay, the number of German towns increased ten-fold in the thirteenth century.[15] Isenmann, following Heinz Stoob, isolates four major epochs in the medieval development of the city (his later epochs run into the early modern and modern periods). In the first phase, until 1150, we find the "mother city," the typical "city" in medieval Europe; between 1150 and 1250 the period of the great foundation cities of the older type; 1250 to 1300 the period of the small cities; and 1300 to 1450 the period of the minor cities.[16] By the end of the Middle Ages there may have been 4,000 cities, the majority (around 2,800, according to DuBoulay), really only "settlements" with fewer than five hundred inhabitants (Isenmann notes that around 94.5% of the cities had populations under 2,000)—such large villages attained city status via central regional functions in trade and production. More than 200 cities (5%) had populations between 2,000 and 10,000; those with between 2,000 and 5,000 included Essen, Ravensburg, Memmingen, and Kiel, while those with between 5,000 and 10,000 included Nördlingen, Esslingen, Schaffhausen, Constance, Basel, Mainz, Freiburg im Breisgau, and Frankfurt am Main. Roughly 15 (16 according to Isenmann) big cities had more than 10,000 inhabitants, including Würzburg, Ulm, Augsburg, Braunschweig, Lüneburg, Erfurt, Hamburg, Stralsund, Rostock, Breslau, and Bremen. Nine cities had populations over 20,000, including Lübeck, Danzig, Hamburg, Strasbourg, Metz, Nuremberg, Augsburg (later), Vienna, Prague, Lübeck, Magdeburg, and Danzig. Cologne, the largest, may have had between 30,000

---

[13] Though not applied to community in this way by Bourdieu, the application suggests itself. See his *Outline of a Theory of Practice*, pp. 73, 76, 82, and 84. See also Calhoun, "Community," p. 106. See also p. 109, where Calhoun argues that community is variable, and that we should not consider individual and community as polar opposites.

[14] Norman Pounds, *An Economic History*, p. 100.

[15] F.R.H. DuBoulay, *Germany in the Later Middle Ages*, p. 115.

[16] Eberhard Isenmann, *Die deutsche Stadt im Spätmittelalter*, p. 27.

(Schubert) and 40,000 (Isenmann) inhabitants at the end of the Middle Ages.[17]

Put in a different perspective, in 1459 Nördlingen had 5,295 inhabitants, including 80 clerics (mostly monks), and eight Jews. In 1430 Nuremberg was home to around 22,800 people, but its population had increased by 1450 to 30,131 people, because of a large influx of people from the countryside (9,912 "Bauern") who fled into the city. Of the 20,219 inhabitants, not including the "farmers," there were: 6,238 women, 5,228 men (1,800 without citizens' rights), 446 clerics, and 150 Jews. The population of Nuremberg continued to rise during the course of the fifteenth century. In 1485, according to the chronicler Sigmund Meisterlin, there were 36,000 inhabitants in the city (although the *Yearbook* for 1483 reports 40,000). Population growth was significant in many cities. In Ulm in 1400 there were 9,000 inhabitants; in 1450, 13,000; in 1500, 17,000; and in 1550, 19,000. Augsburg exploded from between 15,000 and 18,000 inhabitants near the end of the fifteenth century and to 35,000 by 1530. The extent, size and location of the German towns suggests that in the south and west towns served a 40 to 50 square mile region, in central Germany 60 to 85 square miles, and in the "colonial east" 100 to 175 square miles.[18]

Given the old German proverb, "Stadtluft macht frei" ("city air makes free"), it is obvious that the medieval city was viewed as a place of freedom and privilege, but it was also part of a larger structure that involved complex relationships with the countryside, territories, princes, and other cities. Such relationships could be strengthened through trade and production, the sharing of resources, including protection, as well as more strictly cultural traditions or religious connections. Local population development could derive from areas in close proximity to the city or from a broader, more regional base. In Trier, for example, the origin names of people in the 1363 and 1364 tax list suggest that 50% came from within a 30 km radius of the city.[19] Similarly in Frankfurt, most new citizens came to the city from within a 50 km radius. Even the movement of Jews, whether voluntary or forced, from one city to another reflects this regional interrelation, as we will discuss later.

A prince or the emperor formally endowed a city by the grant of a charter. The grant was given because the city could be a valuable asset. Its inhabitants could serve as a source of tremendous income and quick capital. The city itself was often centrally located, and could therefore serve as an important center of administration and communication. It was also at times a point of defense within a territory. The very building structures and topography of the city, which could be well planned, reflected many of the central functions that the city provided. The Jews, as active participants in trade and commerce, were often located along the main streets of the city and typically in the heart of

---

[17] Ernst Schubert, *Einführung in die deutsche Geschichte im Spätmittelalter*, p. 97.

[18] DuBoulay, *Germany in the Later Middle Ages*, p. 119.

[19] Friedhelm Burgard, "Auseinandersetzungen zwischen Stadtgemeinde und Erzbischof (1307–1500)," in Alfred Haverkamp, ed., *Trier: 2000 Jahre*, p. 376.

the city near the marketplace, where the church and city administrative center were also located. The city was surrounded by a wall with towers, and the
progressive expansion of many cities is visible in the extension of the area
enclosed by the walls.[20]

At the same time that the city was a useful tool to its lord, the inhabitants
of the city also demanded special privileges and rights, and a great degree of
autonomy. Inhabitants within a city could form a very cohesive group, joined
together by legal privileges, a degree of social mobility, daily interactions, shared
common customs or values, and drawn together in defense of their autonomy
against outside forces. Legal privileges were often granted to the cities by the
emperor, as in Augsburg (1156), Hagenau (1164), Bremen (1186), Hamburg
(1189), Nuremberg (1219), or Vienna (1237). Similarly, princes could also grant
such legal privileges to cities, as in Brussels (1229), Landshut (1279), or Eisenach
(1283).[21] The city was simultaneously a place of freedom and activity, a legal
entity with inherent structures and external connections and obligations, and
a commune in a variety of ways, glorified by Henri Pirenne, who argued that
in all of the cities, "the burghers formed a corps, a *universitas*, a *communitas*, a
communio, all the members of which, conjointly answerable to one another,
constituted the inseparable parts." For Pirenne, the city was not "a simple collection of individuals; it was itself an individual, but a collective individual, a
legal person."[22] Fritz Rörig similarly saw the medieval German town as a corporation that "could act in its own right and thus bind itself legally by letter
and seal."[23] Of course, Pirenne's and Rörig's legal individual places a great deal
of emphasis on the legal and corporate nature of the city, rather at the expense
of alternate ways of viewing communal identity and the relationships of individuals within and beyond the collectivity.

Some social historians have, in fact, questioned the collective nature of the
city. Erich Maschke noted that a polarization of the social structure of the
German city was developing more intensely at the very end of the Middle
Ages. Capital became ever more concentrated in the hands of a few, and even
the notions of work and poverty began to shift.[24] According to Isenmann, there
were three, not always distinct, social groups within the German cities. At the
highest level was the upper class consisting of urban and knightly patricians or
the merchant elite (including long distance traders, and financiers), followed
by great non-patrician merchants from more recently important merchant fam-

---

[20] For a detailed description of city structures, see Isenmann, *Die deutsche Stadt im
Spätmittelalter*, pp. 41–60.
[21] Armin Wolf, "Die Gesetzgebung der entstehenden Territorialstaaten," in Helmut
Coing, ed., *Handbuch der Quellen und Literatur der neueren europäischen Privatsrechtsgeschichte*,
pp. 606–607.
[22] Henri Pirenne, *Medieval Cities*, pp. 180–181.
[23] Fritz Rörig, *The Medieval Town*, p. 12.
[24] Erich Maschke, "Deutsche Städte am Ausgang des Mittelalters," pp. 14 and 17.

ilies and certain qualified craftsmen (such as goldsmiths and jewelers), and city lawyers. The middle class contained three levels: the middle range of merchants and businessmen, city scribes and notaries, pharmacists, doctors, and artists; the small merchants and shopkeepers, independent master craftsmen, and middling civil servants. The lower middle class was comprised of piece workers and associate craftsmen. Isenmann's reckoning of the lower class includes servants, lower civil servants, day-workers, women without assets, the poor and beggars, the ill, those with dishonorable professions, and other marginal groups.[25]

Within the city an elite—a network of significant families of varying backgrounds—constituting a patriciate, often controlled and at times monopolized city politics.[26] Such patrician families may have maintained their influence longer than their equals in other parts of Europe—at least up to three or four generations in some cases[27]—eventually succumbing to economic reversals, intrigues of marriage and relationship, and general urban demographic instability. In late medieval Strasbourg, the patriciate consisted of episcopal ministeriales, immigrants from the rural nobility, and mercantile families.[28] This patriciate could both compete with and share a common political front with a mercantile aristocracy of guilds.[29] In fact, Thomas Brady has argued that in Strasbourg "the patriciate's renewed strength and prestige depended on two, quite different developments: the steady social pressure of wealthy guildsmen who wanted to become patricians; and the political rehabilitation of the patriciate through its military role in the wars of the mid- and late-fifteenth century.[30]

With the increase in the importance of trade, the older revulsion against the merchant classes was lifted, and the merchant himself could be viewed as the representative of a noble way of life to be emulated.[31] At Nuremberg, for example, merchant families monopolized the city council. The patriciate was long established and the artisan rebellions of the mid-fourteenth century had long been put to rest (by the emperor in 1349). The autonomy of the city had been strengthened as early as the thirteenth century, when it became evident that the power of imperial officials within the city was on the decline, though never thrown off. In fact, the imperial connection in Nuremberg remained of great significance throughout the Middle Ages. Nuremberg was never an episcopal city. It was, however, an imperial city, and its inhabitants refused to take up arms against the emperor. Indeed, the city often served as the site of empire-

---

[25] Isenmann, *Die deutsche Stadt im Spätmittelalter*, p. 254.

[26] DuBoulay, *Germany in the Later Middle Ages*, p. 142; see also Rörig, *The Medieval Town*, p. 123. For an extensive look at the patriciate, see Isenmann, *Die deutsche Stadt im Spätmittelalter*, pp. 269–283.

[27] DuBoulay, *Germany in the Later Middle Ages*, pp. 144–145; See Steven Rowan, "Urban Communities: Rulers and Ruled," p. 209.

[28] Thomas A. Brady, Jr., *Ruling Class*, p. 56.

[29] Ibid., pp. 94 and 96.

[30] Ibid., p. 58.

[31] See Rörig, *The Medieval Town*, p. 126.

wide meetings. Its very autonomy depended on its relationship with the empire. The demise of the empire would have meant the victory of the territorial state and the end of the city's cherished autonomy. The city had been an important area of industry (with an important metal industry) and commerce, and in the later Middle Ages it was known especially as a financial capital.

Unlike in Nuremberg, in Strasbourg, as in Basel and Ulm, guildsmen, representing a broad range of merchants and artisans, gained and continued to hold a great deal of power beginning in the fourteenth century.[32] The guilds themselves have recently been described alternately as political constituencies, units of the urban militia, instruments of social control, religious fraternities, political associations, and drinking societies.[33] Even within the guilds there was no shortage of hierarchy: between guilds representing particular professions or within the same guilds.

In addition to the patricians, there were citizens, non-citizens (including the poor and women), journeymen and apprentices, marginal groups (such as servants), outsiders (such as Jews), and those possessing ecclesiastical and feudal immunities (particularly among the ecclesiastical and charitable institutions). The underprivileged groups could represent a large portion of the city. Of the people obligated in the 1475 surcharge tax in Augsburg, 107 (2.4%) were beggars and 151 (3.4%) were day laborers. The 2,700 "have-not" craftsmen who were to pay a tax of 12 Pfennigs represented over 60% of the tax-bearing population.[34] Similarly in Munich, 60% of the "population" (taxable?) was registered as "have-nots."

Towns could have a variety of lords, often multiple lords, whether territorial, ecclesiastical, or imperial.[35] The complex relationships with such lords, at times relatively harmonious at other times extremely tense, varied according to time and location. Within the city itself, however, there was a certain sense of communal identity, though naturally there was a hierarchy in the city and there were numerous groups of residents or inhabitants, some with civic privileges and accompanying responsibilities—including for example defense and putting out fires—and some with none. The city also had its own communal structures and processes, i.e., bureaucratic government, at times rather independent from and at times contingent upon a myriad of legal considerations, precedents, and pressures both within and beyond the city walls. Many people also traveled into and through the city during the day for business. Given the movement, of both people and goods, between the city and the hinterland, a complex, necessary,

---

[32] Rowan, "Urban Communities," p. 209.

[33] Ibid., p. 215. See also Rubin, "Small Groups," pp. 141–145.

[34] Isenmann, *Die deutsche Stadt im Spätmittelalter*, p. 262.

[35] For a general overview of the legal structure of the German Empire, see Gunter Gudian, "Die grundlegenden Institutionen der Länder," in Coing, ed., *Handbuch der Quellen*, pp. 404–414.

and at times volatile relationship between the city and its residents and the "land" evolved during the later Middle Ages.[36]

The operations of the city were set within the framework of both formal and informal constitutions, at times little more than charters or summaries of such charters granted by the city's lord(s). An oath of loyalty to the council representing the city was typically demanded of citizens. Such an oath possessed social, political, and economic dimensions. Although the formal oath used the term "rich and poor," only a limited percentage of residents actually had citizen privileges or responsibilities, those with means that met community stipulations. In Ulm in 1417, an individual had to present evidence of assets worth a minimum of 200 Pfund Heller; in Munich, at the end of the fourteenth century, the minimum was 90 Pfund Pfennig; in Nördlingen in 1416, 30 Rhenish Gulden; while the Augsburg council demanded that new burghers guarantee 50 Florins (fl.)[37] In some places a further hierarchical distinction was drawn between burghers of the council and burghers of the community.[38] In some cities in the later Middle Ages, however, there was a clear tendency to widen the group of citizens taking oaths. In Constance, for example, 30% of the inhabitants held "Bürgerrecht."[39] With the guild revolutions in Constance, Cologne, and Augsburg, burgher status was tied to acceptance within the guilds.[40] At times, an oath was required for residents without citizenship or visitors, as for example in 1388 and 1428 during periods of crisis in Nuremberg when such people were forced to swear that they would be obedient and not harmful.[41] The very notion of the burgher oath, then, was built upon the concept of peace and obedience. Who was allowed into the peace and who was excluded is quite telling about medieval notions of community and hierarchy. Further, within the city there were multiple associations, multiple communities, and various levels within each. As we will see later in the Jewish communities, community itself could be defined in ways that were simultaneously inclusive and exclusive. Which particular definition or vision of community was implied or used at any given time is suggestive of a broader and extremely significant context. The very concept of such community could be demonstrated in a variety of ways, from civic processions to sumptuary laws, which could be somewhat inclusive at the same time that they maintained rigid hierarchical standards.

The medieval German city was governed internally by a community structure, at the head of which stood the council. The council was still subservient to the lord (in imperial cities to the king himself). In some larger cities there

---

[36] Rolf Kießling, "Markets and Marketing, Town and Country," in R.W. Scribner, ed., *Germany: A New Social and Economic History, 1450-1630*, pp. 145–179.

[37] Isenmann, *Die deutsche Stadt im Spätmittelalter*, pp. 94–95.

[38] Ibid., p. 93.

[39] Schubert, *Einführung in die deutsche Geschichte im Spätmittelalter*, p. 108.

[40] Isenmann, *Die deutsche Stadt im Spätmittelalter*, p. 95.

[41] Ibid., p. 93.

were two councils, the small and large, the latter somewhat more "representative," and the former in some sense more closed and secretive. Throughout the Middle Ages, ending in some places only with successful guild or burgher revolts, the council was comprised of the wealthiest and most influential members of the city, in particular the nobility and some patricians. A member of the council was typically referred to as "Herr" or "dominus."[42] In the later Middle Ages, particularly as the official, and unsalaried, civic positions became more complex and demanding, we find the councils becoming more heavily oligarchic than before.[43] The office of the burgomaster (*Bürgermeister, Ammeister, Stettmeister*) was also introduced, probably in the thirteenth century. The number of council members varied over time and in different cities, though twelve was fairly common. In Worms, early on, there were 40 and then later 15 consuls; in Schwäbisch Gmünd in the fifteenth century 39; and in Augsburg after the 1368 guild revolt, 44. The number of members serving in the large council could vary widely between 40 and 300.[44] A number of servants and officials were also employed in the services of the council and the operation of the city government, as for example in positions related to the militia, the police, taxes and finance, or the recording of court decisions.[45]

Given the vastly divergent and individual developments within the various cities of Germany, it is difficult to generalize. A brief account of the development of Augsburg, however, may help to contextualize the main themes to be pursued in this book. Augsburg, centrally located on the Lech river with easy connections to Flanders and the Lake Constance region, served as a transportation center along both east-west and north-south routes.[46] Augsburg merchants were well represented in Flanders, at the fairs in Frankfurt, and in Venice.

The first extant document that delineated the rights of the city is an imperial document from 1156.[47] Over a century later, in 1276, the city was made a free city through the imperial approval of the Book of Augsburg (*Stadtbuch von Augsburg*). Authority within the city tended to devolve to the Stadtvogt and the episcopal Burggraf (in matters of sales, securities, and debts). The power of these two authorities within the city was a thorn in the side of the city council.

Twelve patricians, not elected, constituted the council. In 1342 it was forbidden for two brothers or a father and son to sit on the council at the same time. In addition to the council of twelve, the old council, there was also a

[42] Ibid., p. 132.
[43] Peter Blickle, *Communal Reformation*, p. 163.
[44] Isenmann, *Die deutsche Stadt im Spätmittelalter*, p. 134.
[45] For a comprehensive treatment of the subject of the city governing structure, and in particular of the council, see Isenmann, *Die deutsche Stadt im Spätmittelalter*, pp. 130–190.
[46] Martha White Paas, *Population Change, Labor Supply and Agriculture in Augsburg 1480–1618*, p. 3.
[47] Ibid., p. 2.

council of twenty-four, the plenum of the small council. A new large council, probably originally consisting of patricians, was also developed and the first document issued by this council was in December of 1290 and allowed the Jews in the city to construct a bath house. At the head of the council the burgomaster stood foremost, first traceable since 1266 (but no longer present in the documents after 1276) quickly succeeded in importance by the position of the Stadtvogt. By 1288 real power was devolved into the hands of two members of the small council in an effort to avoid a dictatorship. In the late thirteenth century social distinctions were clarified and the formula "rich and poor" first appeared in the preamble of the *Stadtbuch* of 1276 to differentiate handworkers who were not yet citizens.

In 1348 Jews in Augsburg were massacred and the debts owed to them were canceled. Despite these cancellations, the city remained incapable of raising sufficient funds to hire troops and was forced to issue new taxes on wine, mead, and beer. The new taxes led to wide-spread resentment amongst the craftsmen, eventually ending in the bloodless guild revolution of 1368, when the guilds were given seats in the council that governed the city. The new civic organization produced 18 guilds that subsumed all of the craftsmen in the city. Twenty-nine guild masters (large guilds had two representatives) along with 15 of the noblest and most important representatives of the burghers made up a new small council (*Kleiner Rat*) of 44.[48] From this small council were elected two burgomasters, one from the guilds and one from the patriciate (note that the reference to "Bürger" and "Gemeinde" in the text refers to a certain privileged group within the city, and that the "most important" refers to the patriciate). Additionally a "Baumeister," two notaries, and six tax collectors were elected, as the document later discusses, on a yearly basis. The two guild letters of late November and mid December 1368, which are cast in the voice of the guilds, coherently spin a self-conscious discourse that emphasizes harmony and friendship within the community, and the allegiance of the city to the Holy Roman Empire.[49] These documents attempt to present the community, both rich and poor as the formula goes, as a cohesive unit. Social tensions within the city escalated after 1383, however, when the patricians closed ranks and membership, isolating themselves to a greater extent from the rest of the city population.[50]

CRISIS?

In a remarkable essay, whose concepts introduced lasting language of analysis for the later Middle Ages and the early modern period, published nearly

---

[48] According to the *Zweiter Zunftbrief* of 16 December, 1368, in Christian Meyer, ed., *Urkundenbuch der Stadt Augsburg*, vol. 2, p. 149. See White Paas, *Population Change*, pp. 10–11.

[49] "... und tun kunt offenlichen an diesem brief für uns und alle unser nachkomen..." (in Meyer, ed., *Urkundenbuch*, p. 148).

[50] White Paas, *Population Change*, pp. 15–16.

twenty years ago, William J. Bouwsma discussed the role of anxiety in the formation of early modern culture. Despite the complexities and problems of the
term, Bouwsma noted that historians examining the transition between "medieval"
and "modern" discovered heightened anxiety throughout late medieval Europe.[51]
Bouwsma asserted that "the unusual anxiety of the period after 1300 is thus
implicit in its novel concern with the passage of time, which found general expression in the familiar new historical consciousness of the Renaissance . . ."[52] He
went on to assert that human anxiety was further fueled by the unreliability
of fortune (death, plagues, famines, or the uncertainties of a depressed economy
or political disorder) as well as the uncertainty of (spiritual) judgment. For
Bouwsma, however, the peculiar anxiety of the later Middle Ages revolved
around the deterioration of social relationships; and at this point he turned his
analysis to the late medieval urban areas.[53] Citing a long tradition of anti-urban
sentiment, he wrote that "towns provoked anxiety above all because they were
greedy; townsmen preyed on others to benefit themselves, and this is what
made them unreliable and dangerous, a threat to the general security of human
existence."[54] Bouwsm argued that here "we are evidently in the presence of
an early formulation of the fruitful modern myth of Gemeinschaft and Gesellschaft;"[55] the new urban environment, with increased social and economic roles,
self-interest, and new rhythms dependent upon unpredictable human will was
opposed to eternal nature. But for Bouwsma there is a deeper transformation,
a deeper anxiety at the root of the transformations of this very transitional age.
The fundamental problem had to do, according to Bouwsma, with the medieval
cosmology, the very ordering of the world:

> Medieval culture was conspicuously successful in the performance of this
> essential task. Applying a common set of distinctions (like other cultures of
> the type described by anthropologists as primitive) to all areas of human
> concern, notably such polarities as inside and outside, high and low, male
> and female, it was able at once to distinguish, to classify, and to relate all
> phenomena, and so to create an intelligible and coherent cosmos, apparently
> rooted in the eternal principles of nature itself, out of the undifferentiated
> chaos of raw experience. The phenomenal world could thus be reduced to
> a kind of orderly map; men could feel at home in it because they could dis-
> tinguish one area from another by clear conceptual boundaries which were
> reflected in the structure of life as well as thought.[56]

---

[51] William Bouwsma, "Anxiety and the Formation of Early Modern Culture," in his
A Usable Past: 157–189, here at p. 158.
[52] Ibid., p. 161.
[53] Ibid., p. 167.
[54] Ibid.
[55] Ibid., p. 168.
[56] Ibid., p. 170.

For Bouwsma it was the social changes of the late medieval urban world that "eventually exceeded the flexibility of the inherited culture and forced men increasingly to violate the old boundaries."[57] Among the many changes and boundary decompositions, he noted that "the distinction between the sacred and the profane was dissolving with the growing responsibility and dignity of lay activity and the secular state."[58]

Bouwsma's assessment raises significant questions that this book will address both directly and indirectly: can we periodize the later Middle Ages as a transitional age and to what extent; what were the cultural and social implications of the urban development in late medieval Europe; to what extent was the boundary between the sacred and the profane dissolving; and, what broader picture can we draw of the later Middle Ages in Germany?

An exploration of the last question leads to an important consideration of a theme that has been much discussed and that means a great deal to the arguments of this work. The disjunctures within a society at any time, but particularly at times of deep-reaching and significant crises, are certainly more obvious than any marks of normalcy and continuity because of their visibility and detailed treatment. Disjunctures and disruptions stand out by definition, and the danger in analyzing such incidents is that they tend to become the standard tool against which the history of an age is measured, rather than as anomalies that may be significant but which present only part of a much broader collage. Nevertheless, it seems reasonable to assume that a close and contextual look at disjuncture can reveal a great deal about particular societies. It is clear that a close look at continuity and disjuncture will afford a heightened opportunity to explore possible changes in Jewish and Christian relations and the conception of community in the fifteenth century.

It has been typical to argue that the German cities of the later Middle Ages experienced deepening fissures and disjunctures in nearly every facet of their existence. The fifteenth century was, according to this view, a time of momentous shifts and crises that witnessed social and political upheaval and disorder. Such a view posits a "feudal chaos" that witnessed increasing "complexity of individual rights and privileges, the increasing differentiation of social classes, the opposition between princes and estates, friction between agriculture and the town crafts, between commerce and industry, that involved the people as a whole in endless strife." Such strife affected the rural folk, whose villages were laid waste and racked by unrest, lawlessness, violence, and insecurity. What is more, this is offered as the same image across Europe, in France and England as much as in Germany; though the German situation has typically been seen as even worse, since it lacked any semblance of effective central government.[59]

---

[57] Ibid., pp. 171–172.
[58] Ibid., p. 172.
[59] Geoffrey Barraclough, *The Origins of Modern Germany*, pp. 338–339.

The presuppositions of such a picture need to be considered. Randolph Starn's discussion of meaning-levels in the theme of historical decline is useful in this regard.[60] In assessing the utility of the term decline in historical thinking, Starn does note that the language of decline, in its affinity for generalization as well as in its comparative assumptions and emphases on "historical process" or "historical development," does have an inherent logic in talking about history. Of course decline, particularly as described from historical distance, takes on a connotation of value judgment. It also creates (contemporary) norms against which history is held, and it tends to move from the limits of single factors to vast generalizations about a period or culture in general. For Starn, the theme of historical decline, as particularly taken up by the Renaissance humanists, is a tactic "of self-definition by which they located themselves and their culture in time and place."[61] It is worth considering, therefore, both how we describe the crises or decline of the later Middle Ages and how contemporaries understood the changes in their own society; in both cases the description defines the descriptor. Along similar lines, Theodore Rabb, in his assessment of "crisis" in the seventeenth century, has attempted to look at a broad array of human experience and relationship, in an effort to locate what he claims is an overarching change in perception. Rabb approaches Europe as a whole, dismissing regional and national histories for his purpose. Rabb's portrayal forces us to remember that issues of perception and of self-identification or reflection are as significant as any events or outward manifestations of change, decline, or crisis.

The traditional picture of decline outlined above has recently been reassessed. This should not be too surprising. After all, Johann Huizinga's famous work on the end of the Middle Ages, originally translated into English as *The Waning of the Middle Ages*, has now been retranslated and retitled *The Autumn of the Middle Ages*, implying its importance in harvesting the positive aspects of the Middle Ages.

According to Ernst Schubert,[62] the concept of the later Middle Ages cannot be found in the nineteenth century; it is, rather an early twentieth century construct, implying the end of the Middle Ages, and so implying a sense of Bouwsma's anxiety or Huizinga's decay. It is only with the Reformation that the beginning of modernity really occurs. For many scholars, the end of the Middle Ages has been posited as a time of great transformation. Among Marxist historians, for example, the period is described as one of early capitalist revolution. Although historians have searched for and found both continuity and discontinuity between the late medieval and early modern periods—here again another rather modern construct—the recent trend has been to see no great

---

[60] See Randolph Starn, "Meaning Levels in the Theme of Historical Decline."

[61] Ibid., p. 28.

[62] See the "Vorfragen" (pp. 1–21) of his *Einführung in die deutsche Geschichte im Spätmittelalter*.

epochal borders, especially in terms of social and economic history, between the two periods.[63] Schubert writes that: "Every definition of an epoch is arbitrary. No period exists in itself, rather it always reflects carry-overs from old and new. 'Later Middle Ages,' as an epochal concept developed by negation."[64] As an example of the continuity he cites general fashions of clothing. Schubert does allow for change, however. Family names and "origin names" reveal an increased mobility in society.[65] In general, however, Schubert questions whether the later Middle Ages in Germany was a period of crisis; and if so to what extent and in what ways. Even in those most standard images of late medieval decline such as agricultural depression and epidemic, Schubert sees no reason to label late medieval Germany a period of crisis or decline.

Wilhelm Abel's negative stereotyping of the late medieval agricultural decline has recently been attacked and revised. According to Abel, famines and pestilence devastated Europe in the fourteenth century, and gave way to feudal crisis; in the fifteenth century they led to late medieval agrarian depression, characterized by a severe population decrease and a long-lasting price slump. However, Abel's theory is based only on an economic context, and it does not account for very positive developments in agricultural technique or transportation. It also does not recognize that crises or famines may have existed in particular years or in specific regions, and that such events do not, of necessity, imply "epochal crisis." Schubert has instead contextualized such epidemics; he sees them as more urban than rural, regional, endemic as opposed to epidemic, and offering important avenues for social opportunity. What is more, Schubert casts the later Middle Ages in Germany as a time of general population rebounding and substantial internationalization, accompanied by important social and geographic mobility. Augsburg, for example, was devastated by recurring epidemics between 1346 and 1408, but virulent plagues were also recorded by chroniclers in 1420, 1430, 1438, and 1450 as well.[66] Even so, the number of tax payers steadily increased during the course of the fifteenth century. New citizens came to Augsburg from towns like Nuremberg, Munich, and Strasbourg; but the largest group of immigrants came from the countryside around Augsburg and nearby villages.[67]

Of course, such a discussion of the nature of continuity, development, or decline in the later Middle Ages, presupposes a rather complex discussion of what exactly is meant by "German." Such a definition must include discussions of culture (mentality), identity, geography, and authority. Indeed, as Schubert makes clear, the idea of the Empire was not synonymous with the concept of the "German Nation."[68]

---

[63] Ibid., p. 2.

[64] Ibid., p. 3.

[65] Ibid., p. 5.

[66] White Paas, *Population Change*, p. 59.

[67] Ibid., p. 73.

[68] See Schubert, *Einführung in die deutsche Geschichte im Spätmittelalter*, pp. 21f.

The areas of "crisis" described here—despite the difficulties of specifying what exactly was in crisis, to what extent, or for that matter what exactly "crisis" is—are telling of the complexity of late medieval urban culture and are significant for our discussion of community and Jewish and Christian relations. In all of the schemes presented so far, it is clear that there existed real possibilities for social tension and transformation within the cities; these involved questions of individual and communal rights and privileges both amongst city residents as well as relations between the urban ruling classes and the landed nobility, and led eventually to attempts to curb the power of the nobility and to strip it of its privileges and authority in some places.[69] In some cases the opposition to landed nobility could result in the banding together of a regional group of cities, though in other cases such organizations also included both secular and ecclesiastical lords.[70] During the 1370s Augsburg joined with other imperial cities against the count of Württemberg. With the defeat in 1374, however, Augsburg had to pay 36,000 Gulden in reparations and its Jews (who had returned to the city in the mid 1350s) were to contribute an [additional] 10,000 Gulden.[71] Again in 1379 Augsburg was forced into a coalition, this time against the advances of the dukes of Bavaria and Württemberg. Augsburg joined the Swabian League with cities such as Ulm, Esslingen, Constance, Nuremberg, and Regensburg—in all 40 cities—in order to protect its independence. Later, in 1381, this Swabian Cities' League joined the Rhine-Alsatian League, thus forming a great south German alliance of cities. The League was, however, defeated in 1387 and the city was forced to pay 10,000 Gulden to the Bavarian dukes and to restore the property of the bishop of Augsburg that had been confiscated. Intermittent wars between dukes and cities continued in Germany, especially in the south between 1450 and 1475, and certainly affected the position of Augsburg both within the south German region and at home.

Economic development in the fifteenth century gave Augsburg a rising position and widespread business. Augsburg itself finally achieved a degree of peace when, joined with imperial forces, it helped to subdue Duke Ludwig of Bavaria-Landshut in 1463. Ulrich Schwartz, a member of the salt guild and a veteran of the war against the duke of Bavaria, became one of the two Augsburg mayors in 1469. Schwartz tried to squeeze the patricians from governmental power and replace them with craftsmen. Schwartz himself became something of a dictator before the other guilds appealed for assistance to the emperor. Schwartz was apprehended by the emperor's forces, accused of treason, found guilty, and

[69] Ibid., p. 136.

[70] Isenmann, *Die deutsche Stadt im Spätmittelalter*, p. 123. Many such leagues were really regional associations, as for example the Swabian League of the early sixteenth century, which included princes, imperial prelates and nobles, and cities. For the actions and fall of this league, see Thomas F. Sea, "The Swabian League and Government in the Holy Roman Empire of the Early Sixteenth Century."

[71] White Paas, *Population Change*, p. 12.

executed in 1478. A new patriciate was instituted that also allowed membership to distinguished guildsmen. The internal dynamics of the city, however, increasingly separated the rich families from the poor. In 1396 the number of taxpayers with disposable assets of 1,000 fl. or more was 2.7%, and they controlled 48.9% of the total disposable assets of the city; by 1492, that number had grown to 4.7%, controlling 80.9% of the assets.[72] In 1492, 22 people, or 0.42%, of the population were in the highest tax category, with disposable assets over 10,000 fl. and controlling over 30% of the total communal assets.

According to Eberhard Isenmann, about ten percent of the imperial cities (*Reichsstädte*) acquired considerable "Herrschaft," exploiting the economic weakness of the lesser nobility.[73] The situation is described generally by Steven Rowan, who notes that although the urban leagues of the fourteenth century had unsuccessfully acted against their lords who sought to restrict their expansion and independence, we find that "by the later fifteenth century the princes were nonetheless rarely able to intervene in the cities' internal affairs, because they lacked sufficiently powerful bureaucratic governments."[74] Peter Blickle has argued that there were a number of stages in the development of a higher degree of political independence for village and urban communities, particularly in Switzerland and southwest Germany, beginning at the end of the thirteenth century and culminating in the fifteenth. For Blickle, the stages included: exemption from the jurisdiction of territorial courts; the curtailment of the power of royal or episcopal lordship; participation in, and eventual exclusive rights over, the appointment of a warden (*Ammann*); acquisition of the rights of high justice; and, the elimination of serfdom in favor of personal freedom.[75] Still, Erich Maschke argues that "the burgeoning territorial state, that included greater regions, was stronger. Nuremberg, that had created for itself a territory of considerable size, was mighty enough to maintain itself against princely pressure; the situation of the imperial cities, however was thoroughly difficult and at times hopeless."[76] This at a time, after 1400, in which the territorial state, with centralized regional power, substituted for imperial representation.[77]

Conflict between the urban population—the citizens or the council—and the bishop or ecclesiastical lords could be equally severe. With the lack of strong central authority the wealthy merchants around Augsburg attempted "to define, defend, and if possible extend their rights in relation to the original city

---

[72] Ibid., p. 190.

[73] Isenmann, *Die deutsche Stadt im Spätmittelalter*, p. 238.

[74] Rowan, "Urban Communities," p. 199. For the importance of this theme into the "early modern period," particularly into the Reformation period, see Heinz Schilling, *Die Stadt in der Frühen Neuzeit*. See also Hans Conrad Peyer, *Verfassungsgeschichte der alten Schweiz* (Zürich, 1978), pp. 21–44.

[75] Blickle, *Communal Reformation*, p. 157.

[76] Maschke, "Deutsche Städte," p. 1.

[77] Rörig, *The Medieval Town*, pp. 55–56.

aristocracy, the Bishop and the nobility."[78] The city eventually freed itself
from the grasp of episcopal power by the beginning of the fourteenth century.
By the end of the thirteenth century most important German cities had shaken
the administrative yoke of ecclesiastical lords and replaced it with rule by a
community council of the urban upper class.[79] In Worms, although the bishop
maintained the title of "Stadtherr,"[80] the city had over the course of the
later Middle Ages slowly removed itself from his yoke. By the beginning of the
sixteenth century the city had denied the bishop his right to install the burgomaster and the council members and had even reconstituted the city council. In the same year, 1505, in an ordinance regarding Jews, the council usurped
the bishop's right to install (and to collect a fee for that installation) the Jewish council.[81] Even among the powerful and multi-faceted bishops of Eichstätt,
who operated in close concert with counts of the region, and who continued
to be important into the nineteenth century, we find that they had, "in political terms, reached their optimum dimension by the middle of the fourteenth
century."[82]

Increasing anti-clericalism, efforts to limit clerical privileges and authority, and
attempts to secularize church property were also all common in the fifteenth
century. In the chronicles of fifteenth-century Augsburg, for example, the clergy,
largely non-native nobility, were attacked for their abuse of the common
people and the damage that they caused the city as a whole. Although the
clerics claimed authority and lorded it over the citizens, they themselves contributed nothing to the well-being of the commune. In the Pomeranian town
of Kolberg, amidst a complex political and economic environment, the town
mayor Hans Schlief, appeared in the cathedral one Sunday in 1442 and dis-
rupted the Mass "by abusing the bishop as a heretic, a traitor, and a profane
perjurer." Robert Scribner described the event: "The mayor went on to have
the bishop's chaplain and notary seized and the episcopal palace stormed and
sacked. Later, the houses of the cathedral canons were stormed and in 1461
Hans Schlief showed his stubborn repentance not only by disrupting the procession held by the Antonine monks in honor of their patron saint, but also
by mishandling the holy relics. The Antonine order was expelled from the town
for the next thirty years."[83]

The widening gulf between rich and poor—in both Jewish and Christian
communities, as we will see—was demonstrated by sumptuary laws (*Das rote*

[78] White Paas, *Population Change*, p. 8.
[79] Hans-Georg Beck, et al., *From the High Middle Ages to the Eve of the Reformation*,
p. 568.
[80] For the late tenth and early eleventh century transfer of power from the emperor
to the bishop, see GJ 1, pp. 437–438.
[81] Fritz Reuter, *Warmaisa*, p. 58.
[82] Benjamin Arnold, *Count and Bishop in Medieval Germany*, p. 174.
[83] Bob Scribner, "Anticlericalism and the Cities," pp. 150–151.

Buch of the city Ulm, for example, stipulated the number of guests that it was reasonable to invite to a wedding,[84] and the *Satzungsbuch* of Nuremberg detailed what could be worn, and at what value)[85] and the hardening of social barriers. Internal friction in governing and citizenship rights were often wide-spread. In Constance, 10% of the families owned 76% of the total taxable assets, and in Schwäbisch Hall, 6% controlled 60%.[86] In the middle of the fifteenth century, 3% to 5% of the population in Frankfurt am Main controlled about half of the means of production.[87] Philippe Dollinger has rightfully cautioned against speaking of social "classes" or social "revolutions" in the modern sense when referring to the Middle Ages. Instead, he suggests that we speak of privileges as a more meaningful determinant in the social world, particularly that of the later Middle Ages.[88] Certainly there is evidence of the important role of privileges and exemptions, and indeed, as we will see later, the position of Jews and clerics as "outsiders" exempt from certain taxes or responsibilities often fueled more popular hostility against them. Nevertheless, there are rather dramatic indications of severe social and economic polarizations in late medieval Germany, throughout the fourteenth and continuing into the fifteenth century. A 1449 census in Nuremberg indicated that a fifth of the population were domestic servants and laborers.[89] In late medieval Trier about 50% of the population lived at or below subsistence, and roughly 42% could be classified as the "lower class" in the 1360s. The 1363 and 1364 tax list reveals that 18.8% of the population paid no taxes (106, or 4.3% were exempt, while 360, or 14.5% were too poor), while 41.7% paid less than 1 pound (lb), 5% paid 1lb, 27.3% paid between 1 and 10lbs, and only 7.2% paid 10lbs or more (the breakdown is more stark, since only 31 individuals (1.25%) out of 2,476 paid more than 60lbs and only 34 (1.35%) paid between 30 and 60.[90]

Waves of internal uprisings fanned across Germany. According to František Graus, every decade between 1301 and 1450 (with the exception of 1311 to 1320 and 1431 to 1440) witnessed at least ten uprisings. Numerous uprisings, with a variety of causes, contexts and effects, could strike the same cities. In Augsburg there were major internal disturbances in 1303, 1348, 1368, 1387, 1397, 1466, and 1478. Würzburg was plagued in both the thirteenth and fourteenth centuries: in 1247 to 1248, 1253, 1265, 1286, 1296, 1353, 1357, 1361, 1372 to 1373, 1374, and 1397 to 1400. The peaks of such social unrest seem to have occurred in the 1340s, 1360s, and the first decade of the fifteenth

---

[84] Mollow, ed., *Das rote Buch*, p. 22.

[85] See for example, the *Luxusordnung* for 1397, pp. 263f.

[86] Schubert, *Einführung in die deutsche Geschichte im Spätmittelalter*, p. 108.

[87] Ibid., p. 112.

[88] Philipp Dollinger, "Die deutsche Städte im Mittelalter: Die sozialen Gruppierungen," p. 269.

[89] Valentin Groebner, "Black Money and the Language of Things: Observations on the Economy of the Laboring Poor in Late Fifteenth-Century Nürnberg," p. 276.

[90] Burgard, "Auseinandersetzungen," in Haverkamp, ed., *Trier*, p. 353.

century. By comparison, the 1320s and 1430s witnessed substantially fewer recorded disturbances. In some instances the high occurrence of social disturbance was reflected in the number of persecutions against and expulsions of Jews, most notably in the 1340s (or the 1370s for Maschke, a time of high imperial taxation of the Jews). Still, there does not seem to have been a precise parallel between general disturbances and attacks against the Jews, which leads us to question the relationship between the two as a key to the Jewish expulsions in late medieval Germany.

Internal conflict could lead to intensification of change within internal social structures, resulting in some cities in the formation of new ruling elites, incorporating previously less powerful guild members, or the reconstitution and broadening of the makeup of the city patriciate or upper class. In Bremen, the "revolution of 1426," in which the city council was expelled, resulted in a new redaction of the civic law in 1428, only to return to the original order of the fourteenth century by 1433.[91] In Mainz and Koblenz, during the fourteenth century, the long-standing patrician upper class was forced from the city and only partially returned. In Augsburg, of the 51 patrician families recorded in 1368 (before the significant guild revolt there), only eight remained in 1538, while 38 new families were recorded, including the Fuggers, Imhofs, and Peutingers.[92] A similar phenomenon is evident in Trier, where opposition to the city "Herren" was voiced in 1396 by the guilds. The subsequent "decentralization of the city administration" was of particular benefit to the nine small guilds.[93] In Cologne a long-standing civil strife between 1396 and 1400 resulted in the overthrow of the city council by the merchants and craftsmen.[94] Similar incidents occurred throughout the fifteenth century as well, as in Mainz in 1444 when the city council was forced out by a committee of guildsmen.[95] In Constance the number of patrician families declined from 60 in 1350 to 15 in 1400 and ten in 1410. Such movements seem to have been particularly common in the southwest in the fifteenth century, though of course no grand generalizations can be made. Certainly some cities, such as Cologne, proved to be exceptions to general trends.[96]

The numerous guild revolutions later in the fourteenth and in the fifteenth centuries were themselves preceded by a series of unsuccessful rebellions by the craftsmen, as in Augsburg in 1303, Speyer in 1304, Strasbourg in 1308, and Erfurt in 1310.[97] But the later guild revolutions did, by and large, alter fundamentally the nature and structure of the ruling bodies in the cities. The excep-

---

[91] Wolf, "Die Gesetzgebung der entstehenden Territorialstaaten," in Coing, *Handbuch der Quellen*, p. 610.
[92] Maschke, "Deutsche Städte," p. 23.
[93] Burgard, "Auseinandersetzungen," in Haverkamp, ed., *Trier*, p. 347.
[94] DuBoulay, *Germany in the Later Middle Ages*, p. 147.
[95] Ibid., p. 149.
[96] Dollinger, "Die deutsche Städte im Mittelalter," pp. 282–283.
[97] Ibid., p. 287.

tion that proves the rule, is Nuremberg, which, after a disturbance in 1348 quickly and effectively suppressed the guilds. As Ernst Schubert has noted, however, the guild revolutions were not social revolutions in the modern sense; that is, they did not strive for social utopias, but rather sought pragmatic and real goals and interests.[98] Eberhard Isenmann, as well, notes that the older description of the guild revolts as revolutions has been discredited and replaced by the language of civil strife.[99]

A HOLY COMMUNITY?

Given the great struggles for independence and privileges undergone by the cities in the twelfth and thirteenth centuries, Bernd Moeller has argued in a landmark essay that by the fourteenth century burghers began to view themselves as a cohesive communal unit, particularly in south and west Germany. It was the burghers' openness to a communal spirit that eventually paved the way for the successes of the reform branches of the Reformation in the early sixteenth century. Moeller has written that:

> The burghers were now openly receptive to the communal idea. With annual elections of the councils, which were often extraordinarily large, a considerable part of the citizenry was able to take part directly and actively in the government of the city and to acquire at least some expertise in political matters. In the course of time, the citizens became proud of their dignity and aware of their obligations. Such sentiments deepened and became gradually more common. Each burgher understood that he was part of the whole, sharing responsibility for his part in the welfare of the great organic community, the 'collective individual,' to which he was tightly bound by laws and duties . . . Material welfare and eternal salvation were not differentiated and thus the borders between the secular and spiritual areas of life disappeared. We can grasp an essential trait of the late medieval urban community if we characterize it as a 'sacred society.' . . . Elsewhere even the lower classes of the urban population, the corporations and guilds, were embued with the communal spirit. They united not only to defend their economic interests but also to work for the eternal salvation of their members by controlling their morals and justice, by supporting altars and masses for the souls of the dead, and so forth.[100]

Moeller is really interested in how such a communalization laid the foundations for a "sacred society" later central in the development of the Reformation. Much of the criticism leveled against him has been related to his view of civic life on the eve of the Reformation.[101] Moeller's attempt to unite theological

---

[98] Schubert, *Einführung in die deutsche Geschichte im Spätmittelalter*, p. 132.

[99] Isenmann, *Die Deustche Stadt*, p. 191, for example.

[100] Moeller, *Imperial Cities in the Reformation*, pp. 44–47. See also his *Das Spätmittelalter* (Göttingen, 1966), p. 34.

[101] Steven Ozment, for example, in his *The Reformation in the Cities*, limits his disagreement with Moeller to issues related to the nature and appeal of Protestantism, as well as the nature of religious life on the eve of the Reformation. See pp. 6–9 and 15.

and sociopolitical analyses has been severely criticized by many social historians for neglecting to account for the serious internal social and economic struggles in the late medieval cities.[102] It was not a cohesive "corpus christianum"
that one finds in the late medieval towns, but rather feudal differentiation. It
was not communalism, but rather class interests that characterized the activity
and ideology of the Strasbourg ruling elite, for example.[103] Recent studies have
shown that the Reformation did not always represent a communal religious zeal,
but often was instituted by the ruling regime of a city in order to moderate
what might have exploded into a more radical revolt. Moeller has also been
criticized for drawing too sharp a distinction between south and north Germany.[104]
Still, some scholars continue to distinguish between northern and southern
cities. In many of the cities to the south "the constitution stipulated that the
commune comprised all sworn citizens, be they patricians, merchants, guildsmen, or workers. However, in many north German cities (both territorial and
imperial) the commune (the *Gemeinde, Gemein, Gemeinheit, Meenheit*) was con-
stitutionally distinct from the incorporated guilds. Craftsmen and merchants,
represented by their guilds, and other citizens, represented by the 'commune,'
enjoyed different legal status in the urban polity in regard to political participation and militia duty."[105]

Despite the fact that he has developed a notion of communal transformation that works beyond the confines of the city, Peter Blickle still notes that
transformations within the Christian community could have radical impact upon
civil life. "According to Heinrich R. Schmidt, 'Zwingli conceived of the sacrament as an oath, by which the believer confessed himself publicly and bind-
ingly to a *Gemeinde* that had committed itself to Christ, its Lord.' In this
way, 'the Eucharist' becomes 'an oath-taking for the Christian community, which
constitutes a *coniuratio*, or sworn union, analogous to the civic *Gemeinde*."[106]
Certainly the question of urban religiosity needs to be explored in greater detail.
Berndt Hamm has noted regarding Moeller's thesis, for example, that "this social
side of urban religiosity was complemented by an individual side, for many
burghers, male and female, cultivated a personal, private penitential piety
focused on the sufferings of Christ and employing the practice of meditation.
This tendency produced some odd shifts, notably in the image of St. Jerome
who was transformed from a paragon of ascetic retreat from the world into a
model of burgher piety of conscience and individual improvement."[107]

---

[102] See also Peter Blickle, "The Popular Reformation," pp. 168–169, for a brief overview
of the Brady-Moeller debate.

[103] R. Po-chia Hsia, "The Myth of the Commune: Recent Historiography on City and
Reformation in Germany," p. 209, citing Brady's work.

[104] Ibid., p. 206.

[105] Ibid., p. 212.

[106] Peter Blickle, "Communal Reformation and Peasant Piety: The Peasant Reformation
and its Late Medieval Origins," p. 227.

[107] Hamm, "The Urban Reformation in the Holy Roman Empire," p. 195.

Lucien Febvre noted that there was "an immense appetite for the divine," and the fifteenth-century Augsburg chronicler Burkhard Zink wrote that "everyone wants to go to heaven."[108] It has been pointed out that there was a proliferation of urban religious institutions in the late medieval cities, as in a variety of brotherhoods or fraternities. In 1350 there were over 70 such associations in Lübeck and around 80 in Cologne. In Hamburg there were 99 brotherhoods on the eve of the Reformation, the majority of them originating after 1450.[109] Some brotherhoods were tied up with particular groups or guilds, others were much larger, as in the Augsburg abbey of SS. Ulrich and Afra which had 5,000 members.[110] In addition to such formalized or institutionalized religion, there were, of course, more popular expressions of urban piety, as in relics, patron saints, and processions.[111] Certainly one could find examples of somewhat more "revolutionary" groups that appropriated religion and religious discourse at different times within different cities. How can we differentiate between the arguments that late medieval burghers were religious and that they formed, in the later Middle Ages, a sacred corporation, a corporation which presupposed substantive transformations in communal identity and organization, and which set the tone for the developments of the reformations of the sixteenth century? To what extent can Moeller's notion of a sacralization of the urban commune, almost a by-product of his larger and more central interest in the communal adaptation of Lutheran teaching in southwest Germany and Switzerland during the early phases of the Reformation, be applied or used to explain late medieval changes?

The boundaries between the laity and the clergy were not always clear; and, many late medieval writers and reformers tried very hard to strengthen the distinctions between them.[112] Such proximity, particularly as mediated through religious confraternities[113] within the cities could allow for a bridging of lay and clerical, and perhaps makes it easier to understand why it is possible to find a burgher appropriation of clerical status in some late medieval cities. The general fusion of canon and Roman Law in other parts of Europe, and beginning at least in the academic circles in Germany in the fifteenth century, laid the foundation for an increased "imitatio sacerdotii" for secular powers that eventually led to the absolutist states of the early modern period. Already for the thirteenth century, Ernst Kantorowicz has located the equation of the "*corpus respublicae mysticum* with the Prince, compared with the mystical body of the

---

[108] Isenmann, *Die deutsche Stadt im Spätmittelalter*, p. 222.

[109] Ibid., p. 223.

[110] Ibid.

[111] For a description of such practices in sixteenth-century Spain, one that focuses primarily on rural areas, however, see William Christian, *Local Religion in Sixteenth Century Spain*.

[112] See Constanin Fasolt, *Council and Hierarchy*, p. 185.

[113] Ibid., p. 187.

church (*corpus ecclesiae mysticum*), headed by Christ."[114] Indeed, conciliarism in
the later Middle Ages helped pave the way for a combination of the theological concept of the mystical unity in the church and the juristic idea of legal
incorporation.[115] Changing urban landscapes, that included an increased sense
of religious and sacerdotal identity within the city and among the burghers,
combined with the solidification of written law, beginning in the middle of the
thirteenth century,[116] in a process that gradually led to the creation of the city
as a sacred community, with very clear religious, legal, and political boundaries.[117]
One example, which wraps together anti-clericalism and efforts to urbanize religious life, may suggest the possibilities.

When the Augsburg chronicler Burkhard Zink describes the bishop's struggle
in Augsburg between 1413 and 1423, he does not malign the clergy openly,
but it is evident that the clergy are a group somehow separated from and
opposed to the civic society Zink envisions. He reports that in 1413 all of the
clerics sided with Nenninger, the contestant to the bishop's position opposed
by the city. In protest against the city's candidate, the clerics left the city and
refused to carry out their offices. Clerics from other areas were, however, brought
in to replace them.[118]

In many sources clerics are charged with numerous offenses.[119] The simony
of which clerics were accused was even compared to usury, the offense most
typically associated with the Jews. According to the "Reformatio Sigismundi"
from the mid-fifteenth century, for example, "everyone is ailed by . . . the great
simony of the clergy which is equal to evil usury; with such simony all of the
clergy poison the city . . ."[120] In some places in the late fifteenth century clerics even seem to have taken over the usurious functions of Jews,[121] and it was

---

[114] Ernst H. Kantorowicz, "Mysteries of State," p. 391. See also Friedrich Meinecke,
Machiavellism, pp. 27–28.
[115] See Brian Tierney, *Foundations of the Conciliar Theory*, p. 246. Antony Black claims
that the fifteenth-century conciliarists "developed a distinctive political theory centered
upon the idea of the guild-like commune, the Christianized *collegium*." See his *Council
and Commune*, p. 2.
[116] For England and France in the thirteenth century, Joseph Strayer speaks of a "laicization" of society, in which leadership passed from the church to the state. See J.R.
Strayer, "The Laicization of French and English Society in the Thirteenth Century," pp.
76–77. Strayer further notes that the thirteenth century witnessed a decided legal theory and movement to justify this laicization. (See p. 81.)
[117] See Chapter Three.
[118] Burkhard Zink, *Chronik*, pp. 76–77.
[119] Wahraus, *Chronik der Erhard Wahraus 1126–1445 (1462)*, pp. 233–234. Even
physical attacks on the clergy, just like attacks on the Jews, are mentioned occasionally in the chronicles. See also *Chronik von der Gründung*, p. 315.
[120] Edith Wenzel, *"Do worden die Judden alle geschant": Rolle und Funktion der Juden
in spätmittelalterlichen Spielen*, p. 101.
[121] The usury and economic exploitation of the clergy was attacked constantly by the
Protestant reformers, see Henry J. Cohn, "Anticlericalism in the German Peasants' War
1525," p. 10.

the clerics' supposed exploitation of the "common man" that many historians have used to explain the swift and violent actions against clerical authorities during the peasant revolts of the early sixteenth century.[122]

The reform programs directed against the clergy in the early sixteenth century are well known,[123] but the concerted efforts to bring the clergy into the civic commune as well as the power struggles between ecclesiastical and civic lords date back to the late fourteenth century. In Augsburg, the attempts to bring clerics under "Bürgerrecht" in the 1380s gave way to peaceful relations until 1413. But the ecclesiastical schism in the city left an ecclesiastical power vacuum into which the secular officials pushed themselves, seizing the opportunity to replace the economic and legal positions of the episcopal territory.[124] The strong rule of Bishop Peter von Schaumberg (r. 1424–1469) was attacked more frequently by the 1450s,[125] and challenges to clerical privileges in Augsburg were again intensified between 1469 and 1495.[126] Two examples will reveal the deep tensions separating the laity and clergy in Augsburg in the middle and later decades of the fifteenth century: the permanent removal of the bishop's residence to Dillingen, outside of Augsburg;[127] and the renewal in 1424 of a 1322 statute in the cathedral chapter which prohibited sons of Augsburg burghers from entering the society of the cathedral chapter.[128] As we will see later, the incident in Augsburg, and in particular the treatment of the clergy, had parallels with the treatment of Jews.

With a clearer picture of the urban scene in late Middle Ages and of the possibilities for communal organization and change, we can now explore the concepts of community that developed in late medieval Christianity, and that may have had particular resonance in the German cities.

---

[122] Ibid., pp. 15–16.
[123] Ibid., p. 29.
[124] Rolf Kießling, *Bürgerliche Gesellschaft*, pp. 28f.
[125] Ibid., p. 30.
[126] Ibid., p. 81.
[127] Ibid., p. 31.
[128] Ibid., p. 30.

2

Religion, Church, and Community

The nature of community that was simultaneously Christian and urban was informed by traditional theological discussions about the Christian community as well as by local conditions of popular lay piety, localized institutional religion, and the local role of customs, rituals, and sacraments.[1] The interplay between what one might call theory and practice was complex and varied, and it could create a dynamic religious practice that affected not only Christian visions of community, but also the place of non-Christians in such communities. Despite the apparent chasms separating the more formal theology from the more mundane ritual and practice, there are at least two significant shifts in the later Middle Ages in Germany, particularly in the fifteenth century, that are of great importance for this study.

First, we find a shift to moralism and legalism. The moral shift is clear in the very production of religious literature at the end of the Middle Ages. A number of influential preachers delivered sermons much more moral than dogmatic, focusing on themes of repentance.[2] According to Lewis Spitz, late medieval confessional and catechetical instructional material leaves the impression that late medieval Christianity was "80 percent morals, 15 percent dogma, and 5 percent sacraments."[3] This point was driven home by Bernard of Siena, who announced that:

> And if, between these two things—either to hear Mass or hear a sermon— you can only do one, you must miss Mass rather than the sermon; the reason for this is that there is less danger to your soul in not hearing Mass than

---

[1] For a nuanced discussion of the appropriation of symbols, ritual, and sacrament, see Miri Rubin, *Corpus Christi: The Eucharist in Late Medieval Culture*. See also Charles Zika, "Hosts, Processions and Pilgrimages: Controlling the Sacred in Fifteenth-Century Germany," and, for the Reformation, Susan C. Karant-Nunn, *The Reformation of Ritual: An Interpretation of Early Modern Germany*.

[2] D. Catherine Brown, *Pastor and Laity in the Theology of Jean Gerson*, p. 21.

[3] Cited in Ibid., p. 265, note 68. See also Beck, et al., eds., *From the High Middle Ages to the Eve of the Reformation*, p. 352.

there is in not hearing the sermon. . . . Tell me: how would you believe in the blessed Sacrament on the altar if it weren't for the sacred preaching which you heard? Your faith in the Mass comes to you only through preaching. Also: what would you know about sin if it weren't for preaching? How would you know about any good act, and how you must go about it, if you didn't learn it through sermons?[4]

Civic sermons also stressed the importance of peace in the community and service for the common good as opposed to egoism and special interest.[5]

The moral preaching of the later Middle Ages could appropriate Thomist theology so that "the proper government and social organisation of the city was seen not merely as a means to a spiritual end, but as an end in itself, that of the pursuit of the common good."[6] Such preaching was wont to emphasize a doctrine of universal obedience[7] and the elect nature of the civic body.[8] This notion of the common good penetrated civic legislation in addition to the moralizing of the preacher. The "common good" of the city was a rather formulaic phrase[9] in many cases, and it could also represent a particular source of authority within the city. Thus, according to *The Red Book* (*das rote buch*) of the city Ulm:

We the burgomaster, the guild master, the councils, great and small, and everyone of the community together of the city Ulm to be advised with each other unanimously for the greater good of our city and it has been decreed . . .[10]

Second we find an increasing laicization of religion, especially in the cities. This was by no means identical to "secularization" but was rather the increasing appropriation of sacred authority and sacred space by the laity, and in particular by the ruling urban authorities. Again, the migration of the sacred into the hands of the laity, within the realm of moralism and legalism, created a community that was simultaneously religious and civic. In part, this laicization may have begun as growing regionalization of the church, with its accompanying increase in local oversight, due in part to the weakening of the late medieval papacy through schism and conciliar conflict.[11] This is not to say that

---

[4] Quoted in Franco Mormando, *The Preacher's Demons: Bernardino of Siena and the Social Underworld of Early Renaissance Italy*, p. 3.

[5] See, for example, Daniel R. Lesnick, *Preaching in Medieval Florence: The Social World of Franciscan and Dominican Spirituality*, pp. 109–111. See also Bernadette Paton, *Preaching Friars and the Civic Ethos: Siena, 1380–1480*, pp. 92, 98, and 135.

[6] Paton, *Preaching Friars*, p. 90.

[7] Ibid., p. 100.

[8] Ibid., p. 119.

[9] Feger, ed., *Vom Rechtbrief*, p. 95; Mollow, ed., *Das Rote Buch*, number 12—"durch besunderen nutz willen gemainer stat," or (number 23, p. 91) "ob er nutzlich in den rat sie oder nicht," or "durch nutz und frides willen unsrer stat."

[10] Mollow, ed., *Das Rote Buch*, p. 82.

[11] John Van Engen, "The Church in the Fifteenth Century," p. 318.

the church became secular; rather civic institutions became sacred[12] and, indeed, the entire community became something more of a sacred entity. Individual guilds and confraternities even wanted to have their own Mass and altar.[13] Similarly, local practices at shrines or pilgrimage spots helped to create unique local, or regional, sacred geography.[14]

This laicization may also have been partially in response to what could only be seen as clerical domineering. In some cities priests and monks might constitute ten percent of the total population but possess as much as half of the property and be immune from taxation and free of lay courts to boot.[15] The fifteenth century in particular witnessed attacks on, and declines in, such clerical privilege; but already in the thirteenth century, precisely when they were attempting to shake ecclesiastical control, the cities sought greater control of church life. In Augsburg the great clerical schism between 1413 and 1423 helped to raise the self-consciousness of the burgher population.[16] During the course of the fourteenth and fifteenth centuries the social and economic power of the burgher population in Augsburg grew steadily, at the expense of the bishop's powers. The city council fought to assimilate both the economic and legal privileges of the clergy and its institutions, and the Augsburg burghers fought to intensify the sacred character of the city.[17] As Rolf Kießling has put it:

> The growing economic power of the burgher city corresponded to a heightening of the self-consciousness against the clergy and their way of life, of landlord and noble character that was brought into the city through the cathedral chapter . . .[18]

According to another interpretation:

> the self-reliance of the now independent bourgeoisie went beyond this to demand its own parish churches or at least its own priest from its own ranks (*plebanus*, people's priest). This priest and often also the pastors were frequently considered to be city officials, like the justice of the peace, school-

---

[12] The guilds are a good example of the sacred functions of what were ostensibly not primarily religious associations. For the case in England in the later Middle Ages, see Gervase Rosser, "Communities of Parish and Guild in the Late Middle Ages." Some institutions or associations were much more religiously oriented. Alfred Haverkamp maintains that from the twelfth century onwards, "the increasing organization of the growing population into brotherhoods expressed itself in new cultic-religious institutions and orientations. This in turn favoured fraternization within the urban community, strengthening social life in a *universitas civitatis* which was often threatened by external as well as internal factors." (Alfred Haverkamp, "Cities as Cultic Centers in Germany and Italy during the Early and High Middle Ages," p. 178).

[13] Beck, ed., *From the High Middle Ages to the Eve of the Reformation*, p. 572.

[14] For a comparison with sixteenth-century Spain, see Christian, *Local Religion in Sixteenth Century Spain*, p. 149.

[15] Beck, ed., *From the High Middle Ages to the Eve of the Reformation*, pp. 567–568.

[16] See Gunther Gottlieb, *Geschichte der Stadt Augsburg*, p. 162.

[17] Kießling, *Bürgerliche Gesellschaft*, pp. 358–359.

[18] Ibid., p. 354.

master, and councillors; they formed part of the *officiales civitatis*, as the Bern municipal law of 1218 expressed it. This led logically to the demand on the part of the citizens or of the party in political control in the cities to elect their pastor like other officials . . . The citizens took care of their churches and in accord with the cooperative principle wanted a share in the administration and supervision of church property . . .[19]

This appropriation shows great similarity to the professionalization of the rabbinate that we will examine later in the book. Although only a small number of cities, probably about 100 out of 3,000, had communal patronage and nomination rights concerning their pastor, the increasing trend in that direction was significant.[20] In fact, throughout the late fifteenth century we find a number of contracts for preachers to serve in a particular city. In Augsburg a contract had carefully stipulated preaching duties, including weekly classes, as well as restrictions on spending time away from the city. The preacher was allowed four weeks of vacation.[21] A similar contract was held by Johann Geiler of Kaysersberg in 1478 in Strasbourg.[22] As we will see with the rabbinate, the convergence of religious instruction and official communal appointment may have standardized the position, while simultaneously weakening its authority. Not only appointments and endowment funds were decided by the city council, however. That body took a more active role in a number of areas that had previously been part of the ecclesiastical hierarchy, such as education and care for the sick.[23]

THE ROLE OF THE SACRAMENTS

The confusion over the definition of community and the relation of thought about the sacraments to community in late medieval Europe has been discussed at length by John Bossy. Against the notion that "the pre-reformation rural parish was a unified community broken up by the progress of economic individualism during the sixteenth century,"[24] Bossy has argued—by examining the Christian rituals that played a part in the construction of group relationships and Christian community—that in the later Middle Ages "the parish was not conceived by the church as a homogeneous unit, but as an assemblage of actually or potentially hostile entities among whom its function was to maintain a precarious peace."[25] Parish priests were, therefore, intermediaries or arbiters of conflict. The sacraments of marriage and baptism, according to Bossy extended and created spiritual kinship in a society and period that was particularly rent by feud and

---

[19] Beck, ed., *From the High Middle Ages to the Eve of the Reformation*, p. 568.

[20] Blickle, *Communal Reformation*, p. 166.

[21] Larissa Taylor, *Soldiers of Christ: Preaching in Late Medieval and Reformation France*, pp. 21–22.

[22] Ibid., p. 21.

[23] Beck, ed., *From the High Middle Ages to the Eve of the Reformation*, p. 569.

[24] Bossy, "Blood and Baptism," p. 130.

[25] Ibid., p. 142.

conflicting systems of friendship and hostility. "The social effect of baptism in
late-medieval Europe was . . . to create what an anthropologist has called a
'polyadic horizontal coalition', a kinship-group partly natural and partly
artificial . . ."[26] Natural kinship did not provide the individual "with adequate
social support." As Bossy paraphrases *Piers Plowman*, "Christ invokes his kinship with Adam and his descendants as entitling him to bring retribution on
Lucifer by rescuing man from hell at the last judgment."[27] It is this emphasis
on artificial kinship and lineage that is particularly important for our story. The
sacraments allow horizontal (i.e., contemporary) society to be extended verti-
cally (i.e., in time).[28] Bossy argues that the later Middle Ages also witnessed
"the tendency to convert the mass from a public ritual offered by those present for themselves and the whole community of Christians, into a private ritual offered by the priest for the benefit of a specific group of individuals, living
or dead."[29] For Bossy, this new commemoration of the living indicates a profound change in the "social constitution of the church," and reveals the church
as "a 'conglomerate of autonomous communities.'"[30] Bossy concludes that the
sense of community in the later Middle Ages was a precarious and transitory
phenomenon.

    Whether or not one accepts Bossy's argument, the question of community
and the function of sacraments in the creation of community is significant. The
example of the development of the host in the fifteenth century suggests that
a closer look at ritual and sacrament will help us to understand communal identity and change in late medieval Germany.[31] According to Charles Zika, the
host attained a new centrality in Germany during the fourteenth and fifteenth
centuries.[32] The host served as a site for resolving conflicting views of legitimate religious behavior and for strategies by some clerics to maintain control
and authority over both public and private access to the sacred.[33] The host,
which remained largely under the power of the clergy, allowed the clergy to
combat the trend of individual laymen appropriating the sacred for personal
use and the increasing tendency of secular authority to expand its influence
upon, and monopoly of, the sacred.[34] Indeed, many of the rituals that evolved

---

[26] Ibid., p. 134.
[27] Ibid., p. 135.
[28] Ibid., p. 136.
[29] Ibid., p. 137.
[30] Ibid., p. 138.
[31] Rituals, whether religious, civic, or a combination of the two, helped to create communal identity. Richard Trexler argues that "it was through ritual that the medieval city
achieved its identity, which it then lost when it surrendered its sovereignty and was
subordinated to international markets and court ritual monopolies. See his *Public Life
in Renaissance Florence*, pp. xxii and xxiv.
[32] Zika, "Hosts, Processions and Pilgrimages," p. 25.
[33] Ibid., p. 27.
[34] Ibid., p. 60.

during the fifteenth century around the host, in particular the procession, reflected conflict over sacred authority and sacred space—the procession took the sacred from the church and the immediate control from the clergy[35]—as well as social tension, while also allowing the possibility for expressions of political power and social cohesion.[36] In the end, Zika asserts that developments of ritual associated with the host reflected the significant attempt to establish a more pastoral clergy in the fifteenth century.[37]

SCRIPTURE AND THE LAWS

According to R. Po-chia Hsia "although Lutheran anti-Semitism assumed many motifs from the medieval polemical texts, a new emphasis was given to the immutable, essentialist, and, to employ an anachronistic concept, the racial character of the German Jews."[38] Hsia goes on to argue that German Lutherans increasingly differentiated between the Jews of the Old Testament and contemporary Jews, essentially de-peopling the Old Testament and appropriating for themselves the idea of a Chosen People and a New Israel. In what follows I will argue that one does not have to wait until the sixteenth century to find the differentiation within Christian thought between the Jews of the Old Testament and contemporary Jews. Fifteenth-century theologians and Christian burghers had already made the distinction and begun to assume new models of identity and community. Through increased use of the literal sense of biblical interpretation, the Old Testament itself was reclaimed, and Christians, by reasserting their role as the Chosen People, extended their history and legitimized their authority by arguing that they were in fact the natural descendants of God's people. Medieval Christians had understood themselves as "Israel according to the spirit," as opposed to the Jews who were merely "Israel according to the flesh."[39] Even radicals such as John Hus appropriated the identity of Old Testament Israelites in traditional Christian ways; he was accused of Judaizing and had himself emphasized the moralizing of the Old Testament or compared himself and his followers to Old Testament figures.[40] We might say that before the period under investigation here, Judaism and the Old Testament were seen to prefigure Christianity and the New Testament. But in the later Middle Ages, Christians now appropriated the Old Testament, and so "Judaism,"

---

[35] Ibid., p. 35.

[36] Ibid., p. 39. See also Rubin, "Small Groups," p. 146.

[37] Zika, "Hosts, Processions and Pilgrimages," pp. 62–63.

[38] R. Po-chia Hsia, "The Usurious Jew: Economic Structure and Religious Representations in an Anti-Semitic Discourse," p. 171.

[39] Daniel Lasker, "Major Themes of the Jewish-Christian Debate: God, Humanity, Messiah," p. 121.

[40] See Louis Newman, *Jewish Influence in Christian Reform Movements*, which however muddies the important distinction between "Jewish" and "Old Testament" influence on Christian thought. For a review of the words used by Erasmus to describe the Jews, see Shimon Markish, *Erasmus and the Jews*, pp. 61–65.

as not merely a prefigurement of the New, but as an important part of it. The
space for contemporary Jews, who were somehow now seen as very different
from the Jews of the Old Testament, was substantially reduced.

The emphasis on the differences between the Old and New Laws, that is
between the Old and New Testaments, that was traditional throughout the
Middle Ages is well-represented in the works of St. Augustine and St. Thomas
Aquinas. In the later Middle Ages, especially in the fourteenth and fifteenth
centuries, however, a greater emphasis on the continuity of the two Testaments
was circulating widely. The continuity suggested that there was a commonality of moral behavior and law in the two works, and so the Old Testament,
although superseded by the New, became of more central concern than it earlier had been. Let me begin here by tracing the main themes of the traditional
interpretation and then outlining briefly the change in perception, a change
that will be taken up more extensively in relation to the question of the Old
and New Testament sacraments.

The ancient Church Fathers had distinguished between the body—words
or letter—of the sacred text and the soul—the spiritual sense—of Scripture.
According to Beryl Smalley,[41] the use of allegorical interpretation marks an
early stage in a civilization. It is a method that allows one to dispose of conflicts
with present moral and intellectual skills, by allowing one to read the past as
an allegory. The literal sense, on the other hand, comes at a much later stage,
when a process of historical development becomes visible. With Jerome, the
Church Fathers began to take a greater interest in the literal sense of biblical
interpretation. Although the Neoplatonist Augustine still valued the spiritual
sense over the literal, he did give the letter a concrete chronological emphasis and he accepted the historical truth of the letter to an even greater extent
than did Jerome. Augustine tried to steer something of a middle exegetical
course, and it was not until the Victorines that the literal sense reemerged in
Christian theology as an important and independent subject of study. Hugh of
St. Victor offered a literal historical sense that gave an historical meaning to
biblical events and a primacy to the words of Scripture. Hugh even planned
his *Summa* along lines more properly historical than theological. In his theology man's history was described as a history of sacraments.

Smalley's discernment of the connection between the literal reading of
Scripture and sacramental ritual as well as the use (or appropriation) of history
in literal exegesis will be important in the analysis that follows. Taking a cue
from her, I begin here with a brief description of the thought of some medieval
Christian theologians about the relation of the Old and the New Laws, in
order to contextualize the developments within late medieval theology that are
of particular concern for this study.

---

[41] See Beryl Smalley, *The Study of the Bible in the Middle Ages*, as well as Henri de
Lubac, *Exégèse médiévale les Quarte Sens de L'Écriture*.

St. Augustine of Hippo (354–430), who was probably the most influential Christian thinker outside the canon of Scripture, held two conflicting views of the Old Testament.[42] On the one hand, there were his old Manichaean, anti-Old Testament views, which found little edification for Christians in the Old Testament—it merely contained literal and historical meaning. On the other hand, Augustine took over from Ambrose a view of the Old Testament as a book of hidden mysteries which referred to Jesus Christ and to the New Testament, and which needed to be interpreted allegorically.[43] According to Augustine, when a passage of the Old Testament did not pertain to virtuous behavior or the truth of faith in its plain meaning, it was to be taken figuratively,[44] because the promises of the Old Testament were merely figures of New Testament promises. For Augustine there was a sharp divide between the two Testaments.[45] In consequence, Old Testament people were only a "figura" of Christians—there was no historical relation between Old and New Testament people, and redemptive history really only begins with the Advent of Christ. Augustine conceded, however, that wherever Old Testament promises alluded to the future covenant, that is to Christ, redemptive history began in the Old Testament period, and the Old Testament itself could function theologically as well as historically.[46] Still, in his *On the Spirit and the Letter* Augustine cautioned that one should not take merely the literal sense, rather one should consider what the words signify, "nourishing the inner man by our spiritual intelligence."[47] These positions also explain why Augustine postulated a contradictory position regarding the Jews that would serve as the basis for their treatment throughout the Middle Ages. On the one hand, he maintained that Jews should be purged from Christian society; on the other, he asserted that they must be tolerated so that they might witness the Second Coming of Jesus and realize the error of their ways in rejecting him as the true Messiah.[48]

St. Thomas Aquinas (1225–1274) made important contributions to the discussion of the relation of the two Laws. Like earlier theologians Aquinas distinguished between the Old Law, which he termed carnal and external, and the New Law, which he contrasted to the Old as spiritual and internal. The

---

[42] For a recent interpretation of Augustine's biblical exegesis, within the context of medieval thinking about the Jews, see Jeremy Cohen, *Living Letters of the Law: Ideas of the Jew in Medieval Christianity*.

[43] Thus, Ambrose himself spent a great deal of ink on the prefigurations of baptism in the Old Testament—for example in the deluge, *Genesis* 7, in *Kings*, and in the life-giving water culled from the desert rock by Moses. See Saint Ambrose, Bishop of Milan, *De Sacramentis*, pp. 443–446.

[44] James Samuel Preus, *From Shadow to Promise: Old Testament Interpretation from Augustine to the Young Luther*, p. 13.

[45] Ibid., pp. 18 and 20.

[46] Ibid., p. 20.

[47] Saint Augustine, *Basic Writings of Saint Augustine*, vol. 1, p. 464.

[48] On the Augustinian doctrine of witness, See Cohen *Living Letters*, pp. 35f.

Old was only a shadow of the New and it ceased, like all law, with the Advent of Christ, at which time the sanctity of the Old Law's sacraments was translated to the New.[49] The New Law is thus the perfection and replacement of the imperfect Old Law. Thomas offered two opinions regarding the Old Law: first, that it was a sign of the sacraments of the New Law and the Passion of Christ, and, second, that it functioned as a testimony of faith. But did the Old Law have any merit, asked Aquinas? One could argue, he wrote, that the sacrifices of the Old Law were not accepted by God, for nothing useless (*inutile opus*) is meritorious. The killing of animals in sacrifices, which served no purpose whatsoever, was therefore not meritorious (*ergo non erat meritorium*).[50] And yet, Aquinas continued, the Old Law did have some merit. Summoning forth the authority of Bede (d. 735), Aquinas rejected the argument for the uselessness of the Old Law.[51] Still, although the carnal sacraments of the Old Law possess a certain merit, they do not themselves lead to grace.

Thomas Aquinas asserted that there are two ways to distinguish the two laws: first, they are ordained to diverse ends, and, second, one is more closely connected with the end and the other more remotely. According to the first distinction, the two are not really different since they have the same end, namely man's subjection to God.[52] Yet according to the second distinction the two are different, since the New Law is the law of perfection and of charity. Faith was united in both testaments, however "faith had a different state in the Old and in the New Law, since that what they believed as future, we believe as fact."[53] The Old Law was given to imperfect men who had not yet received spiritual grace, and it was termed the Law of fear—it induced men to observe its commandments through threats and temporal promises. The New Law, however, "which derives its pre-eminence from the spiritual grace instilled into our hearts, is called the Law of love; and it is described as containing spiritual and eternal promises, which are objects of the virtues, chiefly of charity."[54] There were some people in the time of the Old Testament who possessed charity and grace and looked to spiritual and eternal promises. In essence, however, they really belonged to the period of the New Law.

The Old Testament, for Aquinas, had the capacity to rid the body of uncleanness, but it could not purge the uncleanness of the soul, that is, sin.[55] The expiation of sin could occur only through Christ. The Old Law was, however, not entirely useless. It was not given to the Jews alone, rather it ordained men to Christ—first, by bearing witness to Christ, and second, by instilling a disposition "withdrawing men from idolatrous worship" and directing them "to the

---

[49] Here, in his commentary to the *Sentences*, book IV distinction 1.
[50] IV d. 1, 1497.
[51] IV d. 1.
[52] Saint Thomas Aquinas, *Basic Writings of Saint Thomas Aquinas*, vol. 2, p. 958.
[53] Ibid., pp. 958–959.
[54] Ibid., p. 959.
[55] Ibid., p. 911.

worship of one God, by Whom the human race was to be saved through Christ."[56]

According to Aquinas the New Law fulfilled the Old by supplying what was missing in the Old. The goal of the Old Law may have been the justification of man; however, the Old Law could not attain such a lofty goal, rather, through ceremonial actions it only promised this justification in words.[57] Such ceremonial precepts of the Old were fulfilled only in the New Law, which they foreshadowed, and they were no longer to be observed,[58] because "the promise of a future gift holds no longer when it has been fulfilled by the presentation of the gift. In this way, the legal ceremonies are abolished by being fulfilled."[59]

A significant increase in the weight given to the Old Law in matters of merit could be found in the fourteenth century. According to Durandus of St. Pourçain (1275–1334), the Old Law prior to grace was life-giving—it justified through merit even if that justification was not complete. "Justifying grace was merited because of God's generosity even though the individual was still in a state of sin (*de congruo*); this justification was, however, not complete, because not performed in a state of grace (*de condigno*)."[60] Durandus wrote that

> he who uses well the acts of free will in these things which concern God and his neighbor merits at least *de congruo* divine aid necessary for salvation, for he does what is in him, and God does not fail such people. But the good observers of the [Old] law were people of this sort, and therefore they were meriting, *de congruo*, the conferral of grace upon them by God, without which there is no salvation.[61]

Other scholars in the fifteenth century solidified the bonds holding together the Old and the New Laws. James Perez of Valencia (d. 1490), for example, asserted that although all of the Old Testament was parable, and the deeds of the Old Law were merely signs of sacred things signifying the future mysteries of Christ and the church, the Old and New dispensations were united in "lex:" the "accidents" (rites, ceremonies) of the laws were different, but in essence they were the same.[62] Unlike Peter Lombard, for whom unity of the Testaments lay in the moral law, spiritually interpreted, Perez understood their unity as being founded upon Christ and faith. For Lombard, as for St. Bonaventure and St. Thomas, justification could not occur until the time of Christ. Perez, however, suggested that justification could already have occurred for the Old Testament fathers on the basis of the future, promised Christ.[63]

------

[56] Ibid., p. 809.
[57] Ibid., p. 961.
[58] Ibid., p. 962.
[59] Ibid., p. 962
[60] Preus, *From Shadow to Promise*, pp. 128–129.
[61] Commentary on Book III of the Sentences, distinction 40 question 3 number 8, in Preus, *From Shadow to Promise*, p. 129.
[62] Preus, *From Shadow to Promise*, p. 118.
[63] Ibid., p. 121.

The value of appropriating the Old Law was that it could legitimize Christian authority by fashioning Christians as the true Chosen People at a time of increasing European expansion, heresy, and internal reform. At the same time, however, the discussion paved the way for a serious reconsideration of the role and value of ritual and the nature of community.

RITUAL LAW AND THE SACRAMENTS

The nature of the relationship between the two Testaments examined above takes on greater significance when we consider discussions about the nature of the sacraments of the two Testaments. As in the general discussion above, there is a noticeable and profound theological shift in the late medievals. Augustine asserted that the Old Testament sacraments, like the Old Testament itself, were superseded by those of the New Testament. Similarly, Peter Lombard reiterated that the Old Testament sacraments were carnal, and at best signified grace. But beginning in the thirteenth century with the Mendicants we notice an important shift. While St. Bonaventure did not raise the importance of the Old Testament sacraments above earlier positions, he did change the nature of the distinction. Although the old sacraments do not justify, it is simply because they do not stir the individual to a higher spiritual love. For Bonaventure the purpose of the sacraments was to assist grace spiritually not corporeally. Duns Scotus marked another significant step in the development of the discussion. Utilizing the important nominalist distinction, between efficacy inherent in the rite or sacrament and the efficacy due to the interior disposition of the recipient or administrant, he asserted that while the new sacraments had physical efficacy the old ones were conditional upon the intent of the recipient. For him the old sacraments remedied the law of nature, separated the Jews as a Chosen people, and signified the future, spiritual new Law. The general late medieval nominalist emphasis on the ability of the individual (the pilgrim or *viator*), took powerful root in a number of late medieval theologians' discourses. Gabriel Biel admitted that the old sacraments were external, temporal, and abrogated by the new. Yet he asserted that an underlying moral law remained and connected the two. This moral emphasis, and the centrality of the individual's attempts at salvation, through proper intention, found a home in the arguments of many important late medieval preachers and theologians, such as Geiler of Kaysersberg and Nicholas of Cusa, who stressed both the moral and legal continuity between the Testaments. Let us trace this development in more detail.

According to Augustine, circumcision, like much of the Old Testament, and "other similar legal observances" "are now rejected as shadows of a future substance by Christians who yet hold what those shadows figuratively promised."[64] Augustine accordingly distinguished between circumcision of the body (which comes from the Letter), and a circumcision of the heart (from the Spirit),

---

[64] Augustine, *Basic Writings*, vol. 1, p. 479.

which is assisting and healing.[65] Even if circumcision itself may bring one some benefit, in any event the Jews who circumcise themselves do not keep the Law correctly. Here Augustine quoted Romans 2 at some length:

> . . . circumcision indeed is of value if you obey the law; but if you break the law, your circumcision becomes uncircumcision. So, if a man who is uncircumcised keeps the precepts of the law, will not his uncircumcision be regarded as circumcision? Then those who are physically uncircumcised but keep the law will condemn you who have the written code and circumcision but break the law. For he is not a real Jew who is one outwardly, nor is true circumcision something external and physical. He is a Jew who is one inwardly, and real circumcision is a matter of the heart, spiritual and not literal. His praise is not from men but from God.[66]

It was not the Law which makes one righteous, but grace, which came from faith in the promise of Christ.[67]

The standard medieval interpretation was well represented in the thought of the great systematizer, Peter Lombard. According to him, the letter of the Law (Old Testament) expresses only the "carnal" sense—that which carnal men have and live by.[68] The promises of the Old Testament are earthly and merely signify grace, whereas the promises of the New Testament are heavenly and confer grace.[69] Yet Lombard found a fundamental unity between the Testaments: They are united in the "moralia" that they teach, although they are diverse in "caeremonialia."[70]

In Book IV of his *Sentences*, Peter Lombard examined the sacraments of the Old and the New Laws. The sacraments, he claimed, were instituted as remedies against Original Sin and actual sins. A sacrament, began Lombard, was a sign of a sacred thing, it was a visible form of an invisible grace. Every sacrament was a sign, though not every sign was a sacrament. In the strictest sense, a sacrament was a sign of the grace of God and a form of invisible grace. Sacraments, therefore, did not merely signify, they also sanctified. However, things that were instituted only to signify, such as carnal sacrifice and the ceremonial observances of the Old Law, whose offerings were never able to justify, were only signs and not sacraments.

The sacrament itself consisted of two parts: words—the invocation of the Trinity—and things—such as water, oil, etc. Lombard called "sacraments" what the Old Testament people called sacred things, such as sacrifices, oblations, and the like. The difference between the sacraments of the Old and the New Law, according to Lombard, was that the sacraments of the Old Law only promised

---

[65] Ibid., p. 470.
[66] Ibid., p. 469.
[67] Ibid., p. 487.
[68] Preus, *From Shadow to Promise*, p. 39.
[69] Ibid., p. 40.
[70] Ibid., p. 39.

and signified (salvation) whereas the sacraments of the New Law offered salvation. Regarding circumcision, for example, Lombard argued (citing Augustine and Bede) that it had been ordained by God and imputed a remedy for Original and actual sin in adults and children, but baptism now delivers these remedies. Before circumcision, children were justified by the faith of their parents and adults by the efficacy of their sacrifices, whereas after the giving of circumcision men were justified by circumcision and women by faith and good works, their own if they were adults, or if they were minors through those of their parents. Why was circumcision given at all? To please God who was dissatisfied with the sin of Adam; as a sign of the great faith of Abraham; and to mark off this people (the Jews) as a nation different from others. Circumcision was changed to baptism, however, because the sacrament of baptism was more universal, and more perfect, and it accumulated more grace. Baptism removed sins but also conferred grace and increased virtues—this was not the case with circumcision, through which only sins were remitted. Why, questioned Peter, were these new sacraments not instituted immediately after the fall of man? Because before the advent of Christ, who brought grace, the sacraments of grace could not be granted, for it was through his death and Passion that the sacraments received their virtue. Why did circumcision lose its power? Because all commands of the (Old) Law were terminated by the death of Christ.

I will now turn to some of the important Mendicant writers of the later Middle Ages, whose ideas—given the influence of the Mendicant preachers in the German cities—will be of particular interest in this investigation.[71]

The Franciscan scholastic St. Bonaventure (1221–1274) in his commentary to Book IV of the *Sentences* posed the view that the sacraments were not necessary: God alone was the medicine for man's wounds; faith and virtue were sufficient to repair man's nature; and people were disposed to grace before the institution of the sacraments. Bonaventure then countered these arguments. Medicine, he wrote, if it was to be effective in its reparations, had to contain both corporal and spiritual elements—therefore sacraments were instituted.[72] All

[71] See Paul Nyhus, "The Franciscan Observant Reform in Germany." The reflections of the Mendicants in these matters are particularly important given their importance in south Germany between the end of the fourteenth and the middle of the fifteenth centuries. According to Nyhus the major years of prosperity for the Franciscans were between 1380 and 1450. In Augsburg they were supported by all classes, although in Nuremberg they seem to have been supported more by the patricians. Nyhus argues that the great success of the Franciscans in this period was the fact that "not only were the brothers to adhere more closely to the ideal of poverty, but in addition, their ministry was to garner spiritual benefit for the entire civic community." At the same time that the Franciscan Order was undergoing reform, the domain of their liturgical ministry was reshaped by the urban community. The civic community and their spiritual congregation were coterminous. Nyhus confirms Kießling's argument of "an assimilation of church institutions of the city. . . ."

[72] Saint Bonaventura, *Opera Omnia*, here vol. 4, p. 11.

religions have external signs—God instituted the sacraments for our emancipation (*expediens*), for three reasons: because of his mercy (*misericordia*) to recuperate man with recurring grace; because of his justice (*iustitia*) by which he disposes man to grace by offering him a pact in grace through the sacraments; and because of his wisdom (*sapientia*), which offers a remedy to our occasional lapses.[73]

The sacraments for Bonaventure, as for Lombard, were given for erudition, humiliation, and practice (exercise), but Bonaventure stressed the aspect of practice, which led man to spiritual contemplation.[74] The sacraments assisted grace, which deleted guilt from sin (*culpa*) but did not absolve the punishment for the sin (*a poena*).[75] The sacraments were not instituted for corporal erudition, but for spiritual.[76] By some sacraments we signify what the future (*futurum*) would be, and in others we signify the past Passion.[77] It is only the sacraments of the New Law, however, that bring about grace.[78] The sacraments of the Old Law, by contrast, Bonaventure termed material (*materialiter*).[79] Old Testament man did not attain justification because Old Testament promises did not stir him to spiritual love. Sacraments of the Old Law promised grace but did not give it, whereas sacraments of the New offered what the Old prefigured (*figurant*). Citing Hugh, Bonaventure argued that the sacraments of the Old Law were temporal and that they were given without grace in order to fight concupiscence, but not for a higher spiritual goal. Such sacraments were therefore impotent after the advent of Christ.[80] Bonaventure made an even further distinction between the other sacraments of the Old Law and circumcision. All of the others "were instituted so clearly for the perfection of man and of faith;" circumcision, however, was instituted solely externally to fight the carnal urges. Therefore, "sacraments of the old law signify principally that which is believed . . . through the passion of Christ and through later justification; with the exception of circumcision, which primarily signifies the removal of Original [Sin]."[81] Given the fact that circumcision did not apply to both sexes and to all members or at all times (e.g., Joshua in the desert), Bonaventure wanted to conclude that it was not a remedy (*remedium*), but merely a distinguishing sign (*signum distinctionis*) or covenant (*pactum*), to distinguish the Jews as the people from whom Christ would be born.[82]

---

[73] Ibid., p. 12.
[74] Ibid.
[75] Ibid.
[76] Ibid., p. 13.
[77] Ibid., p. 15.
[78] Ibid., p. 17.
[79] Ibid.
[80] Ibid., p. 25; here he cites the gloss on *Romans* 3. See also his more explicit statement on p. 63.
[81] Ibid., p. 26; he gives a list of sources in the *scholion*, pp. 26–27.
[82] Ibid., p. 40.

What remedy was there against Original Sin before circumcision, asked
Bonaventure? The question, in Bonaventure's line of thought, was no different
from the question of how circumcision (or indeed baptism) could be a remedy
to the child. The answer was through faith—in the case of the child, the faith
of his parents, which "de congrui" may lead to merit. The mere profession of
faith was sufficient for the remission of sins (*peccati*) in the minor,[83] therefore,
faith preceded circumcision.

Along similar lines the Franciscan John Duns Scotus (b. 1266) asked whether
circumcision conferred grace. The first argument that he offered was the negative. Citing Rom. 4, that Abraham received circumcision as a sign or seal (*signa-
culum accepit Circumcisionis*), he argued that only sins were diminished, but grace
was not conferred.[84] Scotus then cited Augustine and Bede (in his commentary on Luke 2) to support this position. One might say that at the time of
the Mosaic law the remission of Original Sin was given for the observance of
the Law—however, one could object that circumcision was given by the Fathers
not by the Law (*ex Patribus, non ex lege*), that is, that it was given before the
written Law. The Law merely confirmed the remedy (*remedium*), contended
Scotus.[85] Scotus then asked, if it is possible that grace was not conferred in
circumcision, then in circumcision was the guilt in fact discharged? Here Scotus
drew a distinction between the two powers of the divine:

> [The power of] God is two-fold, namely following the absolute and the
> ordained power. Therefore according to the first it can be seen that it is pos-
> sible for God by absolute power to annul original [sin] without the infusion
> of grace.[86]

Scotus next marked a debate between those who believed that circumcision
brought about grace on the grounds of the performance of the rite (*ex opere
operato*) and those who believed that it did so solely because of the intentions
of the administrant or the recipient (*ex opere operante*). Scotus noted that some
scholars had argued that "there are two ways to bring about grace *ex opere operato*. The first is through physical efficacy, and in this way the sacraments of the
new law bring about grace; the second is through a conditional medium, and
this is brought about by circumcision."[87] Scotus responded that circumcision
brought about grace *ex opere operantis* and not *ex opere operato*, that is, not on
the grounds of the performance of the rite, but rather on the disposition of
the recipient or administrant at the time of the performance of the rite. Since

---

[83] Ibid., pp. 32–34.

[84] John Duns Scotus, *Opera Omnia*, vol. 16, p. 195.

[85] Ibid., p. 196.

[86] Ibid., pp. 196–197; Scotus next distinguished between faith which leads to *meritum de condigno* (full merit performed in the state of grace) or *meritum de congruo* (half
merit, an act performed in a state of sin). The first depended upon the actions of God,
the second on the powers of the parents in a state of sin.

[87] Ibid., p. 198.

"circumcisio" was performed on minors, the disposition had to be effective in the administrant. This was generally the position taken with regard to the Old Law sacraments in the nominalist tradition.[88]

The infant is incorporated into the synagogue or church, and therefore his sins were wiped away, continued Scotus, through circumcision. Circumcision was necessary for faith to be effective. Scotus cited Genesis 17, where circumcision was instituted as a covenant (*circumcisio statuitur ut pactum*). Here Scotus made a sharp distinction between the efficacy of the sacraments of the Old and the New Law: circumcision was equivalent to the "remedio" of the law of nature and it segregated the Jews as well as signified the future "baptismi" and the spiritual circumcision conferred through Christ. Citing Paul, Scotus noted that all "justitia" was from the merits of Christ, and salvation was to be through faith and the redemption, which was in Jesus Christ and not from the letter of the Law (*ex littera legis*).[89] The Jews, however, were sanctified through the Law and not through faith. Quoting Augustine, Scotus argued that the sacraments of the Old Testament were mere shadows and promises of the New Testament.[90] The sacraments of the Old Law were performed inappropriately (because they lacked good interior motives).[91]

The later nominalists in their emphasis upon the individual doing his best (*facere quod in se est*)—or the ability of man to find God's grace, though not to achieve grace, for which mere fulfillment of the letter of the Law was insufficient—tended to focus more attention on man *prior to*, or *outside of*, justifying grace: "the late medieval concentration on the 'old man' prior to justifying grace brought into the scholastic discussion a new anthropological dimension, which held within it an invitation to closer exegetical and theological scrutiny of the situation of the Old Testament man."[92]

Such interest in the ability of man can be found in Gabriel Biel (d. 1495). In traditional fashion, Biel contrasted the Old Testament and the New in terms of their promises—"the New Testament is more excellent and perfect than the Old, especially because its promises contribute to the God-intended fulfillment of the law by exciting spiritual love."[93] Heiko Oberman has demonstrated at length that the theology of Gabriel Biel was also founded on the notion of the dual powers of God and the ability of the individual "viator" to attain the infusion of grace by doing his best. For Biel and other nominalists, there were two

---

[88] See Heiko Augustinus Oberman, *The Harvest of Medieval Theology: Gabriel Biel and Late Medieval Nominalism*. The question of what exactly constituted nominalism and who should be identified as a nominalist and to what extent remains a vexing question. The general state of the discussion and a useful overview is presented by William J. Courtenay, in his "Nominalism and Late Medieval Religion."

[89] Oberman, *The Harvest of Medieval Theology*, pp. 202–203.

[90] Ibid., p. 206.

[91] Ibid., p. 225.

[92] Ibid., pp. 127–128.

[93] Ibid., p. 123.

powers of God: *potentia ordinata*, by which God can and does "do certain things according to the laws which he freely established" and *potentia absoluta*, whereby "God can do everything that does not imply contradiction, whether God has decided to do these things [*de potentia ordinata*] or not."[94] In *potentia ordinata* man was continually in either a state of "culpa" or "gratia," because of a particular decision of God. In *de potentia absoluta*, however, one could be guiltless with the corresponding infusion of grace.[95] Grace was granted to man only if he did his best, literally what was in him (*facere quod in se est*).[96] Intellectual faith became living faith in man not through acquired faith but through faith as a gift from God, sacramentally infused.[97] In the baptism of children, for example, children were infused with grace not on the basis of their own merits, but rather through the merits of Christ.[98] Similarly, it was by means of the *de potentia ordinata* that God changed the Law of the Old Testament to the Law of the New.

Biel used the image of the two breasts to represent the Old and the New Testaments. For Biel the New was the perfection and fulfillment of the Old. "Moses' Law required exterior acts and ceremonies, whereas Christ calls for interior acts which are not forced but voluntary."[99] Although the ceremonial and judicial laws of the Old Testament have been abrogated, the moral law, centered on the Decalogue, remained and was approved by Christ.[100] The Old Law was largely temporal, the New eternal. Oberman writes, "Quoting Scotus, Biel documents further the quantitative character of the difference between the Old and the New. The sacraments of the New Testament are efficacious, not merely *ex opere operantis* but also *ex opere operato* and confer therefore more grace than the sacraments of the Old Testament."[101] The literal sense of the Law, i.e. without grace, killed, but the spiritual sense of the Law, i.e. the Gospel, saved. The New Law was the Old Law, without the ceremonial and judicial laws, but infused with grace.

In the later fifteenth century many theologians reiterated that the Old Testament laws, sacraments, and promises were only imperfect and incomplete figures of those of the New Testament. Yet the trend of late medieval theology, and of Gabriel Biel in particular, "was to minimize the difference between the sacraments of the old and new laws in such a way that the Old Testament rite of circumcision became more than a mere *figura* of Christian baptism."[102]

---

[94] Ibid., p. 37.
[95] Ibid., p. 48.
[96] Ibid., pp. 72 and 132.
[97] Ibid., p. 74.
[98] Ibid., pp. 84 and 268.
[99] Ibid., p. 112.
[100] Ibid., p. 145.
[101] Ibid., p. 114.
[102] Preus, *From Shadow to Promise*, p. 130.

Unlike Bonaventure and his followers who insisted that the old sacraments came with no covenant attached,[103] Biel found the covenant (*pactum*), to be understood historically, a basis for the real continuity between the Old Testament and New Testament. He wrote:

> Let it not seem bad-sounding and fictitious to anyone that God in the New Law has celebrated this sort of *pacta* with the faithful, since you can read that he did the same thing in the Old Law. For He says: "This is my *pactum* which you shall observe: every male of yours shall be circumcised." And further on "Any man the flesh of whose foreskin has not been circumcised, his soul shall be wiped out from the people." Where, in the converse sense, it can be argued: if he has been circumcised, he shall be saved. And on the basis of the establishment of this pactum God assists this circumcision by remitting original sin, and he causes grace, which is the means of leading man to salvation.[104]

According to Biel there were many ceremonial observances in the Old Law,[105] but as to whether or not these sacraments of the Old Law conferred grace, Biel brought forth three positions—two extreme and one moderate. According to the first, which he identified with Hugh of St. Victor, the sacraments of the Old Law offered grace by the power of the sacrament or *ex opere operato*. According to the second opinion, the sacraments of the Old Law did not confer grace *ex opere operato*, likewise they did not confer faith or *caritas*. The third opinion, held by Alexander (of Hales, *ca.* 1185–1245), Aquinas, and Scotus, seems to have been the one favored by Biel himself: while the sacraments of the Old Law did not confer grace either through their own power or on the grounds of the mere performance of the rite (*ex opere operato*), they did nevertheless provide a certain amount of merit because of the intent of the recipient (*modum meriti ex opere operante*).

Another important late medieval theologian and preacher focused his thought along similar lines, stressing the ability of man to attain grace. Johann Geiler of Kaysersberg (1445–1510) argued, contrary to Scotus, that man prior to original sin enjoyed a peaceful relation between his higher and lower powers.[106] However, God's grace or original righteousness was withdrawn from him, because man was not willing to be obedient to God. According to Geiler, "'we are wounded in *naturalibus*; the *naturalia* are not, however, corrupted—'" the weakness of nature is a result of sin.[107] "It is Geiler's constantly recurring admonition that man has been endowed with a free will, that he alone is the cause of his sins through the misuse of his will, and that he must exercise his freedom to

---

[103] Ibid.

[104] Ibid., pp. 131–132; where he cites Biel, *Expos Lect* 47 X (II, 228).

[105] See *Leviticus, Di, Qiii.*

[106] E. Jane Dempsey Douglass, *Justification in Late Medieval Preaching: A Study of John Geiler of Keisersberg*, p. 106.

[107] Ibid., pp. 108–109.

turn away from sin."[108] At one point Geiler quoted Biel to argue that if the sinner did what was in his power, God would respond and grant him grace. In his later writings, Geiler articulated that through the sacraments moral virtues could even be infused.[109] "In the case of baptism, the only person who could profit from the sacrament *ex opere operato* was the one who was being baptized, for baptism was a spiritual regeneration which could not be repeated. However, *ex opere operantis*, by virtue of the merit either of the administrant or of the person being baptized, the sacrament could be efficacious for the baptismal candidate and for others, just as in the case of other meritorious works."[110] It is the emphasis on the individual's ability and the importance of internal moral virtue, as opposed to the efficacy of the sacrament itself, which was most noticeable in the later Middle Ages.

Nicholas of Cusa (1401–1464), reforming bishop, philosopher, and conciliarist, provides a further (conciliar) development in the assessment of the Old Testament sacraments. Cusa's ideas are of particular importance, given his work against the Jews and his widespread reputation.[111] While Nicholas was not willing to concede that the sacraments of the Christians, of the New Testament, were not central to the salvation of the soul, he still believed that all people shared a common faith. The ceremonies of the Old Law may themselves differ from those of the New, but there was a Law that underlay both. Nicholas stated his assessment of circumcision rather fully in his *De Pace Fidei*, where his Paul, arguing with a Tartar, urged that:

> The acceptance of circumcision is really not pertinent to the truth of salvation. In fact, circumcision does not save any individual, and certainly without it one may attain salvation. Yet whoever does not hold that circumcision is a requisite for reasons of health, but allows it to be performed on his foreskin so that he might be in conformity with Abraham and his followers, will certainly not be condemned for this action, as long as he holds to this basic faith which we are discussing. Thus, for example, Christ was circumcised, as well as many other Christians who lived after Him. The Ethiopians mentioned by St. James and others were not circumcised in the sense that they considered this a sacrament necessary for salvation. The real problem in this matter is how we may preserve peace among the various believers, if some are circumcised and some are not. The fact of the matter is that the great majority of the world's population is not circumcised, and I would contend that circumcision is not a matter of necessity.

At this point, Cusa continued with a discussion regarding unanimity:

---

[108] Ibid., p. 150.
[109] Ibid., pp. 123–124.
[110] Ibid., p. 125.
[111] See Beck, ed., *From the High Middle Ages to the Eve of the Reformation*, pp. 588–589; see also GJ III, pt. 1, "Friedberg," "Halberstadt," and "Hildesheim, and GJ III, pt. 2, "Minden."

In my judgment, peace would be better preserved if the minority would conform to the majority *with whom they are already united in basic belief*. Yet, on
the other hand, if for the purpose of maintaining peace the majority should
conform to the will of the minority and receive circumcision, it should be
done in an arbitrary fashion, so that tranquility might rest on a firmer basis
because of this interchange of common practices. In this way, if some nations
accept the basic beliefs of the Christians, and the Christians, on the other
hand, allow themselves to be circumcised in order to maintain peace, its foundation will be better secured. Nonetheless, I think there will be practical difficulties in this. *It will suffice that there be unanimity in the matter of belief and
the law of charity, and that toleration in the matter of ritual be allowed* [emphasis
added].[112]

The ceremonial aspect of the sacrament was here divorced from actual belief—
it was a mere external sign of a "common" faith that all nations and religions
shared. That faith was based upon faith in Christ. Jews, concluded Nicholas's
Paul, should have had no problem accepting baptism, since they already believed
in the idea of religious ablutions or washings, or indeed of accepting infant baptism, for they already allowed boys to undergo circumcision eight days after birth.
Circumcision should, therefore, merely "be commuted to Baptism." For Cusa,
the individual clinged to the unity of God, *but in Christ*—as Cusa reiterated
his famous dictum (also in *On Learned Ignorance*) that

> ... therefore in Christ it must be held that human nature is so united with
> the Word or divine nature that the human nature does not pass into the
> divine but clings so indissolubly with it that it is a distinct person not in
> itself but in divine nature; so that the human nature, summoned to succeed
> to eternal life with the divine nature, can acquire immortality in the divine
> nature.[113]

Even if the Jews did not believe that Jesus was the "prince of nature in whom
all defects of all men are made up for," it was enough that a majority of the
world recognized him as such.[114] In any event, Cusa concluded, the Jews,
through their strict obedience to the Law, demonstrated that they believed in
an eternal life. Unity in belief and true faith here were more significant than
any ceremonial differences between the Old and the New Law.

This discussion indicates the complexity of the religious thought of the Middle
Ages but also demonstrates the extent to which the rituals that defined Christian
community, and for that matter urban Christian community, were in need of
clarification and were being reconsidered. Not only the role of the sacrament
itself, but even the role and power of the administrant became significant points
of discussion in the fifteenth century. Such discussions, though not grounded

---

[112] Nicholas of Cusa, *Werke*, vol. 1, p. 363. The translation is from John Patrick
Dolan, *Unity and Reform: Selected Writings of Nicholas de Cusa*, pp. 231–232.
[113] Dolan, *Unity and Reform*, pp. 215–216.
[114] Nicholas of Cusa, *Werke*, vol. 1, pp. 356–357; i.e. Christians and Arabs.

in the same intellectual currents, had substantial parallels in the social and political developments of the German cities. Of particular importance was the question of the individual's capacity to free him/herself from sin and the actual value
of the sacraments. As has frequently been maintained, theology and society echo,
but also help to shape, one another. A brief discussion of forced baptism will
lead us closer to the significance of these theological changes for the social standing of the Jews and the internal self-definition of Christian community.

A number of medieval theologians addressed the issue of whether the Jews
could be forced to accept Christian sacraments. Regarding the issue of forced
baptism, John Duns Scotus, countering the Thomistic position, argued that all
Christian princes were required to baptize any children who were in danger of
being reared without the proper religious education and worship. Scotus went
so far as to advise that all Jews, including children, be forced by the temporal
powers to observe the Christian religion.[115] The late medieval canonists however tended to avoid Scotus' argument for mass forced baptism.

Gabriel Biel generally agreed with Scotus regarding the forced baptism of Jews.
For Biel the secular authorities possessed both the power and obligation to prevent not only the physical harm inflicted by a parent on a child, but also the
spiritual damage to the soul caused to a child by a parent who kept him or
her from the true Christian religion.[116] Here again we must consider the question of moral authority.

The issue of forced baptism came to the fore in a number of important
works by the great Freiburg professor of law, Ulrich Zasius (1461–1535). Zasius
argued against a number of authorities who declared against forced baptism
(Aquinas, the author of the ordinary gloss to *Decretum* of Gratian [ca. 1140],
John Zemeke [Teutonicus], Durandus of St.-Pourçain OP, Zabarella [c. 1339–
1417], Jean Gerson [1362–1428], Nicholas de Tudeschis OSB [1386–1445]).
Zasius contended that paternal power could be dissolved if it posed an imped-
iment to the true faith. Everyone must work for the salvation of others, and
a child forced to sin by a parent could and should be emancipated, for to deny
a child baptism was to condemn him to certain perdition.

The case of Jews was similar. Zasius first asserted that Jews were slaves, and
then argued that, as slaves, they also should be compelled to accept Christianity.
Zasius wrote that "Jews are surely slaves, attested in canon law, due to their
crime of deicide, and in the law of the state, due to the conquest of Jerusalem
by [emperor] Titus in 70 A.D. It is always a good work to liberate slaves, but
this comes for Jews only through conversion, especially as children."[117] Jews as
slaves were allowed to hold their goods only by the piety of Christians.[118] Even

---

[115] Steven W. Rowan, "Ulrich Zasius and the Baptism of Jewish Children," p. 19.
[116] Ibid., p. 20.
[117] Ibid., pp. 12–13.
[118] Ibid., p. 14.

though they were really a race of slaves, however, the Jews, in their deeds, were rebellious:

> But today we see that everything has been turned into its opposite, and the Jews are most ungrateful to Christians, whom they curse daily with public curses and public execrations, they despoil with their usuries, they deny their servile dues, they deride our most immaculate faith and proceed to defile it with the blackest blasphemies against our Savior, even in public. And, what is cruelest of all, they lust for Christian blood, which those most cruel blood-suckers seek by day and night, and which has once again occurred in our own day in these very lands (of which we cannot speak without the throbbing of our hearts) . . .[119]

Zasius contended that all Jews should be forcibly converted. Earlier authorities had argued that all Jews could not be converted, for a certain requisite number of Jews had to be on hand as witnesses to the second coming of Jesus. Zasius, however, asserted that even if all Jewish children in Christendom were baptized, the seed of Israel, necessary to witness the second coming of Christ, would not be wiped out since a sufficient number of Jews lived in Muslim lands.[120]

Zasius, however, "never explicitly endorsed his doctrine of general forced baptism."[121] In the end, the question of the forced baptism of the Jews did not, for him, turn on the question of whether or not Jews really were slaves, but rather on the ability of secular authority to overrule paternal powers in general. If the power of the prince to compel the "baptism of children was absolute, then the servitude of the Jews made no difference in this matter. They were on the same footing as all other residents of Christendom." Steven Rowan argues that such a vision of the Christian commune, which insisted on conformity and permitted, even required, forced baptism, "inspired Zasius in his codification of the laws of Freiburg in 1520: he saw the foundation of the town to be the family, and the educational process to be the primary duty of the resident, overseen by the Christian state authorities."[122] Rowan concludes that "once accepted, the notion of the revivified Christian community had room only for an interim toleration for religious minorities. The new Christian community would evangelize the Jews, and the result would be their unification into the faith or their flight."[123] Such a vision of Christian community, with its concomitant discussion of the nature of authority in relation to religion and communal membership is surely significant for the developments within the cities I will discuss below.

---

[119] Ibid., p. 16.

[120] Ibid., p. 15. Scotus had held that the preservation of the Seed on a single distant island would be enough; see pp. 16–17.

[121] Ibid., p. 21.

[122] Ibid., pp. 22–23.

[123] Ibid., p. 24.

CONCLUSION

Significant changes in the reading of Scripture and notions of Law led to new definitions of ritual and community, especially in the works of the nominalists and even later. The theology of the nominalists helped to break down the medieval sacramental system by separating the automatic effect of the sacrament, *ex opere operato*, from the conditional effect, *ex opere operantis*, that is, emphasizing the disposition of the recipient at the time of the performance of the sacramental rite. In their emphasis on the ability of the individual to attain a certain level of grace through his own efforts, the nominalists began to focus more on man outside of justifying grace, on man prior to grace, and on the ability of man rather than the actual rituals that helped one to attain grace. For Cusa, therefore, an internal intellectual conversion superseded any outward adherence to ceremony or ritual. The difficulties brought about by this shift in the understanding of the sacraments afforded the opportunity in the later Middle Ages to revise even further the sacramental system, now that the Law was defined less by the ceremonial or ritual character of the sacraments and more by a certain moral code, which was required by all of the participants within the community. Once such a shift toward moral Law was complete, the objective ties to (and controls from) a larger church became unnecessary, and the local community refashioned itself in the image of the church as a community of grace. Still, a localized church did not possess the capacity to create priests who could administer authentic sacraments. Instead, it began to regulate the beliefs of its members by policing their morals.

Discussion of the sacrament of baptism was particularly relevant to defining community and, eventually, to understanding the role that the Jews were to have in the community. For Ockham and others, baptism was only baptism if the baptized assented, or at the very least did not dissent. In the heated discussion regarding forced baptism in the fifteenth century two contrary schools of thought ended up presenting the same message. For Scotus, Biel, and Zasius, forced baptism was related to paternal power and acceptable; unity in society could be achieved through coerced conformity. For Thomas, Durandus, and Gerson, on the other hand, forced baptism was not acceptable; unity or social cohesion had to be achieved through a certain ecumenical conciliarism. In the end both schools of thought sought the same goal—a uniform Christian society, which, although it could tolerate a degree of difference, became increasingly unable to absorb elements that fell outside more precisely prescribed borders.[124]

As the Old Testament increasingly became more clearly an area of Christian concern, Jews, who had been able to lead something of a segregated existence claiming a unique set of laws pertinent to themselves alone, began to be pushed

---

[124] See the conclusions regarding the Christian sense of organic unity drawn by Jeremy Cohen in *The Friars and the Jews: The Evolution of Medieval Anti-Judaism*.

from their native theological grounds. In the later Middle Ages, membership in Christian society became more firmly rooted in faith in Christ and a specifically defined moral system and not in membership in a church, following a pre-scribed sacramental system. Christians were becoming more Jewish, if by that we mean that they identified themselves more closely with the Old Testament and the people of the Old Testament. They were, however, no longer Jews in a pre-exilic sense, with centralized rituals and institutions; they were instead becoming Diaspora Jews, bound together by moral codes and adherence to law.

The theological discussions about biblical interpretation and sacraments in this chapter could have profound consequences when translated into the realm of urban communal politics or expounded by urban preachers. The expansion and consolidation of the German burghers' identity was accomplished at the expense of "outsiders" such as Jews and clergy. As the sources make clear, both Jews and clerics were being pushed out of the spaces that they had once occu-pied. Important shifts in late medieval theology and religion allowed Christians to turn from an idea of community defined through sacraments to one revolv-ing around a concept of moral law, a moral law which could be manipulated to uproot traditional authority. In the cities the nature of the administration of the sacraments changed. The space occupied by clergy was being taken over by Christian burghers who began to conceive of themselves as something of a priesthood of all Christians. At the same time that a unique sacramental author-ity was being stripped from the clergy, a unique heritage was also appropriated from the Jews in the formation of a new religious identity. In the rural south-west, Peter Blickle has argued convincingly, the political community was begin-ning to be equated with the ecclesiastical community, and the church was adjusted to the existing political culture of rural society; that is, it was com-munalized or localized.[125] This seems to be true of the urban areas as well. Our discussion of rituals also reveals important developments in the ways that Christians imagined Jews and defined themselves and the community of the church. Such definitions were particularly explosive in the cities of the later Middle Ages, where conflicting conceptions of communal and personal piety began to clash, and anticlericalism and burgher animosity toward the landed nobility escalated.

---

[125] Blickle, *Communal Reformation*, p. 165.

3

Language(s) of Community

In the previous chapter I argued that the theological shift that deconstructed the boundaries between the two testaments, and correspondingly between Christian sacraments and Jewish rituals, forced a transformation in Christian ideas of community. It now remains to be seen to what extent and in what ways the transformation of community was manifest in the late medieval German cities, where the majority of Jews lived. At stake in this chapter, therefore, is the notion of community in the cities in both its religious and secular legal senses. But how can the language of the urban evidence, here primarily chronicles and lawbooks, reveal broader social conditions and changes? After a brief review of the nature of both language and law, at least in its written form, which becomes particularly significant in the German cities in the late thirteenth and fourteenth centuries, I will explore the development of legal discussions that could be related to and appropriated by the urban community.

LANGUAGE AND LAW AS SOCIAL ARTIFICE

Mary Douglas long ago recognized that boundaries are important to society.[1] Societies have external boundaries, margins, and internal structure. In such a system, conformity is rewarded and deviation punished. In part, the position relative to boundaries or borders is described in, and in part it is created by, language and representation. Language is not merely a reflection of the spirit and culture of a people, it is intimately intertwined with it. At the end of the eighteenth and in the nineteenth century, it was noted that language was reflective of "people." Wilhelm von Humboldt wrote that "language is, as it were, the external manifestation of the minds of the peoples. Their language is their soul, and their soul is their language."[2]

Language (including writing which is a further representation and transformation of language as an oral system)[3] has the power to represent "events" and

---

[1] See Mary Douglas, *Purity and Danger.*
[2] José Faur, *Golden Doves with Silver Dots,* p. xii.
[3] See Jacques Derrida, *Of Grammatology,* p. 33. On p. 35 he discusses the idea of writing as external "clothing" of speech.

perspectives; it also can affect the course of events and their re-presentation. That is, language both describes and creates.[4] Much has been made of recent attempts to deconstruct language, and for that matter the very act of thinking and representing. It has become increasingly clear that the way that we use, and abuse, language tells a great deal about the object of our linguistic discourse; it also tells a great deal about the subjective assumptions of the agents involved in such discourse. Language reflects social and political developments.[5] Derrida quotes Rousseau:

> but languages, as they change the symbols, also modify the ideas which the symbols express. Minds are formed by language, thoughts take their color from its ideas. Reason alone is common to all. Every language has its own form, a difference which may be partly cause and partly effect of difference in national character; this conjecture appears to be confirmed by the fact that in every nation under the sun speech follows the changes of manners, and is preserved or altered along with them.[6]

In assessing the experiences, and the narration of those experiences, of Europeans traveling to the New World at the end of the fifteenth and the beginning of the sixteenth centuries, Stephen Greenblatt has argued that representation anecdotes belie multiple sites of representation and the movement along and through those sites by both individuals and groups.[7] He speaks of the reproduction and circulation of a mimetic capital. Representation, including representation in language, forces the combination of a stockpile of representations, i.e., previous images, as well as new representations based upon a "social relation to the product." Greenblatt argues that "representations are not only products but producers, capable of decisively altering the very forces that brought them into being."[8] Greenblatt is concerned with the intersection of European identity and vocabulary, the interaction with the Other, and so the creation of a culminating representational discourse that is forced to account for things outside the discursive structures of Europeans but through the European discursive system. As Greenblatt notes, "someone witnessed something amazing, but what most matters takes place not 'out there' or along the receptive surfaces of the body where the self encounters the world, but deep within, at the

---

[4] This point is somewhat different from the argument of J.G.A. Pocock, who asserts that "the language determines what can be said in it, but is capable of being modified by what is said in it . . ." See his "The Concept of Language," p. 20. Here I give freer reign to language as a transformer not only of internal discourse, but also of larger social reality.

[5] Derrida, *Of Grammatology*, p. 169.

[6] Ibid., p. 170.

[7] This seems to push even further the distinction made by Faur regarding two classes of reading: semiotic, which seeks to discern the intended meaning of the author; and semantic reading, which processes the multiple possible readings of a text in creating a "single significant text." See Faur, *Golden Doves*, p. 120.

[8] Stephen Greenblatt, *Marvelous Possessions*, p. 6.

vital, emotional center of the witness."[9] Such language and representation possess the power not only to recast the outside, the Other; they also have the
potential to transform the inside, the producer, be it a culture or an individual witness or writer (Though, of course, it downplays the actual event, the
external intention, in favor of perception!). The way in which Europeans came
to terms with what was outside forced them to reconsider the inside,[10] and in
certain ways to readjust, through the interaction, their own world-view and expectations. Their very experiences, or rather their new experiences, somehow
impelled a new identity.[11]

A similar examination of the role of language in interpretation, that is beyond
mere "representation," can be found in the rather more polemical, and con-
tested, writing of Edward Said. For Said, as for Greenblatt and others, the way
that Europeans describe the Other says a great deal more about the Europeans
than it does about the Other. Still, such representations no doubt affect, at
many levels, the Other; and they also serve as justification for European hege-
mony. Said writes that "European culture gained in strength and identity by
setting itself off against the Orient as a sort of surrogate and even underground
self."[12]

So, language is both a reflection of society and a social artifice, at once
changing and static. Ferdinand de Saussure distinguished between language and
speaking. While speaking is individuated and momentary, language possesses a
social context, a community of speakers.[13] As such, then, according to Saussure,
language must be understood, as all sciences, diachronically and synchronically.
Diachrony is the vertical axis of language "concerned with the evolution and
development of individual elements as they unfold successively through time."
Synchrony, by contrast, corresponds to a horizontal axis and is concerned with
the "static aspect of language at any one time."[14] In applying and then expand-
ing Saussure to rabbinic literature, José Faur assesses the following frequently
cited and highly interpreted passage of Maimonides:[15]

> The wise man had said: 'Golden apples in a silver mesh, this is a word spo-
> ken on its circles [faces].' Hear, now, the significance of what he said.

---

[9] Ibid., p. 16.
[10] A good example is the debate in Spain over the Native Americans. See Anthony
Pagden, *The Fall of Natural Man*. For a broader consideration of the effects of contact
see William Brandon, *Old Worlds for New*; for the biological effects, see Alfred Crosby's
The Columbian Exchange.
[11] Faur quotes Maurice Blanchot along similar lines; see Faur, *Golden Doves*, p. 127.
[12] Edward Said, *Orientalism*, p. 3.
[13] Faur, *Golden Doves*, p. 43.
[14] Faur, summarizing Saussure; See ibid., p. xiv.
[15] See, for example, Colbert I. Nepaulsingh, *Apples of Gold in Filigrees of Silver: Jewish
Writing in the Eye of the Inquisition* (New York, 1995); and, *Apples of Gold in Settings
of Silver: Essays in Medieval Jewish Exegesis and Polemics* (Papers in Mediaeval Studies,
no. 14), edited by Frank Talmage and Barry Dov Walfish (Toronto, 1999).

Maskiyot is a chiseled net, containing places with very finely pierced perforations, as in jewelry work . . . Solomon was saying that a word spoken on its two orbits is like a golden apple in a silver mesh with very fine eyelets. Note how wonderfully this statement describes a meaningful metaphor. He was saying that in an utterance with two faces, i.e., with an outer and an inner one, the outer [face] must be as valuable as silver. However, the inner [face] must be more precious than the outer one, so that the inner [face] in relation to the outer [face] would be as gold is to silver. Moreover, the outer [face] must contain some indication pointing out to the observer the contents of the inner face. In the same fashion a golden apple covered by a silver mesh with very fine eyelets when seen from a distance or carelessly appears to be a silver apple; but on closer examination, to one with sharp sight, its content will be discernible, and he would know that it is of gold.[16]

Faur, remarking on this passage, argues that:

Using the verse 'Golden doves with silver dots' (Songs 1:11) as a metaphor, the rabbis identified 'golden doves' with the divine *oraculum* prior to articulation, and 'silver dots' with the orarculum as processed into language and communicated to the people of Israel. As with gold and silver, ideality and articulation could be equivalent, but ultimately they are not reducible to one another: silver lacks the absolute density of value represented by gold . . . There is a perennial residue—the specific appurtenance of the 'golden doves'— that will always elude the system of value of the silver dots.' Here, iteration involves the *transformation* of the original into a system of values: without transformation, repetition is impossible. The repetition, however, is never identical to the original.[17]

Now this concept of transformation through repetition, and simultaneously repetition as transformation, seems to have a particular relevance to legal language and the solidification of law through the medium of writing. The very act of issuing law simultaneously relates behavior and indicates that a broader social context is at stake; often the repetition of laws, as we find in the late medieval urban lawbooks, suggests that the laws are somehow important in communal definition, and that the laws themselves are not always observed—hence the importance of reiteration. In an extremely clever play on terms, Michel de Certeau argues, in a discussion of writing, that "what is at stake is the relation between the law and the body—a body is itself defined, delimited, and articulated by what writes it."[18] But de Certeau plays here with the concept of body, which is simultaneously the literary corpus of the law and the individual who is subject to the law, both being defined and organized by the law itself. All law, according to de Certeau, is inscribed on bodies; law takes hold of them and makes them into its "texts:" "through all sorts of initiations (ritual,

---

[16] Quoted in Faur, *Golden Doves*, p. 115.
[17] Ibid., pp. xvi–xvii.
[18] Michel de Certeau, *The Practice of Everyday Life*, p. 139.

at school, etc.), it transforms them into tables of the law, into living tableaux of rules and customs, into actors in the drama organized by a social order."[19] Applying such theoretical structures to our theme, we might conclude that the gap between what the law or language signifies as a social construction and how it then realigns and reshapes the social construction itself is where we are likely to find social community. The language and law of community, within a broad social context and representative of change in its reiteration, may allow us to peer deeper into the notion of communal identity and so the position of the Jews in late medieval communities, in instances of both change and continuity. What is more, when a language becomes institutionalized it may be appropriated in a variety of ways. According to Pocock, "the more institutionalized a language and the more public it becomes, the more it becomes available for the purposes of a diversity of utterants articulating a diversity of concerns."[20]

Language and, more specifically, the law have the power to form; they do not merely define. The cultural and discursive world in which communal self-identification, inclusion as well as exclusion, occurs is more than linguistic, however. It is also representational in areas of perspective and expression. In his important work on visual perception, Rudolf Arnheim has suggested that the significance of the visual center depends very much on the work in question as well as the perspective of the viewer. Center often is, but does not necessarily have to be, equivalent to the geometrical middle and may be present without being explicitly visible, that is, it is made visible only through objects.[21] Center according to this definition is not just a fixed point but a dimensional vector or field of forces: "When we speak of a center we shall mean mostly the center of a field of forces, a focus from which forces issue and toward which forces converge."[22] The balance of the composition is worked through the interplay of various visual objects as centers of forces.[23] There is often more than one center in a composition, and so the relation between various objects or structures within the composition exist in a relation that is dynamic, not static. Although a composition is organized around a balancing center the perspective and so the balance of the viewer is centered upon the self.[24] (And although a stray dot might disturb the equilibrium of a circle and its center, the imbalance can be remedied by creating a corresponding imbalance in the opposite direction, creating a directed tension that restores the balance to the center,[25] or by the shifting of perspective.)

---

[19] Ibid.

[20] Pocock, "The Concept of Language," p. 24.

[21] Rudolf Arnheim, *The Power of Center: A Study of Composition in the Visual Arts*, p. 1.

[22] Ibid., p. 2.

[23] Ibid., p. 3.

[24] Ibid., p. 4.

[25] Ibid., p. 6.

In many ways, if we conceive Judaism and Christianity as isolated spheres with centers of "community," this becomes a powerful analogy. The problem is that the isolated spheres come into contact at different points, depending on which set of criteria we examine. In theological interaction, for example, there may be a center of contact that includes conflict such as forced baptism and disputation, but that also includes voluntary conversion, exegetical dialogue, and commonality of approach to religious issues. On an economic plane the Jewish sphere may be nearly wholly circumscribed within the Christian sphere, since it is the minority culture of the Jews that functions within the majority culture of Christianity—on the other hand it is not entirely subsumed since it no doubt adds unique elements to the interaction. The same type of distinctions could be made for political, social or cultural interactions.

How we define the center depends on our perspective as historians and participants; but the fact of the matter is that it is difficult to locate the "center" in one or more three-dimensional fields—particularly so since the human mind travels along a Cartesian grid of horizontal and vertical relationships that lack concentric dimensionality. Although a truly three-dimensional center may be located inside of the visual object it may appear to us as a point external to the object, and may often, therefore, not correspond to the true center of the object—that is, our vision is limited by our fields of perception and the type of object presented. Our vision is further limited in that the placement of the balancing center depends very much "... on whether the building [read object, subject] is seen in isolation or as part of a larger setting. In the broader context the building's perceived center may be some place that would not seem centric if the building were considered by itself."[26] One final observation from Arnheim's work adds to our discussion, namely, that although the visual world—and I would read the historical world as well—is endless, our comprehension requires boundaries—in history based on our perspective and the questions we ask, as well as the sources available. Arnheim writes that "... we can neither perceive nor understand nor act without carving limited areas out of the world's continuity. Not only does the range of the endless whole and the place of each part in it surpass our comprehension, but the character, function, and weight of each object changes with the particular context in which we see it ... This means that the nature of an object can be defined only in relation to the context in which it is considered."[27]

When the isolated spheres of Judaism and Christianity, or better Jews and Christians, collide, in this case in the dimension of religion and law, we are tempted to the see the resulting area of overlap—which is comprised of points of conflict as well as calm—as the center. We frame the entire Jewish-Christian relation and create an artificial center out of the individual's or group's experience or the relation of the two religions—an artificial center which loses the

---

[26] Ibid., p. 8.
[27] Ibid., p. 42.

focus of the independently isolated spheres. This is not necessarily a problem, so long as we recognize it for what it is. Too often, however, this created center becomes the qualifier for at least one of the religions, most typically the minority or Jewish one, and to the exclusion of the "true" center of the original sphere—in this case as we defined it as the "community" in its various and layered meanings. Indeed, it is possible to frame this newly created center so that it does not even include the original center or presents the original center as a mere marginal element within the composition. There are, of course, other options as well. One might visualize three new spheres—one the original Jewish sphere, one the original Christian sphere, both of which appear as degreed crescents, and the new oblique sphere of their interaction. But removing the margins of the original spheres also distorts the true center of the originals in an artificial way. On the positive side such a division allows the continual shading between the parts and does not set the two original and isolated spheres off as dichotomous.

THE LANGUAGE AND STRUCTURE OF LAW IN THE MIDDLE AGES

The *Concordia Discordantium Canonum* distinguishes two basic categories of law (*leges*): divine and human.[28] Included in the divine is the law of nature, and in human law, the customs or mores of humans. As regards justice (*ius*), the *Concordia* distinguishes between natural (*naturale*), civil (*ciuile*), and that of nations (*gentium*).[29] The *ius gentium*,[30] however, which covers a variety of legal interactions between peoples, including war, federated pacts, and religion, also includes a *ius publicum*.[31]

Similar types of distinctions can be found for the entire Middle Ages in the *Oxford English Dictionary*, which offers 23 distinct definitions of "Law." "Law," in the earliest chronological examples delineated "form," or a "body of rules," "body of commandments," "moral or ceremonial precepts," "religious system," or a "class of human institutions." The scientific or philosophical uses of the term seem to belong to the seventeenth century and later. The specific usages and themes that can be dated, to some extent, during the high and late Middle Ages, in particular between the thirteenth and sixteenth centuries, are rather telling, however. In this group we must include: law as custom, customary rule or usage, traced to the end of the twelfth century;[32] law as rule of proper conduct, beginning in the thirteenth century;[33] the law as a (civil) profession, first dated to 1340[34]—though already in the *Digest* of Justinian the Roman jurists

---

[28] Dist. I. C. I.
[29] Ibid., VII.
[30] Ibid., IX.
[31] Ibid., XI.
[32] *Oxford English Dictionary* (OED), definition 14.
[33] Ibid., definition 15.
[34] Ibid., definition 7.

"are deservedly called priests . . .," or in the *Gloss Ordinaria* (thirteenth century), "just as the priests minister and confection things holy, so do we, since the laws are most sacred . . . And just as the priest, when imposing penance, renders to each one what is his right, so do we when we judge;"[35] as rule of action or procedure, with some thirteenth century precedent, but obviously based on biblical passages;[36] law as the specific action of courts in procuring redress of grievances and enforcing claims, beginning in the middle of the fifteenth century.[37] These distinctions hint at the complexity of law, but also at the evolving sense of its meaning, particularly as a professional endeavor with accompanying bureaucratic machinery.

The same is certainly true of the late medieval cities, in which substantial legal books and codifications began to appear at the middle and end of the thirteenth century.[38] A similar transformation spread throughout Germany in the later Middle Ages. Roman Law began to spread throughout Germany in the thirteenth century as evidenced by the creation of a number of significant lawbooks, such as the *Sachsenspiegel* of Eike von Repgow (between 1221 and 1224 in Latin; and 1224 and 1227 for a German edition), the *Deutschenspiegel* (1274/75), the *Schwabenspiegel* (1275/76), and the *Frankenspiegel* (1328 to 1338), as well as a number of city lawbooks such as the *Meissner Rechtsbuch* (1357 to 1387); and by the fifteenth century, particularly in the larger cities, a secular learned class of jurists began to appear.[39] According to Gerald Strauss, "in the course of the fourteenth and fifteenth centuries, the legal and judicial structure of the Holy Roman Empire underwent a major transformation. Known as the "Reception of Roman Law," this sweeping change altered permanently the ways in which Germans thought about law, litigated, judged, and governed. Given the permeation of society by legal attitudes, this change affected, in one way or another, most areas of public and private life."[40]

---

[35] The first quote is from Constantin Fasolt, "Visions of Order in the Canonists and Civilians," p. 36; the second from Ernst H. Kantorowicz, "Mysteries of State: An Absolutist Concept and its Late Medieval Origins," p. 386.

[36] *OED*, definition 16.

[37] Ibid., definition 8.

[38] For the relation between urban records, social order, and communal self identity, see Brigitte Bedos-Rezak, "Civic Liturgies and Urban Records in Northern France, 1100–1400," in *City and Spectacle in Medieval Europe*, edited by Barbara A. Hanawalt and Kathryn L. Reyerson (Minneapolis, 1994 (second printing, 1999)): 34–55.

[39] See Norbert Horn, "Die legistische Literatur der Kommentatoren und der Ausbreitung des gelehrten Rechts," in Helmut Coing, ed., *Handbuch der Quellen und Literatur der neueren europäischen Privatrechtsgeschichte*, pp. 283–284.

[40] Gerald Strauss, *Law, Resistance, and the State*, p. 56. For Strauss, who is primarily interested in the Reformation and its later development, the movement really only begins in the late fourteenth century through the movement of law students north of the Alps from Italy. See pp. 67f.

COMMUNITY AND LAW AS RELATIONAL SOCIAL SYSTEMS

What precisely can we say about the relationship between the language of law and the social context of law? In his effort to fuse social history and *Begriffs-geschichte*, Reinhart Koselleck argues that "within the practice of textual exegesis, specific study of the use of politicosocial concepts and the investigation of their meaning thus assumes a sociohistorical status. The moments of duration, change, and futurity contained in a concrete political situation are registered through their linguistic traces. Expressed more generally, social conditions and their transformation become in this fashion the objects of analysis."[41] Koselleck further asserts, as we have done above, that "a concept is not simply indicative of the relations that it covers; it is also a factor within them."[42] This must particularly be the case since "each word, even each name, displays a linguistic potentiality beyond the individual phenomenon that it characterizes or names at the given moment."[43] J.G.A. Pocock, on the other hand has distinguished between the social and rhetorical generation of language.[44] Quentin Skinner has similarly argued that there is a difference between explaining and understanding a text—that is, the social context does not necessarily help us explain the meaning of a particular text, even though it may supply a context within which to understand the text.[45]

It is true that there is a discernible tension in the very nature of law. On the one hand, law defines the common good and curbs the capricious will of arbitrary rules; on the other hand, law commands what is right and prohibits what is wrong. Put another way, law can be either the means (the expression of common good) or the end (the standard of right and wrong).[46] Further, there is a distinction between instituting and executing laws.[47] The laws that we will examine in this chapter refer to the common good—both as regards general matters and the Jews—and consciously and simultaneously set standards of action and reflect certain communal (how defined?) values underpinning such standards. The question that we must face in what follows is how we can best understand the legal language of community evident in a variety of social legislation. What is the language of community in the fifteenth century? Is this new language, and, if so, how did it change and how was change received and interpreted? To what extent was the language of community institutional and to what extent was it institutionalized from other discursive units, circumstances, or practices?[48] Pocock makes the important observation that "the cre-

---

[41] Reinhart Koselleck, *"Begriffsgeschichte* and Social History," p. 77.
[42] Ibid., p. 84.
[43] Ibid., p. 89.
[44] See Pocock, "The Concept of Language," p. 26.
[45] See Quentin Skinner, "The History of Ideas," p. 46.
[46] Constantin Fasolt, *Council and Hierarchy*, p. 317.
[47] Ibid., p. 165.
[48] See Pocock, "The Concept of Language," p. 28.

ation of new language may take place in the attempt to maintain the old language no less than in the attempt to change it; cases can be found in which a deliberate and conscious stress on change, process, and modernity is among the strategies of those defending a traditional order, and it is in the logic of the concept of tradition that this should be so."[49]

After reviewing some legal constructs, we will examine how some of the urban chroniclers of the fifteenth century, in particular Burkard Zink of Augsburg, understood and processed such language and legal borders. As we have already seen, law is a system of social rules for regulating relationships among people and groups; similarly, community is relational, not substantial or essential.

Throughout the lawbooks and council edicts of the late medieval German cities, a number of "marginal" groups, including Jews, are portrayed in terms opposed to the commune. But what did the commune mean in late medieval Germany? Community in the later Middle Ages was multi-faceted and depended very much for its definition upon the individuals or groups in question, and context. The very uncertainty of community, combined with weak and competing structures of authority both within and outside of the commune, created an uneasiness and a sense of urgency in defining community. The attempts at such definitions eventually left no room for the Jews, who were increasingly seen as outside of, indeed antithetical to, community.

A central theme of many late medieval legal documents is community or association. The very concept of community, of *gemain*, could be rather ambiguous and fraught with deep tensions. The noun *gemain* or the adjective/adverb *gemainlich* could reflect the unity and display the legislating authority of the council.[50] But *gemain(d)* could also represent more generally the inhabitants of the city—a certain section of the population that did not include citizens— "whether he is from the citizens or the community."[51] Many regulations sought to restrict or prevent gatherings of groups that might usurp authority. Such a *gemain* might include two brothers, or doctors—"that no doctor or pharmacist may have a community with another . . ."[52]—or handworkers, or all citizens "together" (*gemainclich*), rich and poor, or even entire city populations. Throughout the documents, the antitheses of community are secret societies or communities, *haimlich puntnuzz*, or individuals out for their own good, *aigennutz*.[53] Any individual or group that was perceived to be outside the communal confines was castigated. As Bernd Moeller has argued, the late medieval imperial cities resembled something of a great organic community, a "collective individual," and "whoever put his own advantage ahead of the public interest, provoked

[49] Ibid., p. 32.
[50] Carl Mollow, ed., *Das Rote Buch*, number 19.
[51] Ibid., number 20: "er sei von den burgern oder von der gemaind."
[52] Otto Feger, ed., *Vom Rechtbrief*, p. 34.
[53] Mollow, *Das Rote Buch*, number 13; see also number 15, which juxtaposes *haimlich* and *öffenlich*.

disobedience, or incited discord, and thereby disturbed the peace, was brought
before the court of God himself. Conspirators against the town were treated
like Judas."[54]

Jews were placed within this field of discourse, and the seemingly private nature
of their religious and social existence marked them as true outsiders (by the
early sixteenth century, the Jews even comprise their own *gemain*),[55] who needed
to be kept apart from the commune. Invariably, Jews were perceived as opponents to the *gemain* or as detrimental to the city. In a letter to the emperor,
the council of Regensburg sought permission to expel the Jews because of the
damage they were thought to cause to the common city and especially to its
citizens.[56]

The nature of community was, of course, in large part shaped by a number
of factors, including the identity of a text's author or the framers of city legislation. Unlike the later monastic account of Clemens Sender, who finds community in religious observance, the fifteenth-century Augsburg chroniclers
generally employed the term *gemain* in a rather politically-oriented manner. As
Lyndal Roper has argued, "arms-bearing and oath-swearing were central to this
notion of collective political belonging."[57] In some ways, then, women, Jews,
and clergy were automatically excluded from a certain meaning of community.
The Reformation, according to Roper, saw a shift away from community as defined
by military capacity to community expressed through a "notion of fatherhood,
both biological and social."[58] But this was certainly true only of the Protestant
reformers, for Sender, as we will see, offered a picture of *gemain* that revolved
around correct religious belief. Yet Roper is certainly correct to point out that
gemain has an ambiguous range of definitions that include political and religious aspects. In the chronicles of the fifteenth-century this dichotomy is often
blurred, as the *gemain* became something of both. Indeed the clergy, as Hektor
Mülich reminded us, were often seen as the enemies of both the political and
the religious community. As religious elements of community were appropriated
it became impossible for Jews to remain a part of communal society, let alone
to exist as nonpartisan bystanders within the civic commune. It was not the
case that Jews were heretics,[59] and in the expulsion rhetoric from Augsburg they
were not accused of false belief. Rather, their religious separation became an
aspect of an inevitable and deep political and social separation, for political

---

[54] Bernd Moeller, *Imperial Cities*, pp. 45–46.
[55] Raphael Straus, ed., *Urkunden*, p. 341, February, 1518, ". . . und einer ganzen gemein
Judischheit und auch einer ganzen gemein Stat R. . . ."
[56] Ibid., number 806, in the year 1514.
[57] Lyndal Roper, "'The Common Man,'" p. 19.
[58] Ibid., p. 20.
[59] Jeremy Cohen argues, however, in the context of exegetical discussions of the Jews,
that given changes within the church, Jews were seen as members of a larger group of
unbelievers and increasingly labeled as heretics in the twelfth century. See his *Living
Letters*, pp. 156f.

and religious concepts of community were no longer so clear, as the German burghers attempted to forge community.

In a number of literary works the confrontation between the Jews and the *gemeind* is clear. In *Des Teufels Netz* (*The Devil's Net*), the author wrote "I hear now of several complaints/Which the "gemain" has with the Jews."[60] Acting against the community, Jews are often accused of coveting the goods of their poor, hapless neighbors.[61] The great distance between Jews and Christians is displayed vividly in a song that notes that the Jews are to be banished from Regensburg to "foreign streets."[62] In other places the presence of the Jews spells disaster for the city. The *Toller Mellodie* records that

> Regensburg was ruined
> Because of the Jews
> The business has completely died . . .[63]

In the same song the Jews were ousted by the council and "gmaine," and contrasted with the common utility, "gmainen nutz."[64] Indeed, if we take seriously the contentions of recent scholars that it was precisely the economic difficulties facing the cities in the later Middle Ages, combined with the specific animosities of the authors of the songs and plays, then economic dimensions of the representations of Jews, particularly the concentration on usury, are significant. Edith Wenzel has argued that

> The previous remarks could demonstrate clearly that Hans Folz in his Reimpaarsprüche (and also in his *Fastnachtspiele*) took up an already-formed literary image of the Jew and intensified it with aggressive-polemical language and action, in which he combined the traditional religious accusations against the Jews with economic reproach, which finds its correlation in the actual daily experience of the public. In the eyes of the petty credit-taker the Jews must appear as exploiters and allies of the ruling upper classes . . .[65]

Wenzel compares three different *Reimpaarsprüche* of Folz over a period of time to document the sharpening polemic of Folz against the Jews and to demonstrate the shift from a more purely formulaic religious diatribe against the Jews to a more purely economic one. Wenzel notes Folz's heightened language against the Jews between the years 1479 and 1491 and particularly after 1486, most especially in his *Ein spil von dem herzogen von Burgund* and *Wahrsagebeeren 9b.*[66]

Certainly there were representational elements that could be construed as economic in character: laziness, unproductivity, draining the poor Christians, destroying the city, and others. But there are also elements that were of

---

[60] Rochus Wilhelm von Liliencron, ed., *Historische Volkslieder*, vol. 3, no. 338, p. 287.
[61] *Jüdische Wucher*, in Hans Folz, *Die Reimpaarsprüche*, p. 312.
[62] Von Liliencron, *Historische Volkslieder*, vol. 3, p. 327.
[63] Ibid., p. 329.
[64] Ibid., p. 331.
[65] Edith Wenzel, "Zur Judenproblematik bei Hans Folz," here at pp. 98–101.
[66] Vv. 127–132.

a religious quality (even in the later plays), elements of criminality, elements that focus on the very difference between Jews and Christians: different rituals, dress, quarters, and the perceived arrogance of the Jews.

Although often excluded, Jews could become burghers in many cities and were often required to take oaths of loyalty to the city. According to the standard formula for the oath, the Jews, who were assembled in their synagogue (*Schul*) would swear an oath on the Pentateuch. The oath could be completely general, or it could pertain to particular matters, for example, pledges, debts, or prison.[67] A good example of such an oath can be found in a formula from the Nuremberg ordinances of the fifteenth century. According to this article:

> Let it be known that any Jew who is a citizen here should vow and swear his Jewish oath, that he will further the greater good ... without all deceit, and that he also will be obedient and subservient to the council in everything ...[68]

It is of interest that the oath that a Jew took was called a "Jewish oath." Even in becoming a citizen of Nuremberg, the Jew entered the community by means of another or distinctive legal instrument, one that put particular restrictions on him. The passage went on to decree that a Jew who took up citizenship in Nuremberg was to follow the laws of the city and the laws of no other cities—that is, he had to swear an oath and become a burgher in no other city.[69] In addition to certain payments for protection and privilege, the Jews who became burghers were compelled to fulfill the functions of citizenship, such as paying additional taxes and supplying men (or money) for the guarding of the city walls and for fire duty during Christian festivals, when Christians would be unable to perform such functions.[70]

And yet Jews shared a certain distance from the commune, as did women[71] and clergy. Despite any rights as burghers that the Jews may have had, an abundance of legislation separating Jews from Christian members of the civic commune was reiterated in the middle decades of the fifteenth century. A 1432 ᵈecree in Augsburg, for example, recirculated earlier anti-Jewish legislation and ᵢ stricted the dress of the Jews.[72] The *Gründung* and Mülich both mentioned that the Jews "must wear the yellow ring."[73] A similar demarcation, however,

---

[67] Feger, *Vom Rechtbrief*, p. 2; Stern, *Bevölkerung*, vol. 3, p. 219; and Straus, *Urkunden*, p. 702.

[68] Joseph Baader, ed., *Nürnberger Polizeiordnungen*, pp. 325–326.

[69] The oath itself is very similar to earlier formulaic versions from the thirteenth century; see Guido Kisch, *Jewry Law*, pp. 282–283.

[70] See Straus, *Urkunden*, number 118.

[71] In certain legal situations; Guido Kisch, *Jewry Law*, notes that Jews and women were offered identical treatment, see p. 263.

[72] Burkhard Zink, *Beilage* III, p. 373; this is a rather formulaic text—compare with the decree from Lateran IV in 1215, given in Kisch, *Jewry Law*, p. 296.

[73] *Chronik von der Gründung*, p. 322. Mülich (p. 76) writes "... ward hie die juden gesetzt, das sie gelb ring mussten vornen an in tragen."

was recorded for heretics, who were earlier forced to wear yellow crosses in 1394 (1393).[74] In Nuremberg in 1458 it was decreed to the Jewish council (*Juden rate*) that all of the Jews who live in the city or come into it are not to wear hats (*pyrret noch hüt*) but rather caps (*cappen*), or a ring, "in order that one may recognize their differences."[75] These ordinances drew attention to the alleged luxuriant behavior of the Jews, as well as to the ease with which Jews could be mistaken for pious Christians. It might be argued that Jews were, in a certain sense, viewed as becoming too much like insiders, and these decrees are a not entirely successful attempt, judging by their frequency, to separate the Jews again. This point comes across clearly in Regensburg in a document dating probably from 1518, in which the Jews were admonished to wear their hats publicly and not to hide them secretly in their capes.[76]

One aspect associated with the Jews' alleged subversion of the community was their activities outside of the city, particularly in relations with other Jewish communities, whether in their commerce with merchants and craftsmen abroad or as is evidenced in the accusations in some of the plays that they distributed goods supposedly baked with Christian blood. Similar comments resounded in guild records, particularly of the early sixteenth century, which complained of the Jews' foreign contacts, and which attempted to limit the entrance of foreign Jews, as well as other foreigners, particularly the less well-to-do.[77] Indeed, in much late medieval German urban legislation interaction with foreigners, both for Jews and Christians, was severely restricted. In Nuremberg, no guests in the city were allowed to go to the Jews without permission from the council,[78] houses were not to be loaned to foreign Jews,[79] foreign Jews were to remain in the city, in some instances, no longer than one week,[80] and in other cases, no more than four weeks.[81] In Constance in 1423, foreign Jews were allowed to remain in the city no longer than overnight.[82] A similar ordinance was passed in Nuremberg in 1407, requiring that foreign Jews be escorted within the city. In 1406 the Jewish school in Nuremberg was to be abolished.[83] By 1462 Jews

---

[74] See Kisch, *Jewry Law*, pp. 206 and 295f; again, compare with Lateran IV.

[75] Moritz Stern, *Bevölkerung*, vol. 3, p. 298.

[76] Straus, *Urkunden*, p. 363.

[77] Such restrictions continue well into the early modern period. In the Judenordnung of the Solms-Laubachisch Guardianship for the city of Münzenberg, in 1562, traditional restrictions, with some new leniencies, emphasize the point here. See Friedrich Battenberg, "Judenordnungen der frühen Neuzeit in Hessen," in *Neunhundert Jahre Geschichte der Juden in Hessen: Beiträge zum politischen, wirtschaftlichen und kulturellen Leben*, edited by the Kommission für die Geschichte der Juden in Hessen (Wiesbaden, 1983): 83–122, here at p. 117.

[78] Stern, *Bevölkerung*, vol. 3, *Nürnberg im Mittelalter*, p. 226.

[79] Ibid., p. 230; see also Werner Schultheiss, ed., *Satzungsbücher und Satzungen des Reichsstadt Nürnberg aus dem 14. Jahrhundert*, p. 280.

[80] Ibid., p. 230.

[81] Schultheiss, *Nürnberg Satzungsbücher*, p. 279.

[82] Mollow, *Das Rote Buch der Stadt Ulm*, p. 90.

[83] Stern, *Bevölkerung*, vol. 3, under the year 1406.

could no longer be sent to Nuremberg for burial, and foreign Jews were banned
from the city.[84] The same strict rules that discouraged burghers from marrying
their daughters to foreigners were also imposed on Jews to discourage them from
marrying Jews from other cities.[85] Ironically, by distinguishing between foreign
and resident Jews, some Jews were simultaneously included in the community
in one sense, though perhaps not in other ways, while other Jews were completely excluded. In a certain sense, Judaism was itself only part of a larger context of exclusion that was grafted onto "outsiders" more generally.

It was not only foreign Jews who were excluded from the city.[86] According
to an ordinance from 1459, foreign beggars could remain in the city of Augsburg
for only three days and they were to wear special clothes identifying them as
beggars.[87] Some ordinances play on the distinctions between native and foreign, and all of the legal documents deal with restrictions on membership to
the community. Given the general changes within the urban communes of the
fifteenth century, outlined earlier, many of these restrictions are not surprising.
In Constance in 1387 it was decreed that no new burghers were to be accepted
into the community for an entire year. Burghers were to swear allegiance to
Constance only, and according to a decree of 1432—a decree immediately following the expulsion of the Jews—citizens were to have no loyalties to other
cities, sovereigns, or laws.[88] The law of the city was to be the focus of the burghers'
allegiance, and fines and other penalties were meted out for those who committed criminal acts (*purkrecht in frevel aufgibt*). Beyond these types of restrictions, however, citizens' business and social dealings with "foreigners" were to
be limited. Restrictions on association between guests and citizens were registered in the same way as were restrictions on a citizen who wanted to marry
his daughter to a foreigner.[89]

Throughout the urban legal documents there was a fear of unrest, of disobedience, and a strong concern for the commune. In the case of ordinances
governing such activities as swearing and gaming, for example, the tension was
between "dangerous games" and "proclamations of the city council."[90] Gaming
was punished with a fine, but the concern over swearing had something to do
with private intriguing. Again, in Constance, the concern expressed in a document from 1432 had to do with the secret (*haimlich*) swearing or oath taking

---

[84] Ibid., under the year 1462, p. 309. For the later cases, see Straus, *Urkunden*, number 845.

[85] Ibid., p. 235.

[86] For a brief treatment of "guests" in the city, see Eberhard Isenmann, *Die deutsche
Stadt im Spätmittelalter*, pp. 101–102.

[87] Rolf Kießling, *Bürgerliche Gesellschaft*, pp. 217–218; a mark because they were
"unnutzlich."

[88] Feger, *Vom Rechtbrief*, pp. 109f.

[89] In Ulm, in Mollow, *Das Rote Buch*, p. 279.

[90] See Feger, *Vom Rechtbrief*, p. 53 for a *schwörverbot*, or prohibition against swearing,
from Constance in 1389.

in the guilds at a time when revolt was brewing in the city.[91] In the *Satzungen* from Nuremberg, swearing is compared with criminal acts (*frevelichen*). Dancing was also to be regulated and unapproved dancing (*ungeordnoten tantz*)[92] or dancing in particular public spaces was prohibited.[93]

THE EXPULSION FROM AUGSBURG

We may be able to define more coherently the concept of the "commune" by examining how the term and its opposites were used in Augsburg's 1438 edict expelling the Jews from the city and in the subsequent recollections of the event by the major Augsburg chroniclers, particularly Burkhard Zink.

In 1438, under the pretext of a letter from King Albert II—which has never been found—the Augsburg city council gave the Jews in their city a period of two years in which to leave the city, a rather gracious gift compared to most other cities. There are some variations between the official council decree of 1438 and several of the chroniclers' accounts, and so it is instructive to compare the different accounts briefly. The reasons behind the expulsion are not entirely clear, but the language of the decrees and chronicles allows us to glimpse the ways in which the expulsion was conceptualized and connected to other events and ideas in the minds of the authors.

By 1440 there were no longer any Jews listed in the city tax books. It has been argued that a large number of Jews settled in the areas outside of Augsburg, and given the fact that Jews were allowed into the city during the day to conduct business and, that we continue to find evidence of Jews in the city after 1440, this would seem to be the case. Some scholars, however, argue that the smaller communities outside of Augsburg were the result of other, larger expulsions of Jews during the 1450s. Certainly, some Jews traveled to other large cities in which Jewish communities were still tolerated, but it is probably impossible to trace the Jews with greater detail, because the documentation is scant until the fifth decade of the sixteenth century.

Most of the chronicles mentioned severe plagues in Augsburg in 1430 and again in 1438 (the one which took the life of one of Zink's children), but in no case, despite close textual juxtaposition, were the Jews directly linked to the plague, nor was the plague given as a pretext for the expulsion, unlike in earlier accounts of the Black Death in other cities.

It is revealing to compare the longest description of the Jews by Zink to that in the city records. According to the edict of 7 July 1438,[94] the Jews were given two years in which to leave the city, after which time they would not be

---

[91] Ibid., p. 105. See also p. 83 for a connection of the *Trinkstuben* of the guilds in 1418.

[92] For example "two and two dancing with each other."

[93] Feger, *Vom Rechtbrief*, p. 19, or p. 36, where regulations against drinking were also in force.

[94] Burkhard Zink, *Beilage*, pp. 377–378.

allowed to remain. There were to be no exceptions, and all Jews, young and old, were to leave. The decision was presented as a unanimous one of the "small and old council," and clearly juxtaposed the Jews to the citizens of Augsburg. The document presented the Jews as a factious group outside of and undermining the unity of the community. The Jews were to be expelled because they were evil, dangerous, and disobedient. As in many legal documents from later in the century, it was precisely disobedience, or the transgression of the common good, which was to be restrained. Jews would no longer be allowed in the city. Spatial separation would mitigate the Jews' disobedience, which manifested itself in their daily interaction and presence. The expulsion, the document insisted, was purely the result of the Jews' own doing. Their machinations against the city, their recruiting and raising of opposition to the city, as well as their own laziness, which contributed nothing to the city, were but a few of their crimes. The document stressed the relationship between the city and the king—first, in an effort to give added authority to the decree and, second, to dissuade the Jews from thinking that they had anything to gain from petitioning the monarch, whom they would have considered their guarantor. It was assumed by the framers of the document that the Jews would desire to remain in the city.

Throughout, the decree is rather unspecific and its language formulaic. Although the decree also betrays the presence of public preaching against the Jews, it is striking that the Jews were not offered the choice of baptism, and that there was no mention of any conversions, at least until five noted in the chronicles for the year 1446. Even if the choice of baptism was understood, it is odd that the document made no mention of the option. Instead, the Jews were merely expelled. The expulsion was not regional, and the Jews who stood under the protection of the bishop were not forced to leave the area.[95]

A number of the Augsburg chronicles mention the expulsion. The *Chronicle of the Founding* notes that in 1440 the Jews departed from Augsburg.[96] While there is no mention of the expulsion decree under the 1438 entry, there is, as we have seen, a reference to King Albert II of Austria as an enemy of the Jews. Why was Albert labeled an enemy of the Jews in 1438? Burkhard Zink mentions that the city of Augsburg possessed, or at least claimed to posses, a letter from Albert allowing them to expel their Jews. The letter, however, never materialized and Albert's successor Frederick III, later fined the city for the unauthorized expulsion. The entry in the *Anonymous Chronicle of 991* is nearly a word-for-word redaction of the Zink text, with no new additions. Mülich, also, merely repeats the essentials of Zink's interpretation: on Saint Kilian's day, 1440, the Jews departed the city, since the council decided that the Jews should never again be permitted residence in the city; the Jews were given two years to ready their affairs, and all of this was permitted by King Albert.

---

[95] Marcus Wenninger, *Man Bedarf keiner Juden Mehr*, here at pp. 115f.
[96] *Chonik von der Gründung*, "zugen die juden aus Augsburg."

Since Zink's chronicle is the central text for the propagation of the expulsion story, particularly so since the two chronicles written before Zink's—those of Wahraus and Fr. Johannes Frank (his chronicle covers the years 1430 to 1462)—do not mention the expulsion at all, it is important to look closely at Zink's account and compare it with the city council's decree.[97] Zink followed the specifics of the edict closely, but he added some new information. Like the framers of the decree, he stated that the Jews were no longer wanted in the city, that they had been ordered to leave and should obey, that they were given a two year period in which to leave, that young and old left, that there were those who wanted to remain, but that in the end all had to go. Zink also added a number of details. He stated that the Jews were given two years to prepare and to sell their houses and possessions that they could not take with them, and that, all told, when they left, the Jews numbered some 300 people. Among this number of Jews there were many rich Jews who, according to Zink, wanted to stay in the city as citizens, and who offered to pay the enormous sum of 1 Gulden per week for lodgings. Finally, Zink added details of the appropriation of the Jewish gravestones for construction purposes, and noted the supposed letter from King Albert II. Zink collapsed all of his information into one account, as if it were one connected episode: 1438, 1440, 1446, and 1456. All of the events that deal with the Jews were taken together. All of the later chroniclers who followed Zink took up the lost letter issue and the subsequent tax penalty instituted by Friedrich,[98] but only Mülich added that the emperor sent a letter to Augsburg in 1456 allowing the council to decide whether they wanted Jews in the city.

Why did Zink focus on these issues? One possible reason is that Zink often focused on economic matters. For example, he noted that the Jews were willing to pay heavily for extended lodgings in the city. He was also concerned about the cost incurred, because of the fines for expelling the Jews, in repairing the steps to the city hall. The very material of the Jews, their gravestones, become a part of the city council steps, yet at the same time their incorporation into the structures of the community created a great deal of trouble. We can perhaps best understand Zink's account by examining more closely his education and the concept of community that he displays in his use of language.

BURKHARD ZINK[99] AND THE LANGUAGE OF THE GEMAIN

From his schooling and the books he copied—he had begun with some works of St. Thomas Aquinas—Zink may well have been familiar with some theology. Certainly, he was well traveled, particularly in Bavaria and Venice, practiced in many trades, especially as a merchant, a seemingly successful financier and

---

[97] Burkhard Zink, pp. 162–163.

[98] See *Chronik von der Gründung*, p. 326 and Hektor Mülich, p. 121.

[99] Zink presents a good deal of his life history in his chronicle, particularly in part three of his four-part chronicle.

a man later to be highly thought of in Augsburg politics. In all of the third book of his chronicle, Zink made only limited mention of persons or groups outside of his immediate family or circle of acquaintants. He seems to have had a high regard for most of these acquaintants, whom he often described as pious; it was their behavior, not religious observance per se, which made them pious. It is, in some sense, surprising, that Zink makes no further reference to Jews here, since he must have encountered them in business, and particularly because there were important Jewish communities in Ulm, Bamberg, Würzburg, Nuremberg, Frankfurt, and Venice, where he spent some time. His later account of the expulsion of the Jews from Augsburg, however, reflected his background—a non-clerical one, in which the central concern was more of an interest in practical economic realities.

Many of the words Zink used over and over again in his chronicle took on varied connotations in different situations. The same word could and did have different shades or aspects in its meaning and could even have very different meanings. We must, therefore, remain relatively open-minded when we begin to examine, more closely, the descriptions of community in Zink's account, for there are layers of meanings that will help us to understand his perception of the Jews. As J.G.A. Pocock has put it:

> The historian is in considerable measure an archaeologist; he is engaged in uncovering the presence of various language contexts in which discourse has from time to time been conducted. I report from my own experience . . . that he grows accustomed to finding many layers of such contexts within the same text, and is constantly surprised and delighted by discovering languages grown familiar from other sources in familiar texts where their presence has been neglected.[100]

In Burkhard Zink's chronicle the term community (*gemain* or *gemein*), as well as its adjectival and adverbial derivatives, had political connotations, as, for example, when Zink wrote of federated cities or the south German confederation (*gemainen stetten*). The term could refer to membership in a specific guild—as when Zink mentioned Jos Kramer who was "from the community of the weavers' guild" (*von der gemain auss der Weberzunft*)[101]—or less explicitly to the civic society more generally—when Zink wrote, regarding a debate in Augsburg over a new consumption tax (*ungelt*), that "the pious people belonged to the commune" (*die frumen leut auss der gemain horten*).[102] When Zink wrote of a "general procession" (*procession gemainklich*) in describing how the citizens of Augsburg appealed to God to withdraw a terrible plague from them, the term referred broadly to the community of Christians in the city. Often, Zink referred almost formulaically to community as inclusive of both rich and poor, except for one

---

[100] Pocock, "The Concept of Language," p. 23.
[101] Burkhard Zink, *Chronik*, p. 128.
[102] Ibid., p. 52.

instance where he used the term "common people" (*gemaine volk*) and "poor people" (*arme leut*) in rather the same sense, or when one senses a distinction in "common people in the city" (*gmain volk in stat*), or more a sense of "common" when Zink described the king as "a common man" (*ain gemainer man*). Similarly, Zink referred to a "general council" (*gemains concilium*), the great Council at Constance in 1414, endowing the term with a specifically ecclesiastical meaning. For Zink "commune" could have economic aspects, as when he wrote about securing grain and meat and the prices for these for the commune, particularly during plague years.

Throughout his chronicle Zink contrasted the welfare of the commune with individual benefit (*aigennutz*).[103] *Gemain* was directly contrasted with *aigennutz*:[104] that is, the need of the "community" was held above the need of the individual.[105] A comparison with the use of *gemain* in two other Augsburg chronicles is insightful. *The Chronicle from 1368 to 1406*, which is anonymous, but which drew heavily from town documents and often used rather juristic language, typically related *gemain* to the city. Generally in this chronicle the term signified actions within the city, such as in the "burgomaster, council, and citizens together" (*burgermeister, raut und burger gemainclich*),[106] or "many respectable people from the community" (*vil erber von der gemaind*),[107] or "the city in common, rich and poor" (*stat gemainclich uz, rich und arm*),[108] or the relation of the city with other imperial cities as in "common imperial cities" (*gemainen reichstetten*).[109] The anonymous chronicler also used the term in a more general sense of "all"—when referring to a procession the chronicler wrote that the clerical participants were "all clad in black" (*gemainclich geclait in schwarz*).[110]

A later chronicler, on the other hand, Clemens Sender, employed an array of meanings that differed from those of Zink and the anonymous chronicler. To be sure, similar constructions such as "the good of the common city" (*gemeiner stat zu gut*, referring to rich and poor)[111] or "council and community at large" (*rat und gantze gemein*)[112] can be found in Sender's work. But nearly forty percent of the instances of *gemein* denoted the concept of the community as a Christian entity. For example, Sender employed the terms "believer" (*gemein glaubiger*)[113] or "communal procession" (*gemein process*).[114] When Sender wrote

---

[103] Ibid., p. 74.
[104] Ibid.
[105] Ibid.
[106] *Chronik von 1368*, p. 41.
[107] Ibid., p. 110.
[108] Ibid., p. 74.
[109] Ibid., p. 30.
[110] Ibid., p. 60.
[111] Ibid., pp. 211, 127, and 111.
[112] Ibid., p. 85.
[113] Clemens Sender, p. 231.
[114] Ibid., p. 153 or p. 83, in order to pray against the Turks.

"common man" (*gemeiner mann*) it was only to tell the reader that the common man was prohibited from entering the church after a procession, while the emperor, king, cardinal, princes, lords, and clerics were allowed in.[115] Again, when he mentioned common people (*gemein volck*), he went on to connect them with "general help of Christendom" (*gemeiner hilf der cristenhait*).[116] The common good also had a close connection with proper Christian belief, as when Sender mentioned the Lutherans, who, he argued, opposed both common utility (*gemeinen nutz*) and "Christian religion" (*christliche religion*).[117] Since he was a clergyman, we should not be too surprised at Sender's emphases. The earlier chroniclers, who were merchants and heads of the urban ruling class, utilized a language of community with less religious overtones, however; they understood community in a more political sense. They did not separate out religious community, but rather integrated religious elements into their very notion of community.

In Zink's chronicle there were a number of words and concepts that denoted unity. In some passages, words such as "unity" (*ainigkait*) reflected the same sense of unity as did *gemain*. The Council of Constance, for example, was called a "commendable unity" (*lobliche ainigkait*), and the burgomaster of Augsburg spoke to the guilds, as Zink reported, and asked them to pay the new taxes and "remain in correct unity" (*bleiben in rechter ainigkait*).[118] "Community" had no simple designation, and we should not, therefore, expect the language describing those outside of the community to be any more simple or uniform. The most important expressions of unity for Zink were expressed through the opposition of "friend" (*freund*) and "enemy" (*feind*). The term *freund* as employed by Zink generally had the connotation of helpful, faithful, or favorable and although typically applied to individuals, it could also be used adjectivally (a positive or friendly answer (*freuntlich antwurt*)). Usually, *freund* represented those who had helped Zink, particularly in book three, where many people were described as "friendly" (*freundlich*) and "pious" (*frum*). But *freund* had a deeper connotation, one that determined the person's relationship to the city of Augsburg.[119] It is rare to find a statement in the chronicle that one person was the other's enemy (though in describing an ambush, Zink wrote, "they waited for their enemies" (*warteten auf ir feinden*)), rather the stress is typically upon one individual's actions towards another. It was what one did that made him an enemy. Generally *feind* had a specific object of enmity: the bishop of Metz

---

[115] Ibid., p. 276.
[116] Ibid., p. 97.
[117] Ibid., p. 172.
[118] Ibid., p. 118.
[119] It has been argued by Heinrich Schmidt that the *burgerliche* consciousness of Zink is focused on Augsburg: The imperial city is the empire in the mind of Zink, and other writers of history in the fifteenth century. Weber also concedes that the focus of Hektor Mülich's outlook was somewhat based on the *Reichsstadt* as well.

was an enemy to the emperor, the people of Freiburg were an enemy to the city Augsburg, or certain bishops or lords were designated as enemies to the city of Augsburg. In other cases, however, there was a more general receptor of the action. For example, when Zink described an evil society of people in Austria, he wrote that "they were an enemy to the whole world" (*sind gewesen aller welt feind*), or in more strictly adjectival uses he used the expressions "hostile power" (*feintlicher macht*) or "hostile war" (*feindlich krieg*).

The actions of enemies were described by a number of terms such as "evil" (*bös, böswicht, böshait, übel*) or "criminal" (*frevenlich*). When Zink wrote about a number of guilds that refused to pay a certain customs tax, he mentioned the "evil weavers." It is clear that all groups exist in a multi-dimensional set of relationships: although the weavers were separated here in regard to the tax, the separation was only in effect in one field of the weavers' relationship with the more general *gemain*. Zink would not have thought to write that the weavers were no longer members of the civic society, or political structure in the city, rather only that their actions marked them off partially—their status as members of the group was partially nullified.

The entire axis of description of *feind* and *freund* involves a certain expectation of order and authority in society: the concept of peace (*frid*), therefore, is central to Zink's thinking through of community. *Frid* has a number of meanings, from a certain administrative quality, as when Zink described the takeover of the guilds in Augsburg in 1368—"when they want to do right and decree good order and good peace with the help of God and all pious men . . ."[120] to a more wide-spread legal institution of peace or "peace of the land in Franconia" (*landfrid in Frankenland*) as opposed to war, to a sense of normal relations between lords or bishops (there was a good *frid* between the bishops)[121] and a certain sense of efficiency. Bishop Peter von Schaumberg was both "noble and peaceful" (*herlich und fridlich*), and the result was that the bishopric became richer than it had been in fifty years. Parallel to *frid* were other terms, notably order (*ordnung*). *Ordnung* had the qualities of administering, organizing, law, public stability, or a certain natural progression or correct sequencing: the burial of people who died in the plague of 1420 "was recorded according to the order of Christendom" (*ward auch besungen nach ordnung der christenhait*).[122] When Zink used the negation of *ordnung* he expressed surprise that things were not as they should be: the imprisonment and finally sale of the old Ludwig to his enemies by the young Ludwig is described as a disorderly or unnatural love (*unordenlichen Leib*).[123] Other terms that centered along the question of authority and obedience reflected similar qualities. The unifying terms included: "obedient" (*gehorsam*), "authority" (*gewalt*), "natural lordship" (*natürlichen herrn* in one

---

[120] Burkhard Zink, p. 1.
[121] Ibid., p. 61.
[122] Ibid., p. 68.
[123] Ibid., p. 167.

case), and "submissive" (*undertenig*); the separating term "disobedient" (*ungehörsam, unwillen*). Zink fondly recalled that his second wife was both "obedient and subservient" (*gehorsam und undertenig*), whereas the Jews were labeled disobedient. Taken together, qualities such as unity, peace, obedience, authority, and order defined community for Zink. The very opposite, in enmity, disobedience, and lack of order denoted lack of community or opposition to community. Such description was applied to the Jews by Zink and many of his contemporaries.

*   *   *

Those who broke the "peace" or opposed authority were to be rounded up and imprisoned. What is particularly striking here is that when Zink describes the Jews he usually mentions that they were imprisoned—generally in order to get them to pay additional taxes. But the concept of jail goes much deeper than just the rounding up of Jews. Those imprisoned included breakers of the peace, murderers, frauds and deceitful businessmen, incendiaries, drunkards, heretics, on occasion women, and even some "pious" men.[124] Jail (*fenknus*) in Zink's account was a place for those disturbing the civil and religious peace—that is, those who stepped outside the boundaries of community being prescribed in fifteenth-century Augsburg. Jews, in particular, do not seem to have been imprisoned for any action on their part. It was rather their very being Jewish that placed them outside of the community. Imprisonment of other groups separated those groups out from community. In the case of the Jews rather the opposite was true: Jews were imprisoned to create a certain kind of bond with the community—the payment of extraordinary taxes. Jews were, therefore, simultaneously included in and excluded from community. The very act of imprisonment recognized that the Jews were in some sense responsible to the laws and boundaries of the city. The Jews, by and large, were not even accused of "false beliefs" or polemically designated as heretics. There was a degree of recognition that they were not Christians, but their physical presence within the borders of the city included Jews in a rather particular way within the community, and the jail itself was a community space—right in the heart of the council chambers—at the center of the physical confines of the city.

CONCLUSION

Throughout this chapter I have maintained that both language and the law are social constructs that simultaneously define and command, and that both have the capacity, through their iteration, to transform and maintain traditional values and relationships. The idea of community and the relationship between individuals and groups within community depend upon a variety of factors and perspectives, and they can change in different contexts and can

---

[124] Ibid., p. 153; a "from Kramer" by the name of Jos was imprisoned.

even be multivalent. Persecution of minority groups simultaneously excludes and includes. But what changes occurred in the later Middle Ages in Germany? After the end of the thirteenth century law certainly took on a new significance within the cities, when written books and ordinances were introduced and, in the later fourteenth and fifteenth centuries, when police ordinances were codified.[125] In some ways such written laws may have simply been the committing to writing of civic customs. Still, the very equation of such customs with the status of "law," and the real effort to define proper behavior through such laws signals a significant change in the late medieval German urban communes. The emphasis on proper conduct, with its parallels to the changes within religious observance that we noted in the previous chapter—the new emphasis on morality over sacrament—reveals changes in the conception of community that made it difficult for Jews to remain. The legislation of community not only demands that members behave in certain ways, it decides what ways they must behave. As "proper conduct" is defined and in turn becomes central to such definition, exclusionary policy grows, that is, the more extreme physical separation of expulsion instead of segregation is carried out.[126] This is precisely why Jews were expelled from so many cities at the end of the fourteenth and throughout the fifteenth century, in most cases without violence.

Unlike the pogroms of the fourteenth century and earlier, which emphasized that Jews constituted an aspect of the general community, the fifteenth century legislation made it clear that Jews were slowly being considered a completely separate entity. The reason may be that the community was imbued with a religious sense, or better that religion became part and parcel of a broader, more multi-faceted definition of community. When religion was somehow separate from urban identity, Jews could remain; as religious self-definition was absorbed into general communal identity, the difference of the Jews became more marked and more central. This may be why Jews were often more frequently persecuted when itinerant Mendicant preachers were in the towns. The preachers sought to galvanize a communal identity that closely interrelated common good and religio-moral ethics.[127] Proper Christian conduct, in the moral if not sacramental sense, became a central identifying criteria for communal membership. Of course, Jews were not completely outside such morally defined community, and so their position was at times rather ambivalent; they could be both included and excluded from the community. Perhaps a more formal separation of civic and religious community occurred in the sixteenth and seventeenth

---

[125] See Isenmann, *Die deutsche Stadt im Spätmittelalter*, p. 83.

[126] Along these lines, consider the "civilizing" argument of Norbert Elias. See his *Power and Civility*, pp. 45f and 229f. Elias finds the beginnings of this civilizing process, which includes the movement from social- to self-constraint, at the beginning of the thirteenth century and culminating in the court societies of the centralizing nation states in the early modern period and then into modernity.

[127] See, for example: Lesnick, *Preaching in Medieval Florence*, pp. 109–111 and 120; see also Paton, *Preaching Friars and the Civic Ethos*.

centuries, with the increasing adaptation of Roman Law in Germany. According to some scholars, Roman Law and Jewish presence increased correspondingly, since Roman Law considered Jews as citizens and because it forced the community to see itself more metaphorically than actually as the body of Christ.[128]

A more detailed examination of the description of the Jews in the later Middle Ages will allow us to expand our understanding of communal identity, and changes within that identity, in the German cities.

---

[128] See Kenneth R. Stow, "Holy Body, Holy Society," p. 152.

4

Anti-Judaism: Between Religion and Community

INTRODUCTION: SHIFTING ANTI-JUDAISM[1]

In *Medieval Stereotypes and Modern Antisemitism* Robert Chazan argues that there are essentially three phases in the evolution of negative Jewish imagery in the Middle Ages. The first phase, the tenth century, saw new immigration of Jews into western Europe (here Chazan's focus is France and Germany). The negative imagery associated with this early immigration revolved around Jews as immigrants, and the crucial newness of early Ashkenazic Jewry was influenced by its own limited size, limited economic outlets, broadly hostile views of the Christian majority, general lawlessness, and common antipathy against urban traders. In the second phase, the eleventh and twelfth centuries, Chazan finds a rapid economic and creative development of Ashkenazic Jewry. The broader commercial revolution forced Jews into a new economic specialization, money-lending instead of trading, and simultaneously strengthened the dependence of the Jews upon ruling elites. Through this second period Chazan sees five anti-Jewish themes, which he divides into two categories. First, Jewish Otherness: including negative imagery of Jews as newcomers and religious dissidents. Second, Jewish harmfulness, as reflected in images of Jews as [economic] competitors, allies of the barony, and historic enemies. For Chazan the latter grouping was most potent and held the greatest possibility for further negative imagery of the Jews that he finds in the third phase.

Beginning in the twelfth century and continuing through the thirteenth century Chazan describes a sharp decline in the fortunes of Ashkenazic Jewry. In particular Chazan notes the central shift and expansion in the Christian sense of Jews as historic enemies to Jews as both historic and contemporary enemies. Chazan traces this transformation to the middle of the twelfth century and the writings of Peter the Venerable.[2] It is the emergence of the stereotype of Jews

---

[1] For an overview of medieval anti-Judaism in Germany, see the very useful book by Michael Toch, *Die Juden im Mittelalterlichen Reich*, pp. 110–132.

[2] For the most recent treatment of Peter the Venerable and the Jews, see Jeremy Cohen, *Living Letters*, pp. 245–270.

as physically harmful that makes possible both accusations of blood libel and host desecration that are found in the twelfth century. Strikingly, it was precisely the renaissance of the twelfth century (in its philosophy, biblical interpretation, and consideration of the human psyche) that heightened Christian awareness of Others.[3] For Chazan, the twelfth century was a time of great change and anxiety in Europe that fostered new negative images of Jews. The new, and according to Chazan, deteriorated image of the Jews eventually influenced the church and the state in their treatment of the Jews.

In sum, Chazan argues that "an earlier period of significant change and dislocation in the West—the dynamic and creative twelfth century—saw the interaction of new societal circumstances and a prior ideational legacy. This interaction produced an innovative view of Jews fated to influence anti-Jewish perceptions down into our own century."[4] His point is further elaborated in his conclusion: "in fact every new stage in the evolution of anti-Jewish thinking is marked by dialectical interplay between a prior legacy of negative stereotypes and the realities of a new social context. Out of this interplay emerge novel anti-Jewish perceptions, which in turn become part of the historic tradition of anti-Jewish sentiment. In this way, anti-Jewish thought maintains a measure of stability and continuity, while in fact evolving considerably over the ages."[5]

Two themes proposed by Chazan will be followed and developed in this chapter. First, if we admit Chazan's general argument, keeping in mind that it contains a number of problematic and unproven assertions, we can conclude that anti-Judiasm takes on specific qualities or elements in particular contexts, and that in all manifestations anti-Judaism mixes an ideational legacy, or well of imagery, with concrete historical events and contexts. How, then, was anti-Judaism expressed in late medieval Germany? What does its expression reveal about the contextual environment in which Jews found themselves? Second, the shift in focus from Jews as historic, and therefore largely religious, opponents to the image of the Jews as enemies in both history and contemporary times may have begun in the twelfth and thirteenth centuries; but it is a process that continued through the reformations of the sixteenth century. The combination, therefore, of anti-Jewish motives that were at once religious and "secular," should not be surprising, but it should force us to stop and consider the nature, reason, and expression of each. If in fact religious elements in anti-Judaism are downplayed in the fourteenth and fifteenth centuries, as I will argue, was it because Jews were no longer viewed as a religious threat, or because Christians cared less about religion, or some other reason? I will argue that, in fact, religious anti-Judaism was as powerful in many ways as it had been throughout

---

[3] There is a growing literature on this theme, building upon the important work of R.I. Moore and others. See, for example, *Other Middle Ages: Witnesses at the Margins of Medieval Society*, edited by Michael Goodich (Philadelphia, 1998).

[4] Robert Chazan, *Medieval Stereotypes and Modern Antisemitism*, p. xi.

[5] Ibid., p. 135.

the high Middle Ages, and earlier. Its expression, however, in tandem with more communal, as opposed to "secular," issues reveals that late medieval German urban communities formed a new identity that was in a very real sense a corporate and sacred entity. It is not the case that the commune was secularized; rather the opposite seems to have been the case. The commune was sacralized, and religion, particularly in its moral as contrasted with its sacramental aspects, became a key aspect of urban communal identity—but only one aspect. Religion was not rejected in the fifteenth century, as many scholars of the reformations would like to argue, it was integrated into communal identity.

In a variety of late medieval sources it is obvious that the anti-Judaism of the fifteenth century could be religious, political, social, or economic. At times, as among the guildsmen who sought to push the Jews out of Augsburg, the reasons for anti-Judaism could combine various elements and rationales. Written, oral, or visual discourse was employed, both consciously and unconsciously, against the Jews, and frequently it implied social protest as much as actual anti-Jewish feeling. Peasants, fools, and other groups could be depicted in similar ways to Jews (hats, physical features), and prostitutes and lepers might be demarcated with badges or other marks in the same way as Jews. The discourse against the Jews was not always directed at Jews because they were Jewish; often it revealed more general concerns and accusations thrown at other communal groups as well. The end result, however, was to cast the Jew as a communal outsider, through the use of metaphors that associated or labeled Jews with particular negative qualities, often times as animals, plants, pestilence, and filth.[6] The manifestation of such representations in urban discourse, taking the form of expulsion edicts, chronicle accounts, carnival plays, and sermons, is the subject of this chapter.

There were two phases in the development and expression of anti-Judaism in late medieval Germany. The first manifestation of anti-Judaism was an attack on Jewish religion and perceived religious practices, and was presented in the form of the defense of Christianity. A second, somewhat later manifestation of anti-Judaism emphasized the offense posed by the Jews to common good and public order; this anti-Judaism focused on alleged Jewish actions to subvert and disrupt the urban community, as in criminal behavior and usury, for example. While both forms and expressions of anti-Judaism existed throughout the later Middle Ages, there is a clear transition toward an heavier emphasis on the latter. In part this transition, which includes both aspects, is most clearly seen in the preaching against the Jews within the cities. Such preaching reveals the consolidation of a communal sacral ethos, as noted in previous chapters. The emphasis in earlier anti-Jewish accounts is on the Jew as the enemy of Christianity. But these early attacks on the Jews are qualitatively different from

---

[6] See Nicoline Hortzitz, "Verfahrensweisen sprachlicher Diskriminierung in antijüdischen Texten der Frühen Neuzeit: Aufgezeigt am Beispiel der Metaphorik," in Rolf Kießling, ed., *Judengemeinden in Schwaben*: 194–216.

the accounts of the fifteenth century, in which the Jews' actions have as much to do with disruption of government as with more general threats to society or the jealousy of local burghers. Many of the late medieval sources that cast anti-Judaism in a more traditionally religious garb, however, suggest the transition to communally-based anti-Judaism, in which the community is subverted through the supposed religious, moral, and criminal behavior of the Jews. Attacks on the Jews as well as the anti-Jewish discourse that spawned such attacks were very much a manifestation of communal change throughout Europe, particularly in the south German cities.

Throughout the Middle Ages, the Jew was seen as a theological enemy. Judaism was attacked as an outdated religion, and Jews were debated, encouraged and forced to convert, and attacked on the basis of their religious differences. Within the context of the late medieval German community such religious opposition was appropriated to clothe internal contemporary concerns. Jews as outsiders were labeled in opposition to the commune, but, of course, they were not just outsiders or minorities, they were Jews. As such, traditional forms of portraying the Jews were melded with new communal concerns described in the previous chapters; and the image of the Jew was slowly reformulated to include both theological and sociological aspects. This seems to go without saying. But the way in which this process developed, the interplay between the theological and sociological, is revealing of the substantive changes within the late medieval communities themselves.

ANTI-JUDAISM AND RELIGION

In the late medieval German chronicles individual Jews were rarely mentioned by name. Instead, Jews were typically presented negatively as a general and unchangeable category. In their very essence, Jews are often portrayed as the exact opposite of Christians, as the anonymous Mainz chronicler (*Chronik 'von alten dingen der Stadt Mainz,'* 1372–1452) divulged in his formulaic positioning of opposites: "poor and rich, Jews and Christians, priests and laymen. . . ."[7]

In rather traditional ways, many fifteenth-century texts concentrated on questions of religion and some *Fastnachtspiele* were presented in the form of disputations between Jews and Christians. These writings focused on the Jewish views of messianism, the Jews' disdain for Christianity, particularly in the Talmud, and the horrific acts allegedly committed by Jews, such as ritual murder and host desecration, acts which struck at the very heart of Christians and attacked central sacraments and beliefs of Christianity. In Regensburg in 1470, a story was told of a Jew sitting in prison who decided to become a Christian. After a long process he converted. Later he was approached by his brother several times in the fishmarket: his brother was dressed in "Christian clothes," and showed

---

[7] *Chronik 'von alten dingen der Stadt Mainz,'* 1332–1452, in CdS, vol. 17, pp. 22 and 186.

him a book against Jesus (a book which young Jews were supposedly not shown until they were firm in their belief). Eventually the convert returned to the Jewish fold and was welcomed back warmly.[8] Such a story revealed the general enmity that Jews were suspected of having for Christians.

In *Kaiser Constantinus* (1474), Hans Folz's Constantine sent for his mother and her rabbi, who were attempting to sway him from his faith in Christianity.[9] What followed was a debate between the rabbi and a Christian theologian. The debate began with a discussion of the Trinity and the Passion, using the Old Testament and the Jewish Prophets, and ended when not only the emperor but the rabbi as well were convinced of the truth of the Christian faith. Before the final baptism of all of the Jews, one Jew conceded to the whole community of Christians that the Jews had indeed been blind, and that he now believed everything that he should, that is, that Christ was the Messiah.[10]

Similar debates occurred in other of Folz's plays, particularly in *Christ und Jude* (1474), and *Pharetra contra iudeos: Der Köcher wider die Juden*. In *Christ und Jude*, the Jew conceded, after a long discussion of the Trinity, the dual nature of Christ, and the time and conditions for the coming of the Messiah. The Jew, for his part, had begun by claiming that Christian belief is a novelty, and that the peace on earth that should be experienced with the coming of the Messiah did not occur when Jesus lived. Yet each of the Jew's accusations was in turn answered based on his own writings.[11] In a later version of the *Pharetra* Folz noted that the birth of Jesus was written in Jewish sources: "that Christ was born and came, as they have written in all of their writings. . . ."[12] According to Folz's logic, all of the Old Testament and the Prophets prefigured the New Testament. Not only was baptism prefigured in the Old Testament—but, the assembly of Christians was the fulfillment of that which was prefigured in the words of the prophets.[13] In the *Pharetra*, the debate was between the synagogue, or Judaism, and the church, or the assembly of Christians. In this piece Folz proceeded from a very structured agenda. He wanted to explain what he saw as the errors and falseness of the Talmud, to make public the teaching of the true belief through the testimony of the Laws and the prophets, and to answer any remaining issues brought forth by the Jews. Folz drew a parallel between the synagogue and an old woman offering outdated sacrifices and between the church and a young woman, nourishing, fruitful, and holy. Drawing a passage from the first chapter of Isaiah and applying it to the synagogue, Folz wrote, in the voice of the young woman: "you should not offer more useless offerings, your smoke is inhuman."[14] Jews themselves were further compared to foxes in

---

[8] Ibid., p. 30.
[9] Von Keller, *Fastnachtspiele*, vol. 3, p. 796.
[10] Ibid., p. 817.
[11] Hans Folz, *Die Reimpaarsprüche*, p. 230.
[12] Ibid., no. 102, p. 392.
[13] Ibid., p. 374.
[14] Ibid., p. 373.

Christian vineyards, and to Goliath, who was destined to be slain by means of his own sword.[15]

The theme of a number of these debates as well as several other plays is the coming of the Messiah. According to Folz the Jews were blind and did not recognize the true Messiah—instead they sold him for thirty pence.[16] Two of Folz's other works played on the Jews' stubbornness in waiting for what they thought was the true Messiah and on a certain naiveté in their expectation of the coming, which they believed would happen soon. In both stories the Jews were convinced rather easily that the time of the Messiah was about to arrive. In both stories they were tricked, disappointed, and left to be mocked. In *Der Falsche Messias* (1482) an eager student living next door to a Jew with the most beautiful of daughters, convinced the Jew that his daughter, with whom the student has, unbeknownst to the family, had an affair and has made pregnant (*swanger*), would give birth to the Messiah. The father relayed the news to a synagogue full of Jews, who were then lectured by the rabbi, thanking God for sending the redeemer after so long. Folz's description of the ruckus caused in the synagogue gave   detailed description of the Jewish prayers that sounded and indeed were so foreign, so different from the reality Folz and other Christians could understand. The Jews' very speech, not merely their belief, seemed to be babbling which made no sense to Christians.[17] As elsewhere in the *Fastnachtspiele*, Jews were portrayed as in league with the Devil and with the Antichrist. In this same piece Folz wrote of the devilish joy of the Jews, and in *Jüdische Wucher* (1491) he argued that the Devil laughed at the Jews' holidays.[18] Indeed, the Jews did not merely associate with the Devil, they were the people of the Antichrist, whom they worshiped with great reverence. In *Des Entkrist Vasnacht* the Jews were made to utter to the Antichrist:

> Oh Messiah, our gentle God/We have long awaited you/Since Jerusalem was destroyed/We have suffered hard life/That we have never been regarded/ Messiah, give us your counsel/You have now come from heaven/From the highest to here/We want to convalesce and die with you/Until we acquire the eternal empire.[19]

At the end of *Der Falsche Messias*, when the daughter gave birth, and the Jews saw that there was no Messiah, they were shocked, and looked as though a pig had taken a bite out of them.[20] Finally, the daughter and child were baptized, and the Jews' shame was made public.[21] The theme of a supposed virgin

---

[15] Ibid.

[16] "*Die Jüdische Wucher*," in Ibid., p. 311.

[17] "*Der Falsche Messias*," in Ibid., p. 94.

[18] "*Die Jüdische Wucher*," in Ibid., p. 311.

[19] Von Keller, *Fastnachtspiele*, vol. 2, pp. 597–598.

[20] Folz, *Die Reimpaarsprüche*, p. 97, "ob es ein sau im ab het pissen/Mit wurcz und all heraus gerissen . . ."

[21] Ibid., p. 98, "Der juden schant wart offenbar."

giving birth to the Messiah was here applied to the Jews, who were thereby shown to be senseless and easily deceived, as well as false, when they accused Christians of accepting something as ludicrous, in this case virgin birth, but secretly believed and distorted the same truths. Similar inversion occurred in the *Pharetra* where Folz's Jews responded to the accusation "that the donkey and the ape are equally the stepmothers of the Jews," that the Christians must equally be the stepchildren of these, since Adam was the father of everyone.[22] Folz then culled a passage from the Talmud, as rendered by earlier Christian scholars, and turned it on the Jews. He wrote, in the voice of the church, that contrary to Rabbi Solomon's argument, Lilith, the house servant of Adam and Eve, who associated with the Devil, was the progenitor of the Jews and not the gentiles.

Throughout the *Pharetra*, Folz continued to attack the "errors" of the Talmud. As in other folksongs and plays, particularly the Simon of Trent song from 1475, the Jews were presented reading from the Talmud a book called *Agoyim*. The Talmud was associated with falseness and the slandering of Christians. According to Folz, the Talmud, in its discussion of Mordechai, talked of the destruction of the Christian empire, and the hatred of the Jews for Christians was very apparent when the Talmud noted that "the best Christian was killed as despicable and a blasphemer" (*Der aller best crist ist zu tötten als ein snoder und lesterer*).[23] Folz pulled out a number of selections from the Talmud,[24] particularly ones touching on the nature of God and attempted to disprove them through a very allegorical reading of the Old Testament. The result, naturally enough, was that the Jews were viewed as heretics and blasphemers.[25] Why else, concluded Folz, did the king of France burn the Talmud, if its errors and dangerous and subverting comments were not evident?

The supposed misdeeds of the Jews also included formulaic accusations of ritual murder and host desecration. When in Überlingen in 1430 Jews were accused of murdering a child, all of the Jews' possessions were confiscated, and the Jews, though they protested innocence, were burned.[26] The Überlingen records also mentioned the visit of a messenger of the Bishop of Trent, who was a teacher of the holy Scriptures, and who informed people of the burning of the Jews in Ravensburg.[27] Jews were more frequently portrayed in the chronicles,

---

[22] August L. Mayer, ed., *Die Meisterlieder des Hans Folz*, p. 379.

[23] Folz, *Die Reimpaarsprüche*, p. 378.

[24] Folz himself seems to have no direct knowledge of the Talmud, and his comments are gleaned from earlier writers.

[25] Similar blasphemies are recounted in the Frankfurt *Fastnachtspiele* of the fifteenth century, which note the Jews' vile speech against Jesus. The plays at the end of the fifteenth century seem to be more anti-Jewish than those at the beginning of the century. See *GJ*, vol. 3, p. 358.

[26] Siegmund Salfeld and Moritz Stern, *Die Israelitische Bevölkerung der deutschen Städtegeschichte*, vol. 1: *Überlingen am Bodensee*, p. 18.

[27] Ibid., p. 21.

however, as the attackers, and in Nuremberg there are two reports that children were sold to Jews.[28] It goes without saying that accusations of Jewish host
desecration and ritual murder had little basis in reality and were part and parcel of Christian imagination that became particularly pressing during debates
about the doctrine of the eucharist or the increase in cases of infanticide.[29]

In Regensburg there were accusations of stealing the host and bringing it
into the Jewish quarter in May of 1470, and the story was retold, around 1475,
of a Jew who had converted to Christianity (on several occasions) and was paid
to bring the host to the Jews, who then stabbed the host three times and
caused it to bleed. In Regensburg in 1474 a baptized Jew accused the head of
the Jewish community, Israel Bruna, of purchasing a Christian child. A chronicle entry for the year 1476 repeats that Rabbi Bruna and another 25 Jews were
responsible for the horrid acts committed upon a young Christian boy named
Simon in the courtyard of the Jewish synagogue.[30] From April 1476 there
existed a list of 25 questions asked regarding the alleged purchase and murder
of a Christian child by the Jews. Such questions as "for what purpose do Jews
need Christian blood?" were posed.[31] The association of the Jews and ritual murder remained strong enough into the sixteenth century to be cited by a chronicler as one of the reasons for the expulsion of the Jews from the city in 1519.

A number of folksongs also focused on acts of host desecration and ritual
murder supposedly committed by the Jews, as well as on the subsequent punishment of the Jewish communities. While very little of this type of representation was to be found in the *Fastnachtspiele*, many of the terms employed in
both the plays and songs had a common ring to them. Host desecration was
described in some detail in two (and mention is made of daily abuse to the
host and to Mary by the Jews in the Rothenburg song) songs. We will begin
by examining these. In the *Deggendorf Lied* a story was told by an ostensibly
pious burgher about the Jews (here opposed to *Cristenhait*). It was a story about
a great murder committed by the "false Jews" in 1337—Closener reported an
apparently unrelated case in which a Jew was accused of murdering a young
woman named Else in 1337.[32] As the song explained, a host was stolen by a
Christian woman and sold to the Jews for money. The Jews gathered together
with false arrogance and then attempted to desecrate the body of Jesus. First
they pierced it, then they tried to burn it in an oven—though the host remained
unburned—and finally a Jew put the host in his mouth. Mary herself appeared
to charge the Jews with having murdered her son.

---

[28] *Jahrbücher*, p. 168 (for 1447), and p. 206 (in 1453).
[29] See Hsia, *The Myth of Ritual Murder*, as well as the recent and controversial work
of Israel Yuval.
[30] Raphael Straus, *Urkunden*, p. 126.
[31] Straus, *Urkunden*, pp. 72–73.
[32] Friedrich Closener, pp. 137–138.

In the same song the Jews were also accused of poisoning the well water, and it was argued that their evil effect was felt in both the city and the countryside:

> The Jews' heretical poison
> They placed in the wells . . .
> Many died suddenly.
> It was because of this a pitiful distress
> In the city and in the country![33]

In response, early one morning Lord Hartman von Degenberg, protector of the city and countryside, arrived in the city, proclaiming to the burghers that he had come to help against the Jews. The Jews (men and women) were overcome and their houses burnt. The host flew back and an altar was erected. Many miracles were subsequently recorded at the spot. The song then concluded with a supplication that God help to keep everyone free from sin.[34]

A similar song detailed the events leading to the expulsion of the Jews from the city of Passau in 1477. Again, according to the song, the Jews purchased a host from a wicked Christian—here a man by the name of Kristof (the "Christ-bearer"). God, however, would no longer allow such evil to be transacted: the Jews were imprisoned and questioned regarding the host. According to the song's Jew, Mandel, the Jews brought the host into their synagogue, gathered around it, held a mass, and then proceeded to pierce the host. The host bled profusely and the Jews left the synagogue to return the next morning to deliberate about what to do with it. The Jews decided to send two pieces of the host to Prague, two to Neustadt, two to Salzburg, and the final two were to remain in Passau. As in the Deggendorf story, the central desecration occurred in the very private space of the Jews' synagogue. What was different, however, was that a larger intra-city conspiracy is revealed, which went far beyond the rather narrow limits of the earlier Deggendorf case.

In the Passau song one Jew suggested that the host be placed in the oven. Immediately after this happened, however, one of the Jews saw an appearance (*Scheinhait*) in the fire in which there was a small child. Two angels then flew out of the oven. The Jews were thereby made aware that the Christian belief wanted to defend itself. Where the oven stood a beautiful church was constructed and a Mass conducted. Ten Jews were burned, some 46 baptized (this is also different from the earlier song), and the rest expelled from the city by the (juxtaposed) "lords and wise council" (*herren und weisen rat*). The same song recorded the purchase of a pious Christian child for his innocent blood.

---

[33] Rochus Wilhelm von Liliencron, *Historische Volkslieder*, vol. 1, p. 47.

[34] Straus, *Urkunden*, no. 1052; When the Jews are expelled, loans are cancelled, and Jewish buildings destroyed. Some of the folksongs from Regensburg depict the tearing down of the Jewish synagogue and the construction, in its place, of a church. The actions against the Jews are, the Jews complain, "wider alle gesatz und natur ist. . . ."

Host crime accusations documented in the city records, and listed in *Germania Judaica*, often reveal geographical and chronological patterns. Serious outbreaks of accusations occurred in parts of Saxony and in Lower Alsace around 1510, in north east and north central Germany around the turn of the fifteenth century, and in Lower Silesia in the 1450s.

The theme of ritual murder, and indeed murder in general, committed by the Jews was also not uncommon in the folksongs. A song proclaiming the expulsion of the Jews from Regensburg, and an end to their tyranny there,[35] emphasized the standard complaints against Jewish usury; indeed the end of the song proclaims "Rejoice all you Christians/in the city Regensburg/about what has happened/the usurer is dead . . ."[36] But to this charge of usury the song also added that Jews had for a long time killed Christian children for their blood: "Six small children were murdered/from the pious Christian people/the blood was needed from them/for a long time." A similar song "in Toller melodie"[37] also proclaimed Jewish murder of Christian children.[38] The Jews, the same song continued to charge, possessed vast chambers under their houses, in which bloody stones were discovered after the Jews were expelled. These chambers were places, the song noted, where the Jews carried out secretly their criminal activities.[39] The same motif was documented more explicitly in another song: "A stone was found/secretly in a place/on which Jewish dogs murdered/many children . . ."[40] The most famous song dealing with the myth of ritual murder was "Vom heiligen Simon." The song attempted to make known the great murder allegedly committed by the Jews in 1475. The Jews, it claimed, in their great need for Christian blood ("they must have Christian blood for the Easter time") set for a Christian child. As in the cases of host desecration, a disgruntled Christian arrived in the Jewish quarter with the goods, the pious son of a cobbler.[41] The "contemptuous Jews" (*snoden Juden*), in their great blindness, tortured and murdered the boy. Then they used his blood to bake their (Passover) bread. They sent this bread to many lands. They read from one of the Jewish books, a tractate of the Talmud by the name of *Agoyim*. In the end, however, the Jews were punished for their use of innocent blood, and miracles occurred in the name of the martyred Simon.

The general accusation of ritual murder can be traced to much earlier in the Middle Ages, but in Germany the accusations hit a peak in the later

---

[35] Von Liliencron, *Historische Volkslieder*, vol. 3, no. 339.
[36] Ibid., p. 336.
[37] Ibid., no. 338.
[38] Ibid., p. 329.
[39] Ibid., p. 331.
[40] Ibid., p. 338.
[41] Here directly contrasted with the other quarter; see Ibid., vol. 2, p. 14. The Jews were also accused of other more general evils. In Regensburg in March of 1474 a certain Jew, Mosse, was burnt as a poison maker: he had taught the skills of making evil poison in the city it was claimed.

Middle Ages. According to Hsia, there were two such accusations in German-speaking lands in the twelfth century, 15 in the thirteenth, ten in the fourteenth, 14 in the fifteenth, and 12 in the sixteenth. I have located 25 such allegations between the end of the fourteenth century and 1518. Fourteen (or 56%) came from cities in the present state of Baden-Württemburg, at a time when the number of Jewish settlements was increasing drastically. There were smaller outbreaks of accusations in Switzerland at the end of the fourteenth century and southern Moravia in the early 1480s. Individual cases can also be found, as for example in Upper Alsace and Saxony.

It is not only in the plays that Jews were seen as servants of the Devil or the Antichrist,[42] and even more significantly, it was not only the Jews who are associated with the Devil. In *Des Entkrist Vasnacht*, for example, a herald announces the arrival of the Antichrist. Only two prophets, Enoch and Elias, challenged the Antichrist who declares that

> I am the Antichrist/Who is powerful over the whole world/Which has no cunning/Heaven and earth and what is in it/That they might withstand me/ It is also done/That I am a lord over all lords/Whether near or far/ Whether poor or rich/Nobody is my equal/I am the true god/Certainly without all scorn . . .[43]

Through promises of wealth and power, the Antichrist won over the emperor as well as a bishop, a priest, and a learned man. The lame and blind appealed to the Antichrist for help. Only at the end was the Antichrist attacked by "Der Bilgram," and labeled a servant of the Devil. While it is interesting to note that the Jews were the first to recognize the lordship of the Antichrist and the ones who had awaited him for so long, the emperor and the bishop were also ensnared. In this sense, however, it was not the Jews as Jews, but the Jews as representative of a particular element, which was seen as squeezing the assets and thereby lifeblood from the city, who were criticized. It was the financial role of the Jew here and elsewhere in the plays that elicited the outpouring of criticism that ensued. As in other works of literature from the period, most notably *Des Teufels Netz*, many groups were associated with the Devil and for various reasons.

Throughout these examples, it is clear that the general accusations of anti-Christian belief and rhetoric as well as the more terrifying accusations of host desecration and ritual murder were grafted onto a communal plane of discourse, in plays produced and performed in the cities, and in chronicles narrating events in the historical development of the cities. This makes sense, since the songs and plays integrated social and political criticism with understandings of popular religious beliefs. The very nature of the urban literature,

---

[42] For example, in the *Volksliedern*, where the Jews are greeted by the Devil, in Ibid., vol. 3, no. 339, p. 336, section 24.

[43] Von Keller, *Fastnachtspiele*, vol. 2, pp. 595–596.

therefore, requires the mixing of religious and communal elements. One clear tension evident in this grafting was that general religious concepts, such as the equation of the synagogue with Judaism and, in a rather unparallel way, the church with the assembly of Christians—identifying Judaism as a religion but Christianity as a sacred community—existed alongside other representations of social issues, as for example in the separation of private Jewish space, especially in the synagogue, Jewish connections outside the city, and details about individual Jews involved in allegedly malefarious deeds.

ANTI-JUDAISM AND COMMUNITY

In the texts that focus on what we might consider more secular and mundane matters, negative attitudes toward Jews may be divided according to anti-Jewish sentiments (accusations of criminality, usury, subversion of the common good) and anti-Jewish actions (taxation, social and economic restrictions, expulsions). To be sure, both are related in a variety of ways, though I would be cautious in assigning any causality. Both actions and sentiments strengthen the separation of the Jews from the community; even the rather generic reports of Zink about taxes imposed upon the Jews by the emperor served to mark the Jews off as a separate entity within the city. In the end, anti-Jewish sentiments and actions reinforced the idea that the Jews were not, indeed could not be, part of the sacred urban community.

Among the various anti-Jewish portrayals of the texts the accusations of criminal, subversive, and usurious acts of the Jews were the most common. Sigmund Meisterlin, the famous fifteenth-century Nuremberg chronicler, reported that during the reign of Charlemagne there was a great crowd of Jews in Nuremberg. There were likely few, if any Jews, in the city at that time, however. Meisterlin's comment, therefore, was an effort to suggest that the Jews had been present in, and, according to him, undermining the city for a long time. These Jews had the best houses and a Jewish school on the Market, narrated Meisterlin. All of the Jews in the world, he continued, sought refuge in the city and they all gave a great deal of money to the emperor, who then protected them and allowed them to secure the choicest spaces on the market[44] (he argued that the Jews were allowed asylum in the city only because of the emperor's avarice).[45] The Jews, Meisterlin rued, committed criminal acts in the city, though he employed only the vague term criminal (frevel).[46] Meisterlin mentioned the great amount of money loaned out by the Jews, not only to the emperor, but to the burghers and the nobles as well. But, the Jews committed treacherous financial manipulations causing the common people in the city to be "undisciplined" and in a state of "masterlessness." Throughout his

[44] Ibid., p. 134.
[45] Ibid., p. 234.
[46] Sigmund Meisterlin, pp. 117–118.

chronicle, Meisterlin envied the Jews and their possessions.[47] He associated the wealth and influence of the Jews with the religious insensitivity of the emperor. Polemically, then, both represented hostility to Christianity and the Christian commune.[48]

Meisterlin recounted efforts to construct a church on the market where the Jews had their synagogue, and he noted a decision to request that the Jews sell all of their houses on the market within a year so that the church could be built,[49] resulting in both the symbolic removal of the Jews from their dominating appearance in the city and perhaps also the loosening of imperial authority upon the city. Throughout the fifteenth century, relations between the south German imperial cities, their imperial lords, and the territorial (particularly Bavarian) lords were complex. The Jews were often trapped within this web of intrigue and utilized both as financial pawns and objects of criticism against outside figures of authority. Many of the chroniclers likened the relationship between the dukes and the Jews to that of the emperor and the Jews. Hektor Mülich connected ducal attacks on the rights of the imperial cities with the negative qualities he found in the Jews. Mülich indicated that a duke who liked Jews consequently had a number of other poor qualities as well.[50] In the mind of Mülich it was believable that a duke, who, as Mülich also informed us, employed Jewish physicians, would be strange, miserly, manipulative, and tyrannical.

Depending on their actions and the context, imperial and territorial rulers might be portrayed favorably or unfavorably. Mülich labeled Albert of Austria, in 1462, "a fool and Jew-king."[51] On the other hand, other chroniclers represented King Albert of Austria, when in 1438 he helped to expel the Jews from Augsburg, as a pious ruler and enemy of the Jews.[52] Relations between lords and the cities could be complex and might change quickly. The sources reveal an uneasy tension between contempt for imperial association with the Jews and the necessity of obtaining imperial permission to sanction the actions of the city councils. Although at times the imperial protection of the Jews was criticized, most cities still required imperial permission to expel and keep out the Jews. Burghers complained to the emperor about the Jews, but often, from their perspective, to no avail. In an effort to gain imperial permission to expel the Jews from the city, the Regensburg city council lodged a complaint against the freedoms granted the Jews by the king (1476).[53] The freedoms granted the

---

[47] Ibid., pp. 200–201.
[48] Ibid., pp. 159–160, Meisterlin reports an exchange between the councilman Stromer and the Emperor.
[49] Ibid., p. 159.
[50] Hektor Mülich, pp. 170–171.
[51] Ibid., p. 195.
[52] *Chronik von der Gründung*, p. 323.
[53] Straus, *Urkunden*, p. 125.

Jews, according to another document, were against all law and nature, because the Jews were lazy and damaged the city through interest-mongering as well involvement with foreign goods and manufactures.

The most common accusation against the Jews was that they practiced harmful and outrageous usury. The description of the Jews in Folz's *Jüdische Wucher* (1491) was quite detailed; Folz mixed a myriad of elements found in nearly all of the plays and songs. He began this play by describing the Jews in both sociological and religious terms: as lazy, unemployed, and therefore unproductive; as robbers and criminals; and, as a people utterly contemptuous even of the Ten Commandments.[54] The Jews did no handiwork, continued Folz, rather, they stayed awake all night during their ridiculous holidays for the mere purpose of secretly blaspheming all of Christendom. The Jews were vermin, they conducted all sorts of criminal business activities. Jews were bloodthirsty, they were murderers, robbers, traffickers in stolen goods and they fed off Christians, whom they constantly sucked dry.

The interest taken on loans by the Jews came to be described, by the end of the fifteenth and beginning of the sixteenth centuries, as an excessive burden on the poor or the common man.[55] Similar characterizations of the Jews were to be found elsewhere, for example in a number of the folksongs, in which the Jews were described as lenders to all strata of society,[56] and destroyers the city through their usury.[57] The correspondence between the emperor and Regensburg, initiated by the city councilmen, for example, associated Jewish usury with laziness, business dealings with foreigners, and the "ruin of the common man" (*verderben des gemainen manns*).[58] The amount of interest that Jews, and for that matter non-Jews, were permitted to charge, however, was usually precisely defined. An ordinance from fourteenth-century Nuremberg prescribed the amount of interest that Jews were allowed to receive on a loan, and it divided the taxes paid by the Jews on such income evenly between the imperial and civil authorities.[59]

The most typical crimes of which Jews were accused were business crimes, including: falsifying surety papers, taking forbidden rates of interest, and most common, counterfeiting.[60] Jews were also commonly accused of buying or receiving stolen goods, and occasionally of themselves stealing goods.[61] There was even

---

[54] Folz, *Die Reimpaarsprüche*, p. 310.

[55] Straus, *Urkunden*, nos. 762 and 979; see Kisch, *Jewry Law*, p. 225. Though it was argued that almost everywhere the Jews have made usurious loans to people from every stratum of society.

[56] Worldly and spiritual as well as poor and rich; see von Liliencron, *Historische Volkslieder*, vol. 3, no. 337, p. 326.

[57] Ibid., no. 338, pt. 14.

[58] Straus, *Urkunden*, no. 979.

[59] Joseph Baader, ed., *Nürnberger Polizeiordnungen aus dem 13 bis 15 Jahrhundert*, p. 325. See also a similar decree from Strasbourg in 1383, in *CdS*, vol. 9, p. 981.

[60] In Pritzwalk in 1392, Braunschweig in 1417, Brandenburg an der Havel and Klosterneuberg in 1485, and Zerbst in the 1480s. See *GJ*, vol. 3.

[61] For example, Baader, ed., *Nürnberger Polizeiordnungen*, no. 349.

a case in Regensburg from 1455 in which a certain Jörg Helkermair from Helkering complained to the Schultheiß that 83 Jews from Regensburg attacked him and his goods with weapons—only one Jew, however, was identified by name.

According to Folz the vast wealth that the Jews had acquired through such usury and theft was the source of their authority, which they used daily to flaunt over Christians. Most of the noble lords, complained Folz, were blind to the destruction wreaked by the Jews, who quickly destroyed the city and exploited the poor Christians: like a wolf in a sheepfold the Jews were against the "poor Christians."

> When a Jew shepherds in a city
> [There are] many great disadvantages and filth
> Because he is a wolf in a sheepfold . . .
> And like the bloodhound sucks and milks
> The poor Christians' blood and sweat . . .[62]

Folz found a few noble lords, such as Bishop Philip of Bamberg, who had engaged in the godly work of expelling the Jews, which he advocated in Nuremberg.

Numerous actions were taken against the Jews throughout the Middle Ages. In addition to the imperial tax-wringing of the late fourteenth century,[63] which caused a great deal of upheaval within the Jewish communities, there were widespread social and economic restrictions and numerous episodes of physical attack and expulsion.

The earliest accounts in Burkhard Zink's chronicle that mention the Jews referred to imperial taxes extracted from them in the eighth and ninth decades of the fourteenth century, the period in which many south German cities were attempting to assert their authority at the expense of the sovereignty of both secular and ecclesiastical lords. In the chronicles, the largest number of cases (some 40%) reported that mention the Jews dealt primarily with questions of taxation—particularly imperial demands for taxes and local responses to those demands, or the raising of taxes in order to pay off debts incurred by military defeat at the hands of the landed nobility.[64] The period between 1374 and 1390 was a particularly important and devastating time for the Jews in Germany.[65] According to most accounts Emperor Charles IV demanded large sums of money

---

[62] Folz, *Die Reimpaarsprüche*, pp. 317–318.

[63] See Ernst Voltmer, "Zur Geschichte der Juden im spätmittelalterlichen Speyer," pp. 112–113.

[64] The large number of cases, however, is not a clear indication, as many historians wish to see it, that the only or the chief role of the Jews in the community revolved around the issue of taxes. To be sure the question of taxation was central to the Jews' relationship to both imperial and local authorities. But to focus exclusively on this issue might distort the image of the everyday reality lived by Jews and of their contacts with Christians.

[65] For an overview of the imperial taxation of the Jews in the later Middle Ages, see Toch, *Die Juden*, pp. 49f.

from the Swabian cities in 1374 (1373 by some accounts). From Ulm he demanded 72,000 fl., 12,000 fl. from the Jews. Nördlingen along with 12 other cities was to supply 70,000 fl. (a sum that had never before been demanded by an emperor, according to the chroniclers). Memmingen was to pay 11,000 fl. Augsburg was to contribute 37,000 fl., 10,000 fl. from the Jews. The *Anonymous Chronicle from 1368* and Hektor Mülich offered fuller accounts of the imposition on the Augsburg Jews of the 10,000 fl. tax in 1374. According to the first chronicle[66] the Jews, both men and women, were gathered up and thrown in jail in an effort to exact the money from them. From Mülich's account we learn that the emperor allowed the city to tax the Jews in order to raise money against the dukes of Bavaria.[67] According to Zink, however, the emperor later brought another letter of privilege (*freihaitbrief*), and he forced the people of Augsburg to give the 10,000 fl. to him. Zink concluded that the emperor "was a true persecutor of Christendom and of all pious men" (*was ain rechter durchachter der christenhait und aller frommen menschen*).[68] The account in the *Founding* added a rather different twist, when it noted that it was the emperor and not the citizens of Augsburg who wanted to imprison the Jews.[69] It was the emperor's instigation that forced the Jews to be mistreated, pleaded the chroniclers.

Other cases of heavy taxation were reported for the 1380s. In 1381, Zink noted, under a single heading, that five heretics were burned in the city and that the Jews were imprisoned and had to give the city 5,000 fl.[70] In 1385 we find a list of 28 Jews who contributed to the 80,986 fl. raised by the Jewish communities for imperial taxes. A similar event was recorded by Ulman Stromer, who noted that in Nuremberg both the rich and the poor Jews were rounded up in the cellar of the townhall and forced to pay 80,000 fl.[71] In the imperial tax campaign of 1384 Zink explained that twice the sum of 1374 was forced from the Jews.[72] Here Zink stressed the emperor's permission granted to the city to extract money from the Jews, because of the many things that the Jews had done, though he offered no catalogue of offenses. Augsburg, continued Zink, was not alone in its ill treatment of the Jews, for the Jews were imprisoned in all of the imperial cities. The extra taxation of the Jews was so impor-

---

[66] *Chronik von 1368*, p. 42.

[67] Hektor Mülich, p. 16.

[68] Burkhard Zink, p. 13. According to the same account the money that was extracted from the Jews later had to be handed over to the emperor. What is different here is the perception of the emperor—transformed in the later accounts as opposed to the city in favor of the Jews. The same twist is echoed in Zink's account, and a similar version in *Chronik von 1368*, p. 35.

[69] *Chronicle from the Founding*, p. 311.

[70] Ibid., pp. 26–27; *Chronik von 1368* (p. 68) does not differ from Zink's account.

[71] In 1373, Zink writes (p. 9) of a war instigated by a certain evil *edelman*, a *bos* and *listig* man, who was a great enemy of the city. *Chronik von 1368* differs only slightly, compare pp. 37–38.

[72] Burkhard Zink, p. 30.

tant for the royal coffers that King Wenceslaus assembled representatives from the imperial cities in Ulm in 1385 to discuss the matter.[73] A few years later in 1390, in exchange for the assistance of the burghers of the imperial cities, King Wencelas canceled any interest that was owed by them to the Jews.[74]

In addition to imperial as well as local taxation—regular and extraordinary— numerous laws restricted the social and economic relations between Jews and their non-Jewish neighbors, as in Ravensburg (1420), Hildesheim (1439[75] and 1451[76]), and Türkheim (1465). In many south German cities Jews were locked in their own houses and quarter during certain Christian celebrations, and prohibited from conducting business during Christian holidays.[77] Jews were often allowed in the market only on specified days—as in Regensburg, where they were permitted only on Wednesdays and Fridays. Jews were restricted in what they were to sell: for example, in Regensburg, Jews were prohibited from trafficking in wine or beer, and from weaving. Interaction between Jews and Christians was restricted, at least in law, and Jews were forbidden to play games with Christians.[78] Not only Jewish actions, but Jewish space as well was severely encumbered.[79] The Jewish quarter[80] in particular was an important divider between Jews and Christians, between public and private, legal and criminal. According to a complaint in Regensburg lodged in 1471:

> Item my lord from Basel is next to the Judengasse in the middle of the city at Herberg, and we cannot pass the house without seeing the Jews and hearing them sing. They have a great quarter with many expensive houses in it . . .[81]

As we have seen above, evil dealings were supposed to have occurred in the Jewish spaces. In Nuremberg, a convert to Christianity was accused of secretly entering and smuggling a host into the Jewish quarter. The Jewish quarter, in another instance, was entered by a cathedral preacher (*Domprediger*), and the Jews complained.[82] Jews might also find protection from hostile citizens in the Jewish quarter, but when they left they were vulnerable: in Regensburg there are two cases of Jews being attacked upon leaving the quarter to shop.[83]

---

[73] According to Burkhard Zink, pp. 31–32.

[74] Ibid., p. 44. Compare Hektor Mülich, p. 39, and *Chronik von 1368*, p. 93.

[75] See Helmut Coing, ed., *Handbuch der Quellen und Literatur der neueren europäischen Privatsrechtsgeschichte*, vol. 1, p. 485.

[76] Connected with clothing and the preaching of Nicholas of Cusa; see also the entries for Magdeburg (for the year 1451) and Friedberg (for 1452) in *GJ*, vol. 3.

[77] See Straus, *Urkunden*, no. 834.

[78] Ibid.

[79] Ibid., p. 295.

[80] Here again, Kisch, *Jewry Law*, argues that the separation of the Jews in their own quarter originated of the Jews' own free will and that such separation facilitated protection and taxation of the community, see pp. 292–293.

[81] Straus, *Urkunden*, p. 33.

[82] Ibid., p. 328.

[83] Ibid., nos. 641 and 693.

The fourteenth century was a period of brutal attacks against Jews throughout Europe, particularly in Germany. Friedrich Closener, like the Augsburg
chroniclers, noted the 1298 massacre of the Jews in Nuremberg, Würzburg,
and many other cities.[84] Königshofen mentioned the expulsion of the Jews from
France in 1317,[85] and he recounted the events in Colmar in 1337.[86] Massacres,
expulsions and restrictions were often the outcome of Jewish and Christian
interaction. The only possible checks on attacks against the Jews were by large
structures of authority that could be relatively insulated from pressures of opinion arising from local life. Large and strong states, particularly in south Germany,
however, were few and far between.

The lack of strong controls protecting the Jews was evident in the widespread
massacres and expulsions associated with the Black Death. Alfred Haverkamp
has conducted an in-depth survey and prepared a detailed chronological list-
ing of these anti-Jewish pogroms.[87] According to Haverkamp the attacks represented sharpening social and political tensions and at times had little to do
with the precise timing of the outbreak of the plague itself.[88] Some attacks
undoubtedly were planned, coinciding with religious festivals or held on the
Jews' Sabbath, and evidently served political functions,[89] and included a broad
cross-section of the city populace—of the 43 Erfurt citizens involved in burning the Jews, nine belonged to the patrician families;[90] they reveal a complex
urban, regional and often imperial context.[91]

The massacre of the Augsburg Jews in 1349 (1348 by some accounts) hit
the Jews of that city much as it did the bulk of the other Jewish communities[92]—quickly and brutally. Whatever Jews were not murdered fled the city.
The entries for these events, however, by the Augsburg mercantile chroniclers,
unlike the chroniclers in other cities, tended to be very concise. An anonymous chronicle entry was typical of this brevity: "in the same year the Jews
were burned here." Wahraus also noted dryly that ". . . the Jews were burned
on Saint Cecilia's Day."[93]

There was mention of the great massacre of 1348, in which large numbers
of Jews in Strasbourg were burned, because they allegedly poisoned the wells.

---

[84] Friedrich Closener, pp. 103–104. Königshofen's account differs at one point; see
pp. 758–759.
[85] In Königshofen, p. 759.
[86] Ibid., pp. 758–759.
[87] Alfred Haverkamp, "Die Judenverfolgungen zur Zeit des Schwarzen Todes in
Gesellschaftsgefüge deutscher Städte."
[88] Ibid., p. 38.
[89] Ibid., pp. 46f.
[90] Ibid., p. 54.
[91] Ibid., pp. 69f.
[92] See Alfred Haverkamp, ed., Zur Geschichte der Juden im Deutschland des späten
Mittelalters und frühen Neuzeit.
[93] Wahraus, p. 220; Hektor Mülich, p. 2; Chronik von der Gründung, p. 308.

Interestingly, the myth of Jews poisoning wells was not limited to the catastrophic events associated with the Black Death. According to Closener's historical recounting, Carl—perhaps referring to Charles the Bald, who was reportedly poisoned by his Jewish doctor in 877—was poisoned in the Alps by a Jew.[94] The Strasbourg chroniclers were quicker than those of Augsburg to focus on the religious deviance of the Jews and the tragedies that arose from the Jews' machinations.[95]

In his chronicle, Closener openly connected the Jews more than once with the poisoning of the water.[96] Königshofen also mentioned that 2,000 Jews were burned in Strasbourg in 1349, the same year that the Jews were burned throughout Christendom.[97] Throughout Germany, Jews were burned, imprisoned, murdered, or expelled.[98] Königshofen writes that the Jews were forbidden from Strasbourg for 200 years, but that they returned in 1368. In 1386 the Jews were forced to pay the city 20,000 fl., but they were soon accused of displaying too much wealth (and with other "disorderly matters," *unordentlichen sachen*).[99] Two years later, in 1388, they were banned from the city forever.

Other attacks were also mentioned in the chronicles. In 1397 Ulman Stromer noted that the Jews in Würzburg as well as the bishop's servants were imprisoned, and that a burgher was killed.[100] Later, in the fifteenth century, there are a number of chronicle entries that documented actions against the Jews.[101] In 1460, according to an anonymous chronicler,[102] a certain margrave imprisoned and executed five Jews, from the "most powerful and learned" among the Jews, because of a murder allegedly committed by them.[103] The same chronicle related the events and accusations of the Trent ritual murder trial.[104]

---

[94] Friedrich Closener, p. 34. See Joshua Trachtenberg, *The Devil and the Jews*, p. 97.

[95] Trachtenberg, *The Devil and the Jews*, p. 104.

[96] Ibid., p. 127.

[97] This number (in terms of population and number burned) seems rather large, though most modern accounts repeat it. For a general overview, see GJ II, part 2, pp. 801–803.

[98] See Königshofen, pp. 759–760.

[99] In CdS, volume 9, p. 985.

[100] Ulman Stromer, p. 57.

[101] There are numerous cases of imprisonment listed in GJ, vol. 3. See: Hagenau (for the year 1391); Archbishop of Mainz (imprisons Jews of Gross-Steinheim, Lorch (1429)); Calbe an der Saale (1514); Dieburg (1429); Dietfurt (1421); Freiberg (1411); Freiburg/ Uechtland (1428); Fulda (1507); Kreuznach (1434); Laibach (1510); Landshut (1450); Rheinber (1409); Cologne; St. Wendel (1381); Treffurt (1452); and, Wil (1469).

[102] *Anonymous Augsburg Chronicle from 991–1483*, p. 520.

[103] Ibid., p. 527.

[104] Among the numerous incidents reported in GJ, vol. 3, we can include the following: the attacks on Jews by the Swiss armies in 1476 and 1477 through Alsace; the attack and plundering of Jewish homes by peasants (Deutz 1445, Reichenweier 1416); the murder of Jews (Kalkar 1443, Villmar 1451), particularly Jews traveling to or from their home cities (Weissenfels 1385/86), and the robbing of Jews.

There were also several cases of Christians accusing Jews of murder (Klingenberg 1461, Lienz 1442, Strakonitz 1503), and even more curiously, reports of Jewish crimes against other Jews and Jewish converts to Christianity. In Dortmund in 1393 converted Jews were attacked; in Schnabelwaid in 1483 a Jew was killed by a foreign Jew; in Löwenberg (n.d.) two Jews killed a third; and there is also mention of a Jewish suicide in Hanover in 1500. Jews were executed because of a number of accused crimes and frequently imprisoned, most often to squeeze additional taxes from them. Jews were frequently reported as the victims of physical attack. There is record, in Nuremberg, of a Jew being beaten with a rod by three assailants in 1497[105] and the mugging of a Jew in 1498.[106] Attacks on Jews may have been on the rise around the time of their expulsion from that city.

There are records of expulsions and attempts at expulsions (see Appendix B), or letters allowing cities not to tolerate Jews, in a large number of German cities between the end of the fourteenth and the beginning of the sixteenth century. Every city cannot be listed here, though some examples will suffice: Heidelberg (1390); Breisach (1421); Cologne (1424); Ehingen (1444); Breslau (1453/54); Hildesheim (1457); Salzburg (1498); Nördlingen (1504). In each of these cases the exact context for the expulsion and the results of the expulsion need to be examined.

In Mainz in 1438 there was an attempted expulsion of the Jews, revolving around a conflict between the bishop and the city.[107] The Landshut chronicler reported that between 1450 and 1451 the Jews in that city were also collected. The men were imprisoned in the *Schergnstuben* and the women in the school. All of their goods were confiscated, and their houses were occupied. In all the Jews were forced to pay 30,000 fl., to clear out the school, and to leave the city within four weeks. Many Jews, however, were allowed to be baptized and remain in the city.[108] Jews were also expelled from many other cities. In Nuremberg the Jews were again expelled in 1498.[109] According to Heinrich Deichsler (1430–1506), the Nuremberg brewer,[110] imperial and local authorities agreed on the action, and the Jews were given three months to leave the city and its territory. It is doubtful that the Jews entirely withdrew from the area, for the same chronicler recorded that three years later, in 1501, four Jewish men and one Jewish woman were apprehended in the city dressed as farmers (*in paurnklaider*).[111] Why were they described as wearing farmers' clothing and

---

[105] "Legt man drei hutergeselen in das loch, heten auf dem Marck einen juden mit airn geworfen," *Heinrich Deichsler's Chronik 1488–1506*, in CdS, vol. 11, p. 592.
[106] Ibid., p. 598.
[107] For an account see CdS, volume 17, pp. 165f.
[108] *Landshuter Rathschronik*, pp. 300–301.
[109] The Nuremberg Council sought imperial permission to expel the Jews as early as 1473, but it was not until 1498 that it was granted; see Edith Wenzel, "*Do worden die Judden alle geschant*", pp. 263–264.
[110] *Heinrich Deichsler's Chronik*, p. 601.
[111] Ibid., p. 633.

how were they recognized? The chroniclers did not divulge answers to these questions, but certainly it was believable that Jews could take up the masks of another group outside of the city community. Similarly, Leonhart Widmann reported that in Regensburg in 1519 the Jews were given eight days to leave the city, that the synagogue was destroyed, that a new church was built where the synagogue had been located, and that Jewish gravestones were unearthed.[112] Whether or not the radical preacher Balthasar Hubmaier was responsible for the actions, the chronicler reports that Hubmaier was preaching at the site.[113]

In many cases, the expulsions had to do with local or regional politics (in some places imperial politics), and there are often clear regional patterns. Nearly all of the Jewish communities in Upper and Lower Austria were expelled in from 1420 to 1421, and somewhere around 60% of the communities in Bavaria were expelled around 1450, in both cases as part of very large regional expulsions. Similarly, 68% of the Jewish communities in Brandenburg were expelled in 1510, as were numerous Jewish communities in adjoining areas in Saxony, while a 1390 through 1391 expulsion in the Palatinate affected Jews in the Upper Palatinate, the Rhineland Palatinate, and parts of modern Baden-Württemburg. There were numerous expulsions in Alsace in the sixteenth century. Areas in west and parts of central Germany seem, on average, to have suffered proportionally fewer expulsions at the end of the Middle Ages. By contrast, regions in the northwest and southwest seem to have suffered proportionally higher rates of expulsion. In some cases the expulsions had a minimal effect on the Jews; while in others the Jewish communities did not revive for several hundred years, if at all.

There were also territorial expulsions. One example of territorial expulsion is Styria, from where the Jews were expelled by the command of Emperor Maximilian in 1496. The expulsion edict stipulated that Jews were to leave Styria as well as the cities of Wiener Neustadt and Neunstadt. The reasons given for the expulsion form a rather formalized litany of accusations, including alleged dishonor, vice, insult to the holy sacrament (Eucharist), the use of the blood of Christian children, as well as the creation of false letters, cheating, and fraud—all bringing devastating economic effects to the general populace. According to the decree, some Jews had already been imprisoned for such crimes. Maximilian objected to the Jews' "coarse, shocking, and intolerable activity," and deferring to his own love of God and subjects, that is, his duty of moral protection, and with learned counsel, Maximilian issued the expulsion. Jews were not to reside in these lands nor to travel there for usurious business. Jews traveling through the region were required to maintain an escort. The imperial decree offered a much broader scope than did the Augsburg expulsion

---

[112] Widmann claims as many as 5,000; see pp. 31–32.

[113] We know that Hubmaier had preached strongly against the Jews there. See R. Po-chia Hsia, *The Myth of Ritual Murder*; and, *The German Peasants' War: A History in Documents*, edited and translated by Tom Scott and Bob Scribner, p. 232.

decree. Religion was referenced first, and the moral protection of the emperor was referred to explicitly.

SACRALIZATION OF THE COMMUNE

The emphasis in the earlier (fourteenth-century) accounts was on the Jew as opposed to Christianity. In the fifteenth-century accounts, the religious element remained, but it was combined with Jews' actions having to do with disruption of government and more general threats to society or the jealousy of local burghers as well. Attacks on the Jews as well as the anti-Jewish discourse that spawned such attacks were very much a manifestation of communal change throughout Europe, particularly in the south German cities.

The terms often employed by the authors of the songs and plays, which focused on ritual murder and host desecration, involved elements of criminality (*frevel, buben/buberei*); stealing; poisoning; or more general descriptions of Jews as bloodthirsty; or evil (*pos* and *ubel*). What stood out in these stories and songs, as in other places, was that the Jews were shown to be set apart from non-Jews in the city. Particularly in their spatial separation, and in their supposed criminal customs, Jews were antithetical to Christianity and to civic community. The Jews had to be described in terms of Christian concepts and ideas, but naturally enough, inverted ones—for the Christians did not have the vocabulary to distinguish the Jews from other marginalized, "evil" groups. As more was learned about the Jews, some of this changed. But the overriding ignorance of Jewish customs and culture, or perhaps the simplicity of relating and describing in a common and familiar language the Jews and their actions, remained.

In the later Middle Ages, such religious inversion was increasingly combined with language of communal subversion, in which Jews were seen as opposed to the very welfare of the city itself. A common thread of discourse runs through these pieces, a common thread that revolves around the opposition between the Jew—his person, his appearance, and his space—and the urban community. One of the most influential preachers of the fifteenth century, Bernardino da Sienna, put it in transparent language. For him, Jews were a plague attacking the body of the civic commune and all of Christianity:

> Money is the vital heat of a city. The Jews are leeches who ask for nothing better than the opportunity to devour an ailing member, whose blood they suck dry with insatiable ardor. When heat and blood abandon the extremities of the body to flow back to the heart, it is a sign that death is near. But the danger is even more imminent when the wealth of a city is in the hands of the Jews. Then the heat no longer flows, as it does normally, towards the heart. As it does in a plague-ridden body, it moves towards the ailing member of the body; for every Jew, especially if he is a moneylender, is a capital enemy of all Christians.[114]

---

[114] Cited in Robert Bonfil, *Jewish Life in Renaissance Italy*, p. 24.

It is certainly significant that Jewish otherness was here opposed to the city and not merely Christianity, and that money was so prominently associated with the welfare of the city. A final similarity in many of the plays and songs that mention the Jews' business was a contrast that the authors frequently drew between the Jews and the urban community. The *Rothenburg Lied* argued that the Jews worked against the commune.[115] What was often decried in these texts was the wealth and laziness of the Jews, and the damage that their usury brought to the community.[116] Such complaints were not, however, limited to the Jews, as a quick glance at the poor ordinances and laws concerning beggars from the late fifteenth and early sixteenth centuries shows.

There is evidence of preaching against the Jews and of debates between Jews and Christians in many cities in the period. A chronicle from Landshut, for example, recorded the preaching in 1449 against the Jews and usury.[117] There was also a case reported by the author of the *Yearbooks* for the year 1478 in Nuremberg, according to which the best Jewish scholars are reported to have engaged in debate with Hebrew-wielding monks familiar with Jewish texts. The Jewish combatants apparently wanted nothing to do with the debate, but eventually Isaac of Prague was brought in to represent the Jews.[118] There seems to have been some unruliness surrounding the debate.

Hatred of Jews could be based on local conditions, but it might also be fanned by itinerant preachers, whose arrival in the city could be greeted with great pomp.[119] The infamous John of Capistrano, for example, may have been behind the ritual murder charges and subsequent executions and expulsions enforced against the Jews in Breslau, and Bernardino da Feltre had a hand in the Trent ritual murder trial in 1475. There are numerous accounts of wandering preachers stirring up the populace against usury and against the Jews. In 1394 Zink noted that a preacher, Peter Engerlin, came to Augsburg from Bamberg and preached exclusively against usurers and heretics, inciting the crowd to action against them.[120]

We know from several of the chronicles that a number of radically anti-Jewish preachers, most notably John of Capistrano, were circulating throughout south Germany in the 1450s[121] and that some Jews were forcibly baptized.[122] A number

---

[115] Von Keller, *Fastnachtspiele*, here vol. 3, p. 357; see also Wenzel, "*Do worden die Judden alle geschant*", here at p. 261.

[116] See Ibid., p. 172, where usury is associated with laziness and slyness, or disputes with clergy.

[117] *Landshuter Rathschronik*, p. 296.

[118] *Jahrbücher des 15. Jahrhunderts*, in CdS, volume 10, pp. 353–354—see also appendix 1, p. 354 for the public brief.

[119] Larissa Taylor, *Soldiers of Christ*, p. 47.

[120] See Zink, pp. 45–46.

[121] See *Nürnberg Kreuzfahrer*, in CdS, vol. 10, p. 412; though he is not mentioned in the context of preaching against the Jews here. A quick review of GJ, vol. 3 reveals that John of Capistrano preached at least in Löwenberg, Olmütz, Forchheim and Magdeburg; Peter Schwarz in Erlangen, and Nicholas of Cusa in Halberstadt.

[122] This is reported in Strasbourg for an earlier period; Jews were given the opportunity

of other itinerant preachers, for example, Peter Schwarz, and later Balthasar
Hubmaier, and notable Church officials—Nicholas of Cusa—are mentioned
throughout the legal records. It was written of Peter Schwartz that he came to
Regensburg to preach to the Jews in their own language.[123] The Jews were
preached to regarding the Messiah or usury, and the "common man" was incited
against them.[124]

But not only words were exchanged. There was a case in Regensburg in which
two Jews complained that they were attacked physically by a certain Dominican
preacher.[125] Such physical danger, whether at the hands of the preacher himself or the angry mob that he aroused against the Jews, was not the only danger that the Jews faced. Jews were also plagued by the danger which intense
fear and constant sermonizing could create within their own communities. For
sermons were given not only against the Jews but to the Jews as well. The Jews
were forced to sit and listen to anti-Jewish conversionary sermons, as the
Nuremberg craftsman Hans Rosenplüt (ca. 1400–1460) noted in his *Order
Preached Against the Jews in Regensburg* (1474). According to Rosenplüt, God
sent a great preacher (a monk) to preach publicly to the Jews in their own
Hebrew language. In addition to the standard theological matters, the preacher
railed at the Jews for their evil and laziness:

> Their treachery and usury/Is so heavy for the Christian/They must be raised
> lazy/Like the obese pig/To watch with cunning/Their work is nothing/. . . and
> dream secrets/What they might do to the Christians/. . ./And instigate evil
> against Christians.[126]

Such preaching did, at times, lead to the conversion and baptism of Jews. Yet
the status of the Jewish convert was still one of extreme ambivalence and suspicion at best. Converts do appear on occasion in the German documents,
and quite frequently are the subject of discussion in the rabbinic responsa. But
the act of conversion itself could have serious practical consequences. In a
case from 1464, for example, in which the father in the household had converted to Christianity, and the mother persisted in her Jewish belief, their child

---

to be baptized before they were killed. See Friedrich Closener, p. 130. See Léon Poliakov,
The History of Anti-Semitism, vol. 1: for Saint Vincent Ferrer (pp. 144–146); for Saint
John of Capistrano, especially the effects of his preaching in Silesia in 1453–54 (pp.
146–147); and, for Bernardino of Feltre (pp. 147–149).

[123] Straus, *Urkunden*, p. 40.

[124] Ibid., p. 335. The Jews of Regensburg could rightfully complain, that "so volgt doch
dem obgezelten übl züe, das die prediger des thümbstifts und Parfüesserordens . . . den
gemainen man . . . wider uns bewegen, under anderm sprechende: die freyhaiten, welche
wir von den Bäbsten, Kaysern und Künigen . . . und sunst herbracht und haben, sollen
nyemants gelten, welher uns schüldig ist . . ., der sey zü kainer bezalüng verbünden,
auch kain richter . . . zü verhelfen."

[125] Ibid., no. 925.

[126] Ibid., p. 307.

was to be taken from the mother at the age of three and handed over to the father.[127]

In some cases the regular clergy may have attempted to direct some of the attention away from themselves by rallying the "common people" against heretics and other marginal groups. But it was itinerant preachers, very often Mendicants, who charted the intersection of moral values and urban identity. In some cases, itinerant preachers often had little or no direct stake, and no authority in the city, and therefore were not a threat to the civic rights of the burghers. Such a distance may have allowed them to enjoy a detachment from the vulnerable position of their clerical peers within the city. In other cities, however, the Mendicants, particularly the Franciscans, were seen as the religious order of the burghers. In fifteenth-century Münster, for example "the burghers saw the friars as their own religious order, a civic counterpart to the traditional religious orders, where aristocratic elements predominated. The magistrates extended protection and patronage to the Franciscans, granted them the use of real properties, honored them with periodic alms. In turn, the friars cared for the sick and poor and opened their cloister to secular use."[128] Indeed, the Mendicant orders were founded as an ostensibly urban institution, and the preaching of the Mendicants struck against notions of the power of wealth and money, while espousing a spiritual, reforming poverty.

According to Lester Little, both the content and the form of the friars' message were shaped by their urban context. The Mendicants discussed issues central to the urban population: "property, interest, credit, insurance, and moneylending."[129] Urban spirituality, like urban professions and existence, "fostered a need for spirituality that would express itself in speech."[130] Particularly in the fourteenth and fifteenth centuries, the Mendicants helped to establish and foster various "group manifestations of lay piety."[131] Little writes that "beyond a favourable moral ethic, new forms of worship, and the encouragement of charitable donations, the friars supplied city people with what may justly be called an urban ideology."[132]

Little notes the paradox, however, that the primary "practitioners of voluntary poverty, themselves city-dwellers, formulated an ethic that justified the principal activities of the dominant groups in urban society."[133] This tension was evident in the work of the Franciscan Peter John Olivi (1248–1298) who held

---

[127] Ibid., p. 21; see also Guido Kisch, *Jewry Law in Medieval Germany*, pp. 200 and 207—Kisch notes that there is only one case of Jews proselytizing Christians that is recorded.

[128] R. Po-chia Hsia, *Society and Religion in Münster 1535–1618*, p. 39.

[129] Lester Little, *Religious Poverty and the Profit Economy in Medieval Europe*, p. 197.

[130] Ibid., p. 199.

[131] Ibid., pp. 209–210.

[132] Ibid., p. 213.

[133] Ibid., p. 216.

realistic ideals, in which "only flagrant and repeated self-indulgence in material goods should be treated as a mortal transgression of the vow of poverty,"[134]
and distinguished between usury and legitimate compensation. According to many
historians, the "pauperes Christi" served the profit economy, resulting in a
decreased need for marginal scapegoats; Jews, according to Little, were expelled
and replaced by Christian bankers.[135] The combination of such an urban theology with an idealized vision of Christianity as an organic unity left no room
for the "infidels,"[136] but also helped create a sacralized urban commune.

But the message of the Mendicants could be rather multivalent. It might attack
wealth and privilege and be very well received in the cities, particularly by members of the urban commune who did not have much if any money at their dis-
posal. Combined with the emphasis on moral and unified community, however,
the message could also strengthen internal hierarchy, intimating that urban
economy was extremely good when used for the correct purposes. The weld-
ing of preaching against wealth and against the Jews, who were often seen as
wealthy, and wealthy at the expense of the common good, helped to reinforce
the image of the Jew as dangerous and subversive, while also providing impetus for internal religious and moral reform at the communal level, and in some
cases the tools with which to criticize the regular clergy, who shared with the
Jews the reputation of being privileged, lazy, and wealthy.

According to the famous Augsburg chronicler Burkhard Zink, in the chaos
after a fire on the town square in 1462 both Jews and priests were the target
of robberies because of their wealth.

> And a house on the square ignited, creating a great fire, and whoever ran
> to the fire choked, and it is said that many people suffocated and were killed
> there piteously. And it was also said that Jews and priests were robbed, since
> many goods were found among them, as is well believable.[137]

What is interesting about this passage is that it mentioned Jews in the city
after their final expulsion in 1440 and grouped them with clergy.[138] What similarities were there in the ways that the two groups are described and how can
we understand hostility to them in the fifteenth century? What do the criti-
cisms brought against the two groups suggest about the social and cultural

---

[134] Steven Ozment, *The Age of Reform, 1250–1550: An Intellectual and Religious
History of Late Medieval and Reformation Europe*, p. 110.

[135] See John Bossy, *Christianity in the West*, p. 77.

[136] Jeremy Cohen, *The Friars and the Jews*, pp. 254–255.

[137] Zink, p. 288.

[138] As in other cases throughout the chronicle one senses a disparity in the "harmony of worldly and spiritual life" seen in Zink's Augsburg by Heinrich Schmidt, *Die
deutschen Städtechroniken als Spiegel des bürgerlichen Selbstverständnisses im Spätmittelalter*.
For a critique of Schmidt, see Dieter Weber, *Geschichtsschreibung in Augsburg: Hektor Mülich
und die Reichsstädte Chronistik des Spätmittelalters*.

transformations in the late medieval German commune, and how can such criticism help us to describe the evolution of religious identity in the south German cities before the Reformation?

Both Jews and clergy were viewed as privileged groups, existing outside of the civic commune. Provoked by an increase in the consumption tax on beer in 1513 in Frankfurt, anger was directed against both "privileged groups":

> Riotous speech such as 'Down with the clerics!' rang out. This cry soon gave way to 'Down with the Jews!' and already they wanted to force their way into the Jewish quarter in order to slay its inhabitants.[139]

It was very often the issues of clerical tithes, exemptions, and privileges that sparked conflict between the laity and the clergy in the late medieval cities. The privileges of the clergy were becoming increasingly open to attack, particularly as a "communal spirit" swept over the city councils as well as the broader urban population, and the councils sought not only to control the clergy, but also to shift ecclesiastical functions to civic officers.[140]

As we have already seen, Bernd Moeller has argued that the conception of the church and the civic community as one body was gaining strength in the late fifteenth century before it reached its supreme articulation in the theological development of Huldrych Zwingli and Martin Bucer in the south German imperial cities.[141] For Moeller, the economic and cultural demands of the burghers were rising in the late fifteenth century. Burghers had learned to read and to write just like clerics,[142] and indeed they were becoming something like self-fashioned clerics and humanists, who set out to reform and absorb the church.[143] Clerics, therefore, who were frequently from outside the city and who possessed a variety of privileges and exemptions, became even further removed from the urban commune.

Whether or not Moeller's thesis is accepted, it is clear that in the discussion of Jews throughout the late medieval urban literature, a sense of communal identity, woven together with religious and moral sensibilities, increasingly tended to view the urban commune as a sacred entity and frequently allowed little room for Jews to remain a part of it.

---

[139] Cited in Wenzel, "*Do worden die Judden alle geschant*", p. 102.
[140] Moeller, *Imperial Cities and the Reformation*, here at p. 47.
[141] Ibid., p. 89.
[142] Ibid., pp. 52–53.
[143] Kießling, *Bürgerliche Gesellschaft*, pp. 356f.

5

The Development of Jewish Communities and Settlements in Late Medieval Germany

INTRODUCTION:
LATE MEDIEVAL JEWISH SETTLEMENTS IN GERMANY

Jews traveled throughout Germany as merchants in the late Roman Empire and in the early Middle Ages. Jews may even have settled in certain cities, such as Cologne, as early as the fourth century, though there are few substantive records or indications of permanent Jewish settlement in Germany before the ninth and tenth centuries, when a number of Jewish families, the most prominent of which was the Kalonymos family from Lucca, likely made their way to the Rhineland from Italy.

From the end of the ninth to the late eleventh century the most important Jewish community was in Mainz. In the 960s and 970s there is mention of royal protection for Jews in Magdeburg and Merseburg, and it is evident that Jews settled in Regensburg in the tenth century, and Cologne, Worms, Trier, and Speyer as well in the eleventh. In general, Jews found homes in old episcopal and trade centers. The famous invitation of the Bishop of Speyer to the Jews of Mainz in 1084 offered Jews protection and numerous privileges for settling in the city at the same time that it made clear the economic benefit the Bishop intended to reap through the Jews' businesses. The charter was thus rather indicative of much of the later development of medieval German Jewry. Similar charters were soon offered to Jews in other cities, such as Worms in 1090. Because of the favorable economic conditions, autonomous self-government, and strong systems of education bolstered by the settlement of important scholars, the Rhineland communities flourished in the high Middle Ages.

Initially, Jews settled in cities and were first involved in international and later, during the eleventh century, in regional business. In the twelfth and thirteenth centuries Jews were also involved in the collection of tolls and taxes, as well as money-handling and credit, in large part because of restrictions prohibiting them from other occupations. Some Jews practiced as doctors, and many also were employed in the service of the Jewish community itself, as teachers, rabbis, and butchers, for example. Despite occupational restrictions, there are traces of Jews in a vast diversity of occupational positions in the later Middle Ages, such as "engineers," glassblowers, barbers, book makers, printers, gold and silver smiths, traders of a variety of products (including precious metals, leather, textiles, wine, fruit, vegetables, saffron, weapons), handworkers, weapon makers, innkeepers, servants, and furriers.

In the ninth century there were only a few dozen Jewish families in Germany, probably a few hundred in the tenth. It has been estimated that there were as many as 4,000 to 5,000 Jews by the end of tenth century, and 20,000 to 25,000 on the eve of First Crusade at the end of the eleventh. Even in the largest Jewish communities, however, Jews typically comprised no more than one to three percent of the total city population. The number of Jewish communities, each rather small in size, increased dramatically during the second half of the thirteenth and the first half of the fourteenth centuries, before the massacres and persecution of the Jews during the Black Death (1348 to 1350). Jews were dispersed throughout Germany in the fourteenth and fifteenth centuries, when we find numerous small Jewish communities and traces of Jews in areas outside larger cities and in rural areas.

In the high Middle Ages Jewish settlement was particularly widespread in the Rhineland, Upper Germany, and Franconia, though much thinner in Bavaria and the north. After the thirteenth century there was a thick settlement in the east, e.g., Silesia, Moravia, and Lower Austria. During the fifteenth century there was a substantial growth in the number of communities and settlements in south and central Germany, particularly in the southwest and parts of Bavaria.

As to the chronological development of the Jewish communities, 50% of the communities mentioned between 1350 and 1519 existed before 1250; 35.5% are first mentioned between 1250 and 1349; only 13.6% are first mentioned after 1350. It is only in the modern state of Baden-Württemburg that we find a substantial number of new settlements after 1350. The general trend is a sharp decline in new communities after the middle of the fourteenth century.[1] In Bohemia and Bavaria the initial settlements were largely there before 1250– 67.5% in Bohemia, 61.7% in Bavaria; on the other hand, the Rhineland area experienced a rather steady and even-paced development until 1349–45.2% in the first phase and 41.2% in the second. Although these are rather constructed periodizations they do at least offer some structure for trying to understand general settlement patterns. In the north, more dramatic growth took place between the beginning of the thirteenth and middle of the fourteenth centuries.

---

[1] For general settlement patterns in the middle Rhineland see Franz-Josef Ziwes, *Studien zur Geschichte der Juden in mittleren Rheingebiet während des hohen und späten Mittelalters*, pp. 25f; for Alsace see Gerd Mentgen, *Studien zur Geschichte der Juden in mittelalterlichen Elsaß*, pp. 25f.

It is very difficult, given the available sources, to ascertain reliable population or settlement information. In Nuremberg the percentage of Jews within
the total population may have climbed over five percent at some points.
Throughout the later Middle Ages large populations of Jews, numbering up to
300, might be found at different times in Bamberg, Braunschweig, Eger, Esslingen,
Frankfurt am Main, Graz, Hildesheim, Cologne, Constance, Landshut, Magdeburg,
Munich, Worms, and Würzburg. Augsburg, Breslau, Erfurt, Nuremberg, Oppenheim
(1440), Rothenburg ob der Tauber, and Wiener Neustadt may have had over 300
Jews each. In the early sixteenth century, Regensburg and Prague were likely
the largest Jewish centers with something like 600 Jews.[2] Over half of the
Jewish settlements in late medieval Germany had no more than one or two
Jewish families. Another 28% had up to 10 families; only 40 settlements, or
6.6%, had up to 20 families. The largest communities, with more than 20 families, and more than about 150 Jews, numbered only 24, or 4%.[3] On the average, therefore, a relatively large Jewish community might have between 30 and
40 members[4] and ten members would constitute a middling community. The
very large number of small Jewish settlements indicates that the dispersal of
the Jewish population through the German countryside can be said to have begun
in the later Middle Ages—earlier than once suspected. It should be noted that
the precise number of Jews living in any given region (or city) could change
dramatically over short periods of time.[5]

The general picture that we have of Jewish settlement in the later Middle
Ages is also affected by the Black Death pogroms and massacres that destroyed
the communal continuity in most regions, with only a band of about 58[6] com-
munities retaining an unbroken Jewish settlement—in a region that included
Bohemia, Moravia, Carniola, Styria, Slovenia, and Upper and Lower Austria.
In many cities, Jews soon returned relatively quickly as in Heidelberg and
Nuremberg in 1349. During the remainder of the fourteenth century numer-
ous Jewish settlements were repopulated as well: Breslau (1350); Nordhausen
(1350); Braunschweig (1352); Worms (1354); Erfurt, Munich, Speyer,[7] Trier, and
Ulm (all in 1355)—in all, 40 settlements were reestablished between 1350 and

---

[2] These figures are from Michael Toch, "Siedlungsstruktur der Juden Mitteleuropas
im Wandel vom Mittelalter zur Neuzeit," p. 35.

[3] Ibid., pp. 33–35.

[4] Using this criteria and the modern geographical boundaries of GJ we have the following number of substantial Jewish communities with populations of 40 or more: Baden-
Württemburg 14; Bohemia 12; Bavaria (including Franconia) 22; modern East Germany
9; North-Rhine Westphalia 5; Rhineland Palatinate 8; Hesse 6; Netherlands 1; Austria
9; Alsace and Switzerland together 16; Lower Saxony 19.

[5] Toch, "Siedlungsstruktur," p. 33.

[6] Thirty-three according to Toch, "Siedlungsstruktur," p. 30.

[7] For a detailed treatment of Speyer, see Ernst Voltmer, "Zur Geschichte der Juden
im spätmittelalterlichen Speyer: Die Judengemeinde im Spannungsfeld zwischen König,
Bischof und Stadt," especially pp. 104–113.

1359; almost 70 between 1360 and 1369; over 60 between 1370 and 1379; nearly 50 between 1380 and 1389; almost 20 between 1390 and 1399.[8] Nearly half of the late medieval Jewish settlements in Germany are traceable to an earlier settlement in the area, primarily in the middle and large communities. When they were resettled, often because of the financial interests of the city ruling classes,[9] Jewish communities could be found in less favorable locations in the city, as in Augsburg, Donauwörth, Frankfurt am Main, Nuremberg, Passau, and Rothenburg ob der Tauber. The majority of communities, however, were resettled in the favorable locations they had inhabited previously, as in Breslau, Erfurt, Heilbronn, Cologne, Constance, Munich, and Prague, to name a few.[10] According to Michael Toch, 82% of the Jewish settlements were centrally located within the city (only 18% were on the periphery).[11]

Between 1350 and the first quarter of the sixteenth century, Jews lived in 1,038 regions—some places contained merely a Jew or two, other places were full blown communities in the structural, and hence legal, way of thinking. Of course, the difference between "settlement" and "community" is not always clear, as we will discuss in the next chapter. Noting that the later Middle Ages is typically seen as a period of crisis for Jewish settlement in Germany, Toch writes that in the period between 1238 and 1350 there was only a slightly smaller number of areas in which Jews lived, numbering over one thousand.[12]

Jewish settlement was continuous throughout the later Middle Ages in about 40% of the regions (largely the biggest communities). Only 9% of the settlements, however, maintained continuous settlement until the eighteenth century.[13]

The largest number of settlements in the broader Holy Roman Empire was in south central, central, and eastern Germany. We find in the northwest (Holland and modern North-Rhine Westphalia) 76 settlements; in the west (Brabant, Lorraine, Luxemburg, and Rheinland Palatinate) 75; in the southwest (Alsace, modern Baden-Württemburg, and Switzerland) 191; in the north (Mecklenburg, Lower Saxony, and Braunschweig) 54; in central Germany (Thuringia, Hesse, Franconia, and Upper Palatinate) 301; in the south (Old Bavaria, Bavarian Swabia, the Austrian Alpine lands, south Tirol, and several communities in northern Italy) 84; in the northeast (Brandenburg and Pomerania) 48; in the southeast (Upper and Lower Austria, Carniola, Styria, and Slovenia) 51; and, finally, in the east (Saxony, Silesia, Bohemia, and Moravia) 139.[14] A very large concentration of settlements could still be found in the Rhineland area, but the clear trend of the later Middle Ages, as opposed to the borders

---

[8] Toch, "Siedlungsstruktur," pp. 30–31.
[9] See Ziwes, *Studien zur Geschichte der Juden in mittleren Rheingebiet*, p. 133.
[10] Toch, "Siedlungsstruktur," p. 32.
[11] Ibid.
[12] Ibid., pp. 29–30.
[13] Ibid., p. 37.
[14] Ibid., p. 36.

of the high Middle Ages, was substantial increase in central Germany, particularly in Franconia.[15]

A large majority of the settlements in the later Middle Ages were in cities (73%); while 11.5% could be found in small cities (regions and markets); and 15% in villages, 88% of those located largely in a band from Alsace, through Rhineland Palatinate, Swabia, and Hesse to Franconia. Given the dramatic increase in small, more rural, Jewish settlements, many scholars have portrayed a terroitorialization, or regionalization, of Jewish community in the later Middle Ages, in some cases in the minds, and more importantly the economic and legal perceptions of both Jews and the non-Jewish authorities.[16] In the southwest, cities with substantial Jewish populations were often surrounded by other, usually smaller Jewish settlements. Within 25 km of Heidelberg were seven settlements and between 26 and 50 km another four. Within 25 km of Freiburg im Breisgau were five Jewish settlements and, at the same distance from Ulm, four. Among the settlements in Hesse, 17 were within 17 km of Frankfurt and an additional 19 between 26 and 50 km. In middle Franconia 16 settlements were within 25 km of Nuremberg, an additional 22 between 26 and 50 km. In the middle Rhineland we find a mass of small Jewish communities (and settlements) around larger city centers, some like Frankfurt am Main and Cologne with relatively large Jewish populations,[17] and others no longer possessing Jewish populations.[18] Similarly, we find an increase in the number of individual privileges and letters of protection, particularly in those territories with no Jewish communities, so that it becomes quite complicated to speak of Jewish settlement, at least outside of the formal Jewish communal centers, in the later Middle Ages.[19]

THE EXAMPLE OF AUGSBURG

Although the settlement of Jews and the development of Jewish community varied between areas and progressed within a unique context of local and regional conditions, the experiences of the Jews in Augsburg is representative of the general contours and characteristics of the history of late medieval German Jewry.

Material traces of the Jews in Augsburg begin in the thirteenth century. The first mention of a Jewish synagogue in Augsburg is from 1276, although the same edifice may have been alluded to in a document from 1259.[20] By 1290

---

[15] Ibid., p. 37.
[16] See Ziwes, *Studien zur Geschichte der Juden in mittleren Rheingebiet*, p. 159, where intra-communal Jewish connections mirrored larger urban political unions. See p. 268 also.
[17] Ibid., pp. 161 and 208.
[18] Ibid., p. 267.
[19] Ibid., pp. 126 and 144–145.
[20] Bernhard Schimmelpfennig, "Christen und Juden im Augsburg des Mittelalters."

there is mention of a bath house[21] and 1298 a Jewish cemetery.[22] Civic laws from 1276 contain a number of regulations regarding the Jews, particularly the constitution of a Jewish court, the role of Jewish and Christian witnesses, the prohibition of sexual relations between Jews and Christians, and the requirement that Jews wear the Jewish hat in public. Despite such regulations, and despite the fact that Jews had to pay handsomely for the protection of the bishop or the city council, the Jewish presence in Augsburg in the thirteenth century seems to have been fairly well tolerated.[23] One recent historian concludes that until 1300 there was in Augsburg widespread tolerance of the Jewish community, which often served as a source of useful and convenient capital.[24]

By the beginning of the fourteenth century, however, the position of the Jews in Augsburg began to change. External changes combined with internal reorientation, evident in the 1276 lawbook. Jews of the small nearby community in Munich were accused of ritual murder in 1285. In 1298 the Rindfleisch massacres swept through southern Germany. The years between 1335 and 1337 witnessed the Armleder massacres, 1337 the murder of the Jews in Deggendorf, and 1348, of course, the massacre of countless Jews in Germany and throughout Europe. It is likely that the sudden massacre of the Augsburg Jews, which is mentioned only in passing in most of the town chronicles, was a planned event.[25] It occurred on a Saturday, and conceivably most of the Jews, 18 taxpayers numbering presumably around 130 people, were killed or chased from the city. The motives for the attack could have been numerous: general enmity, the cancellation of debt, the escalating conflict between the burghers and the nobility, who would have been hurt by the pogrom, or attempts to end the bishop's efforts to strengthen his control over the Augsburg Jews.[26] Even before the massacre of 1348, however, the position of the Jews had been weakening. A document from 1331 demonstrates narrowing tolerance and not coincidentally the importance of Jewish credit was appreciably on the decline, as evidenced by increasing attempts to release Christians from the debts they owed to Jews.[27]

---

[21] See Christian Meyer, *Urkundenbuch*, vol. 1, p. 96; December 5, 1290.

[22] A document from 1290, in which the Jews promise to build a wall from their "churchyard" until the graves at their own expense and within four years, is given in Christian Meyer, *Urkundenbuch*, vol. 1, pp. 129–130.

[23] Though such perversions as forcing Jews to take oaths while standing on pigskin, practiced elsewhere, did not rear their heads until the fifteenth century in Augsburg.

[24] Jews were responsible for maintaining part of the town wall, and they did have to pay to receive civil protection.

[25] See Alfred Haverkamp, "Die Judenverfolgungen zur Zeit des Schwarzen Todes im Gesellschaftsgefüge deutscher Städte," pp. 50 and 57.

[26] Schimmelpfennig, "Christen und Juden im Augsburg des Mittelalters," pp. 33–34. See also Alfred Haverkamp, "Jewish Quarters," p. 18, for the decline in the number of synagogues in this period.

[27] Schimmelpfennig, "Christen und Juden im Augsburg des Mittelalters," p. 30. For documents on the consequences, at least regarding property, of the 1348 expulsion/massacre, see Meyer *Urkunden*, vol. 1, pp. 1–21; 28–30; 32; 35; 41; and 51, for example.

Nevertheless, in 1355 the first Jew was readmitted to Augsburg since the 1348 massacre. Emperor Charles IV allowed the citizens of Augsburg the exclusive privilege of taking in and taxing Jews for a twelve-year period. In that very year 18 Jews are listed in the city tax lists. Four years later, in 1359, the emperor extended the same privilege for 20 more years. From the middle of the fourteenth century on, two different Jewish settlements developed in Augsburg. This was not unheard of in Germany, and in some cities Jews lived outside of one central area. In Ulm, for example, the Jews settled continuously between 1354 and 1499 in the same region that they had occupied before 1349, but two Jewish streets developed within this one area. The area was relatively closed, but Christians did also live there. In Bamberg the Judengasse contained about 20 houses, where both Jews and Christians lived, both as home owners and renters. But Jews also settled in the Kesslergasse by the middle of the fifteenth century, where the new synagogue was located. In Constance, the Jewish quarter was centrally located on an important connecting street, but no wall surrounded the quarter, and Jews also owned homes in other parts of the city.

In many more cases, one was Nuremberg, the Jews were centrally located in the Jewish quarter. Unlike in many other cities, the Jews of Nuremberg did not resettle in the old Jewish quarter after they returned from the Black Death expulsions and massacres. Rather, they were settled in an unfavorable region on the eastern edge of the city. This area was later expanded through the sale of houses between 1364 and 1383 (and then remained fairly much the same until the expulsion of the Jews in 1499). The Jewish houses were constructed around a great court, and although there was no wall, the houses in essence formed an enclosed entity. Within this Jewish quarter could be found the synagogue, bath house, dance hall, two bake ovens, at least one well, and the Spital or *Szelhaus*. These places were only accessible from within the quarter. Another settlement of Jews was added next to the synagogue, but not actually within the enclosed area, comprising another 16 to 18 houses. In Regensburg, the Judengasse was actually deemed a separate entity, and labeled the *Judenstadt*, literally the Jewish city. It was situated in the same location as it had been before the expulsions and massacres of 1350, covering a large area, surrounded by a wall, with six doors, and enclosing 30 Jewish houses, a community synagogue, and three private synagogues. Christians did own several houses in the Jewish Quarter (*Judenstadt*), but no Christians lived there. In fact, Jews had custody of the keys to the doors leading into and out of the *Judenstadt*, and these doors were locked in the evening and opened in the morning. By 1500 the *Judenstadt* may have included multi-level dwellings, which housed members of individual families.

In Augsburg the first of the two late fourteenth-century Jewish communities took root in the Handwerker region, the Judenberg, near today's vibrant Maximilianstrasse, where the community had resided before 1348; the second, beginning in 1361 moved into the Judengasse near Karlsstrasse, some 300 meters northwest of the Judenberg. Christians as well as Jews lived in both of these places, so Jews were not enclosed in a ghetto, but rather they interacted daily with their non-Jewish neighbors,[28] at least until 1370. The younger community was enclosed by ropes in 1434. At the height of settlement each community comprised some 15 Jewish houses. In the newer settlement, Jewish houses stood on both sides of the street. The synagogue continued to be located in the older settlement, at least until 1361. The Jewish bath house was centered in the older quarter near the Christian *Spitalbad*. The cemetery, as before 1348, continued to be located outside of the city on the northwest corner of Frauenvorstadt. The northern community was under the jurisdiction of the bishop, and the other community that of the city.[29]

The number of Jews under the jurisdiction of the city, judging from tax lists, increased until 1383, when the community numbered over 50 taxpayers and presumably about 300 individuals. The toll of imperial taxation between 1374 and 1390 was, however, heavy on the Jews. By 1387 the number of Jews listed in the tax rolls fell to 17 (see Appendix C). Although Jews had been admitted into the city as burghers, and a number of Jews are listed in the city's Bürgerbuch, especially between 1397 and 1419, 1428 was the last year that a Jew was listed as a burgher of the city.[30] The declining position of the Jews can also be demonstrated in the following tax statistics:[31] In 1380, 16.6% of the Jews who paid taxes paid over 20 fl. By 1389 only 7.4% paid over 20 fl., and after 1392 no Jews paid that much. On the other hand, in 1389, 55.5% of the tax-paying Jews paid under 10 fl.; but by 1392 it had increased to 88.8%; in 1400, 89.5%; and in 1424, 92%. The year 1434 also witnessed legal discrimination and the renewed imposition of the yellow ring on the Jews.[32] The attempted and actual expulsions of Jews in other German cities and the general fervor aroused by the Council of Basel added to the impetus to expel the Jews. An expulsion edict was issued in 1438 that gave the Jews of Augsburg two years to leave the city. By that time the Jews contributed a very small amount in taxes. By 1439, of the 24 taxpayers that had been listed the previous year, six had already left. In 1440 no Jews were listed on the city tax lists. By 1445 the stones from the Jewish cemetery were removed and used to make repairs on the steps to the city hall: a practical and symbolic end to the official Jewish presence in Augsburg.

---

[28] See Haverkamp, "Jewish Quarters," p. 22, for comparable situations elsewhere in Germany.

[29] Markus J. Wenninger, *Man Bedarf keiner Juden Mehr: Ursachen und Hintergründe ihrer Vertreibung aus den deutschen Reichsstädten im 15. Jahrhundert*, p. 115.

[30] Ibid., pp. 120–121.

[31] *GJ*, vol. 3, p. 44.

[32] Jews had been granted in 1361 the privilege to be sued in the city only before the Reichvogt; see Meyer, *Urkundenbuch*, vol. 2, pp. 94–95.

PATTERNS OF SETTLEMENT

The general pattern of settlement, population, and economic decline that we find in Augsburg was repeated in many other German cities. In Nuremberg, for example, Jews were readmitted into the city weeks after the attacks of May 12, 1349. Until 1359 there were 10 to 12 male heads of house who possessed the rights of citizens. By 1382 there were 44 individual Jewish taxpayers and 17 money-handlers in 1385 to 1390. The total population in 1449 has been estimated around 150 people. With the help of more detailed tax documents for the year 1489, the Jewish population can be estimated to have been as large as 200 to 250 individuals (including children), including 76 men, 14 boys (presumably 13 years of age or older), 3 foreign students, and 5 poor men. Of the 76 men, 46 grew up in Nuremberg. In Nuremberg, there was a great demand for housing, and the 17 houses possessed by the Jews typically housed more than a single family. A household of 10 was not uncommon, especially given the presence of guests, students, and relatives living there with the permission of the city council.

Reflecting the changing position of the Jews in the later Middle Ages, in Nuremberg there were three main phases in the history of Jewish money-handling. In the first phase from the initial resettlement of the Jews until around 1385, money lending functioned as a family or independent business. Money was loaned against securities/pledges to the city, to secular and ecclesiastical nobles, the landed nobility of Franconia, (less so) to landed nobility in Swabia, the Upper Palatinate, other Franconian cities, and the well-to-do burghers in Nuremberg. Business with handworkers within the city or rural folk in the surrounding areas outside of Nuremberg was much less significant and of secondary importance. In a second phase, around 1390 and the late fifteenth century, the stormy development of the Nuremberg city economy, combined with the rapid increase in the participation of non-Jews in the business of credit, began to marginalize the position of the Jews. In the last phase, at the end of the fifteenth century, the extent of Jewish money-handling shrank considerably, forcing Jews increasingly into business with handworkers and day laborers.

Both the rabbinic literature and civic documents demonstrate rigid social hierarchies within some cities. In Nuremberg, for example, the internal hierarchy was based primarily upon economic considerations. There existed a number of independent Jews, engaged primarily in money-handling, who possessed both citizenship and houses in the Jewish quarter. Among that group, those who were part of the powerful and established families within Nuremberg (for three or more generations) ruled over the rest of the Jews. These people tended to own the majority of Jewish houses and they had the greatest businesses with the largest volumes. Twelve of the 16 money-handlers listed in 1489 belonged to the three families who had been in the community for 20 to 28 years, and were important enough even to be involved in significant ways in city business outside of the Jewish community. Sixteen of the 25 new Jewish citizens the council accepted between 1468 and 1498 belonged to these three main families; sons of those without citizenship were not, however, typically accepted by the council, or for that matter by the Jews themselves. At the lowest level stood the non-native and foreign poor. In Nuremberg the list of professions in which Jews participated is lengthy, though the bulk of Jews were engaged in money-handling. There are records of: an eye doctor, both male and female doctors, a goldsmith and silversmith, a broker, a peddler, saffron-, wine- and vegetable-dealers, a Jew from Frankfurt involved in the knife business, a builder of the model for mill works, a sewage expert, a bookbinder, waiters, barbers, bakers, servants, rabbis, cantors, ritual slaughterers, and heads of schools.

In Regensburg, the number of Jews remained relatively stable at 300 throughout the fifteenth century, though it may have peaked at something over 360 by the end of the century. Around the time of the expulsion there were 500 Jews according to one account, 80 of whom were students studying there. At that rate, Jews would have accounted for three to four percent of the total population in Regensburg. Of these Jews, most seem to have been involved in money-handling and trading—particularly in textiles, feathers, beds, hats, leather, pelts, ironware, salt, oil, and cows, for example—but there are also records of Jews as doctors, midwives, butchers, a watchmaker, a needlemaker, a water carrier, house servants, elementary school teachers, and community professionals. There certainly were some wealthy Jews within this group, at least judging by the libraries that they possessed: Jude Simon von Worms owned more than 30 books; David Eichstätt 43; and Isaac Stein, a considerable scholar, who commented on the *Sefer Mitzvot Gadol* (Great Book of Commandments), possessed 166 books, no small feat for the fifteenth century.

The number of Jews in other cities demonstrates much the same development. In Constance, for example, Jews first resettled in the city in 1375. By 1390 there were 30 (taxpaying) Jews, in 1413, 12, in 1425, 16 and in 1429 a *total* of 80 Jews, more than one percent of the total population in the city. These Jews were apparently mostly engaged in money-handling. In Augsburg there are records of handlers of merchandise, a butcher, a private (house) tutor, doctors, waitresses, a maid, a prostitute (1359), and individuals dealing in cattle. The Jews in Augsburg involved in money-lending typically loaned to Christians at all social strata. Jews in Bamberg similarly loaned primarily to Bamberg citizens and inhabitants of the surrounding land, though seldom to priests or patricians. Their period of greatest activity lasted between the years 1403 and 1415.

Fifty-one percent of the communities were protected by princes; 27% by ecclesiastical lords; 11.5% by the nobility, and 8.5% by the imperial cities.[33] Protection of the Jews and privileges granted to them originated from the imperial authorities, the local duke, or the bishop, and could be delegated to the city council. At times, as in Regensburg, the emperor, the duke of Lower Bavaria, and the city competed with one another to harvest the benefits afforded

---

[33] Toch, "Siedlungsstruktur," p. 37.

by the Jews. As we have seen, the Augsburg city council held from the emperor the privilege to accept and to tax the Jews. This privilege was granted
by the emperor for a certain period of time in return for payment. The first
privilege was in 1355 and extended in 1359 to 1387; then again in 1392, 1401,
and 1415, but not after 1431. Imperial privileges and taxes, regular or extraordinary, could be granted to or extracted from the Jews by the empire. The
primary jurisdiction over the Jews was held by the empire. In cases between
Jews and Christians a parity of 12 Jews and 12 Christians deliberated together
at the Jewish synagogue. After 1436, however, only Christians could deliberate
(the number was increased to 17) and the deliberations were moved from the
synagogue to the city hall, a powerful indication of the changed position of the
Jewish community in the city.

How settlement and population patterns may have affected political attitudes
toward the Jews is difficult to determine, even if we can isolate some general
patterns of expulsions, and accusations of ritual murder and host desecration.
There were substantial regional expulsions at the end of the fifteenth century
in the northeast and southeast; Bavarian territorial expulsions particularly in
the middle of the fifteenth century; and, of course the Austrian expulsion in
1420 and 1421 and the Alsatian expulsions of the early sixteenth century.
Pockets of cities would often expel the Jews at approximately the same time,
though Jews often settled in smaller areas close by, or even within the same
city.

Complaints regarding monetary matters in Augsburg were typically monitored by the Burggraf, who served as a representative of the bishop of Augsburg,
often along with the Vogt. Punishment and police authority were, however, maintained by the members of the city council. In Nuremberg the main protection
of the Jews fell to the empire, but the prince and the city both played key
roles as well. In response to attempts by the city to expel the Jews in 1473,
the empire interceded on behalf of the Jews. Imperial authorities similarly inter-
vened in 1478 against a city council decree forbidding Jews to take interest on
loans to Christians. And although the city council could itself protect the Jews
it might also enact legislation against them. By 1471 the city council began to
function even in internal Jewish matters. In Nuremberg there were occasions
when as much as 8,000 fl. were taken in a single year in the form of collective and extraordinary taxes (1385, 1390, 1419, and 1442; 4,000 fl. in 1371,
1434, and 1453), though by the end of the century the increased impoverishment of the community made this more difficult. The bishop of Bamberg forbade the city of Bamberg to demand greater fees from Jews than from Christians,
and collective privileges granted to the city Jews were extended to include
other Jews within the jurisdiction of the prince-bishopric. Jews could also receive
individual as well as collective privileges or taxes and penalties.

In certain cities, such as Bamberg, the individual tax was standardized for
every Jew in the city. In 1455 a Jew had to pay 10 fl. yearly, while a foreign
Jew was required to pay a nightly sum for his stay in the city. But this was

down from the level of 1445, when each Jew had to pay 20 fl. yearly, indicating diminished prosperity of the Jews in the period.

Often the city did take its role as protector of the Jews very seriously. In Augsburg there are a number of cases indicating that Christian actions against Jews were treated with both warnings and reprimands, in cases of murder;[34] insults;[35] pressing for money;[36] and attempts to stir popular unrest against the Jews.[37] The city even went so far as to punish two foreign Jews who mistreated an Augsburg Jew.[38] In a 1372 case, the Augsburg city council forbade two Christians who had raped a Jewish woman from residing within ten miles of the city, and they also fined them 20 Gulden.[39] But it is not coincidental, I think, that all of these cases date from before the beginning of the fifteenth century, when the position of the Jews began to decline dramatically.

Cities often punished as well as protected. In 1381 the Jew "Hartman" was banned forever from within a six-mile radius of the city, for the "evil" that he committed. According to the order the decision was based on actions against both Jews and Christians.[40] The Jew "Smoe" and his family were similarly banned from ever coming into the city (living or dead) because they broke their oath that they would remain as Augsburg burghers for ten years.[41] In Regensburg, Jews were punished for alleged crimes: making poison (the punishment was burning); stealing (hanging over dogs); blasphemy; and insincere conversion (dunking or burning). In addition to physical punishments monetary ones could also be meted out.

The cohesion of the Jewish communities was attacked on many occasions by the church as well as the city council. As we saw earlier, preaching by renowned clergy such as John of Capistrano in the 1450s or Peter Schwarz in the 1470s may have converted a few Jews, but did even more damage by the hostility that they refocused against the Jewish communities.[42] Preaching might continue against the Jews even in their absence. In 1444, four years after the

---

[34] 1368, 1379, 1386, 1397.
[35] 1372 according to GJ, vol. 3, 1371 according to Achtbuch 81, fol. 103r—"mishandelt mit worten."
[36] 1372.
[37] 1370.
[38] 1372.
[39] Achtbuch 81, fol. 104.
[40] See Juden Regesten, compiled by Dr. Zorn, no. 2, April 30, 1381.
[41] See Schätze 81, Achtbuch, fol. 108r, January 16, 1375.
[42] In Bamberg; the preaching of 1478 led to some family baptisms. Nuremberg hosted Capistrano for four months in 1452; and Schwarz delivered 17 sermons there in 1478. In Nuremberg the playwrights Folz and Rosenplüt could both be found. Regensburg suffered both preachers, as well as an extended and intense period of anti-Jewish Mendicant preaching between 1475 and 1515 leading to a 1475 attempt to expel the Jews and later, perhaps, to the ultimate expulsion in 1519. This preaching may have also contributed to the ritual murder trials in that city. See GJ, vol. 3, under each city listed.

final expulsion of the Jews from Augsburg, there are hints of anti-Jewish preaching in the city.[43]

MIGRATION AND MOVEMENT:
THE FATE OF THE JEWS OF AUGSBURG

Where did the Jews go after they were expelled from the south German cities?
It has been asserted that the bulk of Jews from Augsburg probably traveled to
other large cities with Jewish communities in Swabia, Franconia, and in the
middle Rhine valley. It had also, until recently, been believed that many Jews
settled in the villages around Augsburg.[44] Today, however, it does not seem
likely that, immediately at least, Jews settled in the nearby villages such as
Kriegshaber and Pfersee, where large Jewish communities begin to be documented
only in the middle of the sixteenth century: Jews are first mentioned in Pfersee
around 1530, in Oberhausen in 1555, and in Steppach not until 1570.[45] There
is no real documentation of the fate of the Jews, however, in the one-hundred-
year period between their expulsion from Augsburg and the beginnings of the
rural communities.[46] The lack of evidence about the fate of this Jewish community poses the very important and difficult question of the process of the
shift to a rural Jewry in the early modern period and the transformation of the
Jewish community from a kehillah-based (individual community) to a medinah-
based (regional) entity.[47] Where did the Jews go after the expulsion, and how
did the expulsion affect Jewish life, individually and communally?

As we have seen, the number of Jews in Augsburg was waning by the third
decade of the fifteenth century. According to the tax lists from 1438, 24 Jews
resided and paid taxes in Augsburg. Going back over ten years, however, we
see that the community was fairly stable, at least as far as its tax-paying members (males in general) are concerned (see Appendix D). For the 24 listed the
average length of residence in Augsburg was 12 years. The longest resident was
Josmen at 32 years, the shortest Lemlin Boruch, who was probably a student
of Rabbi Jacob Weil, at only one year. Only one of the tax-payers resided in
Augsburg over 30 years, two over 20 years, five over 15 years, five over 10
years, nine over 5 years, and only two under 5 years. Of the Jews that are traceable, the average length of residence in Augsburg was 12 years, or if those who

---

[43] See Ratsbücher 4: 1442–1447; 1448–1452 added, fol. 110.

[44] See GJ, vol. 3, p. 65.

[45] Ibid. See also Schimmelpfennig, "Christen und Juden im Augsburg des Mittelalters,"
p. 37.

[46] Wolfram Baer, "Zwischen Vertreibung und Wiederansiedlung: Die Reichstadt Augsburg
und die Juden vom 15. bis zum 18. Jahrhundert," in Judengemeinden in Schwaben, p. 117,
and Rolf Kießling, "Einführung," in Judengemeinden in Schwaben, pp. 15–16.

[47] See Stefan Rohrbacher, "Medinat Schwaben: Jüdisches Leben in einer süddeutschen
Landschaft in der Frühneuzeit," in Judengemeinden in Schwaben, and Daniel J. Elazar and
Stuart A. Cohen, Jewish Political Organization: The Jewish Polity from Biblical Times to
the Present.

are questionable are included, 11.5 years. The average residence for the Jews that I have not been able to trace is only slightly higher at 12.6 years. The length of residence, therefore, would seem to have little to do with migration patterns, suggesting that Jews residing in Augsburg conducted business and made contacts in many areas beyond Augsburg.

How many Jews resided in Augsburg is much harder to determine. The 300 listed by Burkhard Zink, the town chronicler, seems too high.[48] A better indicator might be the results of a thorough head tax collected in 1428 to support the war against the Hussites. In that tax list there are, including children, 148 Jews in Augsburg, though only 22 are listed in the city tax lists. Given the general patterns we have seen for other cities, it seems reasonable that the total population of Jews in Augsburg in 1438 could not have exceeded 150 to 200 persons and was probably closer to the lower figure.

Where the Jews went cannot be answered with the help of archival documents alone, which present something of a contradictory message. On the one hand, the Ratsbuch for 1443 reports that the Jews were no longer in the city. On the other hand, we also know that in 1444 preaching against the Jews took place in Augsburg, and that in 1456 the privilege of expelling the Jews was repeated by the emperor,[49] suggesting that Jews may still have been in the city.

It has been suggested that some of the Jews expelled from Augsburg proper may have settled in the bishop's Jewish community nearby.[50] Little is known about this community, except that it must have been substantially smaller than the city community. In 1433 and 1434 an imperial tax of 1,200 fl. was assessed on the city Jews, but only 200 fl. on the bishop's Jews. Still it is conceivable that some Jews merely settled in the bishop's community for a number of reasons: the bishop did not himself expel the Jews; funerals and burials continued in Augsburg until 1445, when the cemetery was destroyed; and according to the chronicle of Burkhard Zink, five Jews were baptized in Augsburg in 1446.[51]

We do know the fate of some individual Jews. Rabbi Jacob Weil, the leader of the community, first settled in Bamberg and finally permanently in Erfurt, no later than 1443, but was, according to family tradition, buried in Nuremberg.[52] Baruch Augsburg, the son of Lämlein,[53] afterwards served as the rabbi in Ulm.

---

[48] Burkhard Zink, pp. 162–163.

[49] In the Urkundensammlung from January 9, 1442, "Välklin the Jew who at this time is resident in Günzburg and Boruch the Jew, son of the Jew Lemlin, who has been resident as a hochmeister (rabbi) came publicly with the letter for us and the Jewish community that had been resident in Augsburg . . ." This probably refers to claims of the Jews who had lived in Augsburg before the expulsion.

[50] Wenninger, *Man Bedarf keiner Juden Mehr*, pp. 115–116.

[51] Ibid., pp. 115–116.

[52] GJ, vol. 3, p. 47.

[53] Who lived in Augsburg between 1411 and 1438 according to GJ, vol. 3, though not the case by my calculations.

Later, in 1442, along with Välklin in Günzburg, he worked as trustee for the expelled Augsburg community.[54] We find mention of Augsburg Jews in a number of different places in the years after the expulsion. In Frankfurt Smoel von Augsburg in 1441;[55] in Nördlingen, Joseph von Werd in 1439 and Veifelmann in 1440; in Rothenburg ob der Tauber, Joseph von Lauingen in 1439—he had left Augsburg already in 1438; Moses Augsburg appears in Würzburg in the middle of the fifteenth century;[56] in Heilbronn, two men from Augsburg are found in 1449;[57] Joseph von Augsburg is mentioned in Mainz in 1449.[58]

It is unlikely that many Augsburg Jews settled in Ulm, given that community's very strict restrictions on settlement[59] and the fact that in 1427 the community had 13 tax payers and in 1441 only eight.[60] Still, the connections between the communities were close. Weil often rendered decisions on cases affecting or involving Ulm, despite the fact that Ulm did have a court of its own.[61] At least three Jews prior to the expulsion are known to have settled in Ulm.[62] Conversely, a number of Ulm Jews are known to have taken up residence in Augsburg.[63] After the expulsion of the Jews from Augsburg, the Jewish court in Ulm was responsible for Swabian Jewry.[64] There was also a close connection between Mainz and Augsburg. After Mainz, a number of Jews are known to have lived in Augsburg.[65] Weil was from Mainz, as was the earlier Augsburg rabbi, a relative of Jacob Molin. The Jews of Mainz were expelled at the same time as the Jews of Augsburg and not readmitted until 1444, however, making it unlikely that Jews would have traveled directly there.[66]

Three Jews with the proper place name of Augsburg lived in Munich in

---

[54] GJ, vol. 3, p. 46.

[55] Baruch von Augsburg was a doctor in Frankfurt between 1399 and 1401, and Smohel von Augsburg appeared for the first time in Frankfurt in 1434, and negotiated there in 1439, ibid., p. 366.

[56] See responsum no. 1 of Joseph Colon, and GJ, vol. 3, p. 1699.

[57] Salomon Mose, Moses (1449–1468) and later Mosse (1471–1474) all from Augsburg and are likely the same person, GJ, vol. 3, p. 538.

[58] Jews can be found in numerous places after leaving Augsburg (see Ibid., pp. 40–41, 46), and the Jews of Augsburg had come from many different places, at least judging by their names of origin (see Ibid., pp. 40, 239, 857, 1192, 1253, 1266, 1418).

[59] Jacob Weil, responsa nos. 106 and 118.

[60] GJ, vol. 3, p. 1498.

[61] See Israel Isserlein, Peskim no. 65; Weil refers to a triad of communities for court matters: Augsburg, Ulm, Pappenheim (see responsum no. 12, regarding giving testimony).

[62] Liebermann von Augsburg, 1398; Abraham von Augsburg, 1418, Samuel, son of Moses von Augsburg, 1418. See GJ, vol. 3, p. 1509.

[63] Jöhlin and his son Suzzkint, 1368; Samuel, 1384; Michel 1384, Simon's son, 1407. See Ibid., p. 1511.

[64] Joseph Colon, responsa nos. 55, pp. 176–178.

[65] Simon v. Mainz, 1389. See also Israel Yuval, Scholars in their Time: The Religious Leadership of German Jewry in the Late Middle Ages, for the scholarly connection.

[66] 1438 and returned 1444 (GJ, vol. 3, p. 793).

1411, 1415, and 1416;[67] and a number of Jews originally from Munich are known to have later resided in Augsburg.[68] Interestingly, the taxes paid by the local Jewish community in Munich soared from 144 fl. in 1438 to 2,000 fl. in 1439.[69] Again, the connection between the communities is problematic, however, since the burghers of Munich were allowed to expel the Jews around 1442.[70] Still, Munich may have served as a temporary residence for members of the expelled Augsburg community.

Jews from Augsburg are also known to have lived in Nördlingen. As we have seen, in 1439 Joseph von Werd appeared in Nördlingen and in 1440 Veifelmann: both had been present on the Augsburg tax lists between 1430 and 1438.[71] In the 1490s Weil's son Rabbi Joslin Weil, who was later found in Regensburg, resided in Nördlingen.[72]

Jews from Augsburg are listed in Nuremberg and Jews from Nuremberg are known to have lived in Augsburg, though the number of Jews listed in Nuremberg declined or remained constant between 1438 and 1442.[73] Still, with a major rabbinical synod there in 1438 and 1439 and the Jewish community in that city enjoying the reputation as a main center of Judaism in the German lands, the possibility exists that some Jews made their way to Nuremberg, at least temporarily.[74] The Nuremberg Rabbi David Tevel Sprinz apparently had lived briefly in Augsburg in 1436, but by 1439 we find him in Salzburg. It is likely that he went to study with Weil and left when the expulsion edict was issued.[75] Weil himself married in Nuremberg and probably lived in Nuremberg between 1417 and 1429.[76] Given the history of interaction between the communities, therefore, there are good reasons to speculate that some Jews made their way to Nuremberg. Although no Jews from Augsburg are recorded in Prague,[77] it was an enormous community that may have been attractive to Jews leaving Augsburg, as it was for Jews in Pfersee one hundred and fifty years later.

The responsa do not give us many clues to the fate of the Jews of Augsburg,

---

[67] Ibid., p. 901.

[68] 1369 (two brothers, Mennlin und Bendith von Munich, although shortly after they returned to Munich) and 1409 (Sanwel von Munich) (Ibid., p. 904).

[69] Ibid., p. 903.

[70] Ibid., p. 904.

[71] Ibid., pp. 989 and 985; In 1406 a Jew from Nördlingen lived in Augsburg briefly, a certain Falk Kohen, possibly a scholar, son of Baruch, Ehemann of Sara, father of Bennet and the father-in-law of Borach; he was a burgher in Nördlingen between 1401 and his death in 1415.

[72] Ibid., p. 985.

[73] Ibid., 1002.

[74] Ibid., p. 1013.

[75] Ibid., pp. 1014–1015.

[76] Ibid., p. 1017; Rabbi Koppelman of Nuremberg settled in Augsburg between 1409 and 1410 and then returned to Nuremberg (Ibid., p. 1018).

[77] See Jacob Weil responsum no. 127; a student of Weil's Rabbi Eliezer of Passau was involved in a rabbinic controversy in Prague.

because they do not deal directly with the expulsion, and they rarely mention Jews by name. Still, some general trends from the responsa and other Hebrew sources may help us to understand the fate of the expelled Jewish community. In responsum 71, Weil treated the case of a woman who was not in the city, but in the suburbs, at the time that her get (bill of divorce) was written, and raises the question of whether the get was valid if she is in the suburbs, that is, were the suburbs considered like the city. While this responsum does not relate that the woman lived in the suburbs, the question seems evident. If so, it may not have been uncustomary for Jews to live outside of the city community in suburbs or in the country as, for example, the author of Leket Yosher described of his parents.[78] In other responsa it is clear that Jews were living in smaller communities outside of Augsburg, in Dillingen, later the residence of the bishop of Augsburg, for example.[79] Another example is Weil's responsum 106, which narrates the story of a woman who was expelled from the town of Coburg and fled to Ulm, where her son lived, intending, it would seem, to move on as soon as she was in better health. Here we have evidence not only that Jews lived in smaller towns but also some insights into strategies Jews employed in the face of persecutions and expulsions.[80]

With all of this information we can account for over forty percent of the tax-paying Jews listed in Augsburg for the year 1438. It is conceivable that death, traveling with family or friends to the same destination, or continued settlement somewhere in Augsburg or the vicinity were all possible fates for the rest of the community.

What were the strategies of Jews who had been expelled from other cities around the same time? Many of the members of the Cologne Jewish community settled in Deutz, a small town not far from Cologne, including a certain Rabbi Susskind, the brother of Rabbi Jacob Molin.[81] According to a Nuremberg chronicler, a number of Jews were apprehended in Nuremberg dressed as farmers shortly after they had been expelled from that city.[82] The point is not necessarily that Jews took up farming or lived in the countryside, but they may have lived within close proximity to the city, even after the expulsion. With a close study of various communities, the cases could no doubt be multiplied. Suffice it here to suggest that, based on the case of Augsburg and other cities, the emigration patterns of Jews followed these major lines: many Jews, although not revealed in archival documents, remained in the cities or very close; some

---

[78] Rohrbacher, "Medinat Schwaben."

[79] Weil, responsum no. 79; Other responsa are also significant in this regard: 106, 107, 118, and 147; Moses Mintz, responsum no. 1; Menachem of Merseberg, no. 33; Joseph Colon, responsum no. 4; Israel Bruna, responsa nos. 267 and 268.

[80] Haverkamp, "Jewish Quarters," gives examples from the second half of the fifteenth century from Hildesheim-Neustadt and Halle-Neuwerk, and from the sixteenth century from Goslar, Göttingen-Weende, and Hanover-Neustadt, pp. 18–19.

[81] Eric Zimmer, Harmony and Discord, p. 135.

[82] See the Chronicle of Deichsler, p. 633.

Jews emigrated to the nearest cities with sizable Jewish populations;[83] others went where they may have had family, where there was a prestigious yeshivah, or where their business or previous contacts had led them before.[84] Many of the Jews that we have seen traveled a good bit in their lifetimes. Still, from the tax lists, it appears as if the wealthier segments of the community had been established in the city for at least five years, even if their business extended beyond the city walls. Two additional examples reinforce these conclusions. Of the six cities in which we know Jews expelled from Heilbronn settled, four were within 15 km south of the city, one was 15 km north of the city, and one was in a different part of Heilbronn itself. Of the eight areas where Jews are known to have gone after the expulsion from Cologne in 1424, two were other parts of the city (Deutz, Mühlheim), three were within 45 km south or southeast of Cologne, and three Jews went to much more distant communities: Frankfurt am Main (150 km southeast), Speyer (200 km southeast), and Salzburg (550 km southeast). Of course, we do not know how long the Jews remained in these new areas. In some cases, we find that Jews returned to the city from which they were expelled within several years, depending upon the political situation.

Jews traveled extensively because of both forced and voluntary migration and business. Jews might travel great distances. There are a number of cases of Jews making their way to Israel (from Höchstadt, Dortmund (1349), Hagenau (1484), Sobernheim), particularly Isaak Halevi of Heidelberg who apparently returned to Germany with messianic works. Within the empire, Jews also traveled quite a bit, and there is one intriguing case mentioned for the village of Münster bei Bingen. In 1495 there was a wedding in that village, which 41 Jews from various parts of the empire attended—illuminating trans-communal relationships at the same time that it demonstrates Jewish travel. These Jews, including three or four local Jews, were imprisoned by the elector Philip for breaking a *Geleit*, law of escort, and were freed only when they swore an oath and agreed to pay a large sum of money (2,100 fl.). Four of the Jews in particular paid a larger share (400 fl.), since they were, presumably, responsible for organizing the wedding. Jews attended the wedding from at least 16 cities or villages (if we include Münster bei Bingen itself), including cities in the Rhineland Palatinate, Hesse, Upper Alsace, modern Baden-Württemburg, and

[83] According to Haverkamp, "Jewish Quarters," p. 17, the following cities had 150 or more Jews living in them, at least temporarily: Originally Cathedral Towns (Cologne, Hildesheim, Magdeburg, Mainz, Worms, Bamberg, Würzburg, Augsburg, Regensburg, Basel, Constance); Royal Boroughs or Imperial Cities (Frankfurt am Main, Nuremberg, Rothenburg ob der Tauber, Esslingen, Erfurt, Eger); Princely Capitals or Residential Towns (Braunschweig, Landshut, Munich, Vienna, Wiener Neustadt, Breslau, Prague).

[84] Burgard argues for the following factors: relatives and marriage; relationships with clients; occupation of pledges and immovables; economic activities, especially money lending and money-lending; religious-cultural connections; letters of protection and escort. See Friedhelm Burgard, "Zur Migration der Juden im westlichen Reichsgebiet im Spätmitelalter," p. 47.

France. Clusters of guests traveled from areas southwest of Mainz, north of Frankfurt am Main, and north of Giessen; but also from near Basel, Stuttgart, and Würzburg.

Jewish mobility may also be demonstrated by tracing the residence patterns of individual Jews. Josef, the son of Jacob of Montabaur, possessed a house in Trier in 1369 and 1377 and also in Koblenz from 1370 to 1385. He also lived in Oberwesel at the end of his life in 1416. A close look at the residences of his family reveal a basically regional, if at times changing, pattern.[85]

A final example is the movement of Jews between yeshivot. Almost all the yeshivot were in large Jewish cities; very few large Jewish populations have no trace of a yeshivah. There was a great deal of continuity in some cities, for example, Mainz and Prague; however, it seems possible to conclude that scholars migrated from city to city and yeshivah to yeshivah frequently and after short intervals. What is more, the actual attraction of students and the establishment of a yeshivah seem to have depended almost solely upon the prestige and motivation of individual rabbinic scholars. That is to say, the yeshivah was most frequently associated with its leader, the rosh yeshivah, rather than the particular city in which it was located. Good examples are the yeshivah of Johanan Luria in Mommenheim, where there was no large Jewish population, and the case of Jacob Weil, who established his own yeshivah in a number of different cities where he resided. This issue is of particular significance, since it has been argued that Ashkenazic yeshivot, at least prior to the middle of the fourteenth century were not considered public, communal institutions, but rather private ones, whose heads were not automatically granted leadership roles within the broader community.[86] According to one recent interpretation "there were no clear guidelines or requirements for the opening of a yeshivah in a particular location, and there was no formal appointment procedure that a prospective academy head had to undergo."[87]

What was the migration pattern of the scholars of a yeshivah? In a recent article on Christian humanists, it has been suggested that the travels of scholars served a number of functions, including acquainting them with different countries, customs, and people as well as establishing contacts with other humanists or maintaining friendships.[88] Similarly, in the Jewish world a good deal has been written about the wandering of scholars.[89] At times travel was forced upon

---

[85] Ibid., p. 55, genealogical table.

[86] See Ephraim Kanarfogel, *Jewish Education and Society in the High Middle Ages* (Detroit, 1992), chapter 4.

[87] Ibid., p. 56.

[88] Eckhard Bernstein, "From Outsiders to Insiders: Some Reflections on the Development of a Group Identity of the German Humanists between 1450 and 1530," in *Renaissance and Reformation Studies in Laudem Caroli, for Charles G. Nauert*, edited by James V. Mehl (Kirksville, Missouri, 1998): 45–64, here at p. 61.

[89] See Mordechai Breuer, "The Wanderings of Students and Scholars—A Prolegomenon to a Chapter in the History of the Yeshivot," p. 446.

Jews. Traveling was also undertaken for learning, or it could be a goal in and of itself. Students and even more established scholars traveled from community to community, region to region in order to study with particular yeshivah heads.[90] Like their humanist counterparts, yeshivah students often traveled from one yeshivah to the next in search of different customs and halakhic decisions regarding certain matters.[91] A good example is the author of *Leket Yosher*, Joseph ben Moses, who wrote down his experiences as well as the decisions of many of his masters.[92] Throughout this period the standard usage of Hebrew facilitated the scholarly movement from place to place.[93] In general, wandering students seem to have caused little friction in the communities in which they settled temporarily.[94] It is, however, nearly impossible to track the students as they moved from yeshivah to yeshivah—some willingly, others like those in Nuremberg in 1499 scattered by the forced expulsion of the Jews from that city.

It is somewhat easier to trace the movements of more prominent rabbis, about whom we have more substantial information, as discussed in the introduction. What is clear is that there was an interconnected network of yeshivot and scholars in late medieval Germany, and that even outside of formal expulsions, Jews, and scholars in particular, wandered extensively through the German empire. As Jacob Katz has argued, this act of scholarly wandering created the consciousness of a broader society and the commitment to the idea of a Jewish nation beyond the local community with its independent customs and traditions.[95]

CONCLUSION

Jewish communities in late medieval Germany existed at a number of levels and for a variety of reasons. How do we assess what appear to be communal or regional customs?[96] The responsa of Rabbi Jacob Weil, for example, vacillate between notions of authority that are regional and local[97] and between ideas of community that are both inclusive and exclusive.

Within the communities, however we define them, Jews were engaged in a diverse spectrum of professions and participated in often rigidly defined social and political structures. In the fourteenth and fifteenth centuries there were over 1,000 Jewish settlements. The number of new settlements in the later Middle

---

[90] Ibid., pp. 447–450; he cites TH 40 regarding a young man wanting to go to another region to study with a particular rabbi. See Jacob Katz, *Out of the Ghetto: The Social Background of Jewish Emancipation, 1770–1870*, pp. 22–23.

[91] Ibid., pp. 459–460

[92] *Leket Yosher.*

[93] Breuer, "The Wanderings of Students and Scholars," p. 467.

[94] Ibid., p. 453.

[95] Katz, *Out of the Ghetto*, p. 23.

[96] Mentgen, *Studien zur Geschichte der Juden in mittelalterlichen Elsaß*, p. 8 on Alsatian minhag.

[97] Compare, for example, Weil, responsa nos. 30, 65, 97, and 113.

Ages was rather small in comparison with the establishment of new settlements especially in the twelfth and thirteenth centuries. The number of new communities was largest in the southwest and in central Germany; but in these regions smaller, often rural, Jewish settlements or communities were more typical. Even in the largest, most well established communities there were typically no more than 150 to 200 Jewish residents. As Alfred Haverkamp has argued, the number of small Jewish settlements was rapidly on the rise by the middle of the fifteenth century.[98] We do not have to wait for the early modern period to find an established, and even somewhat independent, rural Jewry.

While some Jews remained in particular cities or regions for extended periods, the Jewish population tended to be extremely fluid. This was particularly true for several reasons. First, Jewish migration patterns reveal important networks of family, business, religious ritual, and study. Our investigation into the fate of individual Augsburg Jews suggests that Jews, particularly the better off, were likely to settle in one region, barring any unforeseen circumstances, and remain there for a substantial period. Jews continued to seek out large communities as places of refuge and residence, but they also settled in smaller cities or rural areas with few Jews.

It is clear that there were strong and important connections binding Jews in different settlements and cities throughout Germany. The personal, religious, political, and economic connections are at times difficult to define. Still, late medieval Jewry continued to be governed by a somewhat uniform body of law. This, in addition to local customs, and the very movement of Jews between communities as well as their personal interconnection helped to create something of a more cohesive nature than might otherwise have existed had these been largely isolated communities. Even Jews living in rural areas, outside of any large city or Jewish settlement, likely had numerous and multi-faceted interactions with other Jews. The community of Kreuznach, for example, did not possess in 1405 the minimum ten adult men to conduct holiday services. A cantor and additional people were engaged to conduct the services; several Jewish families from the surrounding countryside, who came to Kreuznach for the services were then held responsible for a portion of the expenses.[99] It is interesting that these Jews attended the religious services and that they comprised part of the communal tax structure, a theme that will be treated in more detail in the next chapter. A variety of Jewish institutions, such as ritual baths (*mikvot*) and hospitals, served regional functions. Similar regional interdependencies can be seen in the role of cemeteries. The Jewish cemetery in Hildesheim was used to bury 23 Braunschweig Jews between 1434 and 1457; the cemetery in Frankfurt, at times closely controlled by the city council,[100] and the ceme-

---

[98] Haverkamp, "Jewish Quarters," pp. 19 and 27–28.
[99] Burgard, "Zur Migration der Juden im westlichen Reichsgebiet im Spätmitelalter," pp. 43–44.
[100] Ziwes, *Studien zur Geschichte der Juden in mittleren Rheingebiet*, pp. 80–81. For more

tery in Colmar served similar regional functions.[101] This was a general trend, and the roughly 1,000 Jewish settlements of the later Middle Ages were served by only 150 cemeteries.[102]

The varying, often conflicting levels of non-Jewish jurisdiction over the Jewish communities frequently made Jewish settlement precarious. The increasing marginalization of the Jews during the fourteenth and fifteenth centuries, as reflected in increasing attacks and expulsions made Jewish continuity extremely difficult. The discontinuity and disruption wrought by the massacres and expulsions associated with the Black Death fundamentally altered Jewish social and communal structures. Despite the reconstitution of many communities in the years and decades after 1350, the German Jewry that emerged in the fifteenth century was more easily and more frequently marginalized and excluded from the urban areas where they had previously resided. This, combined with the dramatic changes within the Christian urban communities more generally affected Jewish communal identity and structure in tangible and lasting ways. On the other hand, important changes within the Jewish communities themselves—changes that mirrored more general changes but that also sprang from internal communal issues—helped to make the fifteenth century a significant and transitional period in the history of the Jews in Germany.

Although it has already been suggested that the fifteenth century witnessed a transformation of kehillah-based (individual community) to medinah-based (regional) structures of authority,[103] the process of such a transformation, as well as the impact on Jewish *halakhah* (law) and Jewish daily life has not yet been satisfactorily explained. What, for example, should we make of attempts after the Black Death and on through the fifteenth century, often, though not always, applied from without, to have territorial—as in 1418 when a Jew in Bingen was appointed as director of the Jewry of Rheingau; or in the case of Jacob Molin who was similarly, though for largely *halakhic* issues, recognized as the director of a territory[104]—or even imperial—as in Israel of Rothenburg (1407), Hayim Isaac of Würzburg (1418), Anselm of Cologne (1435), Israel Bruna

---

details see Dietrich Andernacht, *Regesten zur Geschichte der Juden in der Reichsstadt Frankfurt am Main von 1401–1519*; the index for this valuable work is, unfortunately, not yet available.

[101] Burgard, "Zur Migration der Juden," p. 44. Similarly the Jewish cemetery in Nördlingen was used by near-by Jewish communities in the fifteenth century, (including: Baldingen, Bopfingen, Hainsfarth, Kleinerdlingen, Löpsingen, Maihingen, Marktoffingen, Oettingen, Pflaumloch, Wemding) as well as some more distant (including: Dischingen, Donauwörth, Ellwangen, Feuchtwangen, Gunzenhausen, Weissenburg/Bavaria, and Welden). See *GJ*, vol. 3, p. 984.

[102] See *GJ*, vol. 3, pt. 3, "Die jüdische Gemeinde, Gesellschaft und Kultur," p. 7 (in preparation—17.05.99 draft; thanks to the editors for showing me the draft).

[103] Elazar and Cohen, *Jewish Political Organization*, p. 162. See also Stefan Rohrbacher, "Medinat Schwaben."

[104] See *GJ*, vol. 3, pt. 3, "Die jüdische Gemeinde, Gesellschaft und Kultur," p. 33.

(1468), and Levi of Völkermarkt in Nuremberg (1490)[105]—rabbis appointed?[106] Mordechai Breuer has asserted that such appointments and attempts at control helped formalize and undermine the position of the rabbi within the Jewish community.[107] All of the fifteenth-century attempts at centralizing German Jewry ended in failure.[108] Opposition to the centralization of Jewish regulations could come from outside or inside of the Jewish community. Rabbi Weil, for example, related that the King's counselors opposed the union of Jewish communities in Nuremberg in negotiating taxes imposed on the Jews in the empire, presumably because they feared that they would have lost a certain control over defining the sums to be collected.[109] But opposition could also be voiced from within the Jewish communities. In response to the efforts of Rabbi Seligmann Oppenheim of Bingen to set himself up as a superior rabbi or even the Chief Rabbi of Germany in 1455, many communities and rabbis strongly opposed the ordinances that he had passed and his attempts at "supreme authority of interpretation."[110]

Jewish identity and Jewish conceptions of community varied from place to place, but, as the preceding suggests, the fifteenth century was a period of transition from local to regional based communal identity. We must now investigate communal cohesion and conflict in more detail to obtain a more focused picture of the late medieval communities.

[105] Ibid., pp. 34–35.
[106] See Ziwes, *Studien zur Geschichte der Juden in mittleren Rheingebiet*, p. 70.
[107] Mordechai Breuer, "The Position of the Rabbinate in the Leadership of the German Communities in the fifteenth century," pp. 63–65.
[108] See Louis Finkelstein, *Jewish Self-Government in the Middle Ages*, p. 77.
[109] Hayyim Hillel Ben-Sasson, *A History of the Jewish People*, pp. 600–601.
[110] Ibid., p. 601.

6

Toward A Definition of Late Medieval German Jewish Community

In the historiography of the Jews in late medieval and early modern Germany, two important subjects are internal communal history and the transition from an essentially urban to a heavily rural Jewry in the early modern period.[1] Progress on these themes has been particularly weak for southern Germany, where the responsa literature has not been fully combed and where the documentation about the Jewish communities in non-Jewish sources reveals noticeable gaps between the mid fifteenth and the mid sixteenth centuries. This chapter aims to offer some suggestions about the nature of Jewish communal structure and about the transition of the Jewish community in this very important, if difficult to document, period.

TOWARD A DEFINITION OF COMMUNITY

In 1950 Yitzhak Baer argued that the Jewish community of the Middle Ages was a living organism, combining "religious" and secular interests (if, indeed, the two could be separated), simultaneously part of the community of Israel as well as a microcosm within its own particular context.[2] Few historians today see the Jewish community in such idyllic, internal, and immanently religious ways. Israel Yuval, in particular, has criticized this view and has suggested instead that both Jewish and Christian communities in the Middle Ages shared a common reservoir of symbols and motifs used in self-definition, in particular in the appropriation of the image of the Holy Land (the sacred Jerusalem or Rome).[3] Such common images also dipped into more pragmatic communal

---

[1] See Alfred Haverkamp, "The Jewish Quarters in German Towns During the Late Middle Ages," in In and Out of the Ghetto, pp. 16–17.
[2] See Israel Yuval, "Heilige Städte, heilige Gemeinden—Mainz als das Jerusalem Deutschlands," pp. 91–92. See also Menahem Elon, Jewish Law: History, Sources, Principles, vol. 2, p. 667.
[3] Yuval, "Heilige Städte," pp. 92–93 and 96f.

structures. The number of members serving on the Christian and Jewish community councils, for example, was often twelve; a number with very direct religious meaning to Christians (twelve Apostles, the twelve gates to the heavenly Jerusalem depicted in John-Apocalypse 21: 12–14).[4] And although one might justifiably locate Jewish precedents for such numbers, it is clear that often the internal Jewish community structure was modeled upon, if not dictated, by the structure and will of the Christian authorities to which the Jews were subject.

How exactly did Jewish communal structure look in the Middle Ages? According to one recent assessment, Jewish communities in the later Middle Ages were relatively unstructured:

> The physically small Jewish community thus predicated its functions on consent, as, in fact, European Jewish communities were still doing as late as the seventeenth and eighteenth centuries, when their character had also become a distinctly oligarchic one. Communal order was established through binding oaths sworn by each communal member to perform specific acts. Anyone who violated these oaths would be excluded from the community and denied its services. The powers of the kahal in this process were essentially indirect. The kahal could enforce discipline only by resorting to such devices as allowing aggrieved parties to interrupt communal prayers. The reliance on these roundabout tactics indicates how weak and unstructured communal governmental organs actually were.[5]

According to this interpretation, the Jewish community consisted of a small number of Jews who entered into an association based on consensus through binding oaths in order to protect the rights of its members from external authority and to regulate internal communal life according to a shared body of Jewish law. Such associations were, in fact, often oligarchic and more often ineffectual, relying as they did on indirect authority and the revocation of particular ritual services or charity. Internal Jewish communal structures, according to this generalization, were rudimentary, "weak and unstructured."

Hayyim Hillel Ben-Sasson, on the other hand, offered a rather different interpretation in his discussion of the differences between Jewish and Christian community. He argued that:

> The character shaped the uniqueness of the community and is expressed distinctly by important differences in instruments of cohesion and legal sanction between the commune and the community. The Christian city commune is originally and self-consciously a coniuratio; in many towns it continued as a coniuratio, *reiterata*, returning in yearly ceremonies to oath-taking of all citizens, demanding always the oath from new citizens . . . The Jewish community has no such consciousness of having originated in a binding by oath, nor does it have ceremonies of oath-taking, neither upon the acceptance of new citizens, needless to say, nor general, yearly ones. The community of course

---

[4] Ibid., p. 101.
[5] Kenneth Stow, *Alienated Minority*, p. 91.

employs the oath for many and varied purposes. Its total absence as a binding and cohesive element is all the more striking in view of the religious
character of the community . . .[6]

Both of these interpretations, while no doubt partially true, underestimate the
complexity of Jewish communal structure and identity in late medieval Germany.
Recent research has demonstrated repeatedly that Jewish communal life, in its
structure, forms of association, self-identity, as well as geographical dispersal,
was much more diverse than such interpretations allow. The complexity of late
medieval Jewish "community" was due to the fact that "community" was itself
multivalent. In part, this multivalence was due to the fact that the settlement
of Jews could be different from the formation of Jewish communities, particularly at a time when the vast majority of Jewish settlements were extremely
small, perhaps including only a handful of Jews, and when the number of
smaller rural communities, or at least communities outside the large cities, were
beginning to increase dramatically. The relationship between what are more appropriately termed settlements and the larger communities, therefore, requires serious attention.[7] Much recent research regarding the history of Jewish community
in late medieval Germany presupposes that Jewish community must be defined
as a legal or corporate entity within a larger Christian community. Such an
assumption, however, misses the point that Jews could form community, and
identify themselves as a part of a community, in a variety of ways—for example, ritually, through the attendance of religious services or obedience to the
jurisdiction of regional rabbinic courts or judges; economically, through a series
of interconnected business relationships; or intellectually, through the contact
of scholars and students. Community in the broader sense, therefore, went
beyond formal geographical boundaries and could change because of a variety
of both internal and external conditions.

How exactly was "community" defined? What were the communal structures
and how did they function? What tensions existed within the Jewish communities of fifteenth-century Germany, and what do such tensions suggest about
the notion of community as it was developing? More than one scholar has labeled
the late fourteenth and the fifteenth centuries as a transitional period in the
history of the Jewish communities in Germany, between a period in which the
kehillah, or local community, became the prime repository of communal authority and a period, beginning with the communal restructuring after the Black
Death and its ensuing massacres and expulsions, in which the kehillah still constituted the principle locus of organized Jewish life, but in which regional associations (*va'adim*) or federations of kehillot in the form of synods also became

---

[6] Hayyim Hillel Ben-Sasson, "The 'Northern' European Jewish Community and its
Ideals," p. 216.

[7] As for example regarding the nature of leadership in smaller "communities," *chavura*
as opposed to *kehillah* or *kahal*. See Mordechai Breuer, "The Position of the Rabbinate in
the Leadership of the German Communities in the Fifteenth Century," p. 62.

more pronounced and significant.[8] In the first period, partially formed regional structures began to emerge, but external conditions did not allow a regional confederation to supersede the autonomous power of the individual kehillot. As time went on, local custom could become law. Regional jurisdiction of one person tended to become more common, and within the communities the *morah d'atrah* (master of the place, or community rabbi) tended to be given full authority to decide local, even regional, halakhic issues. The period under consideration here was thus very much a combination of the kehillot and *va'adim* epochs. Only the resolution, perhaps in the later sixteenth century, really marks a break from earlier medieval developments. Certainly, however, the movement towards larger structures of greater authority did have a profound effect upon German Jewish life.

Like Christian community, Jewish community was complex. Jewish community was equally difficult to define, since "community" could refer to the entire group of Jews resident in a city, the *bnei 'ir*, the wealthy members of the community, typically those who paid taxes and owned houses, or more "worthy" individuals,[9] such as those who served as members of the community council. In 1498, for example, the community of Regensburg was governed by ten parnasim, but regulations were passed with a body of "thirty-one community members, 'boni viri' of the community and of [the rest of] those who dwell in the streets of the Jews."[10] The council itself, the kahal, was often conceived of as the "community," as was the *tsibur*, literally the "congregation." At times, as in the earlier great council convened by the communities of Speyer, Worms, and Mainz, the idea of "community" took on a very specific legal, jurisdictional, power contrasted with the interest and will of the individual:

> If an individual has a complaint against the community because of taxes or for some other reason he shall pay the Community what they ask him, but the Community must respond to him in Court although they have no personal interest in the matter.[11]

Indeed, the famous eleventh-century scholar Joseph Bonfils had equated the community with a *bet din*, or rabbinic court, with its leadership serving as the rabbinic judges. Communal edicts were, therefore, likened to judicial processes.[12] With the dispersion of authority in Judaism (in which local Jewish communities began to make their own legal decisions apart from those rendered by the Babylonian academies) after the tenth century, local authority gained dominance, in particular in the form of the kehillot. The community came to embody the authority, the legislative competence, and so was seen as a court itself. According

---

[8] This was particularly the case after 1399. See Ben-Sasson, *A History of the Jewish People*, p. 602.

[9] Ibid., p. 501.

[10] Ibid., p. 593.

[11] Louis Finkelstein, *Jewish Self-Government in the Middle Ages*, p. 240.

[12] Stow, *Alienated Minority*, p. 159.

to the Spanish Rabbi Solomon ben Adret (c. 1235–c. 1310), "each community as to its own locality has the same status as the geonim had with respect to all Jewry," and furthermore "the agreement of the inhabitants of a locality has the full force of law; whenever a majority adopt an enactment upon which they have agreed, the views of the minority are disregarded because the majority of every town have the same relation to the minority as the High Court has to all of Israel."[13] Such a view of the community, of course, profoundly affected the relationship between the community and individual members.[14] Before the end of the fourteenth century, the individual local community came to regard itself as possessing an autonomous jurisdiction. "Each community," writes Hayyim Hillel Ben-Sasson, "came to regard itself as an independent region with respect to judicial authority; and whoever came to the community fell within its judicial competence."[15] The power of the local community was well summed up by Joseph Bonfils in a case that we will find again in the fifteenth century:

> they cannot compel the others in any way, even if they are more numerous and greater, except in cases of suppressing transgression or if they [the representatives of the larger community] appear in connection with a charge which may affect them all . . . since all Jews are responsible for one another.[16]

Kenneth Stow cautions, however, that the medieval Jewish community was in no sense a true medieval corporation. The revival of the ancient idea of the *Kenesset Yisrael*, the Assembly of Israel, is more a construction of modern historiography than an accurate reflection of medieval communal identity.[17] Stow argues that the Jewish community in the Middle Ages was governed by the majority, but a majority that was associated with the court. Such emphasis on the majority as a court led not to conciliarism, but rather to the protection of rabbinic authority against lay encroachment, since rabbis headed the courts.[18] As we will see, this situation was altered in the fifteenth century when the rabbinate was professionalized and lay leaders assumed greater authority within the Jewish community.

DEFINING COMMUNITY: THE "TRADITIONAL" SENSE

What was community? In recent literature, the nature of communal authority has been discussed, but the conception and extent of community has received

---

[13] Elon, *Jewish Law*, vol. 2, pp. 699–700.

[14] Ibid., pp. 685 and 704.

[15] Ben-Sasson, *A History of the Jewish People*, p. 505. Ben-Sasson also writes (p. 501) that "from the twelfth to the fourteenth centuries the communities of Ashkenaz underwent extensive institutional and conceptual development. Various provisions and ordinances were instituted to create within the walls of the city its own legal authority to foster the idea of an exclusive right on the part of the community members to live in their place of residence."

[16] Ibid., p. 434.

[17] Stow, *Alienated Minority*, p. 179.

[18] See Kenneth R. Stow, "Holy Body, Holy Society," especially pp. 160–163.

little attention and even less clarification.[19] Given the many and varied uses
of the terms kehillah and kahal—which is more typically associated with the
community council within the community[20]—we may still make some generalizations about the nature of community as reflected in the responsa. Rabbi
Israel Isserlein ruled that "the members of the city and the men of the community who join in paying the taxes have every legal aspect of partnership."[21]
The leaders of the community ruled over the community, therefore, as leaders
of that partnership. Yet for Isserlein, in a case involving an individual Jew,
Abraham, against the community of Posen, membership in the kehillah was
not a partnership from which the individual could disengage himself when
losses were involved. While the community did have something of the feel of
a voluntary association or a partnership, it was, certainly at the very least once
constituted, a necessary association from which one could not remove himself
at will. By disengaging himself the individual would increase the tax burden
on the rest of the community, which he had no right to do.[22] A similarly telling
case was mentioned by Rabbi Jacob Weil, who wrote that a group of Jews in
Neustadt had tried to separate themselves from the community (tsibur) and make
separate tax arrangements with the non-Jewish authorities. For their transgression, they were denied the benefits of ritual slaughtering, praying with the
congregation, and other religious services.[23] The story had further ramifications
inside the synagogue, where a certain Rabbi Meisterlin was forced from the
reader's stand and embarrassed in the midst of synagogue prayers. On the sim-
plest level, therefore, community was a group to which individual Jews were
bound for both ritual as well as economic and social needs.

How was membership within a community determined? In some communities, inclusion was automatic once an individual had resided there for more than
twelve months, bought a house, begun extensive business, or brought his whole
family. Membership in the community, however, extended beyond mere residence. For purposes of taxation, individuals no longer living in a particular city
might be obliged to contribute to that community's financial burdens or might
be responsible for business taking place outside of the specified community.[24]

---

[19] Stow, in Alienated Minority, argues that the Jewish communities of the high Middle
Ages included an homogenous mix of family size and wealth, which he contrasts with
the oligarchical nature of later medieval communities such as Nuremberg in the late
fifteenth century. See also Michael Toch, "The Jewish Community of Nuremberg in the
Year 1489: Social and Demographic Structure."

[20] Jacob Weil, responsum no. 146.

[21] Ben-Sasson, A History of the Jewish People, p. 595.

[22] Cited in Eric Zimmer, Harmony and Discord, p. 199, n. 118; Israel Isserlein, responsum no. 144; see Jacob Molin, responsum no. 71 for a comparable situation.

[23] Weil, responsum no. 140.

[24] See Weil, responsum no. 133. For Rabbi Moses Mintz, the individual could not
separate himself from the community (responsa nos. 62 and 72); though Joseph Colon
rebuked the Würzburg community for trying to force a departed member to pay taxes

Some communities, as we will see, effectively limited membership, but the notion of community could easily transcend a particular residence or city. Community could be more regionally-(*medinah-*)based as well. Smaller communities were often "incorporated" into larger communities nearby.[25] Community, therefore, was a loosely defined concept, having an important ritual element and a sense of a common fate—or at least a common front to external pressures. Jewish community was multilayered. It could include the city in which Jews lived together, along with outlying suburban areas or smaller nearby communities, but community might also be reflected in the association of a number of kehillot within a particular region, or even an entire country.[26]

The Jewish community in medieval Germany was, in a certain sense, a "state" within a "state," or perhaps better put, a semi-autonomous group within a political jurisdiction. On the one hand, the Jewish community possessed the privilege of self-government; on the other hand, Jewish autonomy depended heavily upon the toleration, and often assistance, of the local government. The result was that Jews functioned within two systems of government, which could be overlapping or contradictory. Try as they might, at times leaders of the Jewish community even had difficulty in keeping legal cases that had primarily to do with Jewish law out of Christian courts. Although reluctant to be involved in litigation, Rabbi Jacob Weil, for example, often agreed to judge cases in order that he might prevent the parties from taking their grievances to non-Jewish courts.[27]

The individual community was governed by a council, comprised originally of wealthy and scholarly[28] members of the community and convened to initiate

---

(responsum no. 1). At times, Mintz came close to using the terms kehillah and medinah interchangeably (responsum no. 43). An individual could have obligations to the community even after leaving that community (responsum no. 80). Weil also commented on individuals attempting to separate themselves from the community in cases of taxation (responsa nos. 140 and 81). He dealt with a case in which someone leaving the community was obligated to pay all taxes announced before he left the community, the rationale being that the secular government did not take into account comings and goings, but rather evaluated the tax potential according to the number of residents and the level of their business at one particular time, not making adjustment if the number of Jews resident in the city should change. According to Weil the ordinances enacted in one community did not necessarily apply to another community or area (responsum no. 65, where he cites Maharil). On the other hand, however, the influence of a particular community or rabbi might extend well beyond the boundaries of that specific town.

[25] Menahem of Merseburg, no. 21, and Minz, responsum no. 1.

[26] See Israel Bruna, responsum no. 257 regarding a community in Franconia that refused to participate in an extraordinary tax (see also Mintz, responsum no. 62). In another responsum, Bruna argues that everyone (not just *kehillot*) is responsible to help if one city of the medinah is in danger as was the case in Regensburg in 1456. A similar ruling is brought down by Mintz (Mintz, responsum no. 1).

[27] Bernard Rosensweig, *Ashkenazic Jewry in Transition*, p. 39.

[28] Wealth seems to have been the more important qualification.

and regulate communal policy, and to protect the community and its interests, in economic, judicial, and diplomatic concerns. The members of the council were elected by majority vote and sworn to secrecy, and often only a select group of wealthy and distinguished families served in such offices.[29]

The number of members on the council varied from community to community, as did the exact procedures for electing them. Most communities appointed between 7 and 14 members.[30] In some places councilmen were elected by a majority vote of all residents, in other communities through an indirect election committee. Generally, in theory at least, the length of tenure of office was one year; practically, however, officers were not typically removed from office so long as they continued to fulfill their duties. Elections often required the additional approval of the civil or ecclesiastical authority and often stipulated that the person elected pay an election fee and take an oath of fealty to the civil authority. Community leaders could wield substantial power and lobby for their own personal gain, and yet at the same time they could often be held personally responsible for the vicissitudes facing the community; for example, the payment of ransom for co-religionists held in captivity. The notion of community was at times subsumed under the authority of such councils.

At the head of the Jewish community, in Nuremberg for example, stood the council (*Judenrat*), whose members were elected annually under the direction of (non-Jewish) city officials, by Jews qualified to vote. Typically, the members of this council were wealthy laymen, and the rabbi, at least after 1350, did not sit in this body. The council heard cases between local and foreign Jews, cases regarding Jews who informed to the Christian authorities against other Jews or the Jewish community, information about the declaration and collection of taxes, and at times it might oversee the distribution of charity. In Ulm two curators, again from the group of wealthy laymen, administered the synagogue and the community affairs. Smaller communities had only a few leaders (*parnasim*) who oversaw the numerous administrative functions within the community and between the Jewish and Christian authorities. In larger communities, which could often include such smaller "satellite communities" not directly governed by the community's regulations, certain offices, at times modeled after, or approved by, local non-Jewish structures, dispensed important administrative functions.[31] Among such officials were the supervisor of charity, tax assessors, as well as individuals charged with the upkeep of the cemetery or the synagogue.

The instability and dramatic results of the pogroms following the Black Death had a profound effect upon the Jewish communities in Germany. Old prohibitions on settlement, which Jewish communities had upheld in an effort to limit

---

[29] They are called by a variety of names in the sources: *parnasim, gabbaim, ma'arichim, ba'alai hoda'ot.*

[30] Typically 7, according to Elon, *Jewish Law*, vol. 2, p. 728.

[31] See Alfred Haverkamp, "'Concivilitas' von Christen und Juden in Aschkenas im Mittelalter," pp. 119f and 121.

the entrance of other Jews and maintain the livelihood of their members, were relaxed. More importantly, the threadbare remnants of the Jewish community fell ever increasingly under the purview of the rabbi, whose position became at once more "professionalized" and important, because in the period after the Black Death, with the dispersal of Jews throughout Germany and the disruption of continuous Jewish settlement in many places, the rabbi became, more than ever, the integral lynchpin in interpreting and, perhaps even more significantly, applying the body of Jewish law to the dispersed and complex conditions in which late medieval Jews found themselves in Germany.[32] According to this understanding, the rabbi occupied a more central, even dominant, position within the community immediately after the Black Death.[33]

The first hints of a professional rabbi could be found in the thirteenth century; but not until the end of the fourteenth and beginning of the fifteenth centuries did a professional rabbinate, which began to demand fees for its services, develop.[34] Although some scholars may have received tuition for their instruction earlier, communal rabbis do not seem to have been reimbursed for their work before the fifteenth century. An ordinance from Erfurt granted the community of Schweidnitz the privilege to choose and pay a "master" (*meister*), although there is no confirmation in Hebrew sources that this actually occurred. Due to the devastating effects of the Black Death, Rabbi Meir ben Barukh ha-Levi of Vienna, already at the end of the fourteenth century, adopted a policy of bestowing students with the title of *morenu rav* in order to permit them to establish an academy and perform vital rabbinic functions. Such ordination (*semikhah*) became popular in the fifteenth century, and the more the number of ordinations, the greater the general acceptance of the rabbinic authority that came with them.

By the fifteenth century in Italy and Germany the power and authority of the rabbi was institutionalized by the process of rabbinic ordination. The rite, which shared certain similarities with the ordination of Catholic priests, was more akin to the granting of a university doctoral degree. Indeed, some scholars, particularly in Spain, criticized the development, arguing that the Jews who had instituted it "had copied the Christians who are in the habit of making doctors."[35] According to Robert Bonfil, the similarities between the conferral of the rabbinic ordination and the doctorate are worthy of consideration: both provided for the recipient extraordinary ceremonial protocol, grants of exemptions from taxes, "professional" rights, and financial rewards.[36] Certifications for the two posts were also similarly worded. In the case of the conferral of

---

[32] See Ben-Sasson, *A History of the Jewish People*, pp. 593 and 597.
[33] See Breuer, "The Position of the Rabbinate," pp. 47 and 50–52.
[34] Israel Isserlein, *Peskim* no. 128 and Bruna, responsum no. 277.
[35] According to Isaac Abravanel—quoted in Robert Bonfil, "Aliens Within: The Jews and Anti-Judaism," p. 284.
[36] Bonfil, "Aliens Within," pp. 284–285.

rabbinic ordination, however, the "graduate did not receive a cap, book and ring; rather he was handed a symbolic rod, which represented the power that the rabbi had to punish transgression with excommunication. The rabbinical degree did not fasten its recipient to the world of books or learning in the yeshivah (or to draw the comparison suggested by Bonfil, university), rather it licensed the holder to perform duties within society. A significant point in Bonfil's analysis here emerges: rabbis were needed as not only judges, but also as legal and ritual consultants—"Because it was so intimately tied to the sphere of doctrine and the sacred, excommunication was of fundamental relevance to the legitimate depositories of doctrinal knowledge, the rabbis."[37] Such control of rituals was necessary to maintain the cohesiveness of the community. The rabbi was therefore both a source of power and knowledge. Bonfil concludes that

> it is no wonder that the Christian world's first perceptions of the complex figure of the rabbi were from earliest times charged with uncertainty, as even the earliest testimonials show. The rabbi, in fact, was assigned various names in Latin and vernacular documents: he was magister or doctor (or even more explicitly, sometimes *doctor legis hebraicae*), *Judenbischof*, or *Hochmeister der Juden*.[38]

There existed different types of rabbis and rabbinic authority in the fifteenth century.[39] Important distinctions need to be made between the leading and prestigious rabbis of the age and the majority of other lesser important rabbinic figures.[40] The non-professional rabbi, known as "semikhat haver" or "rav," was granted this title after the completion of a number of years of study. He could join courts of authority, form tribunals, adjudicate certain types of litigation, join community councils, represent the kehillah in inter-communal affairs, and may even have rendered some decisions in ritual matters. He could not function in cases of marriage or divorce. He paid taxes and was usually engaged in business.

The authoritative rabbi for the community, on the other hand, was a rabbinic scholar, who maintained an academy (that is, he had the privilege of instruction) and had authority in all ritual matters. He could appoint ritual slaughterers and inspectors, send inspectors to other communities,[41] deliver public speeches, and perform many of the communal religious functions, such as marriages, divorces, *halizot*, and the administration of oaths to widows in order to collect

---

[37] Ibid., pp. 286–287.
[38] Ibid., pp. 287–288.
[39] See Breuer, "The Position of the Rabbinate," p. 52.
[40] Ibid., p. 66.
[41] See Weil, responsum no. 50, which mentions Weil's power to send inspectors into the province of Neckar and its surroundings to investigate the competence of ritual slaughterers and examiners. Indeed, Weil's later claim to fame was his work on ritual slaughtering. See also Weil, responsum no. 97.

the *ketubot* (money specified at the time of marriage that the woman would collect in the event of divorce or the death of her husband). These authoritative rabbis could also serve as judges of arbitration, either in colleges or as sole judges. Some communities had more than one such rabbi, who was generally invited by the community, had lived in the community for many years, or was appointed by another prominent rabbi.[42] A community could not, however, be forced to accept a rabbi.[43]

In general, Jewish community was organized around the adherence of all of its members to a standardized and traditional body of law, the primary sources of which were the Talmud and the various medieval codifications of Talmudic law, for example, the *Mishneh Torah* of Maimonides and the *Arba'ah Turim* of Rabbi Jacob ben Asher. In addition, local communities were joined by the rulings of important rabbis by their responsa, by the takkanot (ordinances) passed by local, or on occasion regional, authorities, and by the power of local or regional custom, which could often serve the same purpose as legislation.[44] The conception of the rabbis or Jews of "Germany and France" or of "Ashkenaz,"[45] denoting much the same, is frequent throughout the Jewish sources. At the same time, the customs prevalent in a particular region[46] or community might take precedence within a specific community. Rabbi Israel Bruna mentions customs (*minhagim*) that are Ashkenazic,[47] Austrian,[48] specific to the city of Regensburg,[49] and inclusive of all Israel,[50] that is all Jews in the world. Custom could determine which view to accept when halakhic authorities disagreed; it could supplement existing law unable to treat new questions that could arise; and, moreover, as the expression of the will of the people, it could establish new norms contrary to existing (generally only civil, not religious) law.[51] An important Jewish legal concept stipulates that custom, providing it was not contradicted by the laws of the Torah or Talmud, overruled *halakhah* (law).[52] This concept had particular force in the scattered communities of the fifteenth

---

[42] Weil, responsum no. 161. See also Bruna, responsum no. 277.

[43] Weil, responsum no. 146, in Breslau.

[44] See Elon, *Jewish Law*, vol. 2, p. 881.

[45] Bruna, responsa nos. 67 and 211; see also Weil, responsum no. 79.

[46] See Weil, responsum no. 30, where he writes of minhag of the medinah, in a case of deferring to gentile courts, or in the case of delivering punishment in the synagogue between the afternoon and evening prayers (responsum no. 28).

[47] Bruna, responsum no. 14. Weil writes of a leniency extended in all of Ashkenaz to cook for a child on the Sabbath, since the child is generally considered like a sick person. See Weil, responsum no. 46.

[48] Bruna, responsum no. 12. See also Weil, responsum no. 66.

[49] Bruna, responsum no. 98. See also Weil, responsum no. 66.

[50] Bruna, responsum no. 93.

[51] Elon, *Jewish Law*, vol. 2, pp. 896 and 904.

[52] Bruna, responsum no. 23. See Mishnah and Gemara in *Pesachim*. Rashi had much earlier ruled that communities could cancel "decisions made by the ancients according to the needs of the time." See Ben-Sasson, *A History of the Jewish People*, p. 434.

century. Both Bruna and the important Italian legal scholar Rabbi Joseph Colon (1410/20–1480) cite the Palestinian Talmud regarding the power of custom. Colon, commenting on an inheritance case writes that:

> We learn in the Palestinian Talmud that custom cancels law and it is written in [tractate] Avodah Zara, for example, that it is a permanent custom from the mouths of the sages of the place [that cancels law]; as is said in tractate Sofrim, no law will be permanent until it becomes the custom [of the land] and . . . [it is in this context] that it says that custom cancels law, referring to ordained custom; but custom which is not derived from the Torah is like a mistake in reasoning and how many defective customs there are . . .[53]

Certain customs were definitely of a regional sort, such as a custom of eating in Styria that Bruna clearly indicated was not followed elsewhere.[54] Weil mentioned that the Jews of Nuremberg were accustomed to eat with Christians for the sake of peace, but indicated that such was not a general custom elsewhere.[55] In Isserlein's responsa we find a case suggesting that it was customary in one medinah that all Jews went to the non-Jewish court in matters of real property.[56]

There were many connections binding Jews of different communities and regions together in addition to customs. Such connections are particularly significant given the apparent mobility of Jews in the later Middle Ages. Traveling between communities was certainly not uncommon, and it was undertaken for many reasons: according to Bruna a woman might travel alone to another city for a wedding;[57] another woman traveled to Regensburg to give birth;[58] and Isserlein cites the case of a young man who wanted to travel to a different medinah to study with a rabbi, but his father interceded and refused to allow him to go.[59] Obviously individuals from smaller communities might travel to larger communities for burial, provisions, or religious services. According to Isserlein the residents of one settlement wanted to go to an adjoining town to hear the reading of the Megillah on Purim.[60] Many more cases of Jews traveling for business or because of local or regional expulsions can be found in the sources.

---

[53] Colon, responsum no. 8. See also responsum no. 102. See Mintz, responsum no. 6, ". . . each and every *kehillah* ordains the matter according to their needs that are good in their eyes . . ."

[54] Bruna, responsum no. 146.

[55] Weil, responsum no. 49. Jews did apparently dine with gentiles, however, on many occasions. See Isserlein, responsum no. 239, where a Jew, not dressed as a Jew, sat at the table of a hotel with gentiles, who admitted to killing a Jew.

[56] Isserlein, responsum no. 339.

[57] Bruna, responsum no. 24.

[58] Ibid., responsum no. 180.

[59] Isserlein, responsum no. 40.

[60] Isserlein deals with the question of whether these people are also required to be

Although the individual local community, especially before the end of the fourteenth century, came to regard itself as an autonomous jurisdictional area, communities often joined together to enact specific regulations or to judge particular legal cases. Throughout the Middle Ages there were a number of important rabbinic synods that attempted to create centralized authority and legal observance. Of particular importance were the combined synods of the three Rhineland communities Speyer, Worms, and Mainz, known as Shum. Between 1196 and 1250, ordinances were discussed and approved regarding a broad array of topics such as trial procedures, debts, taxation, the ban of excommunication, sumptuary laws, synagogues, and relations with non-Jews. Such synods continued throughout the fourteenth and fifteenth centuries.

BETWEEN STRUCTURE AND COMMUNITY: THE LATE MEDIEVAL YESHIVAH

Communities could be both local and regional; they could share official communal positions and obligations, but might be dispersed geographically or by jurisdiction, as in a number of groups disassociated within the same city—as in Breslau, where two groups formed, each with their own synagogue[61] or in Schweidnitz where there were two Jewish courts in 1431.[62] What connected dispersed communities at difficult times or when communal structures reached beyond the city walls? In part, the foundations of Jewish law and the systematic, if variegated, interpretation of that law at the hands of the rabbis, helped create both a legal and cultural community in the midst of dispersion. The centers of learning, teaching, and application of that law, the talmudic academies or yeshivot, were thus central to the maintenance of Jewish religious, cultural, and communal identity. The yeshivot may serve as a crucial testing ground for the understanding of Jewish continuity and of broader notions of Jewish "community." As Jacob Katz has argued, the act of scholarly wandering created the consciousness of a broader society and the commitment to the idea of a Jewish nation beyond the local community, with its independent customs and traditions.[63]

The 26 yeshivot[64] I have identified were located throughout Germany, but they followed closely the general geographical breakdown of total Jewish

---

in that town in order to hear the Torah reading of "parshat zachor" that must be read on the Sabbath before Purim. This parsha, along with that of "para adumah" are obligations from the Torah, according to the Tosafists, and so are, in this case even more important than the reading of the Megillah. See responsum no. 108.

[61] GJ, vol. 3, pp. 160–161.

[62] Ibid., p. 1346.

[63] Jacob Katz, *Out of the Ghetto*, p. 23.

[64] Yeshivot are noted in GJ in the following cities: Amberg, Augsburg, Bamberg, Bingen, Breslau, Brünn, Eger, Erfurt, Frankfurt am Main, Gotha, Halle, Cologne, Krems, Mainz, Mommenheim, Nördlingen, Nuremberg, Olmütz, Prague, Regensburg, Rothenburg ob der Tauber, Schweidnitz, Ulm, Weinheim, and Würzburg.

communities outlined above.[65] Twenty-one of the 26 cities with yeshivot had
Jewish settlements before 1250, only four before 1350 and only one after 1350,
which, coincidentally was the only small community, really a village, that was
a mere 20 km north of Strasbourg. Almost all the cities with yeshivot had substantial Jewish populations of around 100; only a handful had less—Olmütz had
16 Jews, Halle 20, and Gotha 55.

A cursory look at the yeshivot of fifteenth-century Germany raises a number of questions. What was the nature and structure of the yeshivah, including the internal dynamics of the yeshivah itself, the relationship between the
students and the rosh yeshivah, and the occupation of the rosh yeshivah? What
was the position of the yeshivah in the community, as recognized by other Jews
or by the non-Jewish authorities, for example in issues of settlement, privileges,
and taxation; as well as the subsequent relation between the yeshivah and the
community of the city in which the yeshivah was located? Finally, what was
the nature of the movement of scholars and students and the subsequent relation of scholars and students in geographically diverse areas.

The yeshivah was an institution of advanced talmudic study, unlike the
Judenschul and other institutions that seem to have been directed primarily to
small children.[66] According to Bonfil, it could be designated in a variety of ways
and could refer to

> a group of students gathered around a master who regularly teaches at a
> given place. It might refer to a group of students in some kind of framework
> within the social context of the time (e.g., a company of scholars). It could
> refer to a group who studied together in the synagogue following prayers, or
> any other framework of study, including one supported by a wealthy man in
> his own home and at his expense. Finally, it might mean a meeting-place for
> established Talmudic scholars, who had already mastered the tradition and
> constituted a kind of *collegium* of scholars or jurists.[67]

Unlike the large yeshivot particularly in southern France of the high Middle
Ages (during the period of the Tosafists), the yeshivot described in the German
sources of the later Middle Ages were rather small, often with a limited number of students living in the rosh yeshivah's house, often times, in fact, sup-

---

[65] Eight in Bavaria, 2 in modern Baden-Württemburg, 2 in Lower Saxony, 4 in
Czechoslovakia, 3 near Erfurt, 1 in Lower Austria, 1 in Lower Alsace, and 1 each in
Hesse and North-Rhine Westphalia.

[66] Ephraim Kanarfogel argues that there was no formal system of Jewish elementary
education in the Middle Ages. See his *Jewish Education and Society in the High Middle
Ages.*

[67] The situation is described for Italy in Robert Bonfil, *Rabbis and Jewish Communities
in Renaissance Italy.* Bonfil writes that "the focus of intellectual activity within Jewish
society was the Talmudic academy—the yeshivah. There is a certain confusion regarding the use of this term in the sources from the period. At times, one must refer to
the context in which the term is used in order to understand what is being referred
to ..." See pp. 18–19.

ported by the rosh yeshivah himself.[68] Some yeshivot may have had only a handful of students, such as that of Rabbi Jacob of Ulm, who was a rabbi in Nördlingen between 1462 and 1482. Even the most important yeshivot, such as that of Rabbi Jacob Molin, probably had no more than about fifty students.[69] The number of students, however, could vary drastically from region to region and from year to year. In 1518 in Regensburg there were about 80, presumably foreign, students in a total resident Jewish population of 500, and in Rothenburg ob der Tauber, a community that had about 200 Jews at the end of the fourteenth century, but probably less than one third of that in the late fifteenth century, we find at least ten foreign students per year in the 1460s and 1470s—though the number varied from year to year. Probably representative was the yeshivah of Rabbi Nathan ha-Levi Eppstein (1398–c. 1460), whose yeshivah had six students in 1447.[70]

The yeshivah was a unique institution, that at times seems to have had the appearance of an early medieval university, though with different goals and procedures, and at other times the characteristics of a private tutor or association.[71] The relationship between students and rashei yeshivah, or heads of the yeshivah, could be quite close. Israel Isserlein was, for example, closely involved in many facets of the lives of his students—from daily provisions and housing,[72] to festive celebrations, and even at death; when one of his students died, Isserlein fasted the entire day. Often, in the prayers for the dead, teachers were named along with the next of kin of the deceased.[73] In a letter of protection (*Schutzbrief*) acquired by Rabbi Lebelang in 1365 in Weinheim, the rabbi was allowed residence and granted permission to establish a yeshivah; he was also assured protection for his students.[74] Oftentimes, students within the yeshivah were related to the rosh yeshivah. Israel Isserlein, for example, studied with his uncle Rabbi Aaron Blümlein in Krems an der Donau, and Rabbi Nathan Eger's son studied with his father in Eger.[75] The examples could be greatly multiplied. There were other social and cultural ties between the students and teachers as well. In Regensburg at Chanukah the students and the rabbis of the yeshivah would go together door to door in the Jewish quarter and demand their *Chanukah-geld*.[76]

---

[68] See for example Rabbi Susskind or Jekutiel of Cologne at the end of the fourteenth and beginning of the fifteenth century who housed several students in his own house; see *GJ*, vol. 3, Köln.

[69] See Nördlingen and Mainz.

[70] *GJ*, vol. 3, Frankfurt am Main.

[71] See Mordechai Breuer, "Toward the Investigation of the Typology of Western Yeshivot in the Middle Ages."

[72] For eating with students, see ibid., p. 50.

[73] See Louis Ginzberg, *Students, Scholars and Saints* (Philadelphia, 1928), p. 79.

[74] *GJ*, vol. 3, Weinheim.

[75] Ibid., Eger.

[76] Ibid., Regensburg.

Unlike the yeshivot of mid-sixteenth century Italy, however, whose rashei yeshivah were remunerated for their services by the community,[77] the directors of the yeshivot in late medieval Germany, and for that matter frequently the communal rabbis as well, had to provide for themselves. Some rabbis received tax exemptions, but the majority brought in independent incomes to support themselves, and, frequently, their students as well. Rabbi Moses of Halle, for example, had a yeshivah in the 1440s that was established at his own expense in his own residence.[78]

Ephraim Kanarforgel has noted, in differentiating Sephardic and Ashkenazic support of education and scholars, that Spanish Jewish communities were more likely to support and grant tax exemptions to scholars because these scholars were more directly involved in service to their communities.[79] To what extent does this observation apply to late medieval Ashkenaz? There is, in fact, a lively debate in some of the responsa regarding the question of tax exemption for scholars. In his responsum 163,[80] for example, Jacob Weil attacked what he saw as the abuse of scholarly status in the rabbinate. Some rabbis, he noted, considered themselves scholars[81] and took ancient laws regarding the privileges and exemptions granted to them to apply to themselves. They fancied that they could judge cases alone (without a court), that they could fine anyone who insulted them, that they were exempt from community taxation, and that they might claim a lost article as their own without having to produce witnesses to that effect. According to Weil, however, who cited a long tradition passed on to him by his mentor, the Maharil, scholars should not be too particular about fining those who insult them. Furthermore, because of sins there were no scholars at that time who knew the tractate *Kallah*,[82] one of the requirements given in the Talmud as a prerequisite for receiving the title of scholar.

If not yet a professionalized scholarly class, what occupations did rashei yeshivot practice? The important Rabbi Jacob Molin, the Maharil, was a matchmaker,[83] while other authorities had businesses, such as Rabbi Süssmann and

---

[77] Bonfil, *Rabbis and Jewish Communities*, p. 20.

[78] GJ, vol. 3, Halle.

[79] Kanarfogel, *Jewish Education*, p. 62.

[80] This responsum is mistakenly listed as number 166 by Solomon B. Freehof (*A Treasury of Responsa*), who translates it, pp. 61–65.

[81] For a summary of opinions on this subject in this period, see Yedidya Dinari, *The Rabbis of Germany and Austria at the Close of the Middle Ages: Their Conceptions and Halacha-Writings*, pp. 19–27, and for a discussion of scholars passing judgment by themselves, see Israel Israel Yuval, *Scholars in Their Time: The Religious Leadership of German Jewry in the Late Middle Ages*, pp. 404–423.

[82] The allusion here is to the Talmud, tractate Shabbat 114a. The tractate of *Kallah*, is a minor tractate appended to the fourth order, *Nezikin*, of the Babylonian Talmud. Some commentators, however, question whether the reference quoted above refers to this tractate or a semi-annual assembly by the Babylonian scholars which was termed kallah. See the *Encyclopedia Judaica*, "Kallah" (c. 709–710).

[83] Simon Schwarzfuchs, *A Concise History of the Rabbinate*, p. 19.

Rabbi Moses of Vienna of Amberg who were both involved in money-lending.[84] In some cases, rashei yeshivah were actually taxed based on the number of students that they had.[85] The students themselves most likely did not work on a full-time basis, but some undoubtedly did. Typically students were not citizens of the city and were considered foreign Jews. As such they were often exempt from city taxes as in Cologne. In Amberg, students paid taxes only if they were engaged in businesses. Even when students were not regarded as citizens, they might nonetheless be held responsible for tax payments, as in Rothenburg ob der Tauber.

A yeshivah could have influence in the city in which it was located as well as in smaller satellite communities nearby. Oftentimes, students from the yeshivah would conduct religious services in these smaller communities, or serve as rabbis or cantors (*hazzanim*) during the holidays.[86] In many cases, legal questions were directed to rabbinic authorities, be they communal heads or rashei yeshivah; and in some cases, smaller communities were subject to the authority of a larger community close by—again, at times, depending upon the particular community and individual situation, the yeshivah and its head could play an important role in these matters.

In many of the communities with yeshivot in late medieval Germany, the head of the yeshivah typically served in a similar communal capacity as *av bet din* (head of the Jewish court), *Judenmeister*, or community rabbi.

In Italy, Robert Bonfil has traced the origins of the community-appointed rabbi to the middle of the sixteenth century. For Bonfil, the office of the appointed rabbi needs to be seen within the context of the crystallization of communal organization and the erosion of the rabbi's personal authority, and at the expense of the rosh yeshivah.[87] Bonfil goes on to differentiate the perceived needs reflected in a communally appointed rabbi as opposed to a rosh yeshivah, who often participated in communal functions and courts, but who was not appointed by the community. He writes that:

> in creating the office of the appointed rabbi, Jewish society, which saw the basis of its existence as rooted in a sacred normative system, undoubtedly demonstrated its need to establish fixed and institutionalized organizational frameworks besides the informal authority of a *rosh-yeshiva*. What made the communities feel such a need? As we said, the appeal of the *rosh-yeshiva* depended solely upon the particular characteristics of a given rabbi, the admiration felt towards him by the community, and the sacral aura, which surrounded the yeshiva. We may assume that the fear arose that, in the absence of institutionalized norms in this area, such an appeal might itself not be possible, thereby hampering the proper functioning of the institutions of social organization . . .[88]

---

[84] GJ, vol. 3, Amberg.
[85] See discussion of the *Schülergeld* in ibid., Mainz, for example.
[86] Ibid.
[87] Bonfil, *Rabbis and Jewish Communities*, p. 102.
[88] Ibid., p. 106.

The situation is not so clear for late medieval Germany. Though not explicitly listed in the sources as communal appointments, rabbis and rashei yeshivah in Germany frequently functioned as such. Jacob Weil and others discuss the case of rabbis who fashion themselves as directors of communities but who have not been officially appointed by the community, and therefore have no precedence—in Breslau and Regensburg, for example. Yet the very fact that these discussions were taking place in the responsa suggests that in many cases rabbis and rashei yeshivah were considered community leaders, though perhaps not "community rabbis," even if not appointed by the community in any strictly official capacity. The tensions between communal function and official communal service, however, suggest that significant transformations were brewing within the German communities during the fifteenth century—changes that may eventually have resulted in the same communal structure outlined by Bonfil for mid-sixteenth century Italy.[89]

The rashei yeshivah can not be directly connected to the position of the community rabbi—especially in areas in which there was more than one rabbi. In smaller communities with yeshivot one could, however, expect the community rabbi and the rosh yeshivah to be the same person, as in Weinheim in the 1360s where Rabbi Lebelang established a yeshivah but was also listed as the *meister* and *hochmeister*. Similarly, in Halle around 1430, Rabbi Abraham ben Eliyahu Katz directed the Jewish court, established a yeshivah, and preached in the synagogue. He also offered religious instruction to the Jews of Halberstadt and the surrounding area. In the larger communities the situation was more complicated. Rabbi Aaron Blümlein was called from Krems to be both rabbi of the community and director of the yeshivah in Vienna in 1418—suggesting a connection between the two. Rabbi Pinchas of Schweidnitz was likewise both head of the Jewish court and of the yeshivah around 1450, as was Rabbi Jacob ben Jekutiel Segal Gelnhausen, the nephew of the Maharil, in Augsburg before Jacob Weil settled there. Rabbi Süsskind Jekutiel of Cologne was called "Judenbischof," and he served as community rabbi, a member of the court and had several Talmud students in his house. Rabbi Jacob of Ulm, also with a small yeshivah, was regarded by local Christians as the *hochmeister* of the Jews between 1462 and 1482 in Nördlingen. Rabbi Salman Kohen of Biberach seems to have been recognized as the director of a yeshivah, before 1417, and as community rabbi and member of the court in Nuremberg until his death in 1444. Still, not all cases of rashei yeshivah serving on the Jewish court should be taken to indicate the role of community rabbi, and, many rashei yeshivah are not mentioned in any formal communal function. Even when rashei yeshivah were important communal leaders, they could also remain detached from the community in important ways. Rabbi Nathan Eger, for example, kept his own synagogue and followed his own customs for himself and his students. Similarly,

---

[89] See chapter 7.

Rabbi Weil's students in Erfurt prayed in their own synagogue. In Prague one gets the sense that there was a director of a community yeshivah, who was also the community rabbi; but other yeshivot also existed alongside the community one. In general, one must conclude that in the fifteenth century the yeshivah was not a communal institution.[90]

The situation in the larger communities varied, and seems in many cases to have depended upon the individual rabbi in question. It seems likely that an individual rabbi of great stature who was accepted, though perhaps not yet appointed, by the community would, as a matter of course, establish a yeshivah—perhaps not the only one in the city. So, to assess the relationship of community rabbis and rashei yeshivah is a dangerous and problematic operation. In many cities, we have record of a community rabbi and the hint that he may have had a yeshivah, as for example in Brünn for Rabbi Veybuzz. Some city records do, however, hint at a communal organization indicated for a later period. In that light it may be instructive to review some of the responsa discussion about this issue.

Weil discussed a number of conflicts between rabbis and communities; the Bruna affair, to be discussed at length in the next chapter, as well as the incident of Rabbi Solomon Shapiro, who tried to install himself as community rabbi without the community's approval. Rabbi Weil sided with the community and advised Shapiro to stop his efforts: "You cannot judge anybody against his will, and especially not in Breslau, because they do not want to accept your opinion," he wrote.[91]

Weil's statements imply that the position of "community rabbi" was or could be different from the position of head of a yeshivah. Weil's comments also indicate that the rabbinate was not yet a profession, and, therefore, one scholar could not assume precedence over another, unless appointed by the community; and that seems clearly not to have been the norm.

While cases of communal appointment did exist, it appears that most German rabbis in the fifteenth century were not yet "formally appointed by the communities in which they resided."[92] Instead, it was the teacher who ordained the rabbi who typically directed his student to a new position. Weil's own appointment in Nuremberg, for example, was at the behest of his mentor the Maharil. Later, when Weil moved to Augsburg, it was a relative of the Maharil's whom Weil replaced.[93] Israel Bruna, who himself had been involved in a major struggle for power, issued a certificate to Rabbi David Frank, and noted that:

> I inform you that I have given authority and permission to my relative the eminent Rabbi David Frank, may the Lord save and redeem him, to exercise his supremacy in the city of Nuremberg in all matters pertinent to the

---

[90] Breuer, "The Position of the Rabbinate," p. 63.
[91] Cited in Schwarzfuchs, *A Concise History of the Rabbinate*, p. 30.
[92] Ibid., p. 75.
[93] See Yuval, *Scholars in Their Time*, pp. 80–81.

rabbinate, just as David Sprintz who is related to me by marriage; . . . he may
set up a Yeshiva for himself or arrange divorces, halitsot, deal with weddings,
pronounce blessings of wedding and compel litigants to be judged by him,
judge and instruct, with or without Rabbi David Sprintz's agreement, and
nobody may oppose it.[94]

Of course, this document makes no specific reference to communal functions,
but many of these purely rabbinic functions no doubt were also communal in
some sense. The document also reveals the close relationship between many
of the primary rabbis of the period—relatives and close friends who may have
studied under the same teacher for a certain period of time.[95]

Individual conditions could vary from yeshivah to yeshivah and from individual to individual. Was there a standard body of teaching or a corpus of texts
studied at the yeshivot? Judging from the responsa literature of the fifteenth
century, we can conclude that there were standard works, such as the Mordechai,
writings of the Maharam as well as Maimonides, in addition to more standard
Talmudic works and local takkanot, or ordinances. The books found in a number of individual libraries reveal a wide-ranging scholarship in late medieval
Germany. Indeed, for the period before the middle of the fourteenth century,
Ephraim Kanarfogel has suggested that Ashkenazic scholars were immensely
and broadly learned, much more than their Sephardic counterparts. A number
of libraries and book inventories are mentioned throughout Germania Judaica,
and they do suggest a tremendous diversity of books copied, collected, and, presumably, studied. Individual libraries, though not necessarily part of the yeshivah
itself, may offer some clues. In Eger, for example, a library comprised of ten
books was located, and included prayerbooks and biblical material, in addition
to a copy of Maimonides' Mishneh Torah (with commentary), part of Alfasi's
Talmud commentary, the Semak (Sefer Mitzvot Katan), and a work by Asher
ben Yechiel (the Rosh). A much more substantial library has been found in
Oppenheim. The library belonged to Menachem Menchen ben Nathan, who
may have been Seligman Bing's brother. The library contained more than 100
manuscripts, including several philosophical and kabbalistic works, such as
Sha'are Zedek (Joseph Gikatilla), the Sefer Chasidim, a commentary on the ten
sefirot, as well as works by Maimonides and possibly Judah Ibn Tibbon. Evidence
of a kabbalistic work being copied was also be found in Molsheim, and the
polemical Sefer Nizzahon of Yom Tov Lippman Mühlhausen was found in
Eggenfelden. There is mention of numerous halakhic works being copied
(Mödling, Kaiserstuhl, Brünn, Halberstadt, Andernach, Kreuznach, Wernigrode)
as well as commentaries, including those of Rashi (Görlitz) and David Kimhi
(Oberndorf). This breadth of works suggests that we need further information
about Ashkenazic scholarship and that we must perhaps reassess the scholarly
influence of fifteenth-century German Jews.

---

[94] Cited in Schwarzfuchs, A Concise History of the Rabbinate, p. 33.
[95] See Yuval, Scholars in Their Time.

CONCLUSION

It has been noted that the position of the rabbinate was becoming professionalized by the end of the fourteenth century—indeed that is when semikhah,
or ordination, was introduced into Ashkenazic Jewry, and the period when we
begin to find traces of actual formal appointments of rabbis by communities.
The introduction of semikhah has variously been interpreted as a sign of religious decline, communal decline, or the significant position of academic scholarship within Ashkenazic as opposed to Sephardic Jewry.[96] It is clear from the
information we have available in a number of fifteenth-century responsa, as well
as in the lack of large numbers of rabbinic contracts before the sixteenth century,[97] however, that the transition of the rabbinical position, rabbinic authority, the professionalization of the rabbinate, or whatever one wants to term it,
and so the re-conceptualization of the community began after the Black Death,
perhaps in response to transformed conditions and urgent need, but did not
result in a complete transformation of rabbinic or communal institutions before
the sixteenth century. Mordechai Breuer has argued persuasively that the professionalization, which initially served an important function in maintaining community immediately after the tragedies of the Black Death, later, in
the fifteenth century, helped to undermine the position of the rabbi within the
community, particularly in relation to lay communal authority, even when the
rabbi retained his religious function.[98] The very professionalization seems to
have reflected, or created, deep tensions within the Jewish communities.

As we have seen, the professionalization of the rabbinate had a number of
other important repercussions, including the increased localization of Jewish
structures of authority: despite the example of Jacob Weil, there are numerous
accounts of rabbis attempting to prevent the settlement of a rival in their community. In addition, it has been argued that the professionalization of the rabbinate affected social dynamics within the community, for example the proliferation
of divorce in Jewish communities in the fifteenth century. Combined with professional and social interests the severity of divorce tended to become minimized, particularly with the growing demand for the rabbi's services that
contributed to both his professional and financial well-being. The dramatic
increase in rabbinic literature dealing with issues surrounding divorce, argues
Israel Yuval,[99] offers clear proof that a certain system of theoretical legitimacy
was being constructed in order to extend and enhance the power of the rabbi
and the dependence on his services by the community.

In the fifteenth century lay leaders took over many duties that had formerly
belonged to the rabbinate.[100] The title of *manhig* (leader), previously reserved

---

[96] See Kanarfogel, *Jewish Education*, especially pp. 64–65.
[97] Ibid., n. 50, p. 161. See also Schwarzfuchs, *A Concise History of the Rabbinate*.
[98] Breuer, "The Position of the Rabbinate," p. 63.
[99] See Israel Yuval, "An Appeal Against the Proliferation of Divorce in Fifteenth
Century Germany."
[100] Breuer, "The Position of the Rabbinate," pp. 60 and 66.

for rabbis, was newly applied to lay leaders as well in the fifteenth century; and, in cases where there was no competent rabbi, an experienced communal leader could replace the rabbinic position on the Jewish court.[101] The professionalization of the rabbinate, therefore, in which the community now appointed and paid the rabbi, forced the rabbi into a position of dependence upon the wealthy lay leadership; imperial and territorial Christian intervention in the appointment of rabbis further weakened the standing of the rabbi in the Jewish community, even if it made the position more "official."

The position of the rabbi can, in fact, be seen in many of the responsa to be wavering between one of authority and manipulation; in much the same way the status of the yeshivah seems to have been in a period of transformation as well. We have not yet arrived at the end of the sixteenth century: when the contracts and understandings reached between the rabbis and the Jewish communities, for example in Italy, have been secured;[102] and when the yeshivot were largely community institutions as they were earlier in Spain. The period between the middle of the fourteenth and the beginning of the sixteenth centuries, therefore, witnessed extremely significant transformations within Jewish communal structure, and consequently communal identity. The Jewish community continued to fashion itself as a holy community, yet the real authority in most communities devolved to lay leaders with little or no scholarly Jewish credentials. Unlike the high Middle Ages, when the authority of the rabbi and the sanctity of the community depended upon the renown and influence of the leading rabbinic authorities, the later Middle Ages, with drastically increased dispersion in settlement and communal shifts, was indebted even more to a general identification of the community as a sacred entity in and of itself, and not dependent upon the rabbinic leadership, which, in any event, was slowly pushed from many of its traditional roles.

---

[101] See GJ, vol. 3, part 3 (draft 17.05.99), pp. 16 and 19.
[102] See Bonfil, *Rabbis and Jewish Communities in Renaissance Italy*.

7

Communal Conflict

The complexity and fragility of internal Jewish communal relationships in a potentially, and sometimes actively, hostile environment has been infrequently discussed. There were deep tensions running through the Jewish communities,
however, particularly in an age of forced expulsions, conversions, and secret informing. Recent research on the history of the Jews in late medieval and early modern Germany has begun to focus more extensively on internal Jewish history;
instead of broader Jewish and Christian relations, some scholars have examined the nature of Jewish community and the roles of Jews within both Jewish
and Christian society.

As a result of this new orientation, an entirely new group of poor and under
class Jews has thereby been uncovered and offered for research. Michael Toch
writes that although Jews were very much involved in money-lending, the Jews
as wealthy money-handlers were not at all typical of, nor did they reflect, the
range and diversity of Jewish social stratification and professional occupation
(see Appendix E).[1] Toch tries to show that only a handful of Jews were very
wealthy and privileged, and that a large number of middling and under class
Jews pursued diverse professions.[2]

This new emphasis on the social and economic diversity within the Jewish
communities has allowed scholars to focus on the polarization of Jewish society and internal social structure,[3] particularly during times of internal conflict.
Based on the professional diversity he outlines, Toch notes that the numerous

---

[1] Michael Toch, "Zur wirtschaftlichen Lage und Tätigkeit der Juden im deutschen
Sprachraum des Spätmittelalters."

[2] Toch offers no clue, however, as to how many Jews were actually engaged in these
professions. See also Schimmelpfennig, "Christen und Juden im Augsburg des Mittelalters,"
and Stefi Jersch-Wenzel, "Jewish Economic Activity in Early Modern Times," in Hsia
and Lehmann, eds., In and Out of the Ghetto: pp. 91–101.

[3] Yacov Guggenheim, "Meeting on the Road: Encounters between German Jews and
Christians on the Margins of Society" (pp. 125–136); Deborah Hertz, "Contacts and
Relations in the Pre-Emancipation Period—a Comment" (pp. 151–157); Christopher R.
Friedrichs, "Jews in the Imperial Cities: A Political Perspective" (pp. 275–288); and
Michael Toch, "Aspects of Stratification of Early Modern German Jewry: Population
History and Village Jews" (pp. 77–89), all in In and Out of the Ghetto.

internal conflicts in the Jewish communities, particularly over taxation and symbols of social status, leave unanswered questions about "internal Jewish solidarity in an increasingly hostile environment."[4] Petitions of poorer Jews to the temporal government complaining of unfair tax assessments, for example, were made in some cities.[5] A responsum of Rabbi Israel Isserlein, leader of the Jewish community in Austria and author of the famous work *Terumas HaDeshen*, reflects clearly the tensions that could exist as well as the important position of the wealthy within the community:

> When the wealthy and arrogant choose the judges . . . they are more ready to accept the latter's decisions. Order is maintained and they will not demand more appeals in their arrogance. . . . But there is no reason to be overly cautious with members of the middle class in such matters, since in any case they will accept the decisions and will not cause trouble.[6]

For Isserlein there existed within the Jewish community distinct groups based on both economic and social divisions.

Jewish communities, like non-Jewish communities, were not free of internal discord. Communal conflict could take a variety of forms and involve different individuals and groups. Conflict within the community developed in a number of ways and in various communal institutions and relationships. Power struggles could pit wealthy members of the community against one another. Disagreements also arose between members of the community council and between lay and religious leaders. This is not to suggest that communal conflict was the norm. But the nature and expression of conflict within the communities offers an important portal into those places where the tensions within the community were mounting and help to indicate where changes were occurring.

Attacks within the Jewish community were not new to the fifteenth century. Legislation against such acts was passed at the great Shum synod—the abbreviation for the three communities Speyer, Worms, and Mainz.[7] The same synod declared against slander and defamation of character: "No one shall call his neighbor 'bastard' or revile him with any blemish of birth. All this we have decreed under the herem (excommunication)."[8] Such cases continued, however, to be cited throughout the fifteenth century.[9] Although no deroga-

---

[4] Toch, "Zur wirtschaftlichen Lage," p. 284. Similar internal conflicts are described by Christopher R. Friedrichs for seventeenth-century Frankfurt; see his "Jews in the Imperial Cities."

[5] See Raphael Straus, *Urkunden* for examples.

[6] Hayyim Hillel Ben-Sasson, ed., *A History of the Jewish People*, p. 594.

[7] Louis Finkelstein, *Jewish Self-Government in the Middle Ages*, p. 238.

[8] Ibid., p. 247.

[9] See Weil, responsa nos. 28 and 24 for example. In the latter there was an attempt to disqualify a kohen with the accusation that his mother was wanton and licentious, suggesting that the kohen himself was of illegitimate birth. A similar accusation is leveled in Weil, responsum no. 59.

tory names were exchanged, Moses Mintz recorded a case where two kohanim (men descended from the priestly class that served in the Temple) refused to perform their religious duties together, since they considered one another enemies. Since they disliked each other so much, they argued they would not be able to perform their duties in the spirit of love.[10] Such personal animosity may have had broader communal significance and impetus, but such is often impossible to uncover, given the relatively limited scope of available sources.

Personal animosity could also turn violent. Rabbi Jacob Weil recounts a quarrel between two members of the community, recounting that:

> . . . he hit the man on his head [literally brains] with a sword and the one struck fell to the bed and was sick for four weeks and died, and it was determined that he did not die from the violence upon him . . . [he became well enough] . . . and ate a marriage feast and returned and fell ill and died. . . . I judge that the one who struck submit and will receive upon himself repentance in fasting and in lashes, and if he is rich he will give money and this will atone for him. I already ruled in the region [*medina*] of [Regensburg?] regarding one who struck an old man on the head and blood flowed from his head and I ruled regarding the one who struck [him] that he be lashed in the synagogue between the afternoon and the evening prayers as is deserving . . . I ruled that if he is poor he gives [according to his means?] . . . and if he is rich he gives graciously [at] the Torah and requests forgiveness from the one struck and that it be his intention to ask forgiveness [of the deceased] at the graveside . . .

The community, as a court, had authority to legislate in regard to both civil and criminal law, though the extent to which the Jewish community had jurisdiction in criminal cases or could mete out corporal punishment was prescribed by the Christian authorities that ruled the area.[11] In late medieval Germany, the extent of the Jewish communities' ability to recommend punishment and to punish depended upon the individual situation. In general, punishment could be corporal, social (particularly through the herem, expulsion, disqualification of communal privileges, or loss of honors or titles) or monetary. There is no record of capital punishment being prescribed for a Jew by a Jewish court in fifteenth century Germany, though there are cases of flogging (typically a flogging of humiliation, not of great physical pain).[12]

While one could cite many examples from the responsa of the period, I have elected to present only a handful that address significant and recurring issues and are substantial enough, both in length and content, to warrant closer study. I will only discuss cases of physical,[13] defamatory,[14] and familial[15]

---

[10] Moses Mintz, responsum no. 12.

[11] Menahem Elon, *Jewish Law: History, Sources, Principles*, vol. 2, pp. 696–697.

[12] Eric Zimmer, *Harmony and Discord*, pp. 90–92.

[13] See Jacob Weil, responsa nos. 28 and 87.

[14] See, for example, Ibid., responsum no. 59.

[15] In cases dealing with inheritances, for example. See Ibid., responsum no. 20,

conflict within the Jewish communities where such cases contribute to the
broader discussion of the conflict over communal authority noted at the end
of the last chapter.

Conflict within the communities frequently involved restrictions on business
or settlement, taxation, lay leadership, and rabbinic authority. Discord within
the Jewish community could be communal as well as (or in addition to) personal. Such conflict may have had something to do with the now apparent diversity of Jewish economic life and the growing disparity of wealth within the
communities as well as the shift in communal authority. How was communal
tension manifested in this very transitional period in the history of the German
Jewish commune? What do communal tensions, at least as they are related in
the important rabbinic responsa of the fifteenth century, reveal about internal
communal structure, change, and notions of community?

RESTRICTIONS ON SETTLEMENT

The community council, or the majority of the community as represented by
the council, could enact and, through the herem, enforce a variety of ordinances (*takkanot*). Although some scholars such as Rabbenu Tam in the twelfth
century opposed the principle of majority rule, it seems that the principle was
developed already by the eleventh century, when expansive biblical interpretation suggested that the majority should be followed in the area of communal
enactments.[16] The power of the majority—of taxpayers—was formalized by Meir
of Rothenburg (Maharam) in the thirteenth century. The Maharam argued
that:

> . . . It seems to me that they should gather together in a meeting all the tax-
> payers of the community, who should promise an oath (literally a "blessing")
> that everyone will give his opinion in the Name of God and for the good
> of the community; and that they should follow the decision of the majority
> as to choosing officers, appointing cantors, and fixing the treasury for char-
> ity, and in appointing charity officers, building or dismantling the synagogue,
> adding to or diminishing or acquiring a bakery, building or destroying it, in
> brief, all the needs of the community shall be decided by the majority. If the
> minority refuse and stand off at a distance and not do everything as I have
> said, then the majority shall have the power to appoint heads, to compel
> and to exert pressure, either by the laws of Israel or by the Gentile laws,
> until the minority gives their consent . . .[17]

Based on talmudic precedent, communal members could regulate and limit the
number of Jewish town residents and grant or deny the right of settlement.[18]

---

describing a quarrel between R. Jacob b. R. Shlomo and his [wife] Tsurlin, the daughter of Meir, in Vienna.
[16] Elon, *Jewish Law*, vol. 2, pp. 715 and 717.
[17] Solomon Freehof, *A Treasury of Responsa*, pp. 95–96.
[18] For a discussion of the ban on settlement, and in particular on the relation between

Weil cited a case from the city of Ulm in which the mother of a resident was expelled from her home in Coburg. She fled to her son's residence in Ulm for a number of months, but was too weak to continue on her way. Because of excessive external taxes, a member of the community demanded that she participate in the financial obligations of the community (*kehillah*).[19] Weil, in responsa 106 and 118, ruled that when she was well enough to travel it could be demanded that she leave. Earlier rabbinic authorities (Rabbenu Tam, and later Rabbi Meir of Rothenburg) had denied the legal right of the community to exclude the settlement of others, unless it was necessary to protect the community from risks associated with the entrance of that individual. Originally, this right was exercised in order to keep out dangerous individuals, as in a prohibition of settlement (*herem ha-yishuv*) in Nuremberg in the early fourteenth century attempting to keep out an unsavory Jew by the name of Zalkind of Neumarkt.[20] But one can find cases when this protective right was used for other ends as well. Weil reports that in the community of Ulm an ordinance was passed to the effect that any member of the kehillah was prohibited from attempting to settle a person from outside the community in their midst:

> Should a relative of one of the permanent residents request aid from the latter to persuade the civil authorities to grant him a permanent right to settle, that resident must first notify the community at large. He is obligated to do so in order that the community shall be in the position to counteract the effort with all their power.[21]

What is significant to note here is the attempt at internal cohesiveness within the community and the attempts to keep out both Jewish foreigners and the meddling of Christian authority. It was the right of settlement that allowed one into the community, but this right could only be granted by the members of the community themselves. The community was viewed as a body with particular political and social powers, both in its own sphere but also in negotiations with the non-Jewish authorities.

Jewish autonomy and Christian authority in this regard, see Alfred Haverkamp, "'Concivilitas' von Christen und Juden in Aschkenas im Mittelalter," pp. 132–134.

[19] Weil, responsum no. 106, ". . . Rabbi Zalman against Rabbi Seligman on account of his mother (Seligman's) and demanded that she give for all of the burden of the city. . . ." Later in the same responsum, Seligman argued that the case of his mother was different from that of an individual who was resident in the city, and working, for twelve months, thus becoming "like the people of the city." In responsa nos. 107 and 118 Weil reported that an ordinance was passed in Ulm to the effect that: "the kehillah decreed that he who has a house [in the community] is not authorized to [settle, house?] one who does not have a house." In this case, it was the possession of a house that made one a member of the community, and the community boundaries were very closely regulated.

[20] Kenneth Stow, *Alienated Minority*, p. 172.

[21] Weil, responsum no. 107. Cited in Rosensweig, *Ashkenazic Jewry in Transition*, p. 48.

To help understand this passage it is important to say something more about the Jewish community in Ulm. The earliest documentation referring to Jewish communal establishments dates to the middle of the fourteenth century.[22] The number of Jews in Ulm, however, was always relatively small. In 1427 Ulm had 13 Jewish families, in 1441 eight Jewish tax payers, in 1442 seven taxpayers, in 1457 probably only around three families, and in 1469 only two tax payers. By 1499 the number of Jews increased again to somewhere around 11 families. In the late fourteenth century the community as a whole was offered imperial protection, and in the fifteenth century individual Jews were granted the same, for three to five year periods. The event narrated in this responsum may have had other implications, as there was a major dispute in the community in 1435 that involved the civil authorities.[23] Certainly, the possibility exists that the ban on new residents and an internal dispute between two Jews, Seligman and Simlin, reflected other tensions within the community, which, combined with the small size of the community and its need to protect the volume of its business, would have been ample reasons to define in a very narrow fashion the boundaries of the community.

TAXATION

Tax money could be used for both internal services and external demands.[24] At times the taxes imposed upon the Jews by external authorities could be quite large. In 1414 the Jews of Nuremberg and Cologne contributed 12,000 fl. to Emperor Sigismund. Two years earlier the entire revenue of the empire was only 13,000 fl.[25] Such external taxes were determined by the authorities and might depend on the population, the level of business within the community, or remain fixed independently.[26] As we will see below, the system of tax law within the Jewish communities depended upon both legal principles established in the talmudic period and the "analogy drawn between the legal relations among members of the community and the legal relations among partners,"[27] as well as the provisions and demands of the civil, territorial, and/or imperial authorities. During the fifteenth century community taxes were typically assessed and frequently collected by parnasim,[28] though individual community methods of

---

[22] The first mention of the Judengasse is 1354, the synagogue, 1353. There are also fifteenth-century references to a cemetery, dance hall, and bath house in Ulm.

[23] For general information on the community in Ulm, see GJ, vol. 3, pp. 1498–1522.

[24] Elon, Jewish Law, vol. 2, p. 745.

[25] Bernard Rosensweig, "Taxation in the Late Middle Ages in Germany and Austria," p. 51.

[26] Ibid., pp. 52–53.

[27] Elon, Jewish Law, vol. 2, p. 746.

[28] See Weil, responsum no. 41, which mentions that parnasim were responsible for the assessment and collection of taxes, and that they kept a book of public debt. See also responsum no. 84 which indicates that a committee of assessors was appointed by

assessment and collection varied depending, in part, upon local custom.[29] There existed essentially three methods of tax assessment: a declarative method, in which each individual would declare his taxable possessions under oath but without itemizing them; a committee assessor method, whereby an elected committee of assessors would assess each individual's taxable wealth; or a combination of the first two methods, in which individual declarations would be reviewed by a committee of assessors.[30] Taxes within the community were typically based on the committee of assessors calculations or, in many communities, the declarations of the communal member as to the extent of his assets. According to Weil, in one such case:[31]

> The assessors evaluated M. to possess 800 gulden. Whereupon M. responded that he did not possess that sum. They, therefore, decreased their estimate to 600 gulden. M. retorted that he did not have this much either. Thereupon, they lowered their assessment to 300 gulden. To this M. replied in German: "ich habe sie kaum halber—I have hardly half." I did not want to pay the sum you assessed me. The assessors replied to him in German: "Wir wollen uns es derwahren—we want to clarify the matter for ourselves." Their intention was to bring the matter to [the attention] of the community [council(?)] whether they would agree that he should only pay from 150 gulden.[32]

This responsum demonstrates the interaction between individual members of the community and the assessors[33] and offers a positive picture of the assessors' flexibility. In the end it was to the authority of the community council that the assessors deferred. One logical question is how the assessors arrived at an evaluation apparently so different than what M[eir] himself claimed to have, and how was the truth of the matter determined. That the discussion between the two parties was in German, I will have occasion to discuss more fully in the conclusion of this chapter. The payment of taxes was strictly enforced, and individuals recalcitrant of paying could have business restrictions placed upon them.[34] If it was determined that an individual had indeed made a false tax oath he would not be accepted as a witness in the future and in cases of litigation requiring an oath his opponent would be able to take an oath and receive payment.[35]

---

the community council, and which details the types of property considered taxable and exempt.

[29] Elon, *Jewish Law*, vol. 2, pp. 920f.

[30] Zimmer, *Harmony and Discord*, pp. 31f.

[31] Weil, responsum no. 124, quoted in Zimmer, *Harmony and Discord*, p. 34.

[32] Ibid., responsum no. 84.

[33] Regarding appeal of tax assessment, see Elon, *Jewish Law*, vol. 2, pp. 747f.

[34] Joseph Colon, responsum no. 17, and Weil, responsum no. 147. According to Zimmer, the proliferation of individual tax arrangements with the civil authorities in the fifteenth century is a clear indication of the disintegration of the Jewish community structure and sense of identity in the fifteenth century (*Harmony and Discord*, p. 39).

[35] Finkelstein, *Jewish Self-Government in the Middle Ages*, p. 238.

In general, taxes were collected according to property, not by head, unless extraordinary taxes were levied on the community. Usually, taxes were collected once a year.[36] The taxes of the community were either paid individually or, more typically, pooled as a communal unit, and so the Jewish community was responsible for assessing and administering the collection.[37] Although not generally encouraged, individuals were at times allowed to arrange their own taxes with the civil authorities. Small suburban communities were generally incorporated with the closest large community and treated as an economic unit.[38]

The declaration, assessment, and payment of taxes could be a particularly volatile process. A quarrel arose between the council (*chavurah*) of Landau and an individual Jew by the name of Reuven (Reuven and Shimon are the names generally used to represent different parties in the responsa), who had rented a house in the city but refused to participate in the community's financial obligations to the Christian authorities on the grounds that he did not intend to establish permanent residence in the city. In a very telling interpretation of the situation, Weil ruled that even if Reuven had been exempted by the city council from paying regular taxes, he was nevertheless responsible to contribute for extraordinary taxes: "And even if they [the council] said from the beginning that a certain person would not give, even so he is obliged [in this case of extraordinary taxes] because it is not him alone to whom the steward refers but to Reuven and all of the tax-payers, that they are to give to the rulers at this [particular] time, as if they were regular taxes."[39] Weil goes one step further in this responsum, writing that it was because of these extraordinary taxes of the Christian authorities that Rabbenu Tam permitted Jews to accept interest on loans from gentiles, even if the Jews were wealthy, because the Jews would be obliged to "honor them [the Christian authorities] with taxes," that is the burdens forced upon them by the king and ministers.

Certain objects were exempted from taxation.[40] Objects from which income was generated or potentially generated were taxable, but houses generally were not taxed, unless they were rented or put up for sale. In some communities wealth was taxed whether or not it was idle.[41] Despite the complaints of wealthy community members, vacant houses were generally considered exempt. Still, in

---

[36] Four days were particularly prominent: January 1, May 1, November 11, and December 25; though often the payment could be given in two installments.

[37] Rosensweig, "Taxation in the Late Middle Ages in Germany and Austria," p. 65.

[38] Moses Mintz, responsum no. 1.

[39] Weil, responsum no. 38.

[40] Ibid., responsum no. 133. The issues discussed in this paragraph are based upon Zimmer, *Harmony and Discord* and Rosensweig, *Ashkenazic Jewry in Transition*.

[41] See also Menahem of Merseburg, nos. 11 and 33. For a general discussion, see Rosensweig, "Taxation in the Late Middle Ages in Germany and Austria," pp. 77–78 and 87f. See also Zimmer, *Harmony and Discord*, pp. 40f, for exempted persons; pp. 52f, for exempted objects.

times of emergency all houses might be assessed. Fields and vineyards were taxed but traditionally only about half of their real value because of the high rate of overhead associated with their possession. Precious articles of a personal nature, such as cups and jewelry, were generally not taxed, except in Austria where all household articles, including jewelry, were assessed. Diamonds and precious stones, however, were not exempt. Ordinary household items and wardrobes were not taxed, but they could be assessed if placed for sale, since they would generate income. Books were generally exempt, in order to encourage their production and purchase. Donations were tax exempt.

Some individuals were, however, exempt or partially exempt from taxation, including talmudic scholars (particularly after the thirteenth century), orphans, elementary school teachers, scribes, servants, unemployed or retired people, transients, or those exempted by the civil authorities.[42] Even these exempted or partially exempted persons, however, would be taxed in emergency situations, or when an extraordinary tax was levied on the community. Much, however, depended on the custom of the region. In the Rhineland, for example, talmudic scholars were not exempted from taxation. In the fifteenth century unemployed people probably shared the tax burden, and the attitude to transients such as students, traveling businessmen, and Jews expelled from other cities varied enormously. In general the laws of taxation were based on local or regional customs.

LAY LEADERSHIP

The power of the parnasim increased dramatically during the thirteenth and fourteenth centuries. The council in Worms, for example, became more and more oligarchic. Eventually, in 1312, the parnasim were chosen for life appointments and gained the exclusive right to appoint their successors. In some places, lay communal leaders even began to operate their own courts of arbitration.[43] Such monopolization did not necessarily lead to corruption, but it might. The parnasim elected or, in the following case, appointed by the civil authorities, did not always appear to have the best interest of the community at large in mind. Rabbi Weil lamented that:

> And a parnas that was appointed over the congregation (*tsibur*) and after ten years the people called upon him and challenged him that he needed to make an account for each and every thing . . .
> On account of our sins, a calamity has befallen most communities, inasmuch as the parnasim oppress and despotically rule over the people. Bent upon their personal gain rather than the glory of heaven, they lessen their own burden and shift it upon the shoulders of the unfortunate masses.[44]

---

[42] Ibid.

[43] Stow, *Alienated Minority*, p. 166.

[44] Weil responsum no. 173, quoted in Zimmer, *Harmony and Discord*, p. 21; the first part of the quote is my translation, the second that of Zimmer.

What is particularly intriguing about this brief passage is that the dichotomy of the parnas and the people was created, and the parnasim in general—Weil went so far as to write in "most communities"—were depicted as ruling over the other members of the community (here I take congregation and community to be the same, indicating the extent to which the community was a sacralized entity). Such individuals detached themselves from the community not only in their oppression but in their search for their own personal gain, which, in this case, was not contrasted with the fortune of the community but the glory of heaven. The concept of the "burden" was central to the notion of the shared front of the community, but the addition of the "unfortunate masses" and "despotic rule," seems to have had a rather new ring. To be sure, lording over the community was not novel to the fifteenth century, but the language employed by Weil may have been.[45] We must also mention the distinction that Weil made in this responsum—dealing with the fear that the parnas embezzled community funds—between officials elected by the community and those appointed by the civil government. Weil's language might have something to do with the fact that the official was appointed from outside, and so Weil stresses the oppression of the community in order to distinguish between communal authority and the imposition of external authority. It is also important to remember that the actions of the lay leader were being recounted in a rabbinic responsum. Still, the discussion of authority within the community is significant.

RABBINIC AUTHORITY

It has been argued that because of the increasing power of the parnasim, combined with the growing disputes amongst the rabbis themselves, a professionalized rabbinate came into being.[46] Many of the disputes recorded in the responsa did indeed involve contending rabbis. From the general rhetoric employed in the responsa it seems as if the level of talmudic scholarship and disposition of scholars decreased in the fifteenth century.[47] According to Weil the rabbinic title was often used to extort money and prestige.[48] Often, too, rabbinic titles were merely purchased.[49] The rabbis and their decisions might be opposed. At times, civil authorities had to be enlisted to enforce rabbinic authority. In other cases, lay opposition to this increased rabbinic authority was not always quiet and could be manifest in slandering and interrupting services and classes.[50]

---

[45] Compare with the position of Meir of Rothenburg, the Maharam.

[46] Stow, *Alienated Minority*, pp. 169–170.

[47] Weil, responsa nos. 146, 85, and 128. See also Israel Isserlein, *Peskim* no. 255; and Israel Bruna, responsum no. 7 (to Weil). Responsum no. 85 discusses such a disreputable pseudo-scholar, Abraham, whose divorces Weil invalidated.

[48] Ibid., responsum no. 163.

[49] Ibid., dinim (in his *She'elot u-teshuvot*), no. 68; Isserlein, responsum no. 274.

[50] Ibid., responsa nos. 140, 147, and 152. See also Bruna, responsum no. 231.

According to responsum 157 of Weil, "seeing that many calamities are upon us from mockers and deriders of the Torah and of scholars and they do not heed the preaching, if for example they reproach . . . they stand against us both our bodies and our [material] abundance . . ."[51] Rabbis were often, therefore, afraid to judge cases. At times, it was only after embarrassment and social pressure that rabbis agreed to adjudicate. According to Moses Mintz:

> I did not want to accept the case. Because of my reluctance, the prayers were interrupted evenings and mornings until the members at large began to murmur and gossip saying, 'there is neither judge nor justice in Ulm.' This was very embarrassing. Due to their pressure, I finally accepted to be their judge.[52]

Tensions between would-be rabbinic leaders and the members of community councils could run high. The community in Breslau, for example, complained to Weil that a rabbi tried to force his authority on the community, without being invited to serve as the community rabbi.[53]

A number of controversies over the struggle for authority, particularly between rabbis and communities or competing rabbis, arose in this period. The results of such quarrels could be devastating. Weil could therefore rue that:

> Behold, the result of this controversy is that the country is in a state of disorder and confusion. There is no peace for those who leave or those who come. There is no order in the kehillah. There are so many obstacles to be feared as a result.[54]

Weil argued that such controversies led to disorder within the kehillah as well as the country. Here his notion of community encompassed both the individual community involved in the dispute as well as the larger region (*medinah*), which was necessarily affected by the confusion, both in communal authority and Jewish solidarity. Throughout Weil's responsa there was a very serious effort to maintain the cohesiveness of the Jewish community in the face of communal conflict.

One dispute arose in Nuremberg involving two rabbis. The committee of the city decided that both rabbis be allowed to teach, but on alternate days. Another controversy in Nuremberg occurred when Rabbi Sprinz revoked the permission that he had originally granted to his student Rabbi David Frank to teach. Frank was then accused of reporting Sprinz to the civil authorities.[55] In Prague the resident Rabbi Eliyah did not allow Rabbi Eliezer of Passau, a

---

[51] Ibid., responsum no. 157. For fear of antagonizing powerful litigants, see Weil, responsa nos. 146 and 149.

[52] Mintz, responsum no. 74, quoted in Zimmer, *Harmony and Discord*, p. 71.

[53] Weil, responsum no. 146.

[54] Zimmer, *Harmony and Discord*, p. 127. See Weil, responsum no. 146. See also Bruna, responsa nos. 58 and 86.

[55] See Bruna, responsa nos. 58, 126, 253, 277, and 281; Colon, responsum no. 167; Isserlein, *Peskim* nos. 174 and 175.

student of Jacob Weil, who settled in Prague, to fulfill rabbinic functions or begin his own yeshivah, although he was allowed to teach some students in his own home. In the end Eliezar adjudicated and then disregarded the settlement.[56]

One of the more famous rabbinic controversies of the period was the Anshel-Bruna affair[57] in Regensburg. In 1456 a great conflict broke out between Rabbi Anshel and Rabbi Bruna, when Rabbi Bruna settled in Regensburg, established his own school, and offered his services to the community. Rabbi Anshel, who had been in Regensburg before 1450, viewed Bruna's competition as an intrusion in what he considered to be his sole rabbinic prerogative in the city. Rabbi Bruna, however, refused to acquiesce in the matter and the conflict escalated. A number of Rabbi Anshel's students sought to hasten Rabbi Bruna's exodus from the city and they set out to shame him publicly. They would walk out when he began to lecture, they accused him of heresy, and, it is reported by Rabbi Israel Bruna (responsum 231), a cross was etched on his synagogue seat.

Rabbi Weil, however, judged that both rabbis should be allowed to reside and teach in the city. He cited the permission that he himself had received to establish a yeshivah in Nuremberg although one already existed there. Weil noted that neither of the contending rabbis had been chosen by the Regensburg community to become their rabbi.

> I have written that I know that the community did not choose either Rabbi Anshel or Rabbi Bruna and both need to give [taxes] like one of the community; one does not have precedence in this matter over the other even if Rabbi Anshel was in Regensburg before, *and the position of Rabbi Bruna is no less because the community did not appoint him over themselves as the head* . . . Whether or not the residents in the city receive upon themselves the first scholar or officer . . . the second scholar has the same right as the first. . . .[58] [emphasis added]

According to this interpretation, the rabbinate was not yet a profession. Appointments were typically private not public affairs, and therefore one scholar could not assume precedence over another.

Unlike business dealings, in which restrictive monopolies could be declared, the education of Jews, in Weil's estimation, was not subject to monopoly. Throughout his responsum 131 Weil was gravely concerned to maintain not only the educational integrity but the solidarity of the community as well. The presence of rabbis was essential for the continuation of Jewish learning. From this standpoint, Weil noted that it was common to have more than one rabbi in a given community, a situation that could be found in a number of cities, such as Vienna, Krems, and Nuremberg.

---

[56] Weil, responsum no. 151.
[57] Zimmer, *Harmony and Discord*, p. 124. See Bruna, responsa nos. 253, 25, 167, 193, 195, 196, and 268; Isserlein, *Peskim* nos. 127 and 128; Mintz, responsa nos. 76 and 63c; and Weil, responsum no. 151.
[58] Weil, responsum no. 151.

Weil was, however, at times skeptical of the power sought by rabbinic leaders. In responsum 163 he attacked what he saw as the abuse of scholarly status in the rabbinate. Citing the *Sefer Agudah* of Alexander Cohen Süsslein of Frankfurt, Weil noted that the status of scholar no longer existed when that book was written, and therefore:

> How much the more does it apply in these days when, for our many sins, the minds have shrunk, and many rabbis do not even know the shape of the Law . . . Yet some of them are proud enough to act in lordly fashion and to misuse the crown of the rabbinate. Their whole intention is for their own glory: that they may sit at the head and walk at the head, and there are even some whose intention it is to amass money. They do not have the moral qualities which the rabbis enumerate that a scholar should have. Their whole purpose is to benefit themselves. Some of them are not even careful in their actions. Their reputation is bad and through them the name of Heaven is profaned.[59]

Weil reprimanded such leaders for lording over others and seeking only their own personal gain. Rabbi Weil was disappointed that there were rabbis who were not only poor scholars but who were also "unable to distinguish between their right and their left." His comments on this subject were quite similar to his reflections on similarly dishonest lay leaders, such as we have seen above. Although we must understand that much of the passage is composed of strong rhetoric, the changes rued by Rabbi Weil, given the context I have sketched generally, take on significance.

COMMUNAL AND INDIVIDUAL OBLIGATIONS: THE CASE OF ABRAHAM EZRA

Conflicts could develop within the community or even between communities. One extremely interesting case considered by Rabbi Jacob Weil (responsum 148, which continues into 149 and is also treated by Israel Bruna in his responsum 236) dealt with a dispute between a certain (Rabbi) David Sender,[60] described in glowing terms for his personal traits (at least by the inquirer), and Abraham Ezra, Weil's relative and an extremely wealthy financier to numerous princes. The inquirer claimed to be informed of the details of the case by a reliable and nonpartisan witness who heard the details from officials (non-Jewish), and a witness who was the representative of David Sender sent to Abraham Ezra (informing him that the duke—who is not named in the responsum, but seems to have been Friedrich II of Saxony[61]—could not be mollified and would not lower the 1,000 fl. ransom he had set); contributing to the case was also a series of correspondence.

---

[59] This responsum is listed as number 166 by Freehof (*A Treasury of Responsa*), who translates it, pp. 61–65; here at p. 64.

[60] For David Zenner, see *GJ*, vol. 3, Erfurt, p. 313 which describes him as a wealthy community head in Erfurt.

[61] Ibid., p. 731.

According to the details of the case as presented first in the question and then in Weil's detailed analytical response, the wife and granddaughter of Abraham Ezra were incarcerated and held for a 1,000 fl. ransom by the duke (in 1445). When the ransom had not been paid, after a five-month period,[62] the duke grew greatly agitated and threatened to forcibly convert the girl if Abraham Ezra did not pay the sum demanded. There was some fear that the wife was also in danger, due to her age and the increasing threats from the duke. Abraham Ezra, however, was of the opinion that the more he entered into the matter the worse it would become. Instead he sent his son to the bishop—again, specifics are not offered in the responsum, but this probably refers to the bishop of Merseburg[63]—to inform him of the situation and to ask his advice. The bishop, however, maintained that there was nothing that he could do.

David Sender placed himself in great physical danger and did everything in his power to secure the release of Abraham Ezra's wife and granddaughter from imprisonment. Sender was certain that the women's lives were in danger and he communicated this to Abraham Ezra. The responsum went on to extol the very great merits and positive qualities of Sender, who it concluded took upon himself the burden of getting involved on behalf of the women, and berated Abraham Ezra who repaid the good deeds of Sender, who had secured the release of the women, with evil by not repaying him. According to the inquirer, we do not want the actions of Abraham Ezra to become an example to Jews not to do good deeds. This being said, the inquirer himself wrote to Abraham Ezra instructing him not to desecrate the name of heaven and to repay the 1,000 gold pieces to Sender. Abraham Ezra returned "a flood of words—lies and falsehoods" to the effect that he had been waiting on the promise of the bishop and for the duke to be mollified.

The inquirer, however, cited earlier evidence that the bishop admitted that he had no ability to save the captives. It was clear, wrote the inquirer, that before the land was divided it was possible for the bishop to do something— but such was no longer the case. Although the women had been in captivity for five months, Abraham Ezra insisted that he was waiting for the duke to lower the ransom. Rabbi Sender, argued Abraham Ezra, acted without his permission and paid a ransom greater than he could afford, and not commensurate with the value of the captives. Abraham Ezra, however, continued the inquirer, was very wealthy and the extent of his wealth was well known.

Weil asserted that if one could transgress the Sabbath when there was risk to life, certainly in monetary matters one was required to do whatever necessary to save those whose lives were in danger. Weil noted that Abraham Ezra's wealth was well known (it was so vast that nobody knew his full value). Citing

---

[62] Ibid., p. 732.
[63] Ibid., p. 731.

Maimonides, Weil added that a wealthy person may not exempt himself from monetary obligations through his own oath. Still, Abraham Ezra persisted in trying to make himself out as poor: he claimed that a business venture into which he had entered turned sour. Even so, concluded Weil, an individual was obliged to ransom his friend's wife, and the husband was obliged to pay. Weil cited the case of a neighbor who was not permitted to stand by and watch something bad happen if a friend was drowning in the river, being dragged by wild animals, or pursued by robbers. The case was no less than the biblical one of the shepherd who called other shepherds to his aid. The shepherds who saved him testified to their expenses and the saved shepherd, by an obligation from the Torah, repaid them. In this case, however, Rabbi Sender did not have to swear an oath detailing his actions since there were witnesses present at the negotiations with the duke. Weil seemed concerned that Abraham Ezra might have attempted to take ransom money from his granddaughter's funds—his granddaughter was apparently an orphan. Such transfer of funds might have been permissible, conceded Weil, since in this case it would not have been possible to wait until the girl was old enough to allocate the funds herself and so pay her own ransom.[64]

Because Weil depended so heavily on the rulings of Meir ben Barukh of Rothenburg ob der Tauber (c. 1215–1293), Maharam, and because Maharam was so intimately familiar with cases of ransoming, it is worth considering Maharam's reflections on this subject in some detail. Throughout his responsa, Maharam dealt at great length with ransoming captives as well as issues related to the captivity. Maharam offered the same arguments that Weil would later use regarding the drowning man,[65] even though he did not allow himself to be ransomed from captivity, from which, after a number of years he finally died. Maharam did not want the capturing and ransoming of Jews to turn into a popular business. Still, he did allow for the ransoming of women and children.

Maharam, intimately familiar with the process of ransoming, described its aspects: "For when a person is thrown into prison for purposes of extortion, his rapacious captors first demand a huge sum as ransom, ten times his capital, without knowledge of the actual value of his assets. This is done to frighten him, force him to come to terms quickly, and pay a high ransom." Often the captors are looking to be freed from the debt that they owe to the Jew, but, questioned Maharam, since "the duke did not mind becoming known as a thief, a robber, a highwayman, and an extortionist; why should he object to the

---

[64] The general discussion of the significance of ransoming captives occurs in the opening pages of the Talmud in tractate *Baba Bathra* (in the Gemara—the commentary of the Mishnah). Even here the case is linked closely with the allocation of the funds of orphans.

[65] See Avraham Yaakov Finkel, *The Responsa Anthology*, p. 18. In the Gemara in *Sanhedrin* 73a.

appellation defaulter?"[66] Maharam added that "when a Jew falls into the clutches of gentiles, his life as well as his property is in jeopardy; he can expect from them neither pity, mercy, nor restraint. The gentiles are happy to hold a Jew in their power, and, especially when commissioned by another Jew, their cruelty is boundless. They consider it legitimate and even praiseworthy to rob, maim, and even murder a Jew. Therefore, a person who delivers a fellow Jew into the hands of gentiles is directly responsible for all their cruelties."[67] A Jew should, therefore, be ransomed even against his will,[68] and a husband was directly responsible to ransom his wife[69] and if both have been captured the wife was to be ransomed first for fear of her being outraged. Maharam followed a similar line of logic later to be adduced and extended by Weil: "Moreover, had A acted on his own initiative and ransomed B without being requested to do so, he would still have been entitled to reimbursement, for a Jew should be ransomed even against his express will, and may be charged with the expenses thus incurred."[70]

As Maharam made very clear there existed a very fine line between taxation and ransom:

> Although, in our case, the overlord had incarcerated his Jews, we know that he merely wanted to collect from them an extraordinarily heavy tax and was afraid that they might flee his domain to escape payment. Were he certain that they would not have fled, he would not have incarcerated them and would have collected the same amount in a normal manner. Therefore, the money paid to the overlord was paid as a tax, and not as a ransom; especially so, since A alone was not arrested but together with the rest of the community, and no false charges were brought against him.[71]

This case is of interest for a number of reasons and at a number of levels. First, it highlights the significant danger, as well as the extreme possibilities for success, of Jewish-Christian relations in Germany. Abraham Ezra was both successful and sought after for his financial strength, with a 20 year relationship to the regional princes (between 1422 and 1427 he loaned more than 1,000 fl. to Friedrich IV, count of Meissen and later Friedrich I duke of Saxony from 1425–1428, and in 1428 1,200 fl. to Friedrich II, duke of Saxony) and extensive individual privileges, at the same time that he was extorted for funds. The precarious balance of late medieval Jewry is very much evident here. The case, therefore, reveals the larger political drama upon which Jewish life in Germany was being played.

[66] See Irving Agus, *Rabbi Meir of Rothenburg*, here at no. 609, pp. 564–565.
[67] Ibid., no. 783, p. 678.
[68] Ibid., nos. 572 and 576, p. 541.
[69] Ibid., nos. 493 and 292.
[70] Ibid., no. 573, p. 531.
[71] Ibid., no. 567, pp. 518–519.

This case, however, also indicates something of the disjunction within the Jewish community itself and the tensions between communal obligation and individual position. But what can the responsum tell us about Jewish communal identity? First, it suggests that community must be read at multiple levels. There are, for example, communities defined by familial relations; communities relative to geography, religious and for that matter ethical behaviors; communities of political and economic standing; communities at varying times. The case also reveals that community sits upon a confluence of individual rights and collective responsibilities—to what extent can the individual remain individual, by, for example, declaring his own wealth, and to what extent is he a part of a more "imagined" group based on a variety of defining qualities?

In this case, Weil noted the dangerous environment in which the Jews lived and superimposed a morally defined nature to community, that is, stepping in to assist your "neighbor" when he was in danger of his life. The case was not presented as one of purely halakhic decisions, but rather as one of morally binding dicta. In this analysis, Weil presupposed Maharam's decisions; it was not his interpretation, therefore, that revealed serious transformation within Jewish community. After all Maharam had to deal with very similar issues. The nature of the case in and of itself—in which the logic adduced by the Maharam was played within a different field—one that pitted Jew against Jew in the recovery of ransom money expended, indicated conflict within the community (again as posited to some extent, but not so blatantly, in Maharam) and was reflective of attempts to define community, especially in an age of increased individual privilege and status (see below).

This case suggests finally, that internal communal identities among German Christians were complex—the power of the duke and the bishop and their dynamic and changing relationship that renders them more or less powerful at given times—and interconnected with issues of authority that directly affected the Jews. Jewish interests, as we will see in the next example, could also contribute to the position of any of these external sources of authority, through Jewish contribution or reaction to the actions of authorities, or through the prospects of what could be forced from Jews.

INTRA-COMMUNAL OBLIGATIONS: THE CASE OF WÜRZBURG AND HEIDINGSFELD

In an important responsum of Moses Mintz, which not coincidentally alluded to the case just described in Weil,[72] we find a discussion that is similar in some respects to the one just discussed, but very different in its analysis. Mintz began very humbly arguing that he was not really qualified, given his limited knowledge, to judge in this case that pitted the Jewish community of Würzburg against the Jewish community of Heidingsfeld, a small rural Jewish community

---

[72] See the introduction to Mintz's responsa, p. 4, and the accompanying n. 26.

near Würzburg. Nevertheless, Mintz asserted that this was a very dangerous case that could spawn serious enmity amongst the Jews themselves, and that it was therefore necessary to adjudicate. Briefly stated, the complaint was that the bishop of Würzburg had announced an evil decree to expel the Jews from all his lands in 1450.[73] In an effort to annul the decree, the Jews of Würzburg had attempted to raise money with which to placate the bishop. All communities in the area were asked to contribute to this cause. In the complaint by Heidingsfeld, which we do not have, it was apparently argued that Würzburg had not recently dealt appropriately with it. The Heidingsfeld Jews further argued that the bishop did not request a tax from their community. Rather, he wanted to expel the Jews from his territory, and he did not have the power or the authority to do so in Heidingsfeld. The responsum went on to report information gleaned from inner advisory circles of the bishop that the bishop did indeed intend to expel all the Jews from his territory, but that the act had not been finalized due to conflict within the state. The responsum next more directly responded to the Heidingsfeld argument and made two key arguments: first, that if the Jews in Würzburg were indeed expelled it would also be at least as difficult, if not more so, for the Jews of Heidingsfeld to collect their outstanding debts; for when there were Jews in Würzburg it was possible to pursue the villagers in court, but if there were no Jews in Würzburg the Heidingsfeld position would be severely compromised. Second, regarding the possibility advanced by the Heidingsfeld Jews, that the non-Jewish citizens would allow them to remain, Mintz responded that he did not consider this as a possibility: since the city was very small and so close to Würzburg, being in reality almost a part of Würzburg, and subservient to the bishop, he saw little chance that the Jews of Heidingsfeld would be safe from the local officials without the bishop's protection; alternately he could not understand why the bishop would give the local officials permission to maintain their Jews, if he had himself expelled them from his territory, despite the income that he received from them. In any event, if one stepped outside Heidingsfeld, one was in the territory under the direct authority of the bishop, and so even if Jews were somehow allowed to remain in Heidingsfeld they would not be able to travel to collect their debts or to settle anywhere else in the province.

Mintz concluded that the Heidingsfeld Jews were obliged to try to forestall the danger of the expulsion, since according to the moral precept of Isaiah, a man is obliged to help his brother (Isaiah 41:6: "They helped everyone his neighbor; and everyone said to his brother, Be of good courage."). As we will see below, the case was not only about moral obligation; Mintz believed that the Heidingsfeld Jews were directly involved in and affected by the situation and

---

[73] The Bishop Gottfried Schenk von Limpurg had decreed the expulsion of the Jews from his territory in 1450, and at least 18 Jewish families moved, or planned to move, from Würzburg in that same year. See *GJ*, vol. 3, p. 1704.

were obliged to contribute to the efforts to annul the decree due to the benefit which they would reap if the decree was in fact annulled.

Mintz argued that the Jews of Heidingsfeld must contribute their share, since it would cost much less initially for the effort to save the Würzburg community than the great deal more to collect their debts if the Jews of Würzburg were expelled. The general themes and conclusions outlined early in the responsum were taken up, as Mintz answered the complaint lodged by the Heidingsfeld Jews and assessed a number of talmudic and biblical cases in his attempt to render a decision in the case; in particular, Mintz relied very heavily on discussions in the talmudic tractate *Bava Kamma* and their subsequent elucidation. These cases dealt with questions of liability and legal agreements, and the cases that he cited provide an important insight in to his vision of community.

One case that Mintz found to be different from the case in question was that of the individual in *Bava Kamma* 115b. According to the text of the Mishnah:

> If one man was coming along with a barrel of wine and another with a jug of honey, and the barrel of honey happened to crack, and the other one poured out his wine and rescued the honey into his [empty] barrel he would be able to claim no more than the value of his services; but if he said [at the outset], 'I am going to rescue your honey and I expect to be paid the value of my wine,' the other has to pay him [accordingly]. So also if a river swept away his donkey and another man's donkey, his donkey being only worth a *maneh* and his fellow's donkey 200 *zuz*, and he left his own donkey [to its fate], and rescued the other man's donkey, he would be able to claim no more than the value of his services; but if he said to him [at the outset], "I am going to rescue your donkey, and I expect to be paid at least the value of my donkey,' the other would have to pay him [accordingly].[74]

It is informative that Mintz had to rely largely on biblical and talmudic passages in related subjects, and only occasionally, in particular regarding questions of lending and taxation, on more recent rabbinic interpretations, largely those of Mordechai ben Hillel ha-Kohen (ca. 1240–1298), in his assessment of the case.[75] As Mintz noted repeatedly, this was a serious and very unique case.

---

[74] See Soncino translation of the Mishnah in *Bava Kamma*, 115a–b.

[75] Mordechai ben Hillel ha-Kohen was a student of Maharam and Isaac ben Moses (Or Zarua). His extensive and still famous commentary on the Talmud, *Sefer Mordechai*, is generally referred to as "the Mordechai." Regarding the question whether legislation enacted in Barcelona was binding on the Jews in communities surrounding the city, whose consent was not sought, the Rashba had earlier indicated that although Barcelona and the surrounding villages comprised a single entity in the payment of taxes "we never adopt legislation affecting them, even though we are the majority and the leading province for all matters." See Elon, *Jewish Law*, vol. 2, pp. 669f. Rashba went on to indicate that there were places where the main kehillah did legislate for satellite communities, however. What is noteworthy is that it was local custom that dictated the practices,

There are some obvious implications of the case selected by Mintz and his attempts to fashion it into a related precedent for the case before him. The talmudic case, cited by the Heidingsfeld Jews, suggests that they had no obligation to pay for services that might be rendered to them by the Würzburg community since they did not agree to any such terms. The second half of the passage suggests that if the Würzburg Jews acted on behalf of the Heidingsfeld Jews, the Würzburg Jews were indeed entitled to some payment for the services they performed, if not for the value of the goods they spent in the effort. For Mintz, the talmudic case, even in its broader context, was not comparable to the case in question. The two communities were much more intimately bound together than the residents of Heidingsfeld would admit, and the fate of the Heidingsfeld community was ostensibly that of the Würzburg community. In the talmudic case we are dealing with a question of material goods, in the current case, in the actual existence of the communities themselves. The talmudic case is not one of strict obligation to behave in a certain way, though of course it seems the right thing to do. But the fifteenth-century case was a matter of obligation, implying again no separation in the fate and so in the obligations of the two communities. The two fifteenth-century communities were not really free and independent individuals or agents as in the talmudic case.

Mintz cited another case along the same lines, this time regarding someone chasing away a lion and so preventing the lion from damaging his neighbor's property. The one who chased the lion away did not get any financial compensation for his actions,[76] since he acted voluntarily, but he also did not lose anything, in fact he only stood to gain (spiritually) by acting this way. Mintz contrasted the case before him, however, in which there was a loss to the sacred community in Würzburg because the Jews of Heidingsfeld were "destroying the countryside."

Mintz also considered the case of the Jew who paid a debt on his friend's behalf. The person paying did not gain, but he did suffer a loss; the loss was not entirely clear, however, as he might be repaid in the future. In this case, the individual was not risking his life, only using his money. Again, the Heidingsfeld Jews seem to have been saying that they did not want to be saved, or better, that they really did not need to be saved, and that they should not, therefore, have been asked to pay. But, Mintz noted when an individual says "do not redeem me with my own money" he should not be listened to. This was the case even if he claimed that he would be able to get himself freed. At this point, Mintz cited both Maharam and the case we reviewed above from Weil. Mintz equated the individual not wanting to be ransomed with the

---

and that the inclusion in a tax unit, most likely a definition imposed from without was seen as being different from internal boundaries that affected internal legislation.

[76] See *Bava Kamma* 58a.

Heidingsfeld community; for we did not know how bad things might get or how far the expulsion was likely to go and what effects it might have on all Jews in the region. Mintz took the Jews of Heidingsfeld to task since in their efforts to assert that the situation was not so bad they made Jews of other towns believe that the situation was not so dangerous. By causing an uproar throughout the land they were in a sense dangerous and, rhetorically, enemies of Israel.

Mintz moved to discuss questions of obligations. He cited Maharam to the effect that those with property in a city, but not residing in the city, must still pay taxes like those residing in the city. This was particularly the case for the Heidingsfeld community, which called attention to itself by its usurious conduct in the countryside; Mintz implied that this was in fact the root of the reason why the bishop sought to expel the Jews from his lands. Mintz next discussed the case of taxation, arguing that the current case was not similar. In the case of taxation there was a dispute between Rabbenu Tam and Maharam. Rabbenu Tam held that there was no tax on a loan received (since it was not completely the property of either the lender or the borrower). Maharam, however, maintained that the borrower was the possessor of the money and as such might do what he wanted with the funds, had to pay taxes on them, and may make them heritable. Mintz could have been suggesting here that the salvation that the Heidingsfeld Jews might receive because of their financial contributions was similar to the loan received; since it was theirs, i.e., since the Jews of Heidingsfeld needed and would receive the loan, they should be taxed upon it and were responsible for paying their tax. Returning to the tax issue from a slightly different angle, Mintz noted that when the king set a tax he set a specific amount, and when one individual did not pay the others had unfairly to pay more, since a certain sum was expected. In any event, this case was different since the bishop was not asking for taxes; rather money was being raised to assuage the bishop and bribe his advisors in an effort to annul the burgeoning decree.

Mintz, nevertheless, concluded that the Heidingsfeld Jews could not be obliged equally in this matter, particularly because it was impossible to guarantee the results; on the other hand, they could not be exempted, but rather had to pay a sensible share of the burden. Mintz calculated that every Jew in Würzburg should pay twice the amount of each Jew in Heidingsfeld; but if that was still not enough money, the proportion should be half each. This seemed acceptable, in any case, because this was not a matter of taxes, but rather of other expenditures needed in the effort to have the decree annulled. In any event, the Jews of Heidingsfeld would benefit from the annulment of the decree and, in fact, could not continue if the Jews of Würzburg were actually expelled, as noted earlier. Mintz offered that if the facts of the case changed or other similar cases arose he would judge them according to their individual contexts.

Unlike the previous responsum, the focus here was upon communal relations as a category of business transactions, and the discussion was couched in the language of corporate benefit. Similar to Weil's responsum, however, Mintz utilized discussions of the relations between individuals, only expanded to reflect the relationship between communities—communities here being taken as corporate individuals—and so he examined the moral obligations of communal interaction. The responsum revealed similar political turmoil in the non-Jewish world, and demonstrated clearly the vulnerable position of the Jews themselves, caught between lordly political maneuvers.

The bulk of the responsum dealt with a regional conception of community and detailed the important and interconnected relations between the Jews living in the region, as well as the sensitive issues of internal communal governance and control. This discussion was significant, given the general trend toward regional organization of Jewish community, because of external territorial policies and internal communal shifts. Franz-Josef Ziwes has traced these changes in the middle Rhineland particularly after the resettlement of the Jews after the Black Death pogroms and massacres.[77] Echoing the move toward regional identity, it is informative that Mintz elsewhere and somewhat later (1462) ruled in regard to the reach of the authority of a large Jewish community into neighboring areas that the competence of a community extends as far as its "cemetery region."[78] But the regional transformation, and the overlap of identities and loyalties was not strictly a transformation within the Jewish communities. As Tom Scott has demonstrated there were significant connections and dependencies between rural and urban areas—in this case in the Upper Rhine—as for example, in cases of urban charters incorporating petty rural traders or regional and territorial guilds that embraced both town and country.[79] As Scott notes, complex bonds of interest held regions together and helped craft regional identity at a number of levels.[80] According to Scott, "even when collective economic interests prevailed, the perception of what constituted collectivity underwent a shift as confessional ties linking cities arterially began to overlay the bonds between lords and cities forged by mutual economic interests within the radius of the southern Upper Rhine."[81]

CONCLUSION

The lack of clarity of the nature of community and the boundaries of community, as well as the tensions within the communities, were betrayed by the communal conflict evident in much of the responsa literature. Such communal tension was manifest most readily, and most easily accessible for us, in

---

[77] See Franz-Josef Ziwes, *Studien zur Geschichte der Juden im mittleren Rheingebiet*, pp. 126f and passim for discussion of communal changes after the Black Death; See also the forthcoming *GJ*, vol. 3, part 3, "Gemeinde," pp. 32–36 (draft 17.05.99).

[78] "Friedhofsbezirk"—See Ziwes, *Studien zur Geschichte der Juden im mittleren Rheingebiet*, pp. 82–83.

[79] Tom Scott, *Regional Identity and Economic Change: The Upper Rhine, 1450–1600*, p. 116.

[80] Scott speaks of overlapping regional identities. See Ibid., p. 272.

[81] Ibid., pp. 270–271.

quarrels between individuals in positions of power, such as important councilmen and rabbis. The very nature of the conflict, however, suggests something
more than mere social and economic upheaval. The entire nature of the Jewish
community was undergoing serious transformation in the fifteenth century.
Allow me to cite one final responsum at some length. Weil wrote in responsum 101 the following:

> Regarding a dispute between Rabbi Tuvia and Rabbi Vredel; that Rabbi Tuvia
> wants to testify in German (*lashon ashkenaz*) and Rabbi Vredel responds that
> [by] his heritage he does not know how to write in German; therefore, this
> was one of the many ordinances ordained at the synod [literally band, crowd]
> in Nuremberg. If one of the litigants wants to testify in German and if you
> ordained in your land according to the plain exposition [of the Nuremberg
> takkanah] then the ruling is [with] Rabbi Tuvia, whether Rabbi Vredel him-
> self is expert in German or whether, because of his heritage, he does not
> know how to write German well enough that he would not speak. Thus they
> ordained for every person that even if they are unemployed, someone whose
> heritage does not allow them to write German, and he says so, he will hire
> [someone to write for him]. . . .

This is an important responsum, for it suggests not only that the use of paid
advocates was on the rise in the Jewish communities,[82] but that the very center of community and self-identification was shifting as well. This responsum
suggests that the center of authority was shifting to a *va'ad*-based authority as
we mentioned earlier. But more importantly, the number of people proficient
in Hebrew must have declined significantly by this period. These communities
could more truthfully style themselves Ashkenazic. If it is true that Hebrew as
a communal language was dramatically on the decline, then our discussion of
the emergence of a professionalized rabbinate takes on greater significance.
While the professional rabbi of the late fourteenth century was instrumental
in regrouping and reforming the German Jewish communities after the devastating attacks and dispersions of the Black Death, the position of the rabbi—
particularly in regard to his social and political functions, though likely not as
extensively with regard to his halakhic jurisdiction—came to be challenged, weakened and appropriated throughout the fifteenth century, particularly in the
absence of strong and domineering rabbinic personalities. This was not the situation everywhere, and there is no doubt that some rabbis maintained their
authority in a variety of communal areas and functions. Rabbi Segal could thus
write in the fifteenth century that the "Talmudic scholars have become objects
of sanctity on account of the knowledge of the Torah within them."[83] Rabbi
Moses Mintz could note that "every rabbi and expert has been ordained a rabbi
by a preceding rabbi all the way back to Moses our Master . . . a rod and strap

[82] See Zimmer, *Harmony and Discord*, pp. 83–84. See also Weil, responsum no. 119;
Isserlein, responsum no. 354; and Bruna, responsum no. 132.
[83] Ben-Sasson, *A History of the Jewish People*, p. 597.

had been given in his hand . . . and no householder . . . may in any way question the words of the rabbi."[84] Such statements, however, may have been more
reflective of desired authority than reality.

The conflicts discussed in this chapter reveal the development of new social
and economic pressures mapped onto traditionally defined notions of community. The conflicts recorded for the later Middle Ages were in part responses
to the increasing tensions with the Christian authorities that often resulted in
the expulsion of the Jews. At the same time, however, the conflicts reveal
significant changes within the Jewish communities themselves; regional identity became more imperative, and consequently less clear, and the struggle for
power, that we discussed in the last chapter, increased dramatically in important ways. Increasing social polarization created tensions within and between
communities. While it has been clear that Jewish community developed because
of both internal and external conditions, the latter have not yet been treated
extensively, except to suggest that external conditions played an important role
in changing communal identity. How Jews thought about and interacted with
their Christian neighbors, however, is a theme of great significance that has
not yet been discussed in this book, but must now be addressed. As with
Christian images of Jews, we will find that traditional images of Christians combined with varying relations to produce important catalysts for change, both
in Jewish communal identity and Jewish and Christian relations, in the later
Middle Ages.

---

[84] Ibid., p. 598.

8

Jewish and Christian[1] Relations

Jacob Katz has argued persuasively that despite theoretical theological divisions, Jews, particularly by the end of the Middle Ages, very often did not count Christians among the gentiles referred to in the Talmud, and that they continued to interact with Christians on a regular basis. The relation between practice and theory was not always clear, though both had profound importance for authorities in the later Middle Ages.

The questions we need to address in this chapter, therefore, concern the extent to which the traditional theological model upon which Jews based their interactions with Christians changed or remained the same, the extent to which Jews and Christians interacted at a variety of levels and in a myriad of relations, and finally, how such models and interactions affected the way the Jews defined their communities.

MEDIEVAL JEWISH VIEWS OF CHRISTIANS

It is certain that the Jewish community was never completely isolated from the society that surrounded it. Jews not only spoke Hebrew but were also fluent in the languages of the countries in which they lived. In addition, many famous Jewish writers copied either the form or content of Christian scholarship in the same way that Christians borrowed from Jews. For example, Moses Rieti's *Migdash Me'at* was modeled on Dante's *Divina Commedia*, the *Arba'ah Turim* of Rabbi Jacob ben Asher displays similarities to the *Siete Partidas* of King Alfonso the Wise of Castile, David Gans' *Zemah David* drew heavily from contemporary German chronicles,[2] and Azaria de Rossi's *Meor Enayim* was

---

[1] Throughout this chapter I have used the term Christian when it is obvious from the context of the rabbinic responsa that "gentile" refers to Christian, and in general, gentile and Christian may be taken as interchangeable throughout this chapter. On the one hand use of this terminology allows a more even comparison of Jewish attitudes of and interactions with Christians; on the other, it is misleading, in that general discussions about interactions with gentiles presuppose a much broader tradition of rabbinic discussion and so have a much broader interpretative power.

[2] Robert Bonfil, "Aliens Within," p. 290.

modeled upon classical literature.[3] Even the great polemicist of the fifteenth
century Yom Tov Lipman Mülhausen conceded that:

> And if the slave should say, 'I love my Lord' in Heaven 'and my wife, the
> hind of love, and I study Torah, Talmud and later authorities, and I love the
> Lord and His Unity, and His faith is engraved in my heart and I am able
> to comprehend one thing from another, so I do not need to study others or
> the wisdom of the ancients,' let him take to heart . . . that this will not be
> enough for the great scholar. . . . Many of the degrees of wisdom can be
> found among the sages of Greece . . . and from this do not make the error
> that those degrees are forbidden, namely natural science and astronomy and
> philosophy, for these are branches of our faith and lead us to the love of
> His Blessed Name and fear of Him . . . and this is not Greek wisdom but the
> wisdom of all who are wise.[4]

In administrative structures, tax procedures, and reading material,[5] Jews and
Christians did not always live in mutually exclusive worlds. Christians and Jews
often lived in close proximity and it is certain that they interacted on a daily
basis, not only for business. Judging from the recurring prohibitions of Jews gambling, dancing, and eating with Christians (by both Jewish and Christian authorities), these activities must have occurred frequently.[6] Jews certainly conducted
business with Christians, as a great many of the responsa attest. The majority
of responsa dealing with such business interactions were concerned primarily
with money-handling, but there were also numerous responsa which demonstrated that Jews had other business (often sales) with Christians.[7]

Still, the tensions inherent in Jewish and Christian relations had long-standing theoretical roots that were often equally significant to the dynamic interaction, both positive and negative, experienced by Jews and Christians. The
first Mishnah of the Talmud in tractate *Avodah Zarah* (Idol Worship) states,
for example, that:

---

[3] Amos Funkenstein, "History, Apologetics, and Humanism," in his *Perceptions of
Jewish History*, p. 215.

[4] Hayyim Hillel Ben-Sasson, *A History of the Jewish People*, p. 624.

[5] For the early modern period, see Christoph Daxelmüller, "Organization Forms of
Jewish Popular Culture since the Middle Ages," in *In and Out of the Ghetto*, pp. 29–48.

[6] See, for example, Jacob Weil, responsa nos. 16, 17, and 135; Israel Bruna, responsa
nos. 135 and 136, which deal with card playing, and nos. 71 and 146; and Israel
Isserlein, *Terumas Ha-Deshen*, responsum no. 239. See also Louis Finkelstein, *Jewish Self-
Government*, p. 242. Shum legislation had earlier dealt with the question of dressing like
gentiles (See Finkelstein, *Jewish Self-Government*, p. 233), and the issue was certainly not
dead in the fifteenth century, as responsa nos. 239–241 of Isserlein, *Terumas Ha-Deshen*
make clear. Informing against the Jewish community was also a frequent issue (Finkelstein,
Jewish Self-Government, pp. 238 and in the case of manipulating non-Jewish authority
against other Jews, p. 243.)

[7] See Bruna, responsa nos. 57 and 245; in responsum no. 10 Bruna deals with a case
of Christians hired to stitch clothes during the year when Jews are forbidden to do so
for themselves; see also Isserlein, *Terumas Ha-Deshen*, responsa nos. 206 and 310.

Before the festivals[8] of idolaters[9] for three days, it is forbidden to take and give with them,[10] to lend them money or to borrow money from them, to repay a debt from them. Rabbi Yehuda says: we may accept from them repayment of a debt, since it causes them distress: they [the sages] said to him: even if it cause him distress now, he will rejoice at a later time.

According to the gloss of Rashi (Rabbi Solomon ben Isaac of Troyes, 1040–1105) the reason for this restriction was that the idolater would take any money earned through business with the Jew so close to the time of his idolatrous festival and use it for idol worship. Jews, however, were strictly forbidden to assist anyone to worship idols, and therefore they should be careful not to assist the idol-worshippers indirectly by supplying them with funds for their festivals. The Tosafists (a school of leading scholars whose writings consisted of additions and analytic comments on or explanations of preceding commentators, especial Rashi), however, explained the passage differently. Although in principle Christians, throughout the Middle Ages—particularly up until the twelfth century[11]— were viewed as idolaters (because of their belief in the Trinity, which it was asserted by Jews was contrary to the principles of monotheism), the Tosafists allowed business dealings with Christians based upon the following logic enunciated by the Tosafist Rabbi Jacob ben Meir, or Rabbenu Tam (1100–1171). According to Rabbenu Tam: "It is forbidden to have business dealings with them [idolaters] specifically in matters that would be used for sacrificial purposes. But the ruling does not at all apply to simple buying and selling..."[12]

POLEMICAL THEOLOGY

Not surprisingly, in more polemical treatments Christianity was often presented as heretical or idolatrous. The high medieval *Nizzahon Vetus* (NV) made it clear that the Talmud (or Oral Law) was a correct and necessary supplement to the Torah (Written Law) (i.e., the Old Testament; the New Testament was generally referred to as "their Torah"). According to the author of the NV "the heretics [i.e., Christians] criticize us by saying that the Talmud distorts and spoils our entire Torah and prevents us from realizing the truth by leading us astray.

---

[8] Cited in Kenneth Stow, *Alienated Minority*, p. 157.

[9] Literally worshippers of the stars and constellations, generally substituted for "idolaters" because of Christian censorship, thus giving the abbreviation that would correspond roughly to Hans Folz's book of the Talmud that he called "Agoyim."

[10] That is, transact business.

[11] Here one may cite Jacob Katz's general thesis that leniencies developed in the Jewish tradition which did not, for rather practical reasons, equate Christianity with idolatry. Stow (*Alienated Minority*) has also argued that the exegetical methods employed by the rabbis were able to validate current practice. Even Rashi in the twelfth century, therefore, was able to set up a straw Christian middleman that allowed Jews to take interest from other Jews, a direct prohibition of the Torah. See Hayim Soloveitchik, "Pawnbroking: A Study in Ribbit and of the Halakah in Exile," here at pp. 205–206.

[12] Cited in Stow, *Alienated Minority*, p. 158.

The answer is that the Talmud is a fence and hedge around the entire Torah, for all the commandments are spread through the twenty-four books of the Bible, a little here and a little there, and one who learns a particular commandment is likely to forget it before he reaches the next."[13] Further, the very fact that the Christians did not read or understand the Talmud led them into serious mistakes:

> You may also answer that even they [Christians] would not be able to remain steadfast in their faith if not for the Talmud, for it is written, 'An Ammonite or Moabite shall not enter into the congregation of the Lord' (Deut 23:4), and it is the Talmud which explains that this refers to a male Ammonite but not to a female, to a male Moabite but not to a female. Now, since they do not study the Talmud and are consequently ignorant of this interpretation, how do they explain how David entered the congregation of the Lord or, indeed, how Jesus, who they say was descended from David, could have entered it?[14]

While Christianity is referred to as idolatrous,[15] Judaism is the one true religion. The NV employed a rather pointed logic to argue that we are commanded to "follow the majority."[16] Since only eleven nations to date had erred after Christian belief, and since there were sixty nations, including the Ishmaelites, who considered Christianity a religion of "vanity," and Jews considered Jesus to have been a human being only, Christianity could not be upheld. In addition, continued the NV, a matter was generally established by the testimony of two witnesses (Deut. 19:15). Although both Jews and Christians rejected Islam, and both Jews and Muslims rejected Christianity, all three groups admitted the truth of the Jews' Torah. Therefore "our Torah is true . . . and our God is true and eternal. Blessed is he who chose us."[17] In a rather more poetic and less characteristic argument, the NV related a story in which there was once an emperor who wanted to test the faith of Jews, Christians, and Muslims. He imprisoned one member of each of the three groups and approached each separately with an ultimatum to either change his faith or be decapitated. The Jew did not budge and was willing to die for his Torah. The Christian, after two threats, decided to live and he chose Judaism over Islam—Muhammad, their god, after all "got drunk from wine and was thrown into the garbage, and when pigs came and passed through the dump, they found him, dragged him, surrounded him, killed him, and ate him; how, then, could he be divine?"[18] The Muslim also after two threats agreed to convert and he chose Judaism, because the Torah was true, pure and clear. According to the story's end:

---

[13] David Berger, *The Jewish-Christian Debate*, no. 245, p. 230.
[14] Ibid.
[15] Ibid., no. 210, p. 206.
[16] *Exodus* 23:2.
[17] Berger, *The Jewish-Christian Debate*, no. 204, p. 203.
[18] Ibid., no. 227, p. 217.

Now, when the emperor heard that the Jew was willing to die for his Torah and would not move from his faith one bit, while the priest and the Muslim both denied their vain beliefs and accepted our faith, he himself chose our religion; he, the priest, and the Muslim were all converted and became true and genuine proselytes.[19]

The author of the NV also noted that it was only proper that the uncircumcised and impure should serve the Jews. Here the NV took a typical Christian argument and stood it on its head: Jews were not needed to witness the second coming, rather, the presence of Jews was a necessary requirement for the survival of the world. The author of the NV wrote:

> On the contrary, if not for the fact that they serve the Jews they would have been condemned to destruction, for it is written in Isaiah, 'Arise, shine, for your light has come. . . . For the nation and kingdom that will not serve you shall perish; yea, those nations shall be utterly wasted' [*Isa.* 60:1, 12]. On the other hand, as long as they serve Israel they have some hope . . .[20]

Even the case of conversion shamed the Christian faith according to the NV. For it was very easy for Jews to convert to Christianity; but an apostate from Judaism to Christianity converted only for his own motives and desires, "to give pleasure to his flesh with wine and fornication, to remove himself from the yoke of the kingdom of heaven so that he should fear nothing, to free himself from all the commandments, cleave to sin, and concern himself with worldly pleasures."[21] Converts to Judaism, on the other hand, braved the external threat of being killed, the restriction of many desires of the heart, and even wounded themselves, removing the foreskin through circumcision. "It is evident that they would not do this unless they knew for certain that their faith is without foundations and that it is all a lie, vanity, and emptiness."[22]

Regarding the circumcision of Abraham in Genesis 17, the author of the NV remarked that God did not command Abraham to be circumcised at an earlier age, "so that the people of the world would see and learn from Abraham who, although an old man, did not balk at circumcision."[23] Continued the NV, circumcision, like the Sabbath and all of the commandments of the Torah, were not abrogated with the birth of Jesus, for Jesus himself said "I have not come to destroy the law of Moses or the words of the prophets, but to fulfill them. Heaven and earth shall pass from the words of Moses. Whosoever therefore shall destroy one thing of the words of Moses shall be called the least in the kingdom of heaven."[24] Moreover, "they [Christians] do not follow the ways

---

[19] Ibid., no. 227, p. 218.
[20] Ibid., no. 212, p. 207.
[21] Ibid., no. 211, p. 206.
[22] Ibid., no. 211, pp. 206–207.
[23] Ibid., no. 12, pp. 47–48.
[24] *Matthew* 5:17–19.

of their god Jesus by circumcising themselves and observing the Sabbath and festivals as he did (for he did observe all these commandments)."[25]

The NV went on to offer a critique of Christian baptism. The problem, as the NV saw it, was that the Christians did not even follow their own sacred text, the New Testament's prescription, when they performed the rite of baptism: "they should have imitated that baptism in all of its particulars. In fact, however, Jesus and John were baptized in the Jordan, which consists of fresh water, while they are baptized in drawn water to this day."[26] The author of the NV reminded the Christians to "take care to observe the entire Law which I command you this day; do not add to it or diminish from it." (Deut. 13:1) In addition, although the New Testament taught that a man should be baptized only once, Jesus was sanctified at the hands of a man, "indeed, he was sanctified three times."[27] "What sort of god must be sanctified through removal of his impurity just like a human being?" Here the author of the NV picked up on a critical discussion—the distinction between the baptism of John and the baptism of Jesus—that would undergo serious analysis and challenge at the end of the fifteenth century.[28] If, the NV continued, as the Christians argued, the body was baptized for the sake of the soul, "why do they baptize the crosses in their houses of abomination as well as all other vessels used for their idolatry such as bells and chalices? Do these too have spirit and soul?"[29]

A very important exchange revolved around the discussion of Psalm 15. According to the Christians in the NV's polemic, Jews should not take interest from gentiles, since in their reading the Psalm stated that money should not be lent at interest, without any qualifications, independent of whether a person or a people was circumcised. According to the two parts of Psalm 15 adduced by the Christian set up in the NV, "who shall abide in your tabernacle and who shall dwell in your holy hill? He who walks uprightly and works righteousness, and speaks the truth in his heart. He who does not gossip with his tongue . . . [He who does these things] shall never stumble," and "he who does not lend his money at interest." The rationalization the NV offered here is worth quoting at some length, for the NV argued that gentiles may, at one time, have been considered "brothers," since they were descendants of Esau, but they had since disqualified themselves and were now considered strangers and indeed they defined themselves as foreigners. The entire question of permissibility to loan to gentiles at interest revolved around the break in their descent, their lineage.

---

[25] Berger, The Jewish-Christian Debate, no. 158, p. 173.

[26] Ibid., no. 157, p. 172.

[27] Ibid., no. 160, p. 174.

[28] See David Steinmetz, "The Baptism of John and the Baptism of Jesus in Huldrych Zwingli."

[29] Berger, The Jewish-Christian Debate, no. 160, pp. 174–175.

The answer is: Who gave the Torah to Israel? God. Through whom? Through Moses. Now, Moses said, 'You may take interest on loans to a Gentile, but do not take any on loans to your brother' [Deut. 23:21]. If you then say that the descendants of Esau are also called brethren, as it is written, 'You shall not abhor an Edomite, for he is your brother' [Deut. 23:8], the answer is: It is true that they were once brethren and it was forbidden to take interest from them; now, however, they have disqualified themselves and are considered strangers, for when the Temple was destroyed they did not come to help, as it is written, 'In the day that you stood aside . . . even you were as one of them' [Obad. 1:11]. Indeed, they themselves actually helped destroy it, as it is written, 'Remember, O Lord, the children of Edom in the day of Jerusalem . . .' [Ps. 137:7]. Moreover, they consider themselves foreigners, for they are not circumcised; and it is written, 'Every foreigner who fails to circumcise the flesh of his foreskin' [cf. Exodus 12:43–48]. You may then ask: Even if the fathers sinned, what is the sin of the children? The answer is that this applies indefinitely, as long as they remain rebellious. Indeed, even if they repent and become proselytes, they cannot enter the congregation of the Lord until the third generation. [Here is a real shift in the argument] Moreover, one can respond concerning interest that it represents legitimate gain, for Solomon said, 'He who increases his wealth through usury and unjust gain will gather it for one who pities the poor' [Prov. 28:8]; i.e., his sin can be expiated through charity. Now if this were regarded as robbery, how could charity help? Why, it is written, 'The sacrifice of the wicked is an abomination' [Prov. 15:8]. Moreover, it is written, 'You may not take interest from loans to your brethren, but you may do on loans to a Gentile,' i.e., to one who is uncircumcised.[30]

The central argument here was that Christians were descendants of Esau, and although Esau was the brother of Jacob (who changed his name to Israel), the father of Israel, Christians had become foreigners instead of brothers. They were rebellious and they even helped to destroy Jerusalem. Even if they repented and converted to Judaism they would not actually enter God's congregation until the third generation. Christians were counted out because they did not follow the true line of descent. This was a most significant argument, first, because it was the same line of thought that would be taken up and expanded in the late fifteenth and early sixteenth centuries; and second, because this was the argument that would have disturbed Christians the most, since they considered the "Old Testament" sacred. Why could it not be, they would argue, that Jews were really the descendants of Esau and Christians of Jacob? Such a question begged an answer from the Jews, who claimed to be the Chosen People of God. If they were the chosen people, how could their present suffering be explained?

Were similar views evident in the Jewish polemic of the later Middle Ages? According to Hayyim Hillel Ben-Sasson, the *Nizzahon* of Yom Tov Lipman

[30] Ibid., no. 123, pp. 133–134.

Mühlhausen "sums up the traditional Jewish line of defense in disputation and also puts forward systematically the arguments for attacking Christian views. Written in a rationalistic vein, it evidences signs of the strains present in the Christian church at this time."[31] The same themes outlined in the NV are taken up in the later Middle Ages but seem to have led in a somewhat different direction.

Mühlhausen's polemic was quite similar to that of the NV. He refuted the idea that there existed a new covenant between God and the Christians.[32] He further rejected the notion that the Messiah has already come, since good was not generally found everywhere.[33] Mühlhausen's discussion of circumcision began with the Christians' attack on the practice and concluded with his own defense: "The Christian mocked, saying, females who are uncircumcised have no Jewish character. They [the Christian mockers] do not know that faith does not depend upon circumcision but is in the heart; circumcision does not make a Jew of one who does not believe correctly, and one who believes correctly is a Jew even if he is not circumcised, although he is guilty of one transgression. And circumcision is not possible with women."[34] Mühlhausen insisted that circumcision is a general obligation for each man, just as for Abraham, Isaac, and Jacob, each of whom circumcised himself. The covenant was to "be in the flesh" forever. Indeed, he defended the proposition forever by asserting that in the future Israel would settle in the land of Israel forever and that the kingship of the house of David would last forever.[35] The nations of the world were to be an offering from the Jews to God, they were to be shown the way to the true faith; Mühlhausen cited Isaiah 66:20: "And they shall bring all your brethren from all the nations as an offering to the Lord, upon horses, and in chariots, and in litters, and upon mules, and upon dromedaries, to my holy mountain Jerusalem . . ."

A similar polemic went further. A disputation during a chance encounter between a Jew and a Christian was related later, at the turn of the fifteenth and sixteenth centuries, by Jochanan Luria (c. 1430–c. 1511), the wandering preacher and rosh yeshivah in Alsace who taught Joseph ben Gershon of Rosheim:

It happened to me, as I stood before the Chapter [or: Council] of the Lord Bishop of Strasbourg, and we were ordered to mark our clothes with the colour of 'Gel' [yellow] as it is customary in some places in Ashkenaz [Germany]. There came a priest and spoke to me: Jew, what is this mark that you have on your clothes of 'Gel' colour? And what does it allude to? I said: I don't

---

[31] Hayyim Hillel Ben-Sasson, Trial and Achievement, p. 273.
[32] Yom Tov Lipman Mühlhausen, Sefer Nizzahon, pp. 116–117.
[33] Ibid., p. 94.
[34] Ibid., pp. 19–20. Quoted in Ben-Sasson, Trial and Achievement, p. 273. In arguing with the Christian, Mühlhausen had to revert to a Christian framework.
[35] Mühlhausen, Sefer Nizzahon, pp. 120–121.

know: it is [by] a ruler's command. And if he should order me to carry a
stone [of] two pounds [weight] I would have to do it. Verily, [this law like
other laws that you impose on us is without reason] . . . he [the priest] was
reconciled, and all present were reconciled.[36]

The story is of interest for several reasons: first, because it demonstrates that
Jews did not necessarily "resign themselves to their fate," and second because
it demonstrates the power of the yellow patch and the questioning that it occa-
sioned. Here Luria turned the tables on the priest and, through a certain self-
proclaimed ignorance, showed the ridiculous nature of the badge requirement.
Luria's debate continued when the priest answered that:

> Let me tell you, you have gotten from the Lord Bishop a right judgment
> and just laws. The all-highest has chosen you of all nations and said, 'I have
> separated you from all the peoples to be a nation unto me.' But the works
> of the Law are not continually a mark by which separation is known. For
> you are not occupied uninterruptedly in works. Therefore, he has given you
> an outward mark and a hidden one. The circumcision is seen when one is
> naked, the Tsitsit when one is dressed, the [Jewish] house is known by the
> Mezuzah. All these separations bring you honour, for they have an hon-
> ourable meaning. If someone asks you, 'What are the Tsitsit?' answer him:
> 'The Lord of the world has ordered me, and for an important cause, to
> remember by them the works of Law.' And since you try to prevaricate and
> are ashamed of this mark—worse, you intend to go about dressed in the cloth-
> ing of Gentiles, therefore your God has decreed that you be marked by a
> badge of shame, which has no rime or reason, just as the dress of madmen
> is marked for everyone to know that they are mad.' That is the end of his
> [the priest's] words.[37]

The willingness of the priest to admit the high status of the Jews is somewhat
suspicious, and it seems more likely that Luria created a straw priest from conceptions of the priest that he himself held. At the same time the priest's concern with outward and inward signs is of interest in light of our discussion in
chapter 2. The priest's contention that Jews, although at one time they were
the Chosen People, had forsaken the Law and abandoned the very principles
to which they claimed to adhere and instead went about trumped up like non-
Jews, had a rather sharp logic to it. The priest made no mention of Jesus, and
in a sense the debate was turned entirely upon the Jew. It was because of the
Jews' lack of attentiveness to that which was given to them divinely that the
"modern" Jew suffered the embarrassments that he did. Luria, for his part, went
on to defend the fact that Jews did not openly display items such as *tsitsit* (fringes
worn on four-cornered garments), but that they nevertheless fulfilled the obligation by wearing them under their clothing. He argued that it was only the

---

[36] Cited in Hayyim Hillel Ben-Sasson, "Jewish-Christian Disputations in the Setting
of Humanism and Reformation in the German Empire," pp. 372–373.
[37] Ibid., pp. 378–379.

hooliganism of the Christians that prevented the Jews from bearing their marks openly. If one were to examine the old men who did not go out and thus were under no danger one would find that they wore their *tsitsit* openly. Luria concluded that the priest seemed pacified by this answer.

It is of interest that Luria, in the voice of the Christian, acknowledges that the marks of Jewish chosenness were both external and, more importantly, internal. If, as the Christian priest chided, Jews were negligent in the performance of the commandments, they needed only to act better or, as Luria would suggest, await a time of more favorable social conditions, when they would not be subjected to gentile oppression. Seen from this perspective, the accusation that Jews were not openly practicing the commandments could be either a ruse to inspire Jews to be more observant of the laws or a criticism of the oppressive society in which the Jews lived. But there was also a more fundamental mark of the chosenness of the Jews as a people, and that was circumcision. Here Luria tried to argue that there was something that could not be taken away from the Jew, something which, therefore, was in a sense interior, and which marked him as the chosen one of God. That was circumcision. Circumcision was not challenged here, rather it was assumed that it represented a true and unchangeable demonstration of the Jews' high position.

In another engagement with Christians Luria took up a thread from the previous discussion and turned it upon them. He wrote:

> You [the Christians] have not kept a single sign or testimony, as if you were thieving and ashamed of your descent. On the contrary, you have left us the lineage and nobility. For we keep all those—the law, the script, the language of the Book of Torah, which is the conclusive and main evidence for the Jewish faith. You have left with us the original and taken for yourself a copy. This is inconceivable, for surely there is no avoiding mistakes with copyists; civil contracts need court attestation of the correctness of a copy. With us too, when we want to see that Torah scrolls are without error, [we] take three men who read in three scrolls . . .[38]

According to Ben-Sasson, the language employed here—that of original version and copy—was a clear indication of the Renaissance humanism of the time, with its emphasis on original sources, that may have motivated not only his Christian opponents but Luria as well. The Jews, concludes Ben-Sasson, were not living in an isolated vacuum, rather they shared in the give and take and the cultural climate that surrounded them. More importantly, Luria here hit upon the central tension, which we will outline in the next chapter. Christians had not kept the true laws, the true testimony, instead they lived like thieves and were ashamed of their descent—they were after all descended from Esau and not Jacob, they were therefore not God's Chosen People. While Jews kept the true law, Christians possessed and followed a mere copy, a poor imitation

---

[38] Ibid., pp. 381–382.

strewn with errors. As much as Christians claimed to follow the true law, the original had been entrusted with the Jews. The Jews were the real holders of the true religion, of tradition, which Christians claimed falsely for themselves.

A final issue addressed by Luria regarded peace and unity amongst the world religions. Whereas Nicholas of Cusa, as we have seen, found unity in a religion based upon Jesus, Luria found it in Judaism, not in Christianity. Luria wrote:

> In this too I dispute all the nations, in particular the Christian faith in so far as they agree saying that at the end of time there will be one faith, in their language—one pastor, one flock. This belief is based on the verse 'On that day God will be one and his name one.' It follows that it is impossible for our faith to change its position from the aspect of monotheism, as we are not lacking in any aspect of the monotheistic belief, as there is not [in our faith] any plurality of persons in God, nor does he change, exchange or renew his being. He is for us the self-same in past, present, and future. Should they answer that in their Trinity the Father, the Son, and the Spirit are one too, still they cannot claim that Divine unity will be enhanced if we should accept their faith. But there is a possibility of greater Divine unity if they will accept our faith; all will concede that all religions be abolished and they will believe as we. They have no argument to advance. For if it had been written 'there will be one faith' without saying explicitly which, they could have claimed that we should believe as they do, and eat and drink with them and as they do. But now it says clearly that it [the choice] is to be [made] from the aspect of divine unity, the mouth of all those who speak falsehood will be shut.[39]

Similar lines of thought could be found in the writings of the Maharal of Prague in the sixteenth century. According to the Maharal, the very fact of Israel's Diaspora and the poor treatment of the Jews at that time did not indicate that Israel had been rejected by God. Maharal claimed, on the contrary, that Israel's election was by grace and not by merit: that is, Israel's election was not dependent upon its merits or demerits.[40] Maharal distinguished between the essential and the accidental:

> Unlike the Gentiles, Israel was created in essence by God. Though the Gentiles were also created by God, their creation was not essential. For the essence of creation was Israel. The creation of the [other] nations only follows from the creation in essence which is Israel. It is as if the creation of the nations was accidental and only follows from the formation of the essence of creation.[41]

Here Jews were reattached to the original source, to God's creation. Jews were a part of the essence of creation, and it was the tradition of this essence, a pure line of descent, which connected Jews of the sixteenth century and their

---

[39] Ibid., pp. 383–384.
[40] Byron Sherwin, *Mystical Theology*, p. 85.
[41] Ibid., p. 89.

ancestors so close to God. Despite changes in their historical development,
Jews were innately Jews. Such a conclusion is not too surprising, given the grow-
ing isolation we have outlined, but such a conclusion does demonstrate that
issues of descent and tradition were becoming central at the end of the later
Middle Ages. Jews were as aware of the importance of this issue as were
Christians, who increasingly fashioned themselves the true Jews. It would probably not be too much to say that the same phenomenon was developing in
Spain, except on a larger and more dramatic scale. A central function of the
Inquisition was to clarify and define lineage and privilege.[42] This issue is of some
importance from a comparative perspective, for as I have argued elsewhere, one
of the most important aspects of Martin Luther's discussion of the Jews, and
indeed his criticism of almost everyone, revolved around this question of self-
definition through descent and sanctity.[43]

The very foundations of community were changing in the later Middle Ages,
and the Jews, by all counts, were essential in thinking through new definitions
of descent and, in the end, of community. Some Jews were aware of this, and,
as we have seen, their writings demonstrate the difficult and imperative situation facing them at the end of the Middle Ages. But Jews were not reacting
only to external pressures; they were also dealing with issues of community,
attempting to redefine and resanctify their own identities.

JEWISH AND CHRISTIAN INTERACTION IN LATE MEDIEVAL GERMANY

Beyond theoretical categories, it is clear that Jews and Christians interacted on
a daily basis and in a variety of social, cultural, and economic ways. The political position of the Jews, while frequently compromised and dangerous, also attests
to the closeness that Jews and Christians could share, as well as the sense of
community that Jews might have with their fellow Christian residents. After
the eleventh century Jews were increasingly integrated into the life of many
cities.[44] By the early fourteenth century local Jews seem to have enjoyed the
interaction in communal affairs and protection by the civic authorities.[45] This
was so much the case that in a number of towns new Jewish citizens were recorded along with new Christian citizens in the burgher book—since 1288 in
Augsburg, since 1311 in Frankfurt am Main, and at least since 1344 in Speyer.[46]
The Jews of Budweiss made their real estate transactions before the city court

---

[42] See Henry Kamen, *Inquisition and Society in Spain in the Sixteenth and Seventeenth Centuries* (Bloomington, 1985).
[43] Dean Phillip Bell, "Martin Luther and the Jews: The Reformation, Nazi Germany and Today." For further discussion on this point, see the conclusion to this book.
[44] Alfred Haverkamp, "'Concivilitas' von Christen und Juden in Aschkenas im Mittelalter," p. 124.
[45] Ibid., p. 130.
[46] Ibid., p. 131.

and then had them recorded in the Stadtbuch which listed them under the heading "according to Christian and Jewish Laws."[47] Civic officials were also occasionally mentioned and praised in the responsa, as in Jacob Weil's praise for the Ulm burgomaster Osterreicher, which mentioned the official's fair treatment of both Jews and Christians alike.[48]

There were naturally numerous cases of hostility between Jews and Christians, many reported by Christians, but some also reflected in the responsa literature. There were cases of Christians imprisoning or holding Jews for ransom,[49] of murdering Jews on the road,[50] and of placing extreme financial burdens on the Jews— we have already seen cases of multitudinous taxes levied upon the Jews.[51] Nevertheless, many Jews continued to identify with their urban community, even after they were expelled from the city. In a Passover Haggadah of 1497 from the Jews expelled from Brünn in 1454 a note was appended to the end of the Haggadah's traditional declaration about the wish that the Jews should be "Next year in Jerusalem;" the addendum to the declaration read "and in Brünn."[52]

SOCIAL INTERACTION

There are cases where both rabbinic responsa and urban legislation demonstrate clearly the interaction between Jews and Christians on a daily level. Common participation of Jews and Christians in games of chance was mentioned frequently in the fifteenth century.[53] There was also evidence of Jews and Christians dancing together in Regensburg, and we find a preponderance of Jewish ordinances against gambling or drinking with Christians, and the employment of Christian musicians on the Sabbath or on holidays.[54] Despite long-standing prohibitions, Jews frequently had Christian servants in their houses,[55] or in the service of the community (as servants in the bathing room in Nuremberg and Mühlhausen in Thuringia).

Jews might often receive Christians very warmly. Jacob Weil went so far as to permit Jews to remove their headgear in the presence of a priest as a sign

---

[47] *GJ*, vol. 3, Budweiss.

[48] Weil, responsum no. 147; see Bernard Rosensweig, *Ashkenazic Jewry*, p. 56. See also Isserlein, *Terumas Ha-Deshen*, responsum no. 195; and Bruna, responsa nos. 112, 113, and 275.

[49] See Colon, responsum no. 7 and Weil, responsum no. 79a, and regarding a case in Breslau, nos. 35, 36, 53, 110, and 111.

[50] For insightful examples see Isserlein, *Terumas Ha-Dehsehn*, responsa nos. 239, 240, 241, and 280, where a Jew dressed as a gentile and eating with gentiles at a hotel table learned that they murdered a Jew; see also Bruna, responsum no. 53, which dealt with the issue of valid witnesses that a Jewish man was murdered on the road by non-Jews.

[51] See for example, Colon, responsum no. 16.

[52] *GJ*, vol. 3, Brünn.

[53] See Donauwörth, Mühlhausen, Nuremberg, Regensburg, Schlettstadt, Zurich.

[54] Sidney Steiman, *Custom and Survival*, p. 115.

[55] 1365 and 1372 in Augsburg; other examples include Neustadt and Zurich.

of respect.[56] Maharil allowed Jews to be hosted by Christians, and he allowed Jews to borrow dishes and other vessels from Christians to adorn their homes even on Passover.[57] During Lag be-Omer and Purim or on church festivals, some Jews and Christians even exchanged gifts,[58] and younger patricians at times partook in the Purim festival and in Jewish weddings, as in fifteenth-century Nuremberg. The practice must have been widespread in some places, for we find in Zurich a fine imposed on any Christians dancing with Jews at a Jewish wedding.[59]

There were numerous cases in the urban legislation regarding sexual relations between Jews and Christians in late medieval Germany (in Wiener Neustadt and Zurich, for example). Most often these cases involved Jewish men and Christian women[60] or Christian prostitutes.[61] In the responsa, there were also discussions of inappropriate sexual relations between Christians and Jews. Responsum 8 of Jacob Weil, for example, was concerned with the case of a *sotah*—a woman who was accused of being unfaithful and secluding herself with a Christian even after having been warned to avoid that man by her husband.

BUSINESS RELATIONS

There is evidence that Jews and Christians interacted daily in service trades and business as well. Jewish doctors often had Christian patients, sometimes exclusively, as in Rothenburg ob der Tauber. Christians might also provide services to their Jewish neighbors. Before the middle of the fifteenth century a Christian served as a butcher for the Jews in Nuremberg; the Jews in Regensburg similarly employed a Christian butcher. The Jews in Rothenburg ob der Tauber may have provided for a Christian baker, and a Christian tailor had close contact with the Jews in Trent. The Jews of Regensburg employed a Christian to watch over the cemetery. Given the variety of professions in which Jews were engaged at the end of the Middle Ages there were many different daily interactions between Jews and Christians. There is even evidence that Jews were sometimes instructed in professions typically closed to them; a Christian in Nuremberg, for example, taught Jews the goldsmith trade.

Throughout the responsa there are many references to partnerships between Jews in dealing with Christians, particularly regarding loans that turned sour. The judgments in such cases generally deal with the right of the Jews in regard

---

[56] Weil, *Dinim* 41 and 44; see Rosensweig, *Ashkenazic Jewry*, p. 57. See also Isserlein, *Terumas Ha-Deshen*, responsum no. 196.

[57] Steiman, *Custom and Survival*, p. 115.

[58] Ibid., p. 116.

[59] GJ, vol. 3, Zürich.

[60] 1470 in Nördlingen, as well as in Nuremberg, and Regensburg.

[61] In the second half of the fourteenth century there were frequent cases of relations between Jewish youths and Christian prostitutes in Augsburg, but also in Nuremberg.

to each other, but occasionally they do shed light on internal Jewish relations and Jewish and Christian relations as well.

In a case described by Weil, a certain S[himon] sold to R[euven] a notice of debt that had been written to him by a priest for thirty pounds plus interest for the price of fifty pounds. R[euven] gave to S[himon] a promissory note for the fifty pounds for receiving the debt. R[euven] made many efforts to collect the debt himself from the Christian, but before he could collect the debt S[himon] went to the Christian, collected the debt and gave him a receipt for the payment of the debt. R[euven] lodged a complaint, but S[himon] replied that he had never actually sold the debt to R[euven], rather he had turned it over to him simply in order that he might work to help extract the debt from the Christian. Weil cited Maimonides to the effect that there is no purchase in the handing over alone, but rather only when the transaction consists of writing and actual handing over. Weil argued that even if S[himon] was correct and he had not sold the debt to R[euven], still S[himon] was obliged to reimburse R[euven] for all of the costs that he exerted in attempting to collect the debt from the Christian. If however it was proven that R[euven] had purchased the debt from S[himon], then the fifty pounds that R[euven] paid must be returned to him, though it was not necessary that his exertions be reimbursed. Weil went on to offer a series of hypothetical judgments based on the facts that would be ascertained by the inquirer.[62]

THE CHRISTIAN AND HALAKHAH

While the discussion in the responsa of such business utilized traditional Jewish legal decisions and principles, it is clear that the complexity, and regional variation of the interactions was often unique to the settlement of Jews in the fifteenth century as well as the local conditions imposed upon Jews by civil authorities. The halakhic discussions about Jewish and Christian interactions, particularly in regard to religious ritual, reveal a similar complexity that forced many rabbis to creatively combine previous halakhic rulings, regional customs, and local conditions in their own discussions and deliberations. Throughout the later Middle Ages a number of leniencies were given because of the nature of Jewish and Christian relations at the time. Rabbi Meir of Rothenburg permitted Jews to collect debts from Christians on one of the Christian festivals, a time when Jews were not supposed to have interaction with Christians, if it were necessary to save Jewish money from Christian hands.[63] Other rabbinic decisions that dealt with business dealings with Christians on the Sabbath were more

---

[62] In a similar responsum, Meir of Rothenburg had ruled that although A and B were assigned to collect the principal and interest from a debt owed to C by a gentile, A and B may not collect the interest for themselves, for this belongs to the original creditor (C). See Irving A. Agus, *Rabbi Meir of Rothenburg*, no. 142.

[63] Jacob Katz, *The "Shabbes Goy": A Study in Halakhic Flexibility*, p. 85.

strict.[64] In a case in Regensburg, Rabbi Hayyim Eliezer ben Isaac Or Zarua prohibited a Jew from returning collateral to a Christian on the Sabbath because
it looked like business. He was supported in his decision by another authority,
however both authorities conceded that the collateral could be returned in an
emergency or if the Christian were a violent person. Here the rabbis remained
very firm in the halakhic decisions, but the dangers of the outside world were
also recognized.[65]

Maharil also granted certain halakhic leniencies in order to counteract the
sometimes tense[66] and violent relations between Jews and Christians. In an
effort to stem intentional handling of Jewish wine by Christians, making the
wine forbidden to the Jews, Maharil "suggested that whenever a Jew saw a non-
Jew touch his wine in order to anger him, it was advisable for the Jew to drink
some of the wine immediately while the non-Jew was still present."[67] Maharil
also allowed carrying a certain type of gold coin on the Sabbath in cases of
danger[68] and he allowed Jews to flee beyond the boundaries of the *eruv* (enclo-
sure of an open place into a private one, allowing the carrying of specific
objects during the Sabbath and holidays) to avoid being captured on a Friday
night. He even allowed the sounding of the shofar on Rosh ha-Shanah to be
delayed until later in the morning for fear that the Christians would think that
the Jews were planning a rebellion or an attack if the shofar sounded while
they were still sleeping.[69] Maharil also offered more practical daily advice, when,
for example, he warned Jews against dressing in very expensive clothes while
traveling and not to sleep alone at night.[70]

Although Jews were permitted to appeal to Christians to perform certain labors
on the Sabbath if there was a danger to life, in practice precise definitions of
the qualifications for danger tended to become more rather than less permis-
sive. In the cold weather "a 'Sabbath Gentile' for heating homes became a permanent institution, and only halachic experts were likely to limit its use in
accordance with halachic criteria."[71] The result was, argues Jacob Katz, that
scholars as well as laymen sought ways to circumvent restrictions on "telling a
Gentile" to do something. By reminding a gentile after the Sabbath that he
did not light the fire last Sabbath, one could effectively get the desired action

---

[64] There are cases in the responsa in which the rabbis censured current practices of
giving vessels to Christians (Moses Mintz, responsum no. 116) or clothes (Bruna, responsum no. 173) to Christians to carry or care for during the Sabbath.

[65] Katz, The "Shabbes Goy," p. 28.

[66] Weil, for example, could recall a Sabbath on which the synagogue was closed by
a ban from the local authorities; see Rosensweig, Ashkenazic Jewry, p. 25.

[67] Steiman, Custom and Survival, p. 115.

[68] Although carrying, without an *eruv*, or carrying money, even with an *eruv*, is forbidden; see Steiman, Custom and Survival, p. 115.

[69] Ibid., p. 115.

[70] Ibid., p. 13.

[71] Katz, The "Shabbes Goy," p. 61.

without contradicting the law itself.[72] Similar circumventions could be constructed in order to get a Christian to buy or sell for the Jew on the Sabbath.[73] Not all rabbinic authorities, however, were so lenient. According to the earlier authority of Or Zarua, to which many rabbis still adhered in the fifteenth century, it was forbidden for a Christian to light a candle on the Sabbath, from which Jews might benefit, even if it was for himself; additionally water that a Christian brought on the Sabbath, even on a public way, was forbidden.[74]

Contemporary rulings were also not always lenient. Maharil, for example, wrote that in a city that had no *eruv* there was no *heter* (leniency) for a woman to have a Christian bring hot water to her house. Similarly such carryings of a Christian were forbidden *derabanan* (by decree of the rabbis) even if they were necessary for a mitzvah (commandment)—even though there was a custom of hiring a non-Jew to carry a "body of wine."[75] As a fence to desecrating the Sabbath, Maharam, whose opinions were still heavily cited by Jacob Weil and the other important rabbis of the fifteenth and sixteenth centuries, did not allow Jews to ask Christian friends to hire laborers to do their work on the Sabbath. Maharam also prohibited Jews who bought merchandise from a Christian before the Sabbath to go into the store on the Sabbath and take the merchandise, for example, a hat that one could wear on the Sabbath.[76]

Regarding the question of whether it is proper "to permit a gentile servant to warm the winter house on the Sabbath" even if he did so by his own accord, Maharam had answered that "although in France such practice was not objected to, and Rabbi Jacob of Orleans even permitted one to tell a gentile explicitly to fix the fire, it is not to be permitted in our country where many are accustomed to consider it a desecration of the Sabbath."[77] In the fifteenth century, however, Jacob Weil allowed the heating, which he noted was common throughout all of Ashkenaz, and he compared it to the case of allowing a gentile to cook for a child on the Sabbath, even if the child was not in physical danger, that is even if he was not very sick, because the nature of a child was like that of the sick person.[78]

At all times there existed a web of restriction with regard to the preparation of food by gentiles.[79] Milk, for example, that a gentile milked unsupervised by a Jew was strictly prohibited.[80] The very prohibition of such milk, however,

---

[72] Ibid., p. 62.
[73] Ibid., p. 80.
[74] Or Zarua, *She'elot u-teshuvot*, responsum no. 85.
[75] Jacob ben Moses ha-Levi (Maharil), *She'elot u-teshuvot*, responsum no. 109.
[76] Irving A. Agus, *Rabbi Meir of Rothenburg*, no. 50.
[77] Ibid., no. 47, p. 184.
[78] Weil, responsum no. 46.
[79] See the general restriction in Finkelstein, *Jewish Self-Government*, p. 235.
[80] The same prohibitions held true for cheese. Or Zarua, however, permitted the use of water drawn by a gentile—the fear in the first two cases, that the milk or cheese could be adulterated by milk from non-kosher animals or by contact with meat, did

originated in the Talmud, in tractate *Avodah Zara*: "These items of gentiles are prohibited, but their prohibition is not a prohibition against all benefit: milk that a gentile milked without a Jew watching him, and [their] bread, and oil— Rabbi and his court permitted the oil—and cooked foods, and preserves into which they are accustomed to put wine and vinegar . . ."[81] Rabbi Joseph Colon of Pavia, Maharik, insisted that the law was different in the present, for where the gentile and his product were known, there was certainly no doubt that the gentile would not adulterate his product with impure milk.[82] Rabbi Israel Bruna argued that milk from a gentile was not fit for Jews.[83] Maharil wrote in a rather lengthy responsum that it seemed strange to permit the eating of the butter or cream of the gentiles in places in which such eating was not customary. In Germany, however, Maharil held that it was permissible, since it was customary for the milk to be collected a little bit at a time, unlike the large barrels in the mountains, and so presumably it was easier to detect any adulteration of the contents—in addition there was a custom of allowing this milk in Swabia.[84] Here again the very regional nature of the rabbinic decrees was evident.

As in the case of bread baked by a non-Jew, if the heads of a city allowed it a leniency could be followed, but it was the opinion of Maharil that even in such cases one should remain more strict and make a fence by denying permission.[85] Such local customs were clearly recognized earlier by Maharam, for example, who drew similar analyses.[86]

Other products were also considered by the rabbis. All authorities, with the exception we have cited above, held that wine touched by a non-Jew was prohibited to a Jew, although there seems to have been some discussion as to whether or not a Jew might benefit from such wine (for example, by selling it to a gentile).[87] According to a strict and early ruling of Meir of Rothenburg, a Jew might "derive no such benefit from forbidden wine. The only difference between the 'yayin nesek' (forbidden wine) of the talmudic period and that of our own day

---

not, in this opinion apply to water. See Or Zarua, *She'elot u-teshuvot*, no. 10. See also Bruna, responsum no. 79.

[81] *Avodah Zara*, 2:6.

[82] Colon, responsum no. 42. Along a similar line of thought, Maharil insisted that one not purchase skins from a gentile for the purpose of writing a sefer torah or for making tefilin, since the skins could be from impure animals such as horses or donkeys, *She'elot u-teshuvot hachadoshot*, p. 118.

[83] Bruna, responsum no. 78.

[84] Though the customs of the Swiss were contrasted.

[85] Jacob ben Moses ha-Levi (Maharil), *She'elot u-teshuvot*, responsum no. 35.

[86] Agus, *Rabbi Meir of Rothenburg*, no. 114, pp. 210–211; he also permitted fish smoked by a gentile and the use of gentile flour for the making of bread, see nos. 112–113. Or Zarua offered a leniency regarding the bread of a gentile, which he permitted, provided there was no question regarding the dishes or bowls used to prepare it and that there was no doubt regarding the purity of the bread, no. 94.

[87] See Finkelstein, *Jewish Self-Government*, p. 236.

is that the 'yayin nesek' of today may be taken from a Gentile in payment of his debt, as we thus recover our money from him."[88] Again, stock theological views and legal decisions often combined with unique situations in the decisions reached by the late medieval rabbis.

THE MEETING OF TWO WORLDS: CONVERSION, INFORMING, AND THE HOLY COMMUNITY

A final category of Jewish and Christian relations centered around conversion. The place of converts in both Judaism and Christianity was difficult and at times dangerous. Converts to Judaism could count on severe punishment by the secular or Christian courts if caught. Since the Jewish communities often suffered repercussions for receiving them, converts could also not always rely on the good graces of the Jewish communities, which did their best to discourage converts from taking up their religion. According to Maharil, for example, if a Christian wanted to convert to Judaism it was permissible to report the case to the government.[89] On the other hand, Jewish apostates who wished to return to the Jewish fold were readily admitted by Maharil, though Jacob Weil demanded a certain level of repentance.

The number of Jewish apostates from the late fifteenth and sixteenth centuries was significant, and it included many famous Hebraists and anti-Jewish polemicists. The most famous was Johannes Pfefferkorn (1469– after 1521), Reuchlin's nemesis, a student of Meir Pfefferkorn (the dayan of Prague) and a butcher by profession. Pfefferkorn was convicted of burglary and theft and converted to Christianity with his wife and children in Cologne shortly after his release from prison in 1504. Pfefferkorn's acerbic attacks against the Jews in such works as *The Mirror of the Jews* (*Der Juden Spiegel*, Cologne, 1508), however, revealed his ignorance of the rabbinic literature that he sought so vigorously to suppress, particularly in his examination of Hebrew books in 1509.[90] Equally important for the effect that his writings had on popular and learned attitudes towards Jews was Anthonius Margaritha (b. ca. 1490).[91] Margaritha was the son of Rabbi Samuel ben Jacob Margolioth of Regensburg, and he denounced the Jewish community of Regensburg while still a Jew. He converted to Catholicism in 1522 and later to Protestantism, serving as a lecturer in Hebrew at Augsburg, Meissen, Zell, Leipzig, and Vienna. After his debate with Joseph ben Gershon around 1530—which centered on the *Aleinu* prayer,

---

[88] Agus, *Rabbi Meir of Rothenburg*, no. 128. For rather more detailed accounts of specific cases of accidental handling by gentiles or the taking of wine from Jewish casks by gentiles, see nos. 121, 122, and 124.

[89] Steiman, *Custom and Survival*, p. 114.

[90] *Encyclopedia Judaica* (*EJ*) 13, cc. 355–357; see Joseph ben Gershon of Rosheim's *Chronicle*, section 5, where Joseph notes that the Jews' deliverance from Pfefferkorn's was a miracle of salvation.

[91] Joseph ben Gershon of Rosheim, *Chronicle*, section 15, in particular.

accusations that Jews curse the king and gentiles in their prayers, and the status of "full converts"—Margaritha was deemed dangerous, imprisoned, and then banished from Augsburg. Still, his book *The Entire Jewish Belief* (*Das Gantz Jüdisch Glaub*) was reprinted many times, to the detriment of the Jews.[92] One of the other well-known, earlier, converts was Victor of Karben (Carben) (1422–1515), from whose work Margaritha may have borrowed. Victor claimed to be a rabbi before converting at the age of 49 and leaving his wife and children. It has been questioned whether he actually penned a number of the works attributed to him—some speculate that these works were written by the Dominican Ortwin Gratius—but he did participate in a disputation with Jews at Poppelsdorf which led to their expulsion from the village. Victor became, in 1485, a member of the theological faculty at Cologne.

Particularly in the sixteenth century, there were many other cases of Jewish converts who went on to careers as Christian theologians or lecturers in Hebrew. Paul Staffelsteiner (Nathan Aaron), born in Nuremberg before 1499, converted first to Catholicism and perhaps later to Protestantism, with his children but not his wife, and he filled the long-vacant chair of Hebrew at Heidelberg in 1551, the same year that he published a German speech on the messianism of Christ.[93] Paul Weidner (Asher Judah ben Nathan Ashkenazi) (ca. 1525–1585) was the brother of the physician and diplomat Solomon Ashkenazi. He served as a physician and rector of the university in Vienna. He wrote conversionary sermons and enjoyed extensive imperial patronage, eventually obtaining the title of nobility von Billerburg in 1582.[94] Rabbi Jacob Gipher aus Göppingen (in Swabia), the recipient of Luther's letter of support *That Jesus Christ was Born a Jew* was a lecturer of Hebrew at Wittenberg and in 1522 married the reformer Karlstadt's daughter, who later left him due to suspicions of adultery and theft.[95] There were other converts. Some converts were well known, such as Paul Ricius,[96] Flavius Mithridates,[97] possibly Peter Schwarz (the dynamic anti-Jewish Dominican preacher),[98] Johannes Böschenstein (Hebraist at Wittenberg, who denied that he was of Jewish ancestry),[99] Immanuel Tremellius,[100] Matthäus

---

[92] *EJ* 11, cc. 958–959; Fraenkel-Goldschmidt, *Joseph of Rosheim: Historical Writings*, pp. 26–27.

[93] Gustav Hammann, "Konversionen deutscher und ungarischer Juden in der frühen Reformationszeit," pp. 214–215.

[94] *EJ* 16, c. 375.

[95] Hammann, Konversionen," p. 211.

[96] *EJ* 14, cc. 163–164.

[97] Sander Gilman, *Jewish Self-Hatred*, pp. 26–27.

[98] See Hammann, "Konversionen," p. 209, n. 8 and *EJ* 12, c. 1158; he was an apostate according to the *Sefer Nizzahon*.

[99] *EJ* 4, cc. 1168–1169.

[100] Hammann, "Konversionen," p. 218; See also Salo Baron, *A Social and Religious History of the Jews: Volume 13, Late Middle Ages and Era of European Expansion*, p. 167.

Adrian, Stephen Isaac,[101] Gerhard Veltwyk,[102] and Paul Altdorfer.[103] Other converts were less renowned, but interesting nonetheless. Among this group one might count a young Jewish girl who sought out a priest from Ichtershausen to convert her, took the baptized name of Katharina, and soon after her baptism married the priest Volkmar Froben(ius), living to the ripe old age of 99.[104]

A number of Jews owed their conversions to the work of Protestant missionaries and scholars, such as Andreas Osiander, a reformer who fought particularly strongly against the ritual murder myth but who, nonetheless, managed to bring a number of Jews to the Christian fold: Rabbi Meir's son from Frankfurt,[105] Jacob Wirth,[106] Paulus,[107] and an anonymous twenty-year old with aspirations of being a soldier.[108] There were the numerous and anonymous converts reported in town chronicles and local court documents as well. Two Jews were reported baptized in the Upper Alsatian town of Belfort in 1449.[109] The examples could be multiplied, but it is obvious that Jewish apostasy was a serious and not uncommon phenomenon in late fifteenth- and sixteenth-century Germany, and that it affected a wide range of Jews, even if the most notorious cases seem to come from a particular group of Jews.

Gustav Hammann has argued that after 1521 Jews tended to convert for religious reasons, often regardless of negative social and economic consequences. For the Protestant Hammann the religious discussion and challenge posed by Luther offered the foreground for what appeared to him to be an increase in Jewish conversions to Christianity. The approach of Hammann has been carefully criticized by Hava Fraenkel-Goldschmidt, who notes that Hammann focuses largely on Christian theologians and Hebraists and missionizing but offers no mention of coercion or the role of false accusations such as the blood libel. In turn, Fraenkel-Goldschmidt poses a series of important questions regarding the nature of apostates' interaction with Christian groups and the Jewish community after their baptism; the tendency of known apostates to come from important families; and the lessons that can be learned from the actions of these converts.[110]

---

[101] Selma Stern, *Josel of Rosheim*, p. 228.

[102] Ibid., p. 229.

[103] Elisheva Carlebach, "Converts and their Narratives in Early Modern Germany: The Case of Friedrich Albrecht Christiani," p. 71; see also Franz Xavier von Wegele, *Geschichte der Universität Würzburg* (Aalen, 1969), vol. 2, pp. 42–43.

[104] Hammann, "Konversionen," pp. 212–213.

[105] Ibid., p. 213.

[106] Ibid., p. 214.

[107] Ibid., pp. 215–216.

[108] Ibid., p. 212.

[109] GJ, vol. 3, Belfort.

[110] Hava Fraenkel-Goldschmidt, *Joseph of Rosheim: Historical Writings*.

As Fraenkel-Goldschmidt and Sander Gilman have detailed, many converts described serious ostracism from their former co-religionists. Pfefferkorn, for example complained that:

> ... And they especially hate me and those others who had been Jews and are now Christians. And I know that if I came among them, they would rend me like the wolf rends the sheep, for I have been secretly warned by letter how Jews from various lands have contracted to have me killed. But they know that if I were to be killed, they would not be spared, so they and some false Christians say: 'Yes, Pfefferkorn, you can't believe him. He plays at the Christian as long as he can get money for it.'[111]

But tensions also existed among converts and their new Christian brethren, as Victor of Karben revealed:

> And thus, says the Psalmist, one spends the entire day like a poor dog that has spent its day running and returns home at night hungry. For there are many uncharitable and ignorant Christians who will not give you but will rather show you from their doors with mockery, saying, "Look, there goes a baptized Jew." And then others answer, "Yes, anything that is done for you is a waste. You will never become a good Christian." And thus they are mocked and insulted by the Christians from whom they expect help and solace. And they are also hated by the Jews from whom they have come. Whatever joy or pleasure that one or the other may have had is turned to unhappiness and displeasure.[112]

Obviously, reasons for conversion could be material or spiritual.[113] They may have also been forced. In the sixteenth century, however, conversion may have been particularly facilitated by expectations of the coming of the Messiah around 1500, increased social pressures, religious upheaval, or the declining knowledge of Hebrew, which seems indicative of a decline in social cohesion, amongst Jews. Both Conrad Pelican and Sebastian Münster complained that the lack of Hebrew skills amongst the Jews was widespread, explaining why they could not, in their opinion, find any Jews to assist in their work.[114]

Studies of conversion in Germany after the sixteenth century often contrast with those of the fifteenth and sixteenth centuries. Elisheva Carlebach has suggested that unlike medieval conversion narratives, those in the seventeenth and eighteenth centuries integrated the Jewish past into the Christian persona

---

[111] Cited in Gillman, *Jewish Self-Hatred*, pp. 38–39.

[112] Cited in Ibid., p. 40.

[113] See: Jeremy Cohen, "The Mentality of the Medieval Apostate: Peter Alfonsi, Hermann of Cologne, and Pablo Christiani," in *Jewish Apostasy in the Modern World*, edited by Todd M. Endelman (New York, 1987): 20–47; see also Bernard Rosensweig, *Ashkenazic Jewry in Transition*.

[114] Hava Fraenkel-Goldschmidt, "On the Periphery of Jewish Society: Jewish Converts to Christianity in Germany During the Reformation," p. 653.

of the convert and were less anti-Jewish. She notes that most seventeenth-century autobiographies of converts make at least a cursory statement regarding the convert's Jewish education, that a significant number of converts went on to university careers, and, more significantly, that converts seemed especially prone to be drawn from the fair but not outstandingly-educated Jews who were qualified for functionary positions within the Jewish communities, as teachers, rabbis, or preachers, that is a class of under-respected community servants.[115] This point requires some elucidation, particularly since the pattern may not have been so different in the sixteenth century. But a word of caution is in order, since the picture of the late medieval Jewish apostate that we possess is incomplete and focuses perhaps too much on the most well-known apostates.

Deborah Hertz has suggested similar results for the seventeenth century. According to Hertz the intellectual positions held by converts in the Jewish world paralleled the careers taken up by the converts in Christianity. Most converts, ten of the 12 that Hertz traces in the seventeenth century, were male.[116] Hertz argues that only beginning in the eighteenth century do we find converts from wealthy families and a greater diversity in family position, age, and gender among the converts. If we follow Carlebach, the decisive break in the characteristics of converts occurs in the seventeenth century. If we follow Hertz, the decisive break does not occur until the eighteenth century. In any event the sixteenth century must be seen as a point of passage in the nature of conversion, and a passage that can only be understood in the context of changing notions of community and community membership. As Hertz argues "discovering the dead converts is necessary, because without understanding the 'defecting fringe' of the Jewish universe it is impossible to really grasp the changing condition of the mainstream community."[117] This is a significant observation, though for the purposes of this chapter I would like to explore the notions of community in the sixteenth century and the pressures for change within the Jewish communities as a way to understand the dynamic relationship between center and fringe in the Jewish world of late medieval and early modern Germany.

---

[115] Carlebach, "Converts and their Narratives," p. 71.

[116] Deborah Hertz, "Women at the Edge of Judaism: Female Converts in Germany, 1600–1750," in *Jewish Assimilation, Acculturation and Accommodation: Past Trends, Current Issues, and Future Prospects* (Lanham, 1992): 87–109, here at pp. 95–96. See also B.Z. Kedar, "Continuity and Change in Jewish Conversion to Christianity in Eighteenth-Century Germany," in *Studies in the History of Jewish Society in the Middle Ages and in the Modern Period*, edited by E. Etkes and Y. Salmon (Jerusalem, 1980): 144–160. [Hebrew].

[117] Hertz, "Women at the Edge," p. 88.

REMEMBERING THE PAST: THE ROLE OF INFORMERS AND
CONVERTS IN JOSEL OF ROSHEIM'S SEFER HA-MIKNAH

Fifteenth-century halakhic discussions deal frequently with informers[118] or apostates and their continuing relation with the Jewish community, or at least certain segments of that community—as in issues of bills of divorce, testimony, or
representation.[119] For the fifteenth-century rabbinic scholar Jacob Weil, for
example, the informer was excluded from communal functions, but was not rel-
egated outside of the Jewish sphere. Weil writes of the informer that:

> You shall be disqualified to testify as a witness and to take an oath. When
> the community shall be required to collect money, they shall not accept your
> own assessment by your oath but shall tax you in accordance to their esti-
> mate and their oath.[120]

What is evident, however, is that Jews and apostates continued to interact on
many levels, even if unofficially or against communal edicts.[121]

In more practical daily interaction, Joseph Colon discussed whether a Jew
inherited from his apostate father. Colon seemed to answer in the negative,
but he offered a position of Rabbah in the Mishnah that a Jewish apostate inherited from his father—a view that Rashi rejected.[122] According to Maharam, the
apostate forfeited his rights as an heir, but he retained the power to transmit
his property to his Jewish heirs.[123]

Apostates were often not considered trustworthy. In the case of an apostate
who was sent as a representative of a husband to deliver a *get* to his wife, the
husband's oath that he would not later cancel the *get* was believed, however
the apostate was held in suspicion.[124] In a similar case Jacob Weil declared that
it was not customary to accept the representative for an apostate from Judaism
who was sent to deliver a *get* to the convert's wife. Although a Jew was not
required to give an oath, the apostate was held suspect, and so witnesses were
necessary to confirm the words of the representative.[125] In terms of wine handled by "infidels," such infidels could not be trusted, but they were of a different character than gentiles. According to Maharam "the wine of a (Jewish)
infidel or of a Karaite, who does not trust the teaching of the Rabbis, is 'yayin

---

[118] See for example, Weil, responsa nos. 59f, 129, and 147, or Colon, responsum
no. 21.

[119] Weil, responsum no. 40.

[120] Quoted in Eric Zimmer, *Harmony and Discord*, p. 98.

[121] See Ibid., pp. 165–166. See Bernard Rosenzweig, *Ashkenzic Jewry*, pp. 26–31 for
discussion of apostates, and pp. 31–33 for discussion of informers. See *EJ* 8, cc. 1364–
1373 for informers; *EJ* 3, cc. 201–215 for apostasy.

[122] No. 2.

[123] Agus, *Rabbi Meir of Rothenburg*, p. 686.

[124] Jacob ben Moses ha-Levi (Maharil), *She'elot u-teshuvot*, responsum no. 48; according to no. 100, a husband who sends an apostate is held in suspicion of later cancel-
ing the "get" in order to damage the wife or to increase his own wealth.

[125] Weil, responsum no. 126.

nesek,' for, although they are not idolaters themselves, they do not guard their wine from being handled by gentiles."[126]

The discussion about converts and informers seems to have changed in important ways by the first quarter of the sixteenth century. Joseph ben Gershon of Rosheim (Josel) began the *Sefer ha-Miknah* by noting that:[127]

> noble expressions/words that rescue the persecuted and deliver them, and will destroy informers and traitors against individuals or groups killing them at the hands of the gentiles . . . and in the passage [*Avodah Zara* 26b] informers have the status of those who descend and do not ascend . . . and in the passage of Rosh Hashanah [17a] the sages accounted the informers with the heretics and the apostates that descend to gehinnom and are sentenced there for generation after generation . . . [128]

Joseph stressed the relation of informers and traitors to heretics and apostates mixing many spheres of action and (un)belief. As he noted later "thus informers incite and instigate punishments in the lower level of gehinnom."[129] Throughout the first book, the remains of which included three sections or pillars—the seventh through the ninth—Joseph discussed the nature of the evil brought about by informers and apostates in both a broad philosophical sense—primarily in the seventh and ninth pillars—and in a more concrete sense, describing in detail the events perpetrated by such people in the history of German Jewry in his own time. The eighth pillar focused particularly on the expulsions of the Jews from a number of German towns, including Strasbourg, Augsburg, Ulm, Nuremberg, and Regensburg, as well as specific cases of informers and apostates and their writings. Given the scope of his writings, particularly in reference to the urban expulsions it will be fruitful to compare Joseph's account to other Jewish and non-Jewish chronicles.

Philosophically, Joseph associated the informer and the apostate with pure evil, and he saw two mutually exclusive forces at work in the world. He wrote that:

> . . . the whole world benefits from the righteous and is troubled by the evil, and because the evil and the good and all of their activities and their thoughts are two vessels, it is impossible to unite, attach, and associate the righteous with the evil in name, business or partnership, because they are enemies one to the other . . . the slanderers and informers are evil to heaven and the creation, desecrate God and damage the creation, in everyday speech incite and instigate them [people] from the path of good to the path of evil as explained above . . . [130]

---

[126] Agus, *Rabbi Meir of Rothenburg*, no. 130.
[127] See Joseph ben Gershon of Rosheim, *Sefer ha-Miknah*, p. 3 note 2.
[128] Ibid., p. 1.
[129] Ibid., p. 4.
[130] Ibid., p. 6.

Joseph attributed the expulsion of the Jews from Strasbourg to the machinations of two [wandering] informers. His information, he claimed, had been handed down in oral tradition. He noted that "surely the event was written in the *Sefer Yoshon*, and also the elders that were in the region of Alsace heard it from their fathers, and they remembered what they [their fathers] told them, and we did not receive a lie from our fathers . . ."[131] Joseph here justified his historiography as a part of communal tradition; that is, the very nature of the community was that of historical authority, and the evil was in opposition to the authority, both in the sense that it worked against the community by informing but also in the sense that it challenged the perceptual authority (memory) of the Jewish tradition itself. To the "holy community of Strasbourg" Joseph juxtaposed the filth of the denunciation (brought by Satan) to the lords of Andlau.[132] The juxtaposition was even clearer in the midst of his discussion of Strasbourg, when Joseph mentioned a certain Rabbi Samuel of Schlettstadt, a "pious man" who sentenced two informers to death.[133] One of those sentenced to die escaped and the people of Strasbourg did not heed the gadol's herem, leading eventually, Joseph concludes, to their expulsion from the city and its surroundings.[134]

The expulsion of the Jews from Bamberg that Joseph related had to do with informers against the community who went to the duke to report that certain Jews were not giving imperial taxes truthfully. The house of Eliezer Landshut was subsequently searched and discovered to be full of money (Joseph attributed this to the evil eye). Eliezer's money was confiscated, the heads of houses were forced to pay a fine and then everyone was ordered expelled from the region within eight days.[135] The informers, however, converted and remained in the country.[136] There was a previous history of conversions in Bamberg, particularly in the context of the preaching of Capistrano in 1451 and Dominican preachers (forced sermons) in 1478. There were also records of conversions in 1439 and 1443. In this case as well, however, the center of the issue as Joseph presented it, revolved around issues of wealth. Certainly, the cohesiveness of the small and apparently not wealthy community was questionable, especially given that there were important legal cases between Jews in 1410, 1452, and 1457 that were taken before the city court instead of the rabbinic court. The community was in such disrepair by mid century that Moses Mintz had to reorganize the synagogue ordinances and poor relief around 1470.

In Augsburg[137] an informer instigated two Christian brothers, whom Joseph

---

[131] Ibid., p. 7.
[132] Ibid., p. 8.
[133] Ibid.
[134] Ibid., pp. 8–9.
[135] Ibid., p. 10.
[136] Stern, *Josel of Rosheim*, p. 226.
[137] Fraenkel-Goldschmidt notes that this might actually refer to Bamberg.

likened to wolves,[138] against the Jews—the poor and penniless.[139] The two Christians were arrested, but the Jews were expelled from the city. The Jewish informer got away.[140] In Nuremberg a wealthy Jew from Aubin, whose request to settle in the city was objected to by the Jewish leaders of the city turned against the community and persuaded the city councilmen to issue the expulsion of the Jews.[141] As in Bamberg conversions increased at times of heavy preaching, for example in the 1450s and 1470s; because of intensive preaching between 1478 and 1479 eight cases of conversion were recorded.[142] But again, it is interesting to find a strand of economic tension in many of the accounts that Joseph presented.

In Ulm, Joseph also noted that the expulsion had to do with informing and apostasy.[143] He wrote that:

> The expulsion [of the Jews from] Ulm was caused by tale-bearing in which they strove to outdo one another until Satan helped them lift up their hands to bring great distress to the Gaon Rabbi Moshe Zart. Finally he was forced to abandon his own faith and to fall in with them. Then joy and jubilation swept through the camp of the informers and of his adversaries, and bitter weeping racked the ears of Israel, of the communities, and of the provinces. But the Lord saw it and He knew of the distress of his soul and of the duress under which he lived. Moreover, the heart of the teacher did not forsake him. He was helped to overcome his unbelief, and he succeeded in going to the Holy Land and in returning with true repentance . . . As for those informers, the evil spirit came upon them so that they ended their days in turmoil . . . and their names went down in ignominy. Their descendants met an unnatural death. The citizens of Ulm wandered on the path of their shame to which they had come because of the Gaon's return to his old faith. In their wrath they conspired with nine evil neighbors to have the Emperor Maximilian expel [the Jews] utterly and soon. It was a difficult situation.[144]

Rabbi Moses was the son of a children's teacher Isaac von Lichtenfels. He was rabbi in Ulm probably between 1480 and 1492, and he was one of the five rabbis whom Maximilian ordered to divide the imperial tax in the Jewish communities of the empire. Intellectually, he energetically opposed allegorical exegesis. He was threatened with the ban by Rabbi Jacob Margolioth because he refused to heed a summons before the court of Rabbi Kosman. He converted in Ulm (after 1495) but returned to Judaism in Turkey, and he died either there or in Israel before September of 1518. But the story takes on additional significance given the changes within the Ulm community at the time of Rabbi

---

[138] Joseph ben Gershon of Rosheim, *Sefer ha-Miknah*, p. 11.

[139] Ibid., pp. 10–11.

[140] Stern, *Josel of Rosheim*, p. 226.

[141] Ibid., p. 227.

[142] GJ, vol. 3, Nuremberg, pp. 1001–1044, here at p. 1013.

[143] Joseph ben Gershon of Rosheim, *Sefer ha-Miknah*, pp. 11–12.

[144] Quoted in Stern, *Josel of Rosheim*, pp. 310–311, note 18.

Moses. The number of Jewish taxpayers had fallen to two in 1469, but the population of the community increased drastically by the end of the fifteenth century, with eleven families living there in 1499, the year when the Jews were finally expelled from the city. Still, the obvious legal disputes in which Rabbi Moses was involved combined with the tensions surrounding the city council's earlier attempts to expel the Jews—the expulsion had been first sought in 1490, and after a large payment into imperial coffers, the city received permission to expel the Jews—may have been indicative of deeper communal difficulties both within and imposed from without.

Joseph also mentioned two informers (enemies of the *gadolim*) in Regensburg,[145] who, he said lay in ambush against the Jewish community. The informers reported that the Jews cursed the Christian rulers and Jesus. The Jews of Regensburg did possess the book *Toldot Jeschu*, a polemical and satirical paraphrase of the history of Jesus.[146] There is indeed evidence that two Jews who had converted for economic reasons on different occasions traveled to a variety of regions, eventually making their way to Regensburg. As in other German cities the sermons of Capistrano and Schwarz led to conversions. An infamous case of a baptized Jew who was drowned (or burned) by Christian authorities because of false games, theft, and numerous baptisms is reported for 1474.[147] The Vorbeter Kalman converted to Christianity, later returned to Judaism and was sentenced to death (the formal charge was blasphemy against Jesus and Mary). The Jewish community apparently paid 100 fl. to the Bavarian duke in order to avoid possible complications, since Kalman, perhaps under torture, had accused Jews of host desecration and blasphemy. There is evidence of informing and baptism, at times together, after the middle of the fifteenth century. Conversions in 1456 and 1464 led to custody questions when the wives of the converts refused to follow the lead of their husbands. Throughout his reckoning, Joseph is careful to contrast the holiness of the kehillah with the character of the informers.

Joseph also focused on individual informers and apostates: Pfefferkorn (who Joseph notes associated with impure men to slander and damage, leaving behind the straight and narrow (becoming an infidel) to the damage of all of Israel, and sought to destroy and annihilate the Oral Torah and all of the holy books); Samuel Enschheim who converted at the age of 70, bringing false charges

---

[145] This case has been recently assessed by Elisheva Carlebach. She examines Josel of Rosheim's description of the expulsion of the Jews from Regensburg and discovers that Josel sought to etch out a moral lesson rather than record objective historical facts; further, by focusing on the alleged evil acts of Jews who converted to Christianity, Josel was able to elevate the self-perception of Ashkenazic Jewry as a pure and holy community and criticize anti-Jewish actions, while not confronting Christian authorities directly. See her article "Between History and Myth: The Regensburg Expulsion in Josel of Rosheim's *Sefer Ha-Miknah*."

[146] *GJ*, vol. 3, Regensburg, pp. 1178–1230.

[147] Ibid., p. 1188.

against Jews (according to Joseph, he would go to gehinnom with all of the other informers and sectarians); an unknown man from Frankfurt who apostatized and had his child removed from his wife's custody when she refused to follow (in Frankfurt there were accusations that Jews blasphemed Jesus;[148] the important conversions of Pfefferkorn and Karben also took place there); Gershon Heildorisch, an informer in Worms; Hoechlin of Posen (a Polish Jew responsible for accusing the Jews of proselytizing); and Jacob Boneida (a wealthy Jew from Posen who was arrested on charges of fraud and tale-bearing (he promised to convert to Christianity when his father died and he did so).[149] There were also other anonymous converts "who would not receive *musar* and rebuke to walk in the way of the upright," those who transgressed the decrees of the rabbis, and whose actions affected the Jewish population of entire regions.

CONCLUSIONS: REGIONALIZATION AND SANCTIFICATION

The theological position of Christianity was frequently attacked by Jews in the Middle Ages. If the Jewish polemic against Christianity was fairly consistent from the high through the later Middle Ages, there was some development in the engagement with Christianity. In the fifteenth century there seems to have been a legend of the union of the Jews, Hussites, and King Wenceslaus. In one Hebrew source, the Hussites are even denoted as martyrs, a term probably never otherwise used by Jews to describe the martyrdom of Christians.[150] Although Jews feared the pogroms that accompanied the Hussite uprising, and the crushing of the movement, there seems to have been some affinity with the Hussites on the part of some Jews. Why? Was it because Jews somehow felt common cause with the rebels against the church, or they believed that the Hussites themselves were akin to Judaism or might become Jews?

Jewish business and social relations with Christians were no doubt shaped by practical daily and economic situations as much as by theology. Regarding the use of gentile wine, for example, Byron Sherwin argues that "in general, no practical distinction was made during the Middle Ages between Gentile wine manufactured for sacramental or nonsacramental use."[151] Although in theory one could draw lines of distinction between those items used for sacrificial purposes and those not used for such ends, such as Rabbenu Tam had drawn, in practice actual relations were much less formally regulated. Again, judging from the number of responsa that deal with issues related to *yayin nesek*, this conclusion seems to be justified.[152] It was a different case later in the sixteenth century, however, when authorities such as Rabbi Judah Loewe

---

[148] GJ, vol. 3, Frankfurt am Main, pp. 346–393, here at p. 358.

[149] Stern, *Josel of Rosheim*, p. 311, note 19.

[150] See Israel Yuval, "Juden, Hussiten und Deutsche: Nach einer hebräischen Chronik," pp. 65–66 and 68.

[151] Sherwin, *Mystical Theology and Social Dissent*, pp. 94–95.

[152] See for example, Bruna, responsum no. 154 and Jacob Weil, responsum no. 18.

(c. 1526–1609), the Maharal of Prague, issued restrictions on using non-Jewish wine in an effort to safeguard "the spiritual essence of the people of Israel from penetration by the intrinsically demonic Gentile essence."[153] Social isolation was necessary, according to this reasoning, in order to protect the unique qualities of the Jews from being tainted by the impurities of the gentiles.[154] In the sixteenth century there was a marked attempt to recast the Jewish community as a sacred entity, separate from its surroundings and holy in its own being. It is not by chance that such discussions were further east in Prague, however, or that in the sixteenth century the kehillah was more frequently described as *kadosh*, holy.

The extent of the increasing isolation of the Jews by the mid-sixteenth century is very evident in the somewhat more philosophically oriented writings of the Maharal of Prague. For him, each people had a unique essence. Therefore, an individual could not change his or her essence and convert to another essence or religion. "One cannot alter one's essence by an act of choice."[155] Jews never stopped being Jews and could always be accepted back into the fold. The Maharal did, however, allow conversion to Judaism, because the person who wanted to become a Jew possessed an innate "disposition towards Judaism. The individual is not, therefore, really a convert. He is an individual whose potentiality is realized by the process of conversion. No change of essence is involved—the Jewish essence was always there."[156]

According to Jacob Katz, Jewish polemic against Christianity nearly ceased in the sixteenth century.[157] Katz asserts that Ashkenazic Jewry became a closed system with few or no comprehensive thinkers but a plethora of moralizing and admonishing preachers.[158] Turning inward, polemic against Christianity became less important than restructuring communal structure and identity. The fifteenth-century polemic presented here was a bridge that combined high medieval theology with attempts at separation, resanctification, and moralizing. This is quite evident in Joseph's discussion of informants and converts. Outsiders that seemed somehow still connected to the Jewish community, through legal discourse in the fifteenth century became for Joseph a detached Other that served as a moralizing yardstick to create community and define its boundaries. A close look at the individual contexts of the converts and informants mentioned by Joseph reveals a complex social environment with serious gaps in social and even religious cohesion within the late medieval Jewish communities.

One great benefit of a more broadly, internally conceived community was that it could easily include Jews dispersed geographically. If the community

---

[153] Sherwin, *Mystical Theology*, p. 101.
[154] Ibid., p. 93.
[155] Ibid., p. 103.
[156] Ibid.
[157] See Katz, *Exclusiveness and Tolerance*.
[158] Ibid., p. 136.

itself was based upon inherent sanctity more than daily interactions it is not difficult to see how communal identity could become regional. This analysis suggests that a comparison with the moral shift in the Christian communities that many find fully developed with the reformations is in order. It also invites the comparison of the situation in Spain at the end of the fifteenth century.

9

Comparative Perspectives

Much of this book begs the important question of how the changes described for fifteenth-century Germany were played out in later periods and in different political and geographical regions.

Throughout this book I have largely avoided the question of the effects of the Reformation on the Jews, arguing instead that the important communal transformations of the fifteenth century, which increasingly marginalized the Jews within the urban communes and helped form broader regional communities, made the reformations of the sixteenth century possible and necessary.

In the later Middle Ages, civic community was sacralized and formed as a moral community. With the radical phase of the Reformation the idea of a local and public community was wedded to Christian theology and resulted in the creation of a believing community. The radical Reformation, therefore, represented the logical conclusion to the developments we have been viewing. The radicals, in fact, fashioned themselves as new Jews with the only valid claim to the descent of the people of Israel, the Chosen People of God restored to dignity. The radicals hearkened back to literal readings of the Old Testament. Münster was declared the New Jerusalem. Although some radical reformers, such as Balthasar Hubmaier, preached against the Jews, they themselves, because of their iconoclasm, became something akin to new Jews in the eyes of both Protestants and Catholics, and were often persecuted in the absence of real Jews. While the Jews were often the antagonists in fifteenth-century Augsburg chronicles, it was the Anabaptists who were portrayed as the opposition in early sixteenth-century chronicles. The Anabaptist movement in south Germany reflected well the brewing tensions over authority, piety, and community; in the end it also demonstrated the need for a working program that combined traditional authority, communal identity, and civic reform.

Medieval German Christians defined community through a universalized ritual life governed by centralized institutions. They were neo-Jews in a pre-Diaspora sense. Late medieval German Christians tended to become neo-Jews in a post-Diaspora sense. They identified themselves as a godly people not by ritual, but by legal and moral codes. Ritual was, after all, an external manifestation that could not bind dispersed and factionalized populations; instead, as we have seen with the increasing regional dispersal of the Jews in the later

Middle Ages, community could only be defined through adherence to particular legal and moral behavior that was both internal and external, but that did not, of necessity, begin or end with particular rituals dictated by a centralized authority.

In Spain, because of a variety of factors including the creation of a centralized national state, the transformation of sacred community took place at the national level. In the late medieval German communes, the Jews were presented as opponents of the common good and were expelled. In Spain, there were also local and regional actions against the Jews; but, the language of mass expulsion was one of protecting the true religion and church. In Germany, the local communities fashioned themselves as sacred entities and as such made the Reformation possible. These proto-Protestant communities sacralized the political community. In Spain, on the other hand, sacrality was forged at the national level. Such national sacralization maintained a balance between a centralized secular government and a centralized national church. The Jews were expelled from the nation by the secular government acting on behalf of the church. Such full-scale expulsion was not possible in Germany, where fragmented political realities forced a variety of reactions to the Jews and the local or regional sacralization of the community.

THE REFORMATION AND THE JEWS

In recent years there has been a marked attempt to dislodge Martin Luther from the center of the "Reformation." Nevertheless Luther's position regarding the Jews has remained critical, in part because of his own extensive writings that deal with the Jews, as primarily an historical people but also to some extent as a contemporary people as well, and in part because of the perceived *Sonderweg* between the thought and recommendations of Luther regarding the Jews and the historical events since the sixteenth century, particularly the Holocaust. There have typically been three approaches to the relationship between Luther's writings and the Jews. One approach assumes that there was a profound shift in Luther's attitude toward the Jews, noting that Luther's later writings at the end of the 1530s and the early 1540s belie a virulent anti-Judaism not present in Luther's earlier, presumably much more friendly works, such as *That Jesus Christ was Born a Jew*. A second theory, the theory of continuity, has gained support recently. Briefly stated, it holds that there is an important strand of continuity regarding the Jews in Luther's writings. Finally, a third, somewhat conciliatory theory argues that one finds both change and continuity in Luther's attitude toward the Jews. This interpretation suggests that Luther's fundamental theological teaching remained the same, even if his practical-legal and rhetorical position shifted by his later writings.

Luther's vision of the Jews was largely theological and rhetorical in nature. Jews formed part of a devilish group subverting the true church, or true Judaism, which also helped indicate the end of days. For Luther, Jews of ancient Israel were markedly different from contemporary Jews, who, Luther argued, were not really Jews at all. In fact, for Luther it might be more appropriate to view Catholics or Protestants as Jews in the sense that Luther conceived of them. What is more, the concept of Jew was largely a foil for Luther's attacks on his own society. Even in his later blandishments against contemporary Jews, Luther used the Jews to strike out against those who he believed misused their authority. His later and violent polemics were certainly not restricted to the Jews; at the same time his view of the Jews and the primary issues associated with the concept of Jews remained remarkably salient and consistent throughout his career. The issue of lineage and descent was, even more than apocalypticism, central to Luther's theology, his social and political vision, and the general trends in the late medieval and early modern periods. Beyond a political or social interpretation, it is clear that at the heart of most discussions of Jews for Luther was the question of lineage.[1]

In Luther we notice a conflation of Christian identity with the Israelites of the Old Testament, hence a presupposition of the continuity between the Old and New Laws, and an emphasis on the legal and moral nature of the Old Testament that we have seen in the later Middle Ages. This important shift is even more noticeable in the radical reformers of the sixteenth century.

THE RADICAL REFORMATION

The radical Reformation is often seen as an extended and radicalized version of the theology of Luther. A number of radicals did emerge from Wittenberg. The radical movements were, however, largely centered in numerous areas in southwest Germany and in Moravia, where they were also extensively influenced by the theology of Zwingli.

Discussion of radical reform movements typically focuses on three more or less distinct groups: the Anabaptists, Spiritualists, and Antitrinitarians.[2] Unlike Anabaptism, Spiritualism and Antitrinitarianism "failed to assume a concrete sociological dimension in the first half-century of the Reformation."[3] One of the earliest and most enduring figures of the radical Reformation is Thomas Müntzer (c. 1490–1525). Among the important radicals were Conrad Grebel (1498–1526), Andreas Rudolf Bodenstein von Karlstadt (1486–1541), Balthasar Hubmaier (c. 1484–1528), Hans Hut (c. 1490–1527), Hans Denck (c. 1500–1527), Jakob Hutter (d. 1536), Jan Matthijs in Münster (d. 1534), Menno Simons (1496–1561),[4] Melchior Hoffman (c. 1495–1543/44), Pilgrim Marpeck (c. 1492–1556), and Hans Hergot (d. 1527).[5] Of the Spiritualists, Sebastian Franck

---

[1] For a more complete treatment of this subject, see my "Martin Luther and the Jews: The Reformation, Nazi Germany and Today."

[2] Hans J. Hillerbrand, ed. *The Reformation: A Narrative Related by Contemporary Observers and Participants*, p. 214.

[3] Ibid., p. 273.

[4] Ibid., pp. 217–221.

[5] Lewis W. Spitz, *The Protestant Reformation, 1517–1559*, pp. 166–174.

(ca. 1499–1542) and Caspar von Schwenkfeld (1489–1561) are perhaps the best-known figures; among the Antitrinitarians, Michael Servetus (c. 1511–1553).[6]

The radical Reformation has often been viewed as a fringe or marginal element of the Reformation. Given its nature as a popular movement, and the radicals' desire to Christianize public life beyond devotional practices and ecclesiastical institutions, recent scholars have insisted that the radical Reformation must be seen at the center of the Reformation.[7] Many of the theological elements within the thought of the radicals, such as "biblical literalism, opposition to sacerdotal and sacramental thinking, moral earnestness and reliance on personal experiences and direct revelations" that have generally been seen as unique to the radicals do not, upon closer examination, distinguish them from the magisterial reformers.[8] The radicals did, however, represent a coherent movement within the Reformation. According to Michael Baylor,

> The strategic differences between magisterial and radical reformers were symptomatic of a more fundamental difference in their politics, especially in their attitudes toward the authority of existing secular rulers. Above all, what gave the radicals their coherence as the Reformation's 'left wing' was the rejection of a hierarchical conception of politics in which legitimate authority, whether secular or ecclesiastical, devolved from the top down. Instead, the radicals' vision of politics was rooted in notions of local autonomy and community control which also implied an egalitarianism. The radicals were the most articulate theorists of a 'grass-roots' paradigm of Reformation, one based on principles of communalism that grew out of the late Middle Ages.[9]

The radicals discarded existing distinctions between temporal and spiritual authority. They did not write about political theory per se; rather, "their writings contained a set of norms for living, practical values and principles about how sociopolitical life should be conducted among people who call themselves Christians."[10] A number of the radicals' positions are made clear in the Twelve Articles of the Peasants' Revolt of 1525, combining biblical moralism and demands for social and political reform.[11]

---

[6] Hillerbrand, *The Reformation*, pp. 273–275. See also Spitz, *The Protestant Reformation*, pp. 176–177.

[7] See *The Radical Reformation*, edited by Michael G. Baylor, p. xii. For a discussion of the changing research agenda and orientation to the subject of the Anabaptists since the 1970s, see James M. Stayer, "The Anabaptists," in *Reformation Europe: A Guide to Research*, edited by Steven Ozment (St. Louis, 1982): 135–159. For a discussion of the radicals as the "sect-type" as opposed to the "church-type," see the second volume of Ernst Troeltsch's well-known and significant *The Social Teachings of the Christian Churches*.

[8] Baylor, ed., *The Radical Reformation*, p. xiv.

[9] Ibid., p. xvi.

[10] Ibid., p. xviii.

[11] See the "Twelve Articles," translated in Peter Blickle, *The Revolution of 1525*, pp. 195–201.

In Anabaptism the relation of individual piety and communal responsibility
was addressed, and the objective laws of the sacramental system were smashed,[12]
setting the scene for the implosion of religious communitarianism and the migration of sacral authority via the Bible to the temporal State. In the end the
question of who possessed the authority to regulate moral and religious life (which
were not necessarily the same) was decided on a territorial basis; however, the
course of the discussion and the confusion and competition that sparked that
discussion began in the late fourteenth and fifteenth centuries. The course of
this discussion, in which urban Christian society attempted to define the locus
of power within its confines, draw the boundaries of communal society, and
regulate the structures and morals of its members, turned quickly and significantly to the Jews.

Balthasar Hubmaier (ca. 1480–1528), who stirred up anti-Jewish sentiment
and action in Regensburg in 1519 before turning away from the established
church, and who nevertheless had absorbed a fair amount of nominalist theology, offers a useful port through which to continue into the radical Reformation
discussion begun in chapter 2. Hubmaier's theology revealed much of the late
medieval milieu in which it was steeped.

In his writings one may find at least two nominalist concerns. First, Hubmaier
distinguished between the absolute and ordained powers of God:

> That is a statement about the omnipotent and hidden will of God who owes
> no one anything. Therefore he can without any injustice be merciful to
> whomever he wills or harden the same, save, or condemn. This power or
> will the schools have called the omnipotent power or will of God, which no
> one, as Paul writes, may stand against. Yes, God has the right, power, and
> authority to make of us what he will, a vessel of honor or dishonor, as the
> potter has power over his clay and we cannot rightly say, 'Why do you do
> that?' Now, however, one can also find a revealed will of God according to
> which he wants all people to be saved and to come to recognition of the
> truth.[13]

By this logic certain actions of God cannot be understood by men, whereas
others are ordered according to principles set down for humans to be able to
comprehend. Second, Hubmaier followed the lead of Thomas Bradwardine (ca.
1290–1349) and John Wyclif (d. 1384), who criticized the extrascriptural tradition: that is, they favored the use of Scripture alone, and not the "complementary unwritten tradition . . . transmitted through the apostles and their
successors."[14] Hubmaier claimed to be concerned with the "simple sense" (ain-
feltiger synn) of scripture:

---

[12] For a discussion of ritual in the Reformation, see Susan C. Karant-Nunn, *The
Reformation of Ritual: An Interpretation of Early Modern Germany*.

[13] In *Balthasar Hubmaier: Theologian of Anabaptism*, edited by H. Wayne Pipin and
John H. Yoder, p. 472.

[14] Heiko Oberman, *The Harvest of Medieval Theology*, p. 366; it must be noted, how-

The Scripture should be clear, simple, and understandable in itself if only our fleshly hairsplitting would not seek more out of it than its simple sense could bear.[15]

In place of such "fleshly hairsplitting," Hubmaier wanted to substitute a close reading of Scripture itself.

To these nominalist aspects of his thought Hubmaier did not add the usual nominalist emphasis on the idea of a covenant between man and God. Instead, he emphasized the relationship among men. According to Hubmaier, the apostles held counsel not to decide doctrine but rather to maintain unity among the brethren.[16] For Hubmaier, the value of Mass was that it was a symbol of Christ's love and it allowed people to eat and drink together. Often he spoke of fellowship within the church, and it is precisely in this context that he developed his concept of the ban. The ban was a public separation or exclusion from the fellowship of the church for those who refused to heed fraternal admonition when they had gone astray.[17] The idea of public (*öffentlich*) that Hubmaier used here was also important to his other theological discussions, for example, his consideration of baptism. In baptism the water marked an outward and public act that followed inner conversion and recognition of one's sins.

Hubmaier began to write about baptism seriously only in 1525. For him baptism was a public profession of faith. The Word had to be taught before outward baptism was given. According to Hubmaier, a close reading of Scripture demonstrated that there was a prescribed order for baptism: Word, hearing, change of life/recognition of sin, baptism, works. The inward confession of sins had to occur before the outward baptism with water. That is, faith had to precede baptism, for the water itself did not save. John baptized only those who recognized their sins; he did not baptize children. The very young should not receive baptism (though a prayer for the young could be substituted), because there was no such thing as baptism in future faith: infant baptism was like a vessel without wine.[18] Baptism, therefore, was for believers only, as a pledge of submitting oneself to the brethren.

Much of Hubmaier's discussion of baptism was an attempt to show that Huldrych Zwingli's (1484–1531) argument for infant baptism was unfounded in Scripture, and therefore (since anything not commanded in Scripture should not be done) that Zwingli was mistaken. Although he believed that he needed no other source than Scripture, Hubmaier amassed a great number of

---

ever, that Hubmaier's position on Scripture as the sole basis for authority borrowed equally from the evangelical reformers, especially Zwingli, whom he encountered in the early 1520s.

[15] Pipin and Yoder, eds., *Balthasar Hubmaier*, p. 479.
[16] Balthasar Hubmaier, *Schriften*, p. 92.
[17] Pipin and Yoder, eds., *Balthasar Hubmaier*, p. 410.
[18] Ibid., p. 70.

authorities, ancient and modern, to prove that infants should not be baptized. Surprisingly, perhaps, Hubmaier followed traditional Catholic, and particularly late medieval, teaching in arguing for a sharp distinction between the baptism of John and the baptism of Jesus, whereas Zwingli, in attempting to wipe away the difference between the two baptisms, was the one who broke most sharply from the late medieval theological tradition.[19]

Hubmaier made a good case for reading in a formulaic way biblical passages that dealt with baptism: preaching, hearing, recognition of sins, baptism, and works. He did not so much alter the traditional view of the historical sequence— the baptism of John was followed by the baptism of Jesus—as he changed the meanings behind the categories of the two and so reformulated the historical sense in content but not in time. Hubmaier did not formulate the sequence inner faith (which corresponded to the baptism of the spirit, i.e. the baptism of Jesus) and then outward ceremony (the baptism of water, or the baptism of John), rather the baptism of inner faith was joined with the baptism of outward ceremony, but had to be preceded by a baptism of John which consisted of teaching.

In every case teaching had to precede the rite of baptism, which itself preceded entrance into the community and works. In the world, the harmony of public community, rightly ordained, transcended all else. Hubmaier allowed some latitude for the individual to prophesy and learn, but the believer was always constrained by the moral authority of the community and subject to the ban if the moral power was transgressed. This stress on the unanimity of the community was not surprising, given Hubmaier's attempts to create a more homogenous society in Regensburg by excluding the Jews and in Waldshut by excluding the Catholics.

The community that Hubmaier envisioned was both public (*öffentlich*) and oral (*mündlich*). Hubmaier used this notion of community, based on Matt. 16:18–19, to clarify his view of water baptism. He wrote:

> For through this, as through a visible door, by the public confession of faith, we must enter into the general Christian Church, outside of which there is no salvation. For in water baptism the church uses the key of admitting and locking away, as Christ promises and gives to it the power of the forgiveness of sins.[20]

Hubmaier's reading of the powers of the visible church paralleled the concepts of fraternal admonition and the ban which he developed very literally, based on Matthew's emphasis on humility (Matt. 18:15f). With this disposition it was easy for Hubmaier to redirect the emphasis of interpretation. He analyzed the following passage:

---

[19] See David Steimentz, "The Baptism of John and the Baptism of Jesus in Huldrych Zwingli."

[20] Pipin and Yoder, eds., *Balthasar Hubmaier*, p. 175.

At that time the disciples came to Jesus, saying, 'Who is the greatest in the kingdom of heaven?' And calling to him a child he put him in the midst of them, and said 'Truly, I say to you, unless you turn and become like children, you will never enter the kingdom of heaven. *Whoever humbles himself like this child*, he is the greatest in the kingdom of heaven. "Whoever receives one such child in my name receives me; but whoever causes one of these *little ones who believe* in me to sin . . ."' [emphasis added]

His literal reading of Scripture served his argument well. Against those, and here he meant Zwingli, who interpreted the last part of this passage, "these little ones who believe," to mean that even children have faith and so can and should be baptized, Hubmaier responded that the earlier phrase, "whoever humbles himself like this child," implied that the central message had nothing to do with whether or not children could have faith, but rather demonstrated that only those who were humble, like children, could have faith. Faith, for Hubmaier, required public confession, which was oral and it had to be taught, since it was not inherent in the child but came only through learning (i.e. humility). Faith in this sense allowed one to participate in the community, a community that became a community of believers.

Luther had argued that one could be baptized and assume faith at some point in the future—baptism would in fact promote faith. For Hubmaier, however, the issue was quite different, not primarily whether children could have faith, but whether or not they could actually belong to the "community." After all, this was what baptism was all about—the creation of community—a public (*öffentlich*) sign demonstrating one's affiliation. Since it was true that children did not have understanding,[21] "baptismal scripture does not apply to them but to those who now believe and confess their faith orally."[22] Hubmaier's community was, therefore, a community of believers who could orally articulate their belief. Such a vision of community, particularly as it developed in the south German cities, had severe consequences for Jews and other marginalized groups.

The seeds which allowed Hubmaier to formulate such a communal vision had deep roots stretching back to the early fifteenth century. By the mid-fifteenth and early sixteenth centuries definitions of community were being worked out more fully in a theology centered on community. Hubmaier could therefore write that "it is not enough that one should believe in Christ with the heart. One must confess [to] him also externally in public so that one confesses oneself as a Christian."[23]

Luther suggested that being baptized as a child implied that one did not depend on one's own faith but rather on God's bidding. If one's faith fell away, one was still baptized. For Hubmaier, however, who gave a much freer reign to the human will than did Luther, it was precisely the individual's faith which gave

---

[21] Balthasar Hubmaier, *Schriften*, p. 265.
[22] Ibid., p. 264; see also Pipin and Yoder, eds., *Balthasar Hubmaier*, p. 286.
[23] Pipin and Yoder, eds., *Balthasar Hubmaier*, p. 178.

baptism any meaning at all. God's bidding had nothing to do with the matter, for infant baptism could not be found in the Scriptures. What was most unique in Hubmaier's theology, however, was his emphasis on baptism not merely as an external sign but as a public pledge to the community and a contract with the fraternity.[24] The act of baptism, without the proper instruction, was not good enough. Hubmaier attempted to give greater sacral scope to a moral sacrament that was no longer primarily between God and man but between men.

The community became a central issue to many of the radical reformers of the early sixteenth century. Hans Hut (ca. 1490–1527), an itinerant bookseller residing near Meiningen, who came under the influence of Thomas Müntzer, presented a rather interesting exercise in scriptural exegesis in commenting on the sacrifices of the Old Law. For him the passage had a rather allegorical twist as well as a somewhat literal and definite moral interpretation.

> Thus God's commandments are not based on the language or on the speech he uses but on the power of the spirit. The power of such commandments will always influence those people who are in the same relation to God as such sacrifices are in relation to man. Thus, instead of burnt offerings like rams, cattle, and he-goats, David sacrificed himself to God as a calf (Psalm 51:17). *So, such ceremonial sacrifices are symbols and witnesses that people should give themselves as living sacrifices* (Romans 12:1). Afterward, God commanded that clean animals be eaten (Leviticus 11:4, Deuteronomy 14:3ff), the meaning of which refers to such people who so give themselves to God, to suffer the will of God as such animals must suffer our will. And God forbade unclean animals to be eaten, the meaning of which is that *I should have nothing to do with unclean people*, who are compared with such animals. For it is written (Acts 10:15 and 11:9) that nothing is unclean and everything is good. *The ceremonies show only what the will of God is, and they are presented to us as validly as to the children of Israel.*[25] [emphasis added]

What was most significant for Hut was the faith and sacrifice that the sacraments themselves simply represented (they did not create faith). Such rites were not edifying or even valid in themselves, rather they taught, allegorically, correct behavior. But if Hut read the Old Laws with a certain allegorical strain, he did the same with the New Laws. He noted that ". . . the baptism which follows preaching and faith is not the true essence through which people become pious, but only a symbol, a covenant, a likeness, and a reminder of a person's consent, so that he is reminded daily to expect the real baptism."[26] This real baptism was, for Hut,

---

[24] The idea of baptism as a contract (with God though) goes back to Tertullian (ca. 150–225)—see Joseph Crehan, *Early Christian Baptism and the Creed: A Study in Anti-Nicene Theology*, pp. 96f.

[25] In Baylor, ed., *The Radical Reformation*, p. 159.

[26] Ibid., p. 162.

... an obliteration of all lusts and desires of the heart. That is, baptism is an obliteration of all lusts and disobedience which are in us and which incite us to oppose God. God did this to the ancient world at the time of Noah (*Genesis* 6), when he washed away all evil from the world through the flood, and it also happened to Pharaoh and his Egyptians in the baptismal bath of the Red Sea, when they sank to the bottom like lead. The whole world—including Noah and his household, Pharaoh, and all his followers, and the whole of Israel—is baptized in the same way. But all people do not emerge from baptism alike, nor is baptism equally useful to all. The wicked certainly come to it but do not emerge again, because with their lusts they sink to the very bottom in creaturely things. They have not been able to let go of either worldly things or themselves. But they live continually and happily in lust and love of creaturely things. Thus, they persecute the elect, who do not cling to these things as they do. The elect desire to swim, and they strive unceasingly for the bank or dock, like Peter, so that they come out of the world's violent sea and the water of all grief and adversity ...[27]

For Hut, man was not saved merely by being baptized. Rather the opposite was true. The ceremony of baptism reflected an actual transformation of one's attitudes toward sin and one's actions away from sin. The external ceremony merely marked the internal change that had to precede it.

Although less politically oriented, the Spirituals also demonstrated important continuity with the late medieval theology we have reviewed. The Spirituals' emphasis on internal morality and communities of belief is also important to consider within this context.

Like so many of the theologians whom we have examined until this point, Sebastian Franck, in his *Weltbuch* of 1534, made the standard Pauline distinction between flesh (word) and spirit, between external and internal. However, Franck's inner spirit had an ecumenical, non-legal ring to it. According to Franck "all men are Man. It is all Adam."[28] Franck included Christians and non-Christians alike. Indeed, this was the central point of the *Weltbuch*: all men had the capacity truly to serve God—such men could even be found during the age of the Old Testament. Outward appearance, for Franck, was meaningless. Only correct inner belief was truly valuable. As Franck noted in his *Paradoxa*:

Who is in one city is in the entire world; although he finds different customs, languages, and clothing, the nature, heart, and the senses and the will are the same in all. All men are one Man, the difference is only external, in countenance and appearance before the world; the inner truth is with them all one and the same.[29]

Unlike some of the Anabaptists, such as Hans Denck (ca. 1500–1527), who taught that those who remain outside of the faith of Christ are of no concern

---

[27] Ibid., p. 167.
[28] Sebastian Franck, *Paradoxa*, no. 93, p. 126.
[29] Ibid.

to the community, except for didactic purposes, Franck argued that "God is everything in everything,"[30] the light of God touches everywhere.[31] In a letter of 1531 to his friend John Campanus, Franck admonished him to "consider as thy brothers all Turks and heathen, wherever they may be, who fear God and work righteousness, instructed by God and inwardly drawn by Him, even though they have never heard of baptism, indeed of Christ himself, neither of his stay or scripture, but only of his power through the inner word perceived within and made fruitful."[32]

For Franck, however, the Jews, although disciplined and obedient, had been corrupted in their hearts because of their adherence to the externals, ceremonies, superstitions, and sacraments of their religion, particularly of the Talmud, which Franck claimed, was inundated with foolish fables.[33] As Franck saw them, all ceremonies, whether Christian—the rites of the Roman church, which he labeled sorcery (*zauberei*)—[34] or pagan—he gave the example of the Jews' phylacteries—are changeable and belong to the Devil's realm.[35] According to Franck all sacraments before spiritual rebirth were "ruined and unfit" (*verderbt und untüchtig*). Franck warned John Campanus that "in the meantime the sacraments will also remain but, in respect to their truth and meaning, ensnared by the Antichrist and trampled under his feet—the Antichrist whom the Lord by His advent and by the Spirit of His Mouth will tread on the ground and slay; and (He) will call the scattered church together (as I have said) from the four ends of the world. In the meantime, the Temple, Sacraments, and all services remain with Antichrist."[36]

The world of sacraments and institutions was visible and fleshly, whereas true religion was inward looking. The soul that strove for God was invisible. Like Erasmus, Franck viewed the invisible as a perfection of the visible. He would have agreed that

> you should always try to advance from things visible, which are for the most part imperfect or of a neutral status, to things invisible . . . Here then lies the way to a pure and spiritual life: to gradually accustom ourselves to being alienated from those things which in reality are illusory but which sometimes seem to be what they are not—gross sensuality, for instance, and worldly glory—and which pass away and quickly melt into nothingness; and then to be ravished by those things which are truly lasting, immutable, and true.[37]

---

[30] Ibid., no. 2, p. 16.
[31] Sebastian Franck, *Weltbuch*, fol. i (vor).
[32] Sebastian Franck, "A Letter to John Campanus (1531)," p. 156.
[33] Franck, *Weltbuch*, fol. cl.
[34] Ibid., fol. cxxxivr.
[35] Ibid., fol. clixr.
[36] Franck, "A Letter to John Campanus (1531)," pp. 154–155.
[37] Erasmus of Rotterdam, *Enchiridion*, pp. 101–103.

Yet despite such disdain for the visible, all of the worldly devotions that Franck presented had their place: they all circled around a common and true inner belief—all perhaps helping man fulfill his need to serve God. When men could focus themselves inwardly on the heart and overlook the outward appearance that they viewed through their eyes, they might begin to be able to realize that at base all men were equal. Despite the different customs, clothing, and habitations that he presented, Franck believed that at some level human nature was uniform. All men were, after all, created in the image and likeness of God, and everyone descended from Adam.[38] Franck expressed a hope to return to a natural state in which men could recognize their basic similarity. He did not want to return to the early church, but rather to a period before the rule of Nimrod—before people began to divide up the world and bickered about property.[39] The natural state for which Franck aimed was not an hierarchical one, but rather a communal and harmonious one.

The radicals' emphasis on internal religion emphasizing correct moral behavior continued the development of the late medieval communes. Whereas the late medieval communes were sacralized, absorbing religious identity into the communal ethos, the radicals sought to recast the community as a community of believers absorbing the political and secular aspects of communal existence within a spiritual framework. The radicals were, in the end, unsuccessful; sacralization was a tool in the process of communalization and not an end in itself.

THE JEWS IN LATE MEDIEVAL SPAIN

As much of this book has been comparative it is instructive to offer one final comparison, that between the situation of the Jews in late medieval Germany and Spain. The increasing marginalization of the Jews, the attempts of both Jewish and non-Jewish communities to create larger bodies of authority, and many of the issues related to communal identity seem to resonate in fifteenth-century Spain. To what extent were the changes described throughout this book unique to Germany? Were the situations and experiences of the Jews in late medieval Spain and late medieval Germany comparable? If so, what do such similarities tell us about general European Christian and Jewish development? If not, how can we explain the different developments?

If Germany had been exegetically associated with the Ashkenaz mentioned in Genesis, many rabbinic exegetes, such as the *Targum Jonathan* for example, equated the Sepharad of the biblical Obadia with Spain. Spanish Jews were, therefore, called Sephardim. Although the settlement of the Jews in Spain could be dated with certainty only to the fourth century, later exegetes, such as Don Isaac Abravanel, claimed that Jews had settled in Spain already after

---

[38] Franck, *Weltbuch*, folio iiiir.
[39] Norman Cohn, *The Pursuit of the Millenium*, p. 258.

the destruction of the First Temple.[40] Given the cultural milieu in which the
Jews lived, combining both Islamic and Christian influence, the Sephardim
developed unique language, customs, and literature that marked them as different from the Ashkenazim of western Europe.

The course of Jewish history has been intimately connected with Diaspora
and exile.[41] The forced wanderings of the Jews have had profound effects upon
their religion, culture, identity, and community. The great expulsion of the Jews
from Spain at the end of the fifteenth century, ending possibly 1,500 years of
Jewish settlement, was one particularly significant chapter in the history of
the Jewish people. The results of that and subsequent migrations from Iberia
affected the Jews, as it did their non-Jewish hosts, in deep and lasting ways.
Though not as old, the Jewish communities of Germany had developed significant
communal, religious, and social institutions, particularly since their dramatic
growth after the eleventh century. The results of the expulsions of the Jews
from parts of Germany in the fifteenth and early sixteenth centuries, though
of a somewhat different character and extent, shared some surprising similarities with those of the Spanish expulsions.

Even in terms of mere chronology, the fates of the Jews in Spain and Germany
showed striking similarities.[42] In Spain, the devastating massacres and forced
conversions of 1391 occurred just after the imperial tax campaigns against south
German Jewry. Many of the same anti-Jewish developments that escalated in
fifteenth-century Germany can be found as well in fifteenth-century Spain.
There were waves of conversionary campaigns and religious debates in both
Spain and Germany; in Spain in the second decade of the fifteenth century;
in Germany between the 1430s and 1450s. The ritual murder accusations of the
late fifteenth century, such as that in Trent (1475) and El Niño de la Guardia
(1490–1491) were early versions of a much played-out theme in fifteenth and
sixteenth-century German lands, particularly in the southwest. In both Germany
and Spain Jews suffered social and professional restrictions throughout the
fifteenth century. The Valladolid regulations of 1412 were precursors to increas-
ly severe restrictions beginning in the 1460s. In Germany, the Councils of
i el and Constance initiated and gave force to a variety of anti-Jewish legis-
lati n in individual cities and territories from the 1430s through the 1490s. Jews
were socially segregated in Andalusia in 1480 and in Regensburg in the late
fifteenth-century.

Finally, Jews suffered local and regional expulsions in both places. The Jews
of Andalusia were expelled in 1483. The Jews were expelled from numerous
German imperial and free cities throughout the fifteenth century and from a
variety of territories beginning in the sixteenth century. It has been suggested

---

[40] See the end of his commentary to Kings II.

[41] See Yosef Hayim Yerushalmi, "Exile and Expulsion in Jewish History."

[42] For a general comparison of the fate of Jews under Christian and Muslim rule see
Mark R. Cohen, Under Crescent and Cross: The Jews in the Middle Ages.

that one of the chief motivations in the expulsion of the Jews in Portugal was the prospective marriage between the Portuguese King Manuel and the Princess Isabella, eldest daughter of the Spanish monarchs. Around the same time that the Emperor Maximilian expelled the Jews from Styria, negotiations were in progress for the marriage of Maximilian's son Philip to the Spanish monarchs' daughter Juana.[43]

In intellectual developments there were many cases of interaction between Jews residing in Spain and Germany. Both groups shared common reference works such as the codifications of Alfasi, the Tur, and Maimonides. A number of German Jews such as Asher ben Jehiel emigrated from Germany to Spain, while many others, including Josel of Rosheim,[44] were intimately familiar with the philosophical and polemical works produced by Spanish Jews; indeed, many "Spanish" philosophical and halakhic works could be found in German Jewish libraries and many German Jews were interested in a mysticism that has been more typically associated with Spanish Jewry.[45] Both German and Spanish Jews debated the possibility of resuming rabbinic ordination in the later Middle Ages.[46]

Late medieval Spain, like its German counterpart, was rather fragmented, and the experiences of the Jews depended very much upon local and regional conditions. Medieval Spain was divided into four major political entities, and many of the regions within these divisions retained their own institutions, customs, laws, language, and monetary and judicial systems, even after they were incorporated into one of the larger political units such as the Crown of Aragon. Communal organization and functions varied, therefore, according to geography.[47] Aragonese communities possessed special rituals and spoke a Jewish dialect of Aragonese. They had their own peculiar communal organization as well, which differed from that of the Castilian, Navarrese, or Catalan communities. There was a unique inter-communal organization known as the Collecta that may have been less binding, but was a stronger and more centralized representative body than its Catalan and Valencian counterparts. The representatives of this body met annually in Saragossa, arguably the most important Jewish community in Aragon. Indeed, the charters and duties of Saragossa became models for other Aragonese communities; and Saragossa itself was dominant in

---

[43] See Maria José Pimenta Ferro Tavares, "Expulsion or Integration? The Portuguese Jewish Problem;" and *Quellen zur Geschichte Maximilians I. und Seiner Zeit*, edited by Inge Wiesflecker-Friedhuber, pp. 61f, and, Charles Beard, *The Reformation of the Sixteenth Century*, p. 94.

[44] See Joseph of Rosheim, *Sefer ha-Miknah*, edited by Hava Fraenkel-Goldschmidt, in particular book II.

[45] See Avraham Grossman "Relations between Spanish and Ashkenazi Jewry in the Middle Ages."

[46] See Mordechai Breuer, *The Rabbinate in Ashkenaz during the Middle Ages*; see also Simon Schwarzfuchs, *A Concise History of the Rabbinate*.

[47] Miguel Angel Motis Dolader, *The Expulsion of the Jews from Calatayud 1492–1500: Documents and Regesta*, in the introduction by Yom Tov Assis, p. 5.

communal relations.[48] As in many other communities, however, there was movement for social and communal reform within the community. Similar social
agitation could be found in the fourteenth century in the second most important Aragonese city, Calatayud:[49]

The example of the Jewish community (aljama)[50] of Tortosa is illustrative.
The community was autonomous and legally recognized. Its structure was probably influenced by the Christian municipality in which it was situated. The community was run by a council, whose members, (adelantats and consellers),
represented the three classes (mans). Secretaries of the council executed judgments, and individual members served in positions such as treasurer and tax
collector. The structure of the council did not change after the massacres and
forced conversions of 1391, though the number of councilors rose to seven in
the fifteenth century. Often relations between the highly oligarchical council
and the community were not friendly; sometimes, as well, council elections did
not run smoothly and the non-Jewish authorities might be forced to intervene,
as happened for example, from 1436 through 1437.[51] At times, the community
was involved with suits against members of the community.[52]

Internally, the professional diversity within many of the Spanish communities equaled, and at times surpassed, that in even the largest German communities.
Jews practiced as surgeons and physicians, were moneylenders, dealt in commerce, and even owned property and dealt in real estate. Jews were also engaged
in the crafts; in Tortosa, for example, they frequently worked as tailors.[53]

In Valencia the communities underwent significant geographical and com-

---

[48] Among the important scholars of the city were numbered Hasdai Crescas (d. ca.
1412) and Isaac ben Sheshet Perfet, or Ribash (1326–1408).
[49] Calatayud was the chief community of one of ten Collectas in Aragon, and it
included, like other large cities, smaller satellite communities. Like other Jewish communities it was hit hard by Christian missionary campaigns and the Inquisition. Throughout
Aragon anti-Judaism was on the rise after 1391. Vicent Ferrer began preaching in Castile
in 1411 and then continued on into Aragon.
[50] The Jewish quarter, or the call, in Tortosa had its own entrance and was partly
surrounded by a wall, at least in the fourteenth century, and in general Jews could own
property within the call. There was one major synagogue in the call, where the election of community leaders and delegates took place, as well as hospices. See The Jews
of Tortosa 1373–1492: Regesta and Documents from the Archivo Histórico de protocols de
Tarragona, compiled by Josefina Cubelis I Llorens, pp. viif.
[51] Ibid., p. x.
[52] See documents 219 and 220 in Ibid. In Valencia as throughout the crown of
Aragon, the aljama was ruled by its own particular statutes, which were ratified by the
king of Aragon. The council was under the control of an oligarchy, in which retiring
officials typically appointed their successors. Office holders, therefore, changed but the
office typically remained with the same family. This led to deep social tensions throughout the later Middle Ages. See Jose Hinojosa Montalvo, The Jews of the Kingdom of
Valencia: From Persecution to Expulsion, 1391–1492, pp. 82–83 for election issues and
p. 85 for attempts to democratize the aljama in 1424.
[53] The Jews of Tortosa, p. xix.

munal change after the pogroms and forced conversions of 1391.[54] Throughout
the 1470s the gradual impoverishment of the Valencian Jewish communities
occurred, so that by 1492 the only really important communities were Morvedre
and Jativa. In the city of Valencia after 1391 at least 200 Jews remained, though
the city never again possessed a Jewish quarter. By 1423 there were only 30
Jews. On the other hand, at the time of expulsion there were about 700 Jews
in Morvedre (a third of the total population). Neighboring Burriana, however,
remained practically devoid of Jews and other neighboring communities, such
as Donate Sebastia and Magdalena Nom de Deu, had perhaps around 50 Jews.
Given the close ties between the Castellon and Morvedre communities, we find
an increase in the Castellon population in 1391, probably from Jews escaping
Morvedre.[55] In Castellon there were 27 Jewish residents in 1371 and there may
have been hundreds of Jews in 1391; subsequently, however the number dropped:
in 1433 there were 11 Jews; in 1462, 22; in 1468, 17; 1473, 21; 1479, 18; 1485,
19; and, in 1491, 20 families (expelled).[56]

The anti-Jewish trends that were evident throughout both Spain and Germany
at the end of the fourteenth and the beginning of the fifteenth century are
quite clear in Tortosa.[57] In 1346 the local cemetery was profaned, and Jews frequently suffered attacks during Holy Week (in fact, prohibitions against injur-
ing Jews during this week had to be issued in 1369). The preaching against
Jews in Tortosa was particularly virulent, given the effects of the important disputations held in the city between 1413 and 1414. Pere Cerda was noted in
the 1420s for his volatile sermons against Jews. Such sermons roused the local
population to anti-Jewish behavior and brought about a high number of Jewish
converts to Christianity. Jews could suffer at the hands of secular authorities
as well. In the 1320s we find a significant emigration from royal to baronial
domains of Jews seeking to avoid excessive taxation.[58]

In the fifteenth century the Cortes of Toledo attempted to segregate the
Jews in 1479 through 1480, and in the Andalusian expulsion of 1483, Jews
were accused of collaborating with the Muslims. In January 1486 the municipal council of Valmaseda in the Basque country decided to expel the Jews, following the Andalusian example. Already in 1483, however, the same council
had banned marriages between resident and foreign Jews, moves that suggest

---

[54] Montalvo, *The Jews of the Kingdom of Valencia*, pp. 21f et passim.

[55] The Jewish communities in Valencia retained close contact throughout the fifteenth
century. Morvedre, Castellon and Burriana in particular, which were separated by only
40 km, formed the basic axis of Valencian Jewry. Although each community guarded
its independence, and at times there were altercations between the communities or
within individual communities, still, movement between the communities was not difficult.
See Montalvo, *The Jews of the Kingdom of Valencia*, pp. 66f.

[56] Ibid., p. 69.

[57] See the introduction by Yom Tov Assis in *The Jews of Tortosa*, p. vi.

[58] Ibid., pp. xvif.

similar communal identity questions as those in late medieval Germany.[59] In the late 1480s and early 1490s there was a substantial increase in the taxes demanded of Jews and the seizure of offices of tax farming and collecting taxes held by Jews. But the economic position of the Jews had already deteriorated in many places—instructively, in Navarre, where the Jews seem to have remained central to the economy they were not expelled early—particularly after 1391.

For Navarre, the situation may have been slightly different. Benjamin Gampel has argued that expulsion was not inevitable with the accession of Ferdinand and Isabella, and he therefore uses the term *convivencia* with some justification.[60] Even in the late fifteenth century, city records indicate that Jews continued to play an integral part in the economy. Still, as in Castile and Aragon there was also a clear erosion of Jewish rights and an increase in restrictions against Jews in the 1470s and 1480s. Internally, the communal structure of Navarrese Jewry was similar to other Iberian Jewries, even if the steady immigration of Jews from other communities complicated communal identity and created separate communities within individual cities. In 1495, no doubt in large measure due to the swelling number of refugees, there were about 3,550 taxpaying Navarrese Jews (about 3.5% of the total population).[61]

The Spanish expulsion edict issued by Ferdinand and Isabella focused heavily on religious elements,[62] contending that although Jews had been segregated from their former co-religionists who had since converted to Christianity, they nevertheless continued to exercise undue influence over them, corrupting these New Christians. Such Jewish actions were viewed as transgressions against the holy Catholic faith and the expulsion was issued upon religious and ecclesiastical advice. According to the document:

> Because whenever some grave and detestable crime is committed by some persons of a group or community, it is right that such a college or community be dissolved and annihilated . . . and that those who pervert the good and honest living of the cities and villages, and that by contagion could injure others, be expelled from among the peoples, and even for other lighter causes that are harmful to the states, and how much more so for the greatest of the crimes, dangerous and contagious as is this one.

Although the document reads in some places more like an anti-Jewish sermon of Bernardino of Siena, its emphasis on Jews corrupting the community strikes close parallels with the expulsion discourse of late medieval Germany. Clearly the priority of redefining "community" in a more homogenous way was at stake in the documents.

---

[59] Roth, *Conversos, Inquisition, and the Expulsion of the Jews from Spain*, p. 283.
[60] See Benjamin Gampel, "Does Medieval Navarrese Jewry Salvage Our Notion of *Convivencia*."
[61] This percentage is comparable for the previous century as well. See Benjamin Gampel, *The Last Jews on Iberian Soil: Navarrese Jewry 1479–1498*, pp. 20–21.
[62] See Norman Roth, *Conversos, Inquisition, and the Expulsion of the Jews from Spain*.

The expulsion was to be comprehensive, and Jews were never to return. Still, a grace period was given in which Jews might liquidate the holdings that they would not or could not take with them. The Iberian expulsions affected a very large number of Jews (and *conversos*)—300,000 according to Abravanel, 200,000 according to other chroniclers—and have variously been attributed to the king, the queen, certain advisors, the final expulsion of the Muslims from Granada, and the Inquisition.[63] The goal of the expulsion, it has been argued, was the pacification and ordering of religious life.

Similarly, the Portuguese edict of expulsion from December 1496 expelled all Jews, under the penalty of death and loss of possessions, from all kingdoms and domains. Again, the reason given for the expulsion was that the Jews caused true Christians to depart from the proper way. The great evil and blasphemies of the Jews were also pointed out, as was the royal obligation to protect the church and the people. In addition, however, the edict noted that the action was a way to increase the holy Catholic faith. The Jews were also castigated for maintaining their hardness of heart.

There are a number of similarities in the German and Spanish expulsion discourse that belies efforts at consolidation of communal identity at local, regional, and royal levels; though in some ways the situation of the Jews expelled from Spain was completely different. Many Jews settled in communities that could have been familiar to them, in Portugal and Navarre, for example. Even in more familiar places, however, the emigrants were often forced to create their own communities within the larger Jewish community, and frequently they met the enmity of not only the Christian authorities but of their co-religionists as well. In other places, however, they would have found very different communal situations. Choices of emigration, as in Germany, would have been choices both individual and forced. According to the chronicles of the period, we find Jews settling, some more temporarily than others, in a variety of places, such as: Portugal, Navarre, Italy, Tunis, Fez, Genoa, and Istanbul.[64]

Particularly since 1992, a good deal of literature exploring the position of the Jews in Spain immediately before, during, and subsequent to the expulsion has appeared. These studies indicate, by and large, that Jews were fairly well integrated within many communities even close to the time of the expulsion, though these same studies reveal increasing marginalization of the Jews after the middle of the fifteenth century. Perhaps surprisingly, many studies reveal that the Spanish Jews not only carried with them, but in many ways also continued to value, their Spanish cultural heritage. Miriam Bodian, for example,

---

[63] See: Ibid; Yitzhak Baer, *A History of the Jews in Christian Spain, volume 2: From the Fourteenth Century to the Expulsion; Moreshet Sepharad: The Sephardi Legacy*, 2 volumes, edited by Haim Beinart; and, Haim Beinart, *The Expulsion of the Jews from Spain* [Hebrew]. See also the account of Ibn Verga in *The Expulsion 1492 Chronicles: An Anthology of Medieval Chronicles Relating to the Expulsion of the Jews from Spain and Portugal*, edited by David Raphael, p. 92.

[64] See, for example, Ibn Verga, in Raphael, ed., *The Expulsion Chronicles*.

in investigating the *conversos* who settled in Amsterdam, where they then resumed their Jewish identity, finds that they transplanted their cultural and linguistic identity complete with social hierarchies and traditional outlooks.[65] Bodian points out the difficulty facing the *conversos*, who wished to identify with the prevalent values of Iberian society and who nonetheless needed to defy them. Such Jews combined an acceptance of Iberian esteem for lineage along with insistence on special merit of their Jewish ancestry. It might not be to unreasonable to draw a comparison between the transformation and continuity with Spanish Diaspora communities after the 1492 expulsion and the transformations and continuities of identity among the increasingly territorialized Jewish communities in Germany in the fifteenth and sixteenth centuries.

The nature of the community established in Amsterdam, and its later interactions with Ashkenazic Jews indicates the strength of such traditions as well as the complexity of relations with other Jewish segments and populations. The Diaspora could affect individual Jews, families, and even large portions of old communities in various ways—philosophical outlooks, religious customs, halakhic discussions, economic roles, and social standing.[66] The role of the rabbinate seems to be one particularly significant area to pursue in more detail, and in many ways, parallels the developments noted within Germany.[67]

CONCLUSION

Although Anabaptism in the end failed to create its own sacral community— and the religious communitarianism of the Anabaptists, divorced from ecclesiastical and sacramental law (except in the experiment at Münster, or later in the Hutterite and Mennonite communities), became self-destructive and socially dangerous—the result was that such communitarianism, or spiritualization, could only be restrained by a migration of sacral authority into the temporal power of the state.

In fifteenth-century Germany sacralization occurred at the local urban level. Slowly, throughout the sixteenth century this process expanded into the regional state level, explaining why Jews were expelled from the cities in the fifteenth century and from many territories in the sixteenth. The migration of sacral authority to the state was also an important element in the expulsion of the Jews from Spain. However, this sacralization occurred at the national level. With stronger centralized identity it is not surprising that when Spanish Jews were expelled they maintained both religious and ethnic identification.

The Spanish expulsion edict's heavy emphasis on issues of religion seems to confirm a more general theory that the assumption of sacred authority by the

---

[65] Miriam Bodian, *Hebrews of the Portuguese Nation*, p. 17, for example.
[66] See *Crisis and Creativity*, edited by Benjamin Gampel, and *In Iberia and Beyond*, edited by Bernard Dov Cooperman.
[67] See Breuer, *The Rabbinate in Ashkenaz*; Schwarzfuchs, *A Concise History of the Rabbinate*; and Robert Bonfil, *Rabbis and Jewish Communities in Renaissance Italy*.

secular authority makes tolerance of religious minorities impossible. In a sense, then, Spain on a national, monarchical, level was moving in a very similar direction to the cities and territories of Germany in the later Middle Ages. The sacralization in Spain occurred at the national level; such was, of course, impossible in Germany given the territorial fragmentation and rudimentary forms of political authority in many regions. The net result of expulsion, however, was the same in both places. For the Spanish Jews, who were forced to create a communal identity that could survive serious rupture and displacement, we again find striking parallels with the German Jewish communities that were becoming increasingly regional, rural, and dispersed at the end of the Middle Ages. Identity was based on moral codes and inherited social structures.

In Germany, with the consolidation of the sacralized State at the end of the sixteenth century, Jews were able to begin the process of reintegration. The need to accommodate minority religious groups in England and France in the sixteenth and seventeenth centuries made the re-absorption of the Jews possible there. Given strong regionalization and the role of the Roman church, the case of Italy was an admixture of different developments. In Catholic Spain, however, where the state was not fully sacralized, but rather paralleled the centralization of a national church, Jews were not re-admitted.

Conclusion

Jewish and Christian communities in fifteenth-century Germany underwent significant and, in some ways, parallel transformations that affected their notions of themselves as well as their views of, and interactions with, each other. These transformations had both internal and external—to the degree that they can be separated—causes and consequences. Urbanization, territorialization, and the reordering of centralized religious structures, along with the ensuing struggles to define and wield authority, affected both Jews and Christians. Given that the concept of community could be multi-valent and could alter its meaning according to circumstances, it was possible for both Christians and Jews to refashion their sense of community to strengthen traditional communal understanding or create new communities to adapt current understandings to changed circumstances.

In south German cities during the fifteenth century, the urban Christian sense of community was being restructured along civic and religious lines. The outcome was a miniature local version of a *corpus christianorum*, a "sacred society" that integrated material and spiritual well being into a moral and legal society, stressing the common good and internal peace. Jewish community also emphasized its sacrality, but given the increasing dispersion of the Jewish population, the territorialization of the political powers governing the Jews, as well as changes in internal communal structures, Jewish community came to be defined through regional, not local, communal structures and through a moral and legal discourse that allowed for broader geographical communal identity. The developments examined in this book both preserved and built upon older relations and adapted to new conditions. They flowed, on the one hand, from the general transformation of European politics, religion, and culture and, on the other, promoted the downward spiral, increasing social isolation in older residential areas but promoting the integration of Jews into new parts of Europe.

* * *

Urbanization in late medieval Germany offered a forum in which social tensions could be played out. The cities, with their historic privileges and self-awareness, encouraged the creation of new forms of communal identity. The self-awareness of urban Christian communities was informed by the powerful social, economic, and cultural conditions that they created and to which they reacted. The burghers also molded traditional theological discussions about the Christian community to local conditions of popular piety, localized institutional religion, and the role of customs, rituals, and sacraments. Two important changes helped to forge the burghers into a sacred community: the increasing power of moral and legal definitions of community and lay appropriation of clerical religious authority.

The idea that a certain moral code was required of community members became central in the self-understanding of the late medieval German commune. The completion of this shift toward the moral law as the center of religion relativized ties to and controls by the larger church and opened them to burghers' criticism. The local moral community refashioned itself in the image of the church as a community of grace, regulating the beliefs of its members by policing their morals. The way toward a complementary revision of the understanding of the sacramental system had been paved by the nominalists, who defined the Law less in terms of the ceremonial or ritual character of the sacraments and more by a certain moral code. The Mendicant friars delivered the message home more directly, by preaching morality and the common good throughout the cities.

Beginning in the thirteenth century and continuing through the fifteenth, the city councils, dominated by wealthy laymen, increasingly appropriated authority in the cities from the noble and ecclesiastical lords. About the same time, the cities anchored their rights and identity in written lawbooks that gave them new communal meaning and tradition. Combined with increasing anti-clerical sentiment, such identification inclined lay leaders to take over and monopolize the sacred, in effect forming the urban community into a sacral body. In both religion and politics, emphasis on the common good was stressed over its antithesis, individual benefit and separation. Everything foreign was more closely monitored and distanced. The Jews were placed, to some extent, in this category, and seen as standing outside of community and opposed to the common good. As "proper conduct" was defined in moral treatises and the law (police ordinances, for example) and in turn became central to such definition, exclusionary policy intensified, and exile frequently became the fate of the Jews.

*   *   *

While a large majority of the Jewish settlements in the later Middle Ages were in the cities, a growing number of settlements were located in small towns and villages spread across central and southern Germany. The resulting territorialization, or regionalization, of Jewish community had a significant impact on Jewish and Christian interaction but also upon Jewish communal structures and identity. This transformation has been described as a shift from kehillah-based to medinah-based structures of authority. Jewish communities, in large measure because of increasing dispersion and the increasing authority of lay leaders at the expense of the rabbinate, required Jews to identify themselves as a broader and geographically dispersed collectivity, different from earlier models.

Jews living in rural areas, outside of any large city or Jewish settlement, fashioned community and maintained numerous and multi-faceted interactions with other Jews in religious services, communal tax structures, and the use of ritual baths (*mikvot*), hospitals, and regional cemeteries. It is clear that strong and important connections bound Jews in different settlements and cities throughout Germany. Late medieval Jewry continued to be governed by a fairly uniform body of law and ritual. In addition to this, regional customs, and the very movement of Jews between communities as well as their personal inter-connection helped to create something of a more cohesive nature than might otherwise have existed had these been completely isolated communities.

The process of social change that affected Jews and Christians in the fifteenth century worked to polarize the Jewish social structure. Deep tensions ran through the Jewish communities, particularly in an age heightened by forced expulsions, conversions, and secret informing. One important tension arose from the chang-ing role and status of the rabbi.

In the era after the coming of the Black Death the rabbi's position within the Jewish community was becoming professionalized. In this age, indeed, *semi-khah*, or ordination, was introduced into Ashkenazic Jewry, and we begin to find traces of actual formal appointments of rabbis by communities. The pro-fessionalization of the rabbinate forced the rabbi into a position of dependence upon the wealthy lay leadership, however. Imperial and territorial Christian intervention in the appointment of rabbis further weakened the standing of the rabbi in the Jewish community, even if it made the position more "official." The responsa often reveal, in fact, the rabbi's position to be wavering between one of authority and manipulation.

The Jewish community continued to fashion itself as a holy community. In the high Middle Ages the authority of the rabbi and the sanctity of the com-munity depended upon the renown and influence of the leading rabbinic author-ities. During the later Middle Ages, however, drastically increased dispersal of the Jews and changes within the communities promoted a general identification of the community as an entity sacred in and of itself and weakened the sense of dependence on the rabbi, who, in any event, was slowly being pushed from many of his traditional roles.

*   *   *

The ways in which Jews were conceived and described by Christians in the later Middle Ages shared a great number of features with the concepts ascribed to other outsiders; by applying such discourse to them, Jews were included in the late medieval urban community in very tangible, if not always very favor-able, ways.

Beginning in the twelfth and thirteenth centuries Jews were seen not only as a historic people, and therefore largely a religious people, but increasingly as enemies, both historical and contemporary. This process, which reflected the new, Christian sense of communal identity, continued through the reformations of the sixteenth century. Religious anti-Judaism remained in many ways as pow-erful as it had been throughout the high Middle Ages and earlier. Its expres-sions, however, reveal their dependence on the formation of a new corporate, religious sense of identity among the communally organized burghers of late medieval Germany. It is not the case that the commune was secularized; rather the opposite seems to have been the case. The commune was sacralized, and religion, particularly in its moral as contrasted with its sacramental aspects, became a key aspect of urban communal identity. But only one aspect, for religion was not rejected by the burghers—as many modern scholars have argued— but was integrated into communal identity and became its normative center. Burghers themselves became clerics, who set out to reform and absorb the church. In earlier times, when religious and urban identities had been distinct, Jews could remain in the cities; later, when communal identity absorbed religious self-understanding, the different character of the Jews became more noticeable and less tolerable.

In this process of sacralization Jews were first increasingly excluded and then expelled. They had to be, for symbolic space had to be made for a new type of Jew, the new children of the New Israel, who claimed direct descent from the old, biblical Jews as God's Chosen People. The Christian burghers, in fact, in a sense co-opted the Jewish sacred identity and became themselves a kind of Jew, just as they became a kind of clergy. This change was a profound shift in the self-understanding of medieval Christians. In earlier centuries, Christians had defined their community in terms of a universal sacramental life governed by a central institution, the church, which made them neo-Jews, but in a pre-Diaspora sense. Late medieval urban Christians in the German lands became something quite different: neo-Jews in a post-Diaspora sense. They identified themselves as a godly people not by ritual—corresponding to the daily sacrifices performed in the Temple at Jerusalem—but by legal and moral codes. In the Christian communities, the domestication of sacrality tended to lessen the role of universal rituals, or at least to create local rituals distinct from a more universal system. This reformulation became, in the sixteenth century, central to the introduction and spread of Protestantism.

If in the later Middle Ages, civic community was sacralized and formed as a moral community, the radical phase of the Protestant Reformation attempted to create a believing community by replacing legal norms with theological belief. The radical Reformation of the sixteenth century Anabaptists and Spiritualists, therefore, represented the logical conclusion to the whole process studied in this book. The radicals, in fact, fashioned themselves as new Jews who possessed the only valid claim to the descent of the people of Israel. The Anabaptist movement in south Germany not only reflected the ferment over authority, piety, and community; in the end it also demonstrated the need for a new vision, one that combined traditional authority, communal identity, and civic and religious reform.

If Christian discussions of Jews combined changing theological constructs with practical daily interaction, the same could be said of Jewish representations of Christians. Despite theoretical theological divisions, Jews, particularly by the end of the Middle Ages, very often did not count Christians among the idol-worshipping gentiles referred to in the Talmud, and they continued to interact with Christians on a regular basis. Jewish business and social relations with Christians were no doubt shaped by practical daily and economic situations as much as by theology.

Social isolation of Jews from Christians did, nonetheless, increase in the sixteenth century, when there was a marked attempt to recast the Jewish community as a sacred entity, separate from its surroundings and holy in its own being, as revealed in the writing of Josel of Rosheim and Maharal of Prague. Ashkenazic Jewry became a closed system with few or no comprehensive thinkers but a plethora of moralizing and admonishing preachers. As Jewish sense of community turned inward, polemic against Christianity became less important than reorganizing communal structure and identity. The late medieval polemic presented here was a bridge that combined high medieval theology with attempts at separation, moralizing, and resanctification. One great benefit of a more broadly, internally conceived community was that it could easily encompass geographically dispersed Jews. If the community itself was based upon inherent sanctity more than daily interactions it is not difficult to see how communal identity could become regional.

Like the urban Christian communities, the Jewish communities refashioned and resacralized themselves as well, at both the regional and universal level. On one level, Jewish community was defined through regional customs and institutions. On another level, however, universal ritual, as described in common bodies of law, and in particular in the Talmud, maintained cohesion among Jews. Jews employed ritual and law to fashion a broader communal identity beyond the local or regional structures of community.

*   *   *

The process of religiously understood intensification and closure of community, which we observe in the late medieval German cities, resembled in some ways the later formation of national communities analyzed by Ernst Gellner. According to Gellner, in this process it is at first in the state's interest to protect minority groups, which are easy to exploit. But as the process of nationalization begins, the state becomes more interested in depriving the minority of the economic monopolies that it had once lavished upon them. It is the very visibility of the minority that affords their dispossession and persecution as a means to buy off a great deal of discontent in the state's wider population. According to Gellner "the national 'development' requires precisely that everyone should move in the direction which was once open only to a minority and stigmatized group."

In Germany, communities were sacralized at the local urban and later at regional levels. This contrasts diametrically with what happened in Spain, where the Jews were expelled from the nation by the temporal government acting on behalf of the church. Such full-scale expulsion was not possible in Germany, where fragmented political realities forced a variety of reactions to the Jews and the local or regional sacralization of the community. A migration of sacral authority into the temporal power of the state took place at different times and levels in Germany and Spain. In Germany, with the consolidation of the sacralized state at the end of the sixteenth century, Jews were able to begin the process of reintegration. According to some scholars, the adaptation of Roman Law and Jewish reintegration increased correspondingly, since Roman Law considered Jews as citizens and because it forced the community to see itself more metaphorically than actually as the body of Christ. In any event, the need to accommodate minority religious groups in England and France in the sixteenth and seventeenth centuries helped to facilitate the re-absorption of the Jews. Italy represented an admixture of different developments, while in Spain, Jews were not re-admitted.

* * *

In the end, this book demonstrates the necessity of comparative study, taking both common history and different histories together. Jewish and Christian history and community informed one another and helped each to create its own self-understanding and boundaries. Neither can be viewed in a vacuum. In the same way, the history of late medieval Germany gains greater clarity when compared and contrasted with developments in other regions at the same time. Such comparisons throw into relief the outlines of an age that was extremely complex and yet central in German, Christian, and Jewish history. Finally, this book has argued for, and attempted to practice, a kind of history that takes ideas, including theology, as a necessary and complementary component of social history. Ideas do not simply record social, political, cultural, economic, and religious developments; they also influence such developments and offer important keys to understanding them. Perhaps it is no longer possible to separate histories of Jews and Christians or intellectual and social change in the history of medieval and early modern Germany or in history in general.

Glossary of Terms

aigennutz	(German) individual self interest
Arba'ah Turim	(Hebrew) "four rows;" comprehensive codification of Jewish law in four parts written by Jacob ben Asher (c. 1270–1340)
Bauer	(German) farmer
Bürgerrecht	(German) civic right
Burggraf	(German) overseer of a city
Bürgermeister	(German) mayor, burgomaster
chametz	(Hebrew) an agent of fermentation, which Jews are forbidden to own or consume on Passover
coniuratio	(Latin) alliance, conspiracy
contritio	(Latin) contrition; repentance for sins out of love for God
conversos (pl.)	(Latin) Christians of Jewish descent; frequently accused of secretly maintaining Jewish rites; also known as anusim or marranos
convivencia	(Latin) living together; often used to describe the multicultural existence of medieval Spain
corpus christianum	(Latin) "body of Christendom;" sacred society
cortes	(Spanish) Spanish courts
culpa	(Latin) guilt; sin remitted through penance
eruv	(Hebrew) extension of the private domain into the public domain, typically by using a wire, to allow carrying on the Sabbath that is otherwise forbidden
ex opere operantis per modum meriti	(Latin) efficiency of a rite as related to interior disposition of administrant or recipient
ex opere operato	(Latin) on the grounds of performance of the rite
facere quod in est	(Latin) to do all that is one's natural power unaided by grace
Fastnachtspiele	(German) carnival plays
gadolim (pl.)	(Hebrew) literally, great ones; leaders
gaon (pl. geonim)	(Hebrew) "excellency;" title of heads of the two leading Babylonian academies between the end of the 6th and end of the 12th centuries
gehinnom	(Hebrew) valley outside the western wall in Jerusalem; assumed status of hell in post-biblical literature
Geleit	(German) law of escort
gemein	(German) common, communal

Gemeinde	(German) community
Gemeinschaft	(German) community
Germania Judaica	(German) central synthetic study of Jewish settlements and communities in Germany until the beginning of the sixteenth century. See appendix and bibliography
Gesellschaft	(German) society
get	(Hebrew) bill of divorce
Gulden	(German) since the fourteenth century a gold coin in Germany; 1500 until the nineteenth century a silver coin in Germany and neighboring states
halakhah	(Hebrew) Jewish law
halizah	(Hebrew) the act of "drawing off;" freeing a woman from the biblical injunction to marry the widow whose husband died without offspring and the brother of the deceased (Levirite Marriage)
herem	(Hebrew) excommunication
herem ha-yishuv	(Hebrew) ban on settlement
Herr	(German) lord
Herrschaft	(German) lordship
heter	(Hebrew) leniency
Judenrat	(German) Jewish council in a city/community; often modeled on the Christian council
kadosh	(Hebrew) holy
kahal	(Hebrew) community
kehillah	(Hebrew) community
ketubah	(Hebrew) Aramaic document of bridegroom's obligations toward the bride as a prerequisite to marriage
kohen (pl. kohanim)	(Hebrew) descendants of Aaron who served as priests in the Temple
Maimonides	(Hebrew) Moses ben Maimon (1135–1204); also known as the Rambam
manhig	(Hebrew) leader
medinah	(Hebrew) region
meritum de condigno	(Latin) "full merit," meeting standard of God's justice and performed in state of grace and worthy of divine acceptance
meritum de congruo	(Latin) "half merit," meeting standard of God's generosity, performed in state of sin in accord with natural or divine law and accepted by God to satisfy requirement for infusion of first grace
mikvah (pl. mikvot)	(Hebrew) ritual bath
Mishnah	(Hebrew) the Oral Law, divided into six orders and redacted in the third century CE by Rabbi Judah ha-Nasi
Mishneh Torah	(Hebrew) Mishnah commentary of Maimonides

morah d'atra	(Hebrew) master of the place; community rabbi
morenu	(Hebrew) "our teacher;" title given to distinguished rabbi
musar	(Hebrew) moral and religious ethical instruction
parnas (pl. parnasim)	(Hebrew) "presider;" religious or administrative functionary
poena	(Latin) punishment; sin transmuted from eternal to temporal by penance
potentia dei ordinata	(Latin) ordained power of God; order established by God and way in which God has chosen to act
potentia dei absoluta	(Latin) absolute power of God subject only to law of non-contradiction
Reichstädte (pl.)	(German) imperial cities
responsa (she'elot u-teshuvot) (pl.)	(Latin (Hebrew)) "questions and answers;" answers to questions on Jewish law and observance given by halakhic and talmudic scholars in reply to inquiries addressed to them
rosh yeshivah (pl. rashei-yeshivah)	(Hebrew) head of a talmudic academy
Satzungsbuch	(German) book of (civic) ordinances
semikhah	(Hebrew) "laying on" of hands; rabbinic ordination
Sonderweg	(German) "special way;" unique development
sotah	(Hebrew) wife suspected of being adulterous
Stadtbuch	(German) medieval compilation of civic law
Stadtrecht	(German) city law
takkanah (pl. takkanot)	(Hebrew) ordinance
Talmud	(Hebrew) literally "Teaching," used to denote the Mishnah and Gemara ("completion," or comment on and discussion of the Mishnah) as a single unit. It exists in Babylonian and Palestinian versions and includes both halakhah and midrash
tsibur	(Hebrew) community
tsitsit	(Hebrew) "fringes" attached to four-cornered garments. See Deut. 22.12
va'ad (pl. va'adim)	(Hebrew) committee
viator	(Latin) the pilgrim
Vogt	(German) overseer
Volkslieder	(German) folksong
Vorbeter	(German) leader of prayers; cantor
Wucher	(German) usury
yayin nesek	(Hebrew) "libation wine;" wine consecrated by gentiles for idol worship and so forbidden from consumption and benefit by Jews
yeshivah (pl. yeshivot)	(Hebrew) talmudic academy

Appendix A: *Germania Judaica*: History and Scope

Our understanding of the nature and development of German Jewish communities and settlements has increased significantly due to the publication of important materials in *Germania Judaica* (*GJ*), now in its third volume. Begun early last century, *GJ* offers an extensive and much needed resource for the history of the Jews in Germany from "the oldest times" until the early sixteenth century. Volume 1 (edited by M. Brann, I. Elbogen, A. Freimann, and H. Tykocinski), reaching to 1238 was republished by the Leo Baeck Institut in 1963. Volume 2 (in 2 parts, edited by Zvi Avneri) was published in the late 1960s and volume 3 (part 1 edited by Arye Maimon and Yacov Guggenheim; part 2 by Arye Maimon, Mordechai Breuer and Yacov Guggenheim) in the late 1980s and mid-1990s (part 3, edited by Mordechai Breuer and Yacov Guggenheim, is in press).

The first part of volume 1, letters A-L first appeared n 1917; part 2 did not see print until 1934. The working plan for the edition (see vol. 1, pp. x–xi) was laid out in Breslau in June of 1905, dictating that, among other things:

1. *GJ* has the task of representing all of the areas of the German Empire, where Jews had settled from the most ancient times until the Viennese agreements, in alphabetical order;
2. the work was to include all the regions that constituted the Empire at that time as well as the states that formed the *imperium romano-germanicum*, including modern day France, Netherlands, Belgium, Austria, Luxemburg, and in some cases, Switzerland;
3. initially the project was to extend until the beginning of the nineteenth century, in 3 volumes: the first until 1238, the second examining the period between 1238 and 1500; and the final volume to consider 1509–1815;
4. each entry was to examine the internal life of the particular community in question, while also setting a broader historical context.

The introduction to volume 1 offers a thorough orientation to the: early settlement of the Jews in Germany; legal position of the Jews; organization of the Jewish communities; taxation of the Jews; economic activity of the Jews; relations between Jews and Christians; and, Jewish cultural and religious endeavors.

When volume 2 was published in 1967, 1348 was chosen instead of 1500 for the *terminus ad quem*. Volume 2 included a large amount of material that had been collected before World War II but that had only made its way to London and then to Jerusalem in the 1950s. A brief introduction in volume 2 gives some information for the period from 1238 to 1350 according to the same rubric of the introduction to volume 1. Volume 3 covers the period from 1350 to 1519, with 2 parts published to date: part 1 includes articles on settlements (cities and regions) beginning with the letters A through L (1987); part 2 on settlements between M to Z (1995), with no introductory materials. Volume 3 is also scheduled to include a third part examining German territories in addition to the cities and villages of the first two parts. Throughout, GJ uses modern place designations, for example it utilizes the modern state of Baden-Württemburg and regions of modern East Germany.

Appendix B: Selected Regional and Urban Expulsions of Jews in Late Medieval Germany

Area	Period	Area	Period
Major Regional Expulsions		*Major City Expulsions*	
Palatinate	1390/91	Trier	1418/19
Thurinigia	1401	Vienna	1421
Austria	1420/21	Cologne	1424
Trier			
(Archbishopric)	1418/19	Zurich	1435/36
Breisgau	1421	Heilbronn	1437
Cologne			
(Archbishopric)	1429	Ausgburg	1438/40
Bavaria-Munich	1442	Mainz	1438, 1470
Bavaria-Landshut	1450	Munich	1442
Bohemian Cities	1454	Würzburg	1450
Mainz			
(Archbishopric)	1470	Breslau	1453/54
Bamberg			
(Hochstift)	1478	Erfurt	1453/54
Mecklenburg/			
Pommerania	1492	Hildesheim	1457
Magdeburg			
(Archbishopric)	1493	Bamberg	1478
Carniola	1496	Salzburg	1498
Styria	1496	Wiener Neustadt	1498
Brandenburg	1510	Nuremberg	1499
Alsace	ca. 1520	Ulm	1499
Saxony	1540	Nördlingen	1504
		Regensburg	1519
		Rothenburg ob	
		der Tauber	1520

Source: GJ, vol. 3

Appendix C: Number of Jews Listed in the Augsburg Tax Books 1355 to 1440

Year	Number of Tax-Paying Jews	Year	Number of Tax-Paying Jews
1355	23 (4 stricken)	1411	17
1356	22 (2 stricken)	1412	20
1357	24 (3 stricken)	1413	20
1358	24	1414	21
1359	24	1415	21
1362	19 (2 stricken)	1416	22
1363	17 (2 stricken)	1417	23 (1 stricken)
1364	20 (3 stricken)	1418	20
1367	23	1419	17
1377	27	1420	20
1382	50+ (3 stricken)	1421	19
1383	56+	1422	21
1384	19	1423	22 (1 stricken)
1386	18	1424	20
1389	30 (4 stricken)	1425	21
1390	14	1427?	23 (1 stricken)
1391	21	1428	22
1392	6/9	1429	23 (2 stricken)
1393	10	1430	25/27?
1394	11	1431	25
1395	14	1432	24/25 (4 stricken)
1396	14	1433	24 (1 stricken)
1398	14	1434	26
1400	19	1435	27 (5 stricken)
1401	17	1436	23
1402	17	1437	24/25
1404	17	1438	24/25
1405	11		
1406	12		
1407	14		
1408	17		
1409	22 (1 stricken)		
1410	19		

Source: Augsburg Steuerbücher

Appendix D: Jews Paying Taxes in Augsburg, 1438

Name	First Mentioned in Tax Lists	Traceable after 1438
1. Jacob Hochmeister	1429	Bamberg, Erfurt (1443)
2. Merlin his son	1436 at latest	
3. Lemlin Boruch Välklin	1421	Rabbi in Ulm?
4. Perma his son	1433 (not 1437)	
5. Abraham son of Lemlin	1434	
6. Josep son of Lemlin	1434	Mainz (1449)?
7. Mosse (recessit)	1423 (possibly 1420 if brother of Lemlin Abrahams, 1409 if Moses von Laugingen)	Würzburg (mid 15th-century)
8. Abraham his son	1433	
9. Liepma(n)	1421	
10. Josep his son (recessit)	1433	Mainz (1449)?
11. Salkind von Werd	1420	Nördlingen (1440)?
12. Josep his son	1430	Nördlingen (1439)
13. Hayem . . .	1424 (son of Salkind)	
14. Salman von Werd	1412	Heilbronn (1449)?
15. Josmen (recessit)	1407 (not 1419); father listed before 1413	
16. Mair his son	1416 (not 1419)	
17. Jäcklin his son (recessit)	1434	
18. Old Vällkin (recessit)	1426 (Wölfin?)	Günzburg (1442)?
19. "Ungehorend" Boruch	1426	
20. Josep von Laugingen (recessit)	1426	Rothenburg ob der Tauber (1439)
21. Schmul Sechtes	1428	Doctor in Frankfurt am Main (1441)
22. Feyvelman	1430	Nördlingen (1440)
23. Säcklin his son	1433	
24. Lemlin Boruch	1438	Rabbi in Ulm?

Source: Augsburg Steuerbücher, GJ, vol. 3

Appendix E: Professions Practiced by Jews in Late Medieval Germany

Profession	Area
Alchemist	Kassel
Baker	Friedberg
Barber	Nuremberg, Prague
Bookbinder	Erfurt, Nuremberg
Box-maker	Mühlhausen
Broker	Nuremberg
Butcher	Augsburg, Breslau, Friedberg
Carpenter	Regensburg
Cereals, dealer	Steyr
Clock-maker	Regensburg
Cloth, dealer	Luxemburg, Prossnitz
Clothing (used) dealer	Erfurt
Cook	Erfurt
Cow breeder	Spandau
Cow trader	Augsburg
Currency worker	Prague
Die/cube-maker	Friedberg
Doctor (f)	Colmar, Mainz
Doctor (m)	Augsburg, Dresden, Mainz
Doctor (horse)	Karburg
Doctor (eye)	Esslingen am Neckar, Colmar, Rottenburg am Neckar
Furrier	Prague
Fur trader	Friedberg
Glazier	Lüben, Kölin, Komotau, Winterthur, Wulfingen
Goldsmith	Kölin, Nuremberg, Prague
Goose dealer	Prague
Guitar player (Zitherspieler)	Prague
Handworker	Laun
Herring business	Prague
Horse trader	Lüben, Mühlhausen
Inn servant	Mainz, Prague
Maid	Augsburg
Merchandise, dealer (including: wine, cereals, knives, tin)	Frankfurt am Main, Laibach, Laun, Mühlhausen, Regensburg
Midwife	Breslau
Needle-maker	Regensburg
Painter	Munich
Precious metals, leather, textiles, dealer	Prague
Printer	Gunzenhausen, Prague
Procurator	Prague
Prostitute	Augsburg, Frankfurt am Main
Provisions, dealer	Prague

Appendix E (*cont.*)

Profession	Area
Saffron, wine, vegetable, handler	Friedberg, Mainz, Nuremberg
Servant	Nuremberg
Sewage expert	Nuremberg
Spice dealer	Friedberg
Surgeon	Freiburg/Uechtland
Swordsmith	Kölin, Komotau, Pardubitz, Prague
Tailor	Prague
Toll taker	Villach
Waitress	Augsburg
Water drawer	Regensburg
Weapons dealer	Mühlhausen
Weapons master	Karburg
Wool, dealer	Friedberg

Source: GJ, vol. 3

[*Note: Communal Positions (e.g., Shochet, Mohel, Teacher (schoolmaster)) and some business professions (e.g., money-handling, money-lending) are not included*]

Bibliography

Primary Sources

Altmann, Wilhelm, ed. *Die Urkunden Kaiser Sigmunds (1410–1437)*. 2 vols. Regesta imperii, vol. 11. Innsbruck, 1896–1900.

Ambrose, Saint. *De Sacramentis*. In *Patrologiae cursus completus; omnium ss. patrum, doctorum scriptorumque, ecclesiasticorum sive latinorum, sive graecorum [series latina]*, edited by J.P. Migne, vol. 16: 435–482.

Andreas von Regensburg. *Sämtliche Werke*. Edited by Georg Leidinger. Aalen, 1969 (reprint). [Originally published as Quellen und Erörterungen zur bayerischen und deutschen Geschichte, neue Folge, vol. 1 (Munich, 1903)].

Aquinas, Thomas, Saint. *Basic Writings of Saint Thomas Aquinas*. Vol. 2. Edited by Anton C. Pegis. New York, 1945.

———. *Divi Thome Aquintas in tertio sententiarum libro*. Venice, 1497.

Arnpeck, Veit. *Sämtliche Chroniken*. Edited by Georg Leidinger. Aalen, 1969 (reprint). [Originally published as Quellen und Erörterungen zur bayerischen und deutschen Geschichte, neue Folge, vol. 3 (Munich, 1915)].

Augustine, Saint. *Basic Writings of Saint Agustine*. Vol. 1. Edited by J. Whitney Oates. New York, 1948.

———. *Sancti Aurelii Augustini Quaestiones Evangeliorum cum appendice Quaestionum xvi in Matthaeum (Aurelii Augustini Opera, XIII:3)*. In *Corpus Christianorum series Latina 44B*, edited by Almut Mutzenbecker. Brepols, 1980.

Aventinus, Johannes. *Baierische Chronik*. Edited by Georg Leidinger. Jena, 1926.

———. *Sämtliche Werke*. 6 vols. Edited by the Royal Academy of Science. Munich, 1881–1908.

Baader, Joseph, ed. *Nürnberger Polizeiordnungen aus dem xiii bis xv Jahrhundert*. Bibliothek des Litterarischen Vereins in Stuttgart, Nachdruck 63. Stuttgart, 1966 (reprint). (orig., 1861).

Balthasar Hubmaier: Theologian of Anabaptism. Classics of the Radical Reformation, vol. 5. Edited and translated by H. Wayne Pipin and John H. Yoder. Scottdale, Pennsylvania, 1989.

Barack, K.A., ed. *Des Teufels Netz: Satirisch-Didaktisches Gedicht: Aus der ersten Hälfte des Fünfzehnten Jahrhunderts*. Bibliothek des Litterarischen Vereins in Stuttgart, vol. 70. Stuttgart, 1863.

Basler Chroniken. 8 vols. Edited by The Historical and Antiquarian Society in Basel. Leipzig, 1872–1945.

Bastian, Franz and Josef Widemann, eds. *Regensburger Urkundenbuch*. 2 vols. Monumenta Boica, vols. 53–54. Munich, 1956.

Berger, David, ed. and trans. *The Jewish-Christian Debate in the High Middle Ages*. Philadelphia, 1979.

Bergsten, Torsten. *Balthasar Hubmaier: Anabaptist Theologian and Martyr*. Edited by William R. Estep. Translated by Irwin J. Barnes and William R. Estep, Jr. Valley Forge, Pennsylvania, 1978.

Biel, Gabriel. *Inventarium seu repertorium generale*. Cologne, 1504.

Blois, Peter of. *Contra Perfidiam Judaeorum*. In *Patrologiae cursus completus; omnium ss.*

patrum, doctorum scriptorumque, ecclesiasticorum sive latinorum, sive graecorum [series latina], edited by J.P. Migne, vol. 207: 825–70.

Böhmer, Johann, Friedrich, ed. *Acta Imperii selecta*. 2 vols. Insbruck 1866–70.

———. *Regesta imperi inde ab anno 1314 usque ad annum 1347*. Frankfurt am Main, 1839.

Bonaventura, Saint, Cardinal. *Opera Omnia*. 10 vols. Edited by the College of Saint Bonaventura. Quarracchi, 1882–1901.

Brinckus, Gerd, ed. *Eine bayerische Fürstenspiegelkompilation des 15. Jahrhunderts*. Münchener Texte und Untersuchungen zur deutschen Literatur des Mittelalters, vol. 66. Munich, 1978.

Bruna, Israel b. Hayyim. *She'elot u-teshuvot rabbi Yisroel me-Bruna*. Jerusalem, 1960.

Bucer, Martin. "De Regno Christi." In *Melanchthon and Bucer*, edited by Wilhelm Pauck (Philadelphia, 1969): 174–394.

———. *Martin Bucers Deutsche Schriften, Volume 1: Frühschriften 1520–1524*. Edited by Robert Stupperich. Gütersloh, 1960.

Caesarius von Heisterbach. *The Dialogue of Miracles*. Vol. 1. Translated by H. von E. Scott and C.C. Swinton. London, 1929.

Die Chroniken der deutschen Städte vom 14. bis ins 16. Jahrhundert. 36 vols. Edited by The Historical Commission for the Royal Academy of Science. Leipzig, 1862–1931.

Chrysostom, John, Saint. *Saint Chrysostom: Homilies on the Gospel of Saint Matthew*. Edited by Philip Schaff. Grand Rapids, 1956 (reprint). [Originally published as A Select Library of Nicene and Post-Nicene Fathers of the Christian Church, vol. 10 (New York, 1888)].

Clement of Alexandria. *Christ, the Educator of Little Ones*. The Fathers of the Church, vol. 23. Translated by Simon P. Wood. New York, 1954.

Colon, Joseph ben Solomon. *Sefer She'elot u-teshuvot Maharik*. Edited by Shmuel Baruch ha-Kohen Doitsch and Elyakim Shlezinger. Jerusalem, 1989.

Cusa, Nicholas of. *Werke*. 2 vols. Edited by Paul Wilpert. Quellen und Studien zur Geschichte der Philosophie, vols. 5–6. Berlin, 1967.

Cyprian, Saint. *Treatises*. Translated by Roy J. Deferrari. Fathers of the Church, vol. 36. New York, 1958.

Denck, Hans. *Schriften*. Vol. 2. Edited by Georg Baring. Quellen zur Geschichte der Täufer, vol. 6:2. Quellen und Forschungen zur Reformationsgeschichte, vol. 24:2. Gütersloh, 1956.

———. *Selected Writings of Hans Denck, 1500–1527*. Texts and Studies in Religion, vol. 44. Translated by E.J. Furcha. Lewistown, New York, 1989.

Denis Le Cahrtreux. *De his qvae secvndvm sacras scripturas et orthodox patrum sententias, de sanctissima et indiuidua trinitate semper adorada, catholice credantur, liber primus [-qvarvvs]*. Cologne, 1535.

Deutsche Reichstagsakten: Ältere Reihe (1376–1486). 22 vols. Edited by The Historical Commission for the Royal Academy of Science. Munich, 1867–1957.

Diehl, Adolf, ed. *Urkundenbuch der Stadt Esslingen*. 2 vols. Württembergische Geschichtsquellen, vol. 4. Stuttgart, 1899 and 1905.

Dirr, Pius, ed. *Denkmaler des Münchener Stadtrechts von 1158–1403*. 2 vols. Bayerische Rechtsquellen, vol. 1. Munich, 1934–1936.

Duns Scotus, John. *Opera Omnia*. Vol. 16. Paris, 1891.

Durandi a sancto Porciano. *In Petri Lombardi Sententias Theologicas Commentariorum Libri iiii*. Venice, 1586.

Eisenstein, Judah David. *Ozar Wikuhim: A Collection of Polemics and Disputations*. New York, 1928. [Hebrew].

Engel, Wilhelm, ed. *Urkunden und Regesten zur Geschichte der Stadt Würzburg 1201–1400*. Regesta Herbipolensia, vol. 1. Quellen und Forschungen zur Geschichte des Bistums und Hochstifts Würzburg, vol. 5. Würzburg, 1952.

———, ed. *Urkundenregesten zur Geschichte der Städte des Hochstifts Würzburg (1172–1413)*.

Regesta Herbipolensia, vol. 3. Quellen und Forschungen zur Geschichte des Bistums und Hochstifts Würzburg, vol. 12. Würzburg, 1956.

Erasmus of Rotterdam. *The Enchiridion.* Translated by Raymond Himelick. Bloomington, 1963.

Fabri, Fratris Felicis. *De civitate Ulmensi, de eius origine, ordine, regimine, de civibus eius et statu.* Bibliothek des Litterarischen Vereins in Stuttgart, vol. 186. Edited by Gustav Veesenmeyer. Tübingen, 1889.

Feger, Otto, ed. *Vom Rechtebrief zum Roten Buch: Die ältere Konstanzer Ratsgesetzgebung.* Konstanzer Geschichts- und Rechtsquellen, vol. 7. Constance, 1955.

———. *Die Statutensammlung der Stadtschreiber Jörg Vögeli.* Konstanzer Stadtrechtsquellen, vol. 4. Constance, 1951.

Finke, Heinrich, ed. *Acta concilium Constantiense.* 4 vols. Münster, 1896–1928.

Finkel, Avraham Yaakov, ed. *The Responsa Anthology.* New York, 1991.

Fischer, Hanns, ed. *Die deutsche Märendichtung des 15. Jahrhunderts.* Münchener Texte und Untersuchungen zur deutschen Literatur des Mittelalters, vol. 12. Munich 1966.

Folz, Hans. *Spruch von der Pest: 1482.* Edited by Karl Strassburg. Trübner, 1879.

———. *Die Reimpaarsprüche.* Edited by Hanns Fischer. Münchener Texte und Untersuchungen zur deutschen Literatur des Mittelalters, vol. 1. Munich, 1961.

Franck, Sebastian. *Chronica Zeitbuch und Geschichtsbibel.* Strasbourg, 1536.

———. *Krieg Buchlin des Friedes.* Frankfurt am Main, 1550.

———. *Paradoxa.* Edited by Heinrich Ziegler. Jena, 1909.

———. *Weltbuch.* Tübingen, 1534.

———. "A Letter to John Campanus (1531)." In *Spiritual and Anabaptist Writers: Documents Illustrative of the Radical Reformation,* edited by George Williams. The Library of Christian Classics, vol. 25 (Philadelphia, 1957): 147–160.

Geiler von Kaysersberg, Johann. *Die Emeis.* Strasbourg, 1516.

Gengler, Heinrich, ed. *Codex Iuris Municipalis Germaniae: Medii aevi. Regesten und Urkunden zur Verfassungs- und Rechtsgeschichte der deutschen Städte im Mittelalter.* Erlangen, 1867.

———. *Deutsche Stadtrechte des Mittelalters.* Erlangen, 1852.

———. *Deutsche Stadtrechts-Altertümer.* Erlangen, 1882.

———. *Die Quellen des Stadtrechts von Regensburg aus dem 13, 14 und 15. Jahrhundert.* Beiträge zur Rechtsgeschichte Bayerns, vol. 3. Erlangen, 1892.

Haemmerle, Arthur. *Die Hochzeitsbücher der Augsburger Bürgerstube und Kaufleute bis zum Ende der Reichsfreiheit.* Munich, 1936.

———. *Die Leibdingbücher der freien Reichsstadt Augsburg 1330–1500.* Munich, 1958.

Harder, Leland, ed. *The Sources of Swiss Anabaptism: The Grebel Letters and Related Documents.* Classics of the Radical Reformation, vol. 4. Scottdale, Pennsylvania, 1985.

Hayyim Eliezer ben Isaac Or Zarua. *She'elot u-teshuvot.* Jerusalem, 1860.

Holkot, Robert. *Super quattuor Libros sententiarum questiones.* Cologne, 1505.

Hopkins, Jasper. *Nicholas of Cusa's Dialectical Mysticism: Text, Translation and Interpretative Study of De Visione Dei.* Minneapolis, 1985.

Hubmaier, Balthasar. *Schriften.* Edited by Gunnar Westin and Torsten Bergsten. Quellen zur Geschichte der Täufer, vol. 9. Quellen und Forschungen zur Reformationsgeschichte, vol. 29. Heidelberg, 1962.

Hugh of St. Victor. *De Sacramentis.* In *Patrologiae cursus completus; omnium ss. patrum, doctorum scriptorumque, ecclesiasticorum sive latinorum, sive graecorum [series latina],* edited by J.P. Migne, vol. 176: 173–618.

Hus, John. *Super iv Sententiarum.* 3 vols. in 1. Edited by Vaclav Fladshans. Sbírka pramenu ceského hnutí nábozenského ve XIV. A XV. století, cís. 4–6. Prague, 1904–1906.

Isidore of Seville. *De Fide Catholica Contra Judaeos.* In *Patrologiae cursus completus; omnium ss. patrum, doctorum scriptorumque, ecclesiasticorum sive latinorum, sive graecorum [series latina],* edited by J.P. Migne, vol. 83: 449–538.

Isserlein, Israel. *Terumas Ha-Deshen*. 2 vols. Edited by Shmuel Avitan. Jerusalem, 1990.
Jacob ben Moses ha-Levi (Maharil). *She'elot u-teshuvot*. Cracow, 1881.
——. *She'elot u-teshuvot hachadoshot*. Jerusalem, 1977.
Jerome, Saint. *Saint Jerome: Dogmatic and Polemical Works*. Translated by John N. Hritzu. Fathers of the Church, vol. 53. Washington D.C., 1965.
The Jews of Tortosa 1373–1492: Regesta and Documents from the Archivo Histórico de pro-tocols de Tarragona. Compiled by Josefina Cubelis I. Llorens. Sources for the History of the Jews in Spain, vol. 3. Jerusalem, 1991.
Joseph of Rosheim. *Joseph of Rosheim: Historical Writings*. Edited by Hava Fraenkel-Goldschmidt. Jerusalem, 1996. [Hebrew].
——. *Sefer ha-Miknah [me'et] Yosef Ish Ros'heim*. Edited by Hava Fraenkel-Goldschmidt. Jerusalem, 1970.
Keller, Adelbert von, ed. *Fastnachtspiele aus dem fünfzehnten Jahrhundert*. 3 vols. Bibliothek des Litterarischen Vereins Stuttgart, vols. 28–30. Stuttgart, 1853–1858.
——. *Hans Sachs*. Vol. 1. Bibliothek des Litterarischen Vereins Stuttgart, vol. 102. Tübingen, 1870.
Keutgen, Friederich. *Urkunden zur Städtischen Verfassungsgeschichte*. Ausgewählte Urkunden zur deutschen Verfassungsgeschichte, vol. 1. Berlin, 1965 (orig., 1901).
Kolb, Christian, ed. *Geschichtsquellen der Stadt Hall*. 2 vols. Württembergische Geschichts-quellen, vols. 1 and 6. Stuttgart 1894–1904.
Kracauer, Isidor, ed. *Urkundenbuch zur Geschichte der Juden in Frankfurt am Main 1150–1400*. 2 vols. Frankfurt, 1911–1914.
Langton, Stephen. *Der Sentenzenkommentar des Kardinals Stephen Langton*. Edited by Artur Michael Landgraf. Beiträge zur Geschichte der Philosophie des Mittelalters, vol. 37:1. Münster, 1952.
Liliencron, Rochus Wilhelm von. *Historische Volkslieder der Deutschen vom 13. bis 16. Jahrhundert*. 5 vols. Leipzig, 1865–1869.
Linder, Amnon. *The Jews in Roman Imperial Legislation*. Detroit, 1987.
Lombard, Peter. *Sententiarum Libri IV*. In *Patrologiae cursus completus; omnium ss. patrum, doctorum scriptorumque, ecclesiasticorum sive latinorum, sive graecorum [series latina]*, edited by J.P. Migne, vol. 192: 519–964.
Lyra, Nicholas of. *Glossae seu Postilla perpetuae in veterum et novum*. Venice, 1485.
Mayer, August L., ed. *Die Meisterlieder des Hans Folz aus der Münchene Originalhandschrift und der Weimarer Handschrift Q 566 mit Ergänzungen aus anderen Quellen*. Berlin, 1908.
Meyer, Christian, ed. *Das Stadtbuch von Augsburg, insbesondere das Stadtrecht von 1276*. Augsburg, 1872.
——. *Urkundenbuch der Stadt Augsburg*. 2 vols. Augsburg, 1874–1878.
Migne, J.P., ed. *Patrologiae cursus completus; omnium ss. patrum, doctorum scriptorumque, ecclesiasticorum sive latinorum, sive graecorum [series latina]*. 221 vols. Paris, 1844–1864.
Mintz, Moses. *She'elot u-teshuvot Rabbenu Moshe Mintz (Maharam Mintz)*. 2 vols. Edited by Yonathan Shraga Dumav. Jerusalem, 1991.
Mollow, Carl, ed. *Das Rote Buch der Stadt Ulm*. Württembergische Geschichtsquellen, vol. 8. Stuttgart, 1905.
Monumenta conciliorum generalium saeculi XV: Concilium Basilense. Scriptores. 4 vols. Edited by The Academy of Science. Vienna, 1857–1937.
Mühlhausen, Yom Tov Lipman. *Sefer Nizzahon*. Edited by Theodorico Hackspan. Altdorf, 1644.
Ockham, Guillelmi de. *Venerabilis Inceptoris Guillelmi de Ockham Quaestiones in Librum Quatrum Sententiarum (Repurtatio)*. In *Opera Theologica*, vol. 7. Edited by Rega Wood and Gedeon Gal. New York, 1984.
Pressel, Friedrich, ed. *Ulmisches Urkundenbuch (bis 1378)*. 2 vols. Stuttgart 1873–1900.

Puchner, Karl, ed. *Die Urkunden der Stadt Nördlingen (1233–1399)*. 4 vols. Schwäbische Forschungs-gemeinschaft bei der Kommission für bayerische Landesgeschichte Veröffentlichungen Reihe 2a: Urkunden und Regesten, vols. 1, 5, 9, and 10. Augsburg, 1952–1968.

Quellen zur Geschichte Maximilians I. und seiner Zeit. Edited by Inge Wiesflecker-Friedhuber. Darmstadt, 1996.

Rapp, Adolf, ed. *Urkundenbuch der Stadt Stuttgart*. Württembergische Geschichtsquellen, vol. 13. Stuttgart, 1912.

Richental, Ulrich von. *Das Konzil von Konstanz*. Edited by Otto Feger. Constance-Starnberg, 1964.

Roth, Friederich, ed. *Des Ritters Hans Ebran von Wildenberg Chronik von den Fürsten aus Bayern*. Munich, 1969 (reprint). [Originally published as Quellen und Erörterungen zur bayerischen und deutschen Geschichte, neue Folge, vol. 2, pt. 1. (Munich, 1905)].

Rüster, Peter, ed. *Die Steuerbücher der Stadt Konstanz, Volume 2: 1470–1530*. Konstanzer Geschichts- und Rechtsquellen, vol. 13. Constance, 1963.

Salfeld, Siegmund and Moritz Stern. *Die Israelitische Bevölkerung der deutschen Städtegeschichte. Volume 1: Überlingen am Bodensee*. Frankfurt am Main, 1890.

———. *Die Israelitische Bevölkerung der deutschen Städte, Volume 3: Nürnberg im Mittelalter*. Kiel, 1894–1896.

Schultheiss, Werner, ed. *Die Acht-, Verbots- und Fehdebücher Nürnbergs von 1285–1400, mit einer Einführung in die Rechts- und Sozialgeschichte und das Kanzlei- und Urkundenwesen Nürnbergs im 13. und 14. Jahrhundert*. Quellen und Forschungen zur Geschichte der Stadt Nürnberg, vol. 2. Nuremberg, 1960.

———, ed. *Satzungsbücher und Satzungen des Reichsstadt Nürnberg aus dem 14. Jahrhundert*. Quellen zur Geschichte und Kultur der Stadt Nürnberg, vol. 3. Nuremberg, 1965.

Stern, Moritz. *Urkundliche Beiträge uber die Stellung der Papste zu den Juden mit Benutzung des päpstliche Gheimarchivs zu Rom*. Kiel, 1893.

Straus, Raphael, ed. *Urkunden und Aktenstücke zur Geschichte der Juden in Regensburg, 1453–1738*. Quellen und Erörterungen zur bayerischen Geschichte, neue Folge, vol. 18. Munich, 1960.

Süssmann, Arthur, ed. *Das Erfurter Judenbuch (1357–1407)*. In Mitteilungen des Gesamtarchivs der deutschen Juden, edited by Eugen Täubler (Leipzig 1915): 1–126.

Vietzen, Hermann, ed. *Das Lehenbuch des Hochstifts Augsburg von 1424*. Kempten, 1939.

Wagenseil, Johann. *Tela Ignee Satanae*. Altdorf, 1681.

Weil, Jacob. *She'elot u-teshuvot*. Jerusalem, 1958 to 1959.

Die Welt zur Zeit des Konstanzer Konzils. Edited by Konstanzer Arbeitskreis für Mittelalterliche Geschichte. Constance, 1965.

Wesselski, Albert, ed. *Heinrich Bebels Schwänke*. 2 vols. Munich, 1907.

———. *Mönchslatein: Erzählungen aus geistlichen Schriften des 13 Jahrhunderts*. Leipzig, 1909.

Zwingli, Hulrych. *Huldreich Zwinglis Sämtliche Werke*. Vol. 4. Edited by Emil Egli, Georg Finsler, Walther Köhler, and Oskar Farner. Leipzig, 1927.

SECONDARY SOURCES

Abel, Wilhelm. *Agricultural Fluctuations in Europe: From the Thirteenth to the Twentieth Centuries*. Translated by Olive Ordisch. London, 1980.

Abraham, Israel. *Jewish Life in the Middle Ages*. Philadelphia, 1920.

Agus, Irving A. *Rabbi Meir of Rothenburg: His Life and his Works as Sources for the Religious, Legal, and Social History of the Jews of Germany in the Thirteenth Century*. 2 vols. Philadelphia, 1947.

———. *Responsa of the Tosaphists*. Min haganuz leor, no. 2. New York, 1954. [Hebrew].

Albert, Bat-Sheva. "Isidore of Seville: His Attitude Towards Judaism and his Impact on Early Medieval Canon Law." *Jewish Quarterly Review* 80, nos. 3–4 (January-April, 1990): 207–220.

Alberts, Werner. *Einfache Verbformen und Verbale Gefüge in zwei Augsburger Chroniken des 15. Jahrhunderts: Ein Beitrag zur Frühneuhochdeutschen Morphosyntax.* Göttingen, 1977.

Andernacht, Dietrich. *Regesten zur Geschichte der Juden in der Reichsstadt Frankfurt am Main von 1401–1519.* 3 vols. Forschungen zur Geschichte der Juden, Abteilung B, Quellen, vol. 1. Hanover, 1996.

Anderson, Benedict. *Imagined Communities: Reflections on the Origins and Spread of Nationalism.* London, 1983.

Angermeier, Heinz. *Königtum und Landfriede im deutschen Spätmittelalter.* Munich, 1966.

———. *Die Reichsreform 1410–1555: Die Staatsproblematik in Deutschland zwischen Mittelalter und Gegenwart.* Munich, 1984.

Arnheim, Rudolf. *The Power of Center: A Study of Composition in the Visual Arts.* Berkeley, 1971.

Arnold, Benjamin. *Count and Bishop in Medieval Germany: A Study of Regional Power 1100–1350.* Philadelphia, 1991.

Ashley, Benedict M. *The Dominicans.* Religious Order Series, vol. 3. Collegeville, Minnesota, 1990.

Bader, Karl S. "Approaches to Imperial Reform at the End of the Fifteenth Century." In Gerald Strauss, ed., *Pre-Reformation Germany* (New York, 1972): 136–161.

———. *Der deutsche Südwesten in seiner territorialstaatlichen Entwicklung.* Stuttgart, 1950.

Baer, Wolfram, ed. *Augsburger Stadtlexikon: Geschichte, Gesellschaft, Kultur, Recht, Wirtschaft.* Augsburg, 1985.

Baer, Yitzhak. *A History of the Jews in Christian Spain: Volume 2, From the Fourteenth Century to the Expulsion.* Translated by Louis Schoffman. Philadelphia, 1971. (orig., 1959).

Baron, Salo. *The Jewish Community: Its History and Structure to the American Revolution.* 3 vols. Philadelphia, 1942.

———. *A Social and Religious History of the Jews: Volume 13, Late Middle Ages and Era of European Expansion.* New York, 1969.

Barraclough, Geoffrey. *The Origins of Modern Germany.* New York, 1984.

Barth, Reinhard. *Argumentation und Selbstverständnis der Bürgeropposition in städtischen Auseinandersetzungen des Spätmittelalters: Lübeck 1403–1408; Braunschweig 1374–1376; Mainz 1444–1446; Köln 1396–1400.* Kollektive Einstellungen und sozialer Wandel im Mittelalter, vol. 3. Cologne, 1974.

Battenberg, J. Friedrich. "Jews in Ecclesiastical Territories of the Holy Roman Empire." In *In and Out of the Ghetto*, edited by R. Po-chia Hsia and Hartmut Lehmann (Cambridge, 1995): 247–274.

Bauer, Johannes Joseph. *Zur Frühgeschichte der Theologischen Fakultät der Universität Freiburg im Breisgau, 1460–1620.* Freiburg, 1957.

Baylor, Michael, ed. *The Radical Reformation.* Cambridge Texts in the History of Political Thought. Cambridge, 1991.

Bazak, Jacob, ed. *Mishpat ve-halakah.* 2 vols. Tel Aviv, 1971–1975. [Translated as *Jewish Law and Jewish Life: Selected Rabbinical Responsa* by Stephen M. Passamaneck (New York, 1978)].

Beard, Charles. *The Reformation of the Sixteenth Century.* Westport, Connecticut, 1962.

Beck, Hans-Georg, Karl August Fink, Josef Glazik, Erwin Iserloh, and Hans Wolter. *From the High Middle Ages to the Eve of the Reformation.* Translated by Anselm Biggs. Handbook of Church History. Edited by Hubert Jedin and John Dolan. Vol. 4. London, 1970.

Beinart, Haim. *The Expulsion of the Jews from Spain.* Jerusalem, 1994. [Hebrew].

Beinart, Haim, ed. *Moreshet Sepharad: The Sephardi Legacy*. 2 vols. Jerusalem, 1992.
Bell, Dean Phillip. "Gemeinschaft, Konflikt und Wandel: Jüdische Gemeindestrukturen im Deutschland des 15. Jahrhunderts." Translated by Melanie Brunner. In *Landjudentum im deutschen Südwesten während der Frühen Neuzeit*, edited by Rolf Kießling and Sabine Ullmann. Colloquia Augustana, vol. 10 (Berlin, 1999): 157–191.
——. "Martin Luther and the Jews: The Reformation, Nazi Germany and Today." In *The Solomon Goldman Lectures*. Vol. 7. Edited by Dean Phillip Bell (Chicago, 1999): 155–187.
Below, Georg von. *Die Enstehung des deutschen Städtgemeinde*. Düsseldorf, 1889.
Ben-Sasson, Hayyim Hillel. "Jewish-Christian Disputations in the Setting of Humanism and Reformation in the German Empire." *Harvard Theological Review* 59 (1966): 369–390.
——. "The 'Northern' European Jewish Community and its Ideals," in *Jewish Society Through the Ages*, edited by Hayyim Hillel Ben-Sasson and Samuel Ettinger (New York, 1971): 208–219.
——. "The Reformation in Contemporary Jewish Eyes." *The Israel Academy of Sciences and Humanities Proceedings*, Vol. 4, no. 12, Jerusalem, 1970.
——. *Trial and Achievement: Currents in Jewish History (from 313)*. Library of Jewish Knowledge. Jerusalem, 1974.
——, ed. *A History of the Jewish People*. Cambridge, Massachusetts, 1994. (orig., 1976).
Berliner, Abraham. *Aus dem inneren Leben der deutschen Juden im Mittelalter*. Berlin, 1900.
Berman, Harold J. *Law and Revolution: The Formation of the Western Legal Tradition*. Cambridge, Massachusetts, 1983.
Beyerle, Konrad. "Die deutschen Stadtbücher." *Deutsche Geschichtsblätter* 11, nos. 6–7 (1910): 145–200.
Biersack, Aletta. "Local Knowledge, Local History: Geertz and Beyond." In *The New Cultural History*, edited by Lynn Hunt. Studies on the History of Society and Culture, vol. 6 (Berkeley, 1989): 72–96.
Black, Antony. *Council and Commune: The Conciliar Movement and the Fifteenth Century Heritage*. London, 1979.
——. *Monarchy and Community: Political Ideas in the Later Conciliar Controversy 1430–1450*. Cambridge Studies in Medieval Life and Thought, 3rd series, no. 2. Cambridge, 1970.
Blendinger, Friedrich. "Versuch einer Bestimmung der Mittelschicht in der Reichsstadt Augsburg vom Ende 14. bis zum Anfang des 18. Jahrhunderts." In *Städtische Mittelschichten: Protokoll der 8. Arbeitstagung des Arbeitskreises für Südwestdeutsche Stadtgeschichtsforschung, Biberach, 14.–16. Nov. 1969*, edited by Erich Maschke and Jürgen Sydow. Baden-Württemberg. Kommission für Geschichtliche Landeskunde, Veröffentlichungen, Reihe B: Forschungen, vol. 69 (Stuttgart, 1972): 32–78.
Blezinger, Harro. *Der Schwäbische Städtebund in den Jahren 1438–1445, mit einem Überblick über seine Entwicklung seit 1389*. Darstellungen aus der württembergische Geschichte, vol. 39. Stuttgart, 1954.
Blickle, Peter. "Communal Reformation and Peasant Piety: The Peasant Reformation and its Late Medieval Origins." *Central European History* 20 (September/December, 1987): 216–228.
——. *Communal Reformation: the Quest for Salvation in Sixteenth Century Germany*. Translated by Thomas Dunlap. Studies in German Histories. Atlantic Highlands, New Jersey, 1992.
——. "The Popular Reformation." In *Handbook of European History 1400–1600: Late Middle Ages, Renaissance and Reformation*, Vol. 2, edited by Thomas A. Brady, Jr., Heiko A. Oberman, and James D. Tracy (Leiden, 1996): 161–192.
——. *The Revolution of 1525: The German Peasants' War from a New Perspective*. Translated by Thomas A. Brady, Jr. and H.C. Erik Middelfort. Baltimore, 1981. (orig., 1975).

Blickle, Peter, and Renate Blickle. *Schwaben von 1268 bis 1803.* Dokumente zur Geschichte von Staat und Gesellschaft in Bayern, vol. 2:4. Munich, 1979.

Blumenkranz, Bernhard. *Die Judenpredigt Augustins: Ein Beitrag zur Geschichte der jüdisch-christlichen Beziehungen in den ersten Jahrhunderts.* Basler Beiträge zur Geschichtswissenschaft, vol. 25. Basel, 1946.

——. *Juden und Judentum in der mittelalterlichen Kunst.* Franz Delitzsch-Vorlesungen, 1963. Stuttgart, 1965.

Bodian, Miriam *Hebrews of the Portuguese Nation: Conversos and Community in Early Modern Amsterdam.* Modern Jewish Experiences. Bloomington, 1997.

Bonfil, Robert. "Aliens Within: The Jews and Antijudaism." In *Handbook of European History 1400–1600: Late Middle Ages, Renaissance and Reformation,* Vol. 1, edited by Thomas A. Brady, Jr., Heiko A. Oberman, and James D. Tracy (Leiden, 1996): 263–302.

——. *Jewish Life in Renaissance Italy.* Translated by Anthony Oldcorn. Berkeley, 1994. (orig., 1991).

——. *Rabbis and Jewish Communities in Renaissance Italy.* Translated by Jonathan Chipman. Littman Library of Jewish Civilization. London, 1993. (orig. 1979).

de Boor, Helmut and Richard Newald. *Geschichte der deutschen Literatur von den Anfänge bis zur Gegenwart.* Munich, 1949.

Borst, Arno. *Der Turmbau von Babel: Geschichte der Meinungen über Ursprung und Vielfalt der Sprachen und Völkern.* 4 vols. Stuttgart, 1957–1963.

Bosl, Karl. *Die bayerische Stadt in Mittelalter und Neuzeit: Altbayern, Franken, Schwaben.* Regensburg, 1988.

——. *Die wirtschaftliche und gesellschaftliche Entwicklung des Augsburger Bürgertums vom 10. bis zum 14. Jahrhundert.* Sitzungsberichte der Bayerischen Akademie der Wissenschaften, Philosophisch-Historische Klasse, no. 3. Munich, 1969.

Bossy, John. "Blood and Baptism: Kinship, Community and Christianity in Western Europe from the Fourteenth to the Seventeenth Centuries." In *Sanctity and Secularity: The Church and the World: Papers read at the eleventh summer meeting and the twelfth winter meeting of the Ecclesiastical History Society,* edited by Derek Baker. Studies in Church History, no. 10 (Oxford, 1973): 129–143.

——. *Christianity in the West 1400–1700.* Oxford, 1985.

Bourdieu, Pierre. *Outline of a Theory of Practice.* Translated by Richard Nice. Cambridge Studies in Social Anthropology, vol. 16. Cambridge, 1977. (orig., 1972).

Bouwsma, William J. *A Usable Past: Essays in European Cultural History.* Berkeley, 1990.

Brady, Thomas A., Jr. "From the Sacral Community to the Common Man: Reflections on German Reformation Studies," *Central European History* 20 (September/December, 1987): 229–245.

——. "In Search of the Godly City: The Domestication of Religion in the German Urban Reformation," in *The German People and the Reformation,* edited by R. Po-chia Hsia (Ithaca, 1988): 14–31.

——. *Ruling Class, Regime and Reformation at Strasbourg 1520–1555.* Studies in Medieval and Reformation Thought, vol. 22. Leiden, 1978.

——. "'You Hate Us Priests:' Anticlericalsim, Communalism and the Control of Women at Strasbourg in the Age of Reform." In *Anticlericalsim in Late Medieval and Early Modern Europe,* edited by Peter A. Dykema and Heiko Oberman. Studies in Medieval and Reformation Thought, vol. 51 (Leiden, 1993): 167–207.

Brady, Thomas A., Jr., Heiko A. Oberman and James D. Tracy, eds. *Handbook of European History 1400–1600: Late Middle Ages, Renaissance and Reformation.* 2 vols. Leiden, 1996. (orig., 1994–1995).

Brandon, William. *New Worlds for Old: Reports from the New World and Their Effect on the Development of Social Thought in Europe, 1500–1800.* Athens, Ohio, 1986.

Brettinger, Friedrich. *Die Juden in Bamberg*. Bamberg, 1963.

Breuer, Mordechai. "The Position of the Rabbinate in the Leadership of the German Communities in the Fifteenth Century," *Zion* 41, nos. 1–2 (1976): 47–67. [Hebrew].

———. *The Rabbinate in Ashkenaz during the Middle Ages*. Jerusalem, 1976. [Hebrew].

———. "Toward the Investigation of the Typology of Western Yeshivot in the Middle Ages." In *Studies in the History of Jewish Society in the Middle Ages and in the Modern Period: Presented to Prof. Jacob Katz*, edited by E. Etkes and Y. Salmon (Jerusalem, 1980): 45–55 [Hebrew]

———. "The Wanderings of Students and Scholars—A Prolegomenon to a Chapter in the History of the Yeshivot." In *Culture and Society in Medieval Jewry: Studies Dedicated to the Memory of Haim Hillel Ben-Sasson*, edited by Menahem Ben-Sasson, Robert Bonfil, and Joseph R. Hacker (Jerusalem, 1989): 445–468 [Hebrew].

Browe, Peter. *Die Judenmission in Mittelalter und die Päpste*. Rome, 1942.

———. *Die Verehrung der Eucharistie im Mittelalter*. Munich, 1933.

Brown, D. Catherine. *Pastor and Laity in the Theology of Jean Gerson*. Cambridge, 1987.

Brunner, Otto. *Land and Lordship: Structures of Governance in Medieval Austria*. Translated by Howard Kaminsky and James Van Horn Melton. Middle Ages Series. Philadelphia, 1984. (orig. 1939).

Buc, Philippe. "Potestas: Prince, Pouvoir et Peuple dans les Commentaires de la Bible (Paris et France du Nord, 1100–1350)." Ph.D. dissertation, University of Paris, 1989.

Buchanan, Harvey. "Luther and the Turks, 1519–1524." *Archiv für Reformationsgeschichte* 47 (1956): 145–160.

Burgard, Friedhelm. "Auseinandersetzungen zwischen Stadtgemeinde und Erzbischof (1307–1500)." In *2000 Jahre Trier, Volume 2: Trier im Mittelalter*, edited by Hans Hubert Anton and Alfred Haverkamp (Trier, 1996): 295–398.

———. "Zur Migration der Juden im westlichen Reichsgebiet im Spätmitelalter." In *Juden in der christlichen Umwelt während des späten Mittelalters*, edited by Alfred Haverkamp and Franz-Josef Ziwes. Zeitschrift für historische Forschung, no. 13 (Berlin, 1992): 41–57.

Burke, Peter. *Popular Culture in Early Modern Europe*. New York, 1978.

———. "A Survey of the Popularity of Ancient Historians, 1450–1700." *History and Theory* 5 (1966): 135–152.

Burr, Davis. "Eucharistic Presence and Conversion in Late Thirteenth-Century Franciscan Thought." *Transcations of the American Philosophical Society* 74, no. 3 (1984).

Calhoun, C.J. "Community: Toward a Variable Conceptualization for Comparative Research," in *Social History* 5, no. 1 (1980): 105–129.

Carlebach, Elisheva "Between History and Myth: The Regensburg Expulsion in Josel of Rosheim's *Sefer Ha-Miknah*." In *Jewish History and Jewish Memory: Essays in Honor of Yosef Hayim Yerushalmi*, edited by Elisheva Carlebach, John M. Efron, and David N. Myers (Hanover, New Hampshire, 1998): 40–53.

———. "Converts and their Narratives in Early Modern Germany: The Case of Friedrich Albrecht Christiani." *Yearbook of the Leo Baeck Institute* 40 (1995): 65–83.

Caro, Georg. *Sozial- und Wirtschaftsgeschichte der Juden im Mittelalter und in der Neuzeit: Grundriss der Gesamtwissenschaft des Judentums*. 2 vols. Frankfurt am Main, 1908–1920.

Cassirer, Ernst. *The Individual and the Cosmos in Renaissance Philosophy*. Translated by Mario Domandi. Philadelphia, 1972. (orig., 1963).

de Certeau, Michel. *The Practice of Everyday Life*. Translated by Steven Rendall. Berkeley, 1984.

Chazan, Robert. *Medieval Stereotypes and Modern Antisemitism*. Berkeley, 1997.

Chrisman, Miriam Usher. *Bibliography of Strasbourg Imprints 1480–1599*. New Haven, 1982.

———. *Lay Culture, Learned Culture: Books and Social Change in Strasbourg, 1480–1599*. New Haven, 1982.

Christian, William A. Jr., *Local Religion in Sixteenth Century Spain*. Princeton, 1981.

Cohen, Jeremy. *The Friars and the Jews: The Evolution of Medieval Anti-Judaism*. Ithaca, 1982.

——. *Living Letters of the Law: Ideas of the Jews in Medieval Christianity*. The S. Mark Taper Foundation Imprint in Jewish Studies. Berkeley, 1999.

Cohen, Mark R. *Under Crescent and Cross: The Jews in the Middle Ages*. Princeton, 1994.

Cohen, Susan Sarah. *Antisemitism: An Annotated Bibliography*. 3 vols. Garland Reference Library of Social Science, vol. 366. New York, 1987–1994.

Cohn, Henry J. "Anticlericalism in the German Peasants' War 1525." *Past and Present* 83 (1979): 3–31.

Cohn, Norman. *The Pursuit of the Millenium: Revolutionary Millenarians and Mystical Anarchists of the Middle Ages*. Oxford, 1970. (orig., 1957).

Coing, Helmut, ed. *Handbuch der Quellen und Literatur der neueren europäischen Privatsrechtsgeschichte, Volume 1: Mittelalter (1100–1500)*. Munich, 1973.

Cooperman, Bernard Dov, ed. *In Iberia and Beyond: Hispanic Jews Between Cultures: Proceedings of a Symposium to Mark the 500th Anniversary of the Expulsion of Spanish Jewry*. Newark, Delaware, 1998.

Courtenay, William J. "Nominalism and Late Medieval Religion." In *The Pursuit of Holiness in Late Medieval and Renaissance Religion*, edited by Charles Trinkaus and Heiko Oberman. Studies in Medieval and Reformation Thought, vol. 10 (Leiden, 1974): 26–59.

Crehan, Joseph. *Early Christian Baptism and the Creed: A Study in Anti-Nicene Theology*. London, 1950.

Crosby, Alfred Jr. *The Columbian Exchange: Biological and Cultural Consequences of 1492*. Contributions in American Studies, no. 2. Westport, Connecticut, 1972.

Culler, Jonathan. *On Deconstruction: Theory and Criticism after Structuralism*. Ithaca, 1982.

Davis, R.H.C. and J.M. Wallace-Hadrill, eds. *Writing History in the Middle Ages: Essays Presented to R.W. Southern*. Oxford, 1981.

Daxelmüller, Christoph. "Die deutschesprächige Volkskunde und die Juden: Zur Geschichte und den Folgen einer Kulturellen Ausklammerung." *Zeitschrift für Volkskunde* 83 (1987): 1–20.

——. "Jewish Popular Culture in the Research Perspective of European Ethnology." *Ethnologia Europea* 16 (1986): 97–116.

Derrida, Jacques. *Of Grammatology*. Translated by Gayatri Chakrabarty Spivak. Baltimore, 1976. (orig., 1967).

Dicker, Hermann. *Die Geschichte der Juden in Ulm: ein Beitrag zur Wirtschaftsgeschichte*. Rottweil, 1937.

Dinari, Yedidya Alter. *The Rabbis of Germany and Austria at the Close of the Middle Ages: Their Conceptions and Halacha-Writings*. Jerusalem, 1984. [Hebrew].

Dolan, John Patrick, ed. *Unity and Reform: Selected Writings of Nicholas de Cusa*. Chicago, 1962.

Dollinger, Philipp. "Die deutsche Städte im Mittelalter: Die sozialen Gruppierungen." In *Altständisches Bürgertum, Volume 2: Erwerbsleben und Sozialgefüge*, edited by Heinz Stoob. Wege der Forschung, vol. 417 (Darmstadt, 1978): 269–300.

——. *The German Hansa*. Translated by D.S. Ault and S.H. Steinberg. Stanford, 1970. (orig., 1964).

Douglas, Mary. *Purity and Danger: An Analysis of Concepts of Pollution and Taboo*. New York, 1966.

Douglass, E. Jane Dempsey. *Justification in Late Medieval Preaching: A Study of John Geiler of Keisersberg*. Studies in Medieval and Reformation Thought, vol. 1. Leiden, 1966.

DuBoulay, F.R.H. *Germany in the Later Middle Ages*. London, 1983.

Ehrismann, Gustav. *Geschichte der deutschen Literatur bis zum Ausgang des Mittelalters*. Vol. 2. Munich, 1935.

Eidelberg, Shlomo. *Jewish Life in Austria in the Fifteenth Century: As Reflected in the Legal Writings of Rabbi Israel Isserlin and his Contemporaries.* Philadelphia, 1962.

Elias, Norbert. *Power and Civility.* Translated by Edmund Jephcott. The Civilizing Process, Vol. 2. New York, 1982. (orig., 1939).

Elm, Kaspar, ed. *Reformbemühungen und Observanzenstrebungen im Spätmittelalter Ordenswesen.* Ordensstudien, vol. 6. Berliner historische Studien, vol. 14. Berlin, 1989.

Elon, Menahem. *Jewish Law: History, Sources, Principles.* 4 vols. Translated by Bernard Auerbach and Melvin J. Sykes. Philadelphia, 1994. (orig., 1973).

Emery, Richard W. *The Jews of Perpignan in the Thirteenth Century: An Economic Study Based on Notarial Records.* New York, 1959.

Fasolt, Constantin. *Council and Hierarchy: The Political Thought of William Durant the Younger.* Cambridge Studies in Medieval Life and Thought, 4th series, vol. 16. Cambridge, 1991.

———. "Visions of Order in the Canonists and Civilians." In *Handbook of European History 1400-1600: Late Middle Ages, Renaissance and Reformation,* Vol. 2, edited by Thomas A. Brady, Jr., Heiko A. Oberman, and James D. Tracy (Leiden, 1996): 31–59.

Faur, José. *Golden Doves with Silver Dots: Semiotics and Textuality in Rabbinic Tradition.* Jewish Literature and Culture. Bloomington, 1986.

Febvre, Lucien. *The Problem of Unbelief in the Sixteenth Century: The Religion of Rabelais.* Translated by Beatrice Gottlieb. Cambridge, Massachussets, 1982. (orig., 1942).

Feilchenfeld, Ludwig. *Rabbi Josel von Rosheim: Ein Beitrag zur Geschichte der Juden in Deutschland im Reformationszeitalter.* Strasbourg, 1898.

Finkelstein, Louis. *Jewish Self-Government in the Middle Ages.* Abraham Berliner Series. New York, 1924.

Fleckenstein, Josef and Karl Stackmann, eds. *Über Burger, Stadt und städtische Literatur: Bericht über Kolloquien der Kommission zur Erforschung der Kultur des Spätmittelalters 1975-1977.* Abhandlungen der Akademie der Wissenschaften in Göttingen, Philologisch-Historische Klasse, vol. 3. Göttingen, 1980.

Foucault, Michel. *Power/Knowledge: Selected Interviews and Other Writings, 1972-1977.* Edited and translated by Colin Gordon. New York, 1980.

Fraenkel-Goldschmidt, Hava. "On the Periphery of Jewish Society: Jewish Converts to Christianity in Germany During the Reformation." In *Culture and Society in Medieval Jewry: Studies Dedicated to the Memory of Haim Hillel Ben-Sasson,* edited by Menahem Ben-Sasson, Robert Bonfil, and Joseph R. Hacker (Jerusalem, 1989): 623–654. [Hebrew].

Frank, Moses. *The Jewish Communities and their Courts in Germany from the Twelfth to the End of the Fifteenth Centuries.* Tel-Aviv, 1937. [Hebrew].

Freehof, Solomon B. *The Responsa Literature and A Treasury of Responsa.* Philadelphia, 1973.

Freytag, Gustav. *Bilder aus der Deutschen Vergangenheit.* 4 vols. Leipzig, 1892–1893. (orig., 1876).

Friedman, Jerome. *The Most Ancient Testimony: Sixteenth-Century Christian-Hebraica in the Age of Renaissance Nostalgia.* Athens, Ohio, 1983.

Funkenstein, Amos. *Perceptions of Jewish History.* Berkeley, 1993.

Gampel, Benjamin. "Does Medieval Navarrese Jewry Salvage Our Notion of Convivencia." In *In Iberia and Beyond: Hispanic Jews Between Cultures,* edited by Bernard Dov Cooperman (Newark, Delaware, 1998): 97–122

———. *The Last Jews on Iberian Soil: Navarrese Jewry 1479-1498.* Berkeley, 1989.

———, ed. *Crisis and Creativity in the Sephardic World 1391-1648.* New York, 1997.

Gaupp, Ernst Theodor. *Deutsche Stadtrechte des Mittelalters.* 2 vols. Breslau, 1851–1852.

Gay, Ruth. *The Jews of Germany: A Historical Portrait.* New Haven, 1992.

Geertz, Clifford. *The Interpretation of Cultures: Selected Essays.* New York, 1973.

Geiger, Gottfried. *Die Reichsstadt Ulm vor der Reformation: Städtisches und kirchliches Leben am Ausgang des Mittelalters.* Forschungen zur Geschichte der Stadt Ulm, vol. 11. Ulm, 1971.

Gellner, Ernst. *Nations and Nationalism. New Perspectives on the Past.* Ithaca, 1983.
Germania Judaica, Volume 1: Von den ältesten Zeiten bis 1238. Edited by M. Brann, I. Elbogen, A Freimann, and H. Tykocinski. Tübingen, 1963 (orig., Breslau, 1917–1934); Volume 2: Von 1238 bis zur Mitte des 14. Jahrhunderts. Two Parts. Edited by Zvi Avneri. Tübingen, 1968; Volume 3: 1350–1519, Part 1. Edited by Arye Maimon. Tübingen, 1987; Volume 3: 1350–1519, Part 2. Edited Arye Maimon, Mordechai Breuer, and Yacov Guggenheim. Tübingen, 1995; Volume 3: 1350–1519, Part 3. Edited by Mordechai Breuer and Yacov Guggenheim. Tübingen, in press. Veröffentlichung des Leo Baeck Instituts.
Ginzberg, Louis. *Students, Scholars and Saints.* Philadelphia, 1928.
Ginzburg, Carlo. *The Cheese and the Worms: The Cosmos of a Sixteenth-Century Miller.* Translated by John and Anne Tedeschi. New York, 1982. (orig., 1976).
——. *Ecstasies: Deciphering the Witches Sabbath.* Translated by Raymond Rosenthal. New York, 1991. (orig., 1989).
——. *Night Battles: Witchcraft and Agrarian Cults in the Sixteenth and Seventeenth Centuries.* Translated by John and Anne Tedeschi. England, 1983. (orig., 1972).
Gottlieb, Gunther. *Geschichte der Stadt Augsburg von der Römerzeit bis zur Gegenwart.* Stuttgart, 1984.
Gow, Andrew Colin. *The Red Jews: Antisemitism in an Apocalyptic Age 1200–1600.* Studies in Medieval and Reformation Thought, vol. 55. Leiden, 1995.
Graf, Roland. *Augsburg. Geschichte einer zweitausendjährigen Stadt.* Augsburg, 1954.
Grau, Wilhelm. *Antisemitismus in späten Mittelalter: Das Ende der Regensburger Judengemeinde 1450–1519.* Munich, 1934.
Graus, František. *Pest-Geisler-Judenmorde: Das 14. Jahrhundert als Krisenzeit.* Veröffentlichung des Max Planck Instituts für Geschichte, vol. 86. Göttingen, 1987.
——. "Randgruppen der Städtischen Gesellschaft im Spätmittelalter." *Zeitschrift für Historische Forschung* 8, no. 4 (1981): 385–437.
Greenblatt, Stephen. *Marvelous Possessions: The Wonder of the New World.* Chicago, 1991.
——. *Renaissance Self-Fashioning: From More to Shakespeare.* Chicago, 1980.
Greyerz, Kaspar von, ed. *Religion, Politics and Social Protest: Three Studies on Early Modern Germany.* London, 1984.
Groebner, Valentin. "Black Money and the Language of Things: Observations on the Economy of the Laboring Poor in Late Fifteenth-Century Nürnberg." *Tel Aviver Jahrbuch für deutsche Geschichte* 22 (1993): 275–291.
Grossman, Avraham. "Relations between Spanish and Ashkenazi Jewry in the Middle Ages." In *The Sephardi Legacy,* Vol. 1, edited by Haim Beinart (Jerusalem, 1992): 220–239.
Grundmann, Herbert. *Geschichtsschreibung im Mittelalter.* Göttingen, 1965.
Güde, Wilhelm. *Die rechtliche Stellung der Juden in den Schriften deutscher Juristen des 16. und 17. Jahrhunderts.* Sigmaringen, 1981.
Guggisberg, Hans R. *Basel in the Sixteenth Century: Aspects of the City Before, During, and After the Reformation.* St. Louis, 1982.
Haas, Peter J. *Responsa: Literary History of a Rabbinic Genre.* Semeia Studies. Atlanta, 1996.
Hailperin, Herman. *Rashi and the Christian Scholars.* Pittsburgh, 1963.
Hall, Basil. "The Reformation City." In *Bulletin of the John Rylands Library* 54 (1971–1972): 103–148.
Hall, Thor. "Possibilities of Erasmian Influence on Denck and Hubmaier in their Views on the Freedom of the Will." *Mennonite Quarterly Review* 35 (1961): 149–170.
Haller, Johannes, ed. *Concilium Basilense: Studien und Quellen zur Geschichte des Konzils von Basel.* Basel, 1896–1926.
Hamm, Berndt. "The Urban Reformation in the Holy Roman Empire." In *Handbook of*

European History 1400-1600: Late Middle Ages, Renaissance and Reformation, Vol. 2, edited by Thomas A. Brady, Jr., Heiko A. Oberman, and James D. Tracy (Leiden, 1996): 193–227.

Hammann, Gustav. "Konversionen deutscher und ungarischer Juden in der frühen Reformationszeit." *Zeitschrift für Bayerische Kirchengeschichte* 39 (1970): 207–237.

Haverkamp, Alfred "Cities as Cultic Centers in Germany and Italy during the Early and High Middle Ages." In *Sacred Space: Shrine, City, Land*, edited by Benjamin Z. Kedar and R.J. Zwi Werblowsky (New York, 1998): 172–191.

――. "'Concivilitas' von Christen und Juden in Aschkenas im Mittelalter." In *Jüdische Gemeinden und Organisationsformen von der Antike bis zur Gegenwart*, edited by Robert Jütte and Abraham P. Kustermann (Vienna, 1996): 103–136.

――. "Die Judenverfolgungen zur Zeit des Schwarzen Todes in Gesellschaftsgefüge deutscher Städte." In *Zur Geschichte der Juden im Deutschland des Späten Mittelalters und der Frühen Neuzeit*, edited by Alfred Haverkamp (Stuttgart, 1981): 27–93.

――, ed. *Zur Geschichte der Juden im Deutschland des späten Mittelalters und der frühen Neuzeit*. Monographien zur Geschichte des Mittelalters, vol. 24. Stuttgart, 1981.

Headley, John M. *Luther's View of Church History*. Yale Publications in Religion, vol. 6. New Haven, 1963.

Helmrath, Johannes. *Das Basler Konzil 1431-1449. Forschungsstand und Probleme*. Kölner historische Abhandlungen, vol. 32. Cologne, 1987.

Herde, Peter. "Von der mittelalterlichen Judenfeindschaft zum modernen Antisemitismus: Juden und Nicht-Juden in Deutschland vom Mittelalter bis zur Neuzeit." In *Begegnungen, Judentum und Antisemitismus in Zeit und Geist*, edited by Peter Herde (Munich, 1986): 7–55.

Hillerbrand, Hans J., ed. *The Reformation: A Narrative Related by Contemporary Observers and Participants*. Grand Rapids, 1987.

Hinnesbusch, William A. *The History of the Dominican Order: Origins and Growth to 1500*. 2 vols. New York, 1965 and 1973.

Holborn, Hajo. *A History of Modern Germany: The Reformation*. Princeton, 1959.

Homeyer, Karl Gustav. *Die deutschen Rechtsbücher des Mittelalters*. Berlin, 1856.

Hörburger, Hortense. *Judenvertreibungen im Spätmittelalter: Am Beispiel Esslingen und Konstanz*. Campus Forschung, vol. 237. Frankfurt am Main, 1981.

Hsia, R Po-chia. *The Myth of Ritual Murder: Jews and Magic in Reformation Germany*. New Haven, 1988.

――. "The Myth of the Commune: Recent Historiography on City and Reformation in Germany." *Central European History* 20 (September/December 1987): 203–215.

――. *Society and Religion in Münster 1535-1618*. Yale Historical Publications, Miscellany, vol. 131. New Haven, 1984.

――. *Trent 1475: Stories of a Ritual Murder*. New Haven, 1992.

――. "The Usurious Jew: Economic Structure and Religious Representations in an Anti-Semitic Discourse." In *In and Out of the Ghetto*, edited by R. Po-chia Hsia and Hartmut Lehman (Cambridge, 1995): 161–176

Hsia, R. Po-chia and Hartmut Lehmann, eds. *In and Out of the Ghetto: Jewish-Gentile Relations in Late Medieval and Early Modern Germany*. Publications of the German Historical Institute. Cambridge, 1995.

Huppert, George. *After the Black Death: A Social History of Early Modern Europe*. Interdisciplinary Studies in History. Bloomington, 1986.

Iancu, Danièle. *Les juifs de Provence (1475-1501): De l'insertion à l'expulsion*. Marseille, 1981.

Iggers, Georg. *The German Conception of History: The National Tradition of Historical Thought from Herder to the Present*. Hanover, New Hampshire, 1968.

Irsigler, Franz, und Arnold Lasotta. *Bettler und Gaulker, Durnen und Henker: Randgruppen und Aussenseiter in Köln 1300-1600*. Aus der Kölner Stadtgeschichte. Cologne, 1984.

Isenmann, Eberhard. *Die deutsche Stadt im Spätmittelalter, 1250–1500: Stadtgestalt, Recht, Stadtregiment, Kirche, Gesellschaft, Wirtschaft.* Stuttgart, 1988.
——. "Reichsfinanzien und Reichssteuern im 15. Jahrhundert." *Zeitschrift für historische Forschung* 7 (1980): 1–76.
Iserloh, Erwin. *Johannes Eck (1486–1543): Scholastiker, Humanist, Kontroverstheologe.* Katholisches Leben und Kirchenreform im Zeitalter der Glaubensspaltung, no. 41. Münster, 1981.
Israel, Jonathan. "Germany and Its Jews: A Changing Relationship (1300–1800)." In *In and Out of the Ghetto*, edited by R. Po-chia Hsia and Hartmut Lehmann (Cambridge, 1995): 295–304.
Jacobs, Louis. *Theology in the Responsa.* The Littman Library of Jewish Civilization. London, 1975.
Jahn, Joachim. *Augsburg Land.* Historischer Atlas von Bayern, Teil Schwaben, no. 11. Munich, 1984.
Joachimsohn, Paul. *Geschichtsauffassung und Geschichtsschreibung in Deutschland unter dem Einfluss des Humanismus, Part 1.* Leipzig and Berlin, 1910.
——. *Hermann Schedels Briefwechsel 1452–1478.* Bibliothek des Litterarischen Vereins in Stuttgart, vol. 196. Tübingen, 1893.
——. *Die Humanistische Geschichtsshcreibung in Deutschland, Part 1: Die Anfänge-Sigismund Meisterlin.* Bonn 1895.
——. "Zur städtischen und klösterlichen Geschichtsschreibung Augsburgs im fünfzehnten Jahrhundert." *Alemannia* 22 (1894): 1–32 and 123–159.
Kanarfogel, Ephraim. *Jewish Education and Society in the High Middle Ages.* Detroit, 1992.
Kantorowicz, Ernst H. *The King's Two Bodies: A Study in Medieval Political Thought.* Princeton, 1957.
——. "Mysteries of State: An Absolutism Concept and its Late Medieval Origins." In *Ernst Kantorowicz, Selected Studies* (Locust Valley, New York, 1965): 381–398.
Karant-Nunn, Susan C. *The Reformation of Ritual: An Interpretation of Early Modern Germany.* Christianity and Society in the Modern World. London, 1997.
Katz, Jacob. *Exclusiveness and Tolerance: Studies in Jewish-Gentile Relations in Medieval and Modern Times.* Scripta Judaica, vol. 3. New Jersey, 1983. (orig., 1961).
——. *Out of the Ghetto: The Social Background of Jewish Emancipation, 1770–1870.* Modern Jewish History. Syracuse, 1998 (orig., 1973).
——. *The "Shabbes Goy": A Study in Halakhic Flexibility.* Translated by Yoel Lerner. Philadelphia, 1989. (orig., 1983).
Keyser, Erich, ed., *Bibliographie zur Städtegeschichte Deutschlands, unter Mitwirkung zahlreicher Sachkenner.* Acta Collegii Historiae Urbanae Societatis Historicorum Internationalis. Cologne, 1969.
Kibre, Pearl. *Scholarly Privileges in the Middle Ages: The Right, Privileges, and Immunities of Scholars and Universities at Bologna, Padua, Paris, and Oxford.* Medieval Academy of America, publication no. 92. London, 1961.
Kießling, Rolf. "Bürgerliche Besitz auf dem Land: ein Schlüssel zu den Stadt- Land-Beziehung im Spätmittelalter, aufgezeigt am Beispiel Augsburgs und anderer ostschwäbischer Städter." In *Bayerisch-schwabisch Landesgeschichte an der Universität Augsburg*, edited by Pankraz Fried (Sigmaringen, 1979): 121–140.
——. *Bürgerliche Gesellschaft und Kirche in Augsburg im Spätmittelalter: Ein Beitrag zur Strukturanalyse der oberdeutschen Reichsstadt.* Abhandlungen zur Geschichte der Stadt Augsburg, vol. 19. Augsburg, 1971.
——, ed. *Judengemeinden in Schwaben im Kontext des Alten Reiches.* Colloquia Augustana, vol. 2. Berlin, 1995.
Kießling, Rolf and Sabine Ullmann, eds. *Landjudentum im deutschen Südwesten während der Frühen Neuzeit.* Colloquia Augustana, vol. 10. Berlin, 1999.

Kirchgässner, Bernhard and Fritz Reuter, eds. *Städtische Randgruppen und Minderheiten, 23. Arbeitstagung in Worms, 16.-18. November 1984.* Stadt in der Geschichte, vol. 13. Sigmaringen, 1986.

Kisch, Guido. *Jewry Law in Medieval Germany: Laws and Court Decisions regarding Jews.* American Academy for Jewish Research, Texts and Studies, vol. 3. New York, 1949.

——. *The Jews in Medieval Germany: A Study of their Legal and Social Status.* Chicago, 1949.

Knowles, David. *The Evolution of Medieval Thought.* New York, 1962.

Koselleck, Reinhart. "Begriffsgeschichte and Social History." In Reinhart Koselleck, *Futures Past: On the Semantics of Historical Time.* Translated by K. Tribe. Studies in Contemporary German Social Thought (Cambridge, Massachusetts, 1985 (orig., 1979)): 107–129.

Kracauer, Isadore. "Rabbi Joselmann de Rosheim," *Revue des Étude Juives* 16 (1888): 84–105.

Kramer-Schlette, Carla. *Vier Augsburger Chronisten der Reformationszeit: Die Behandlung und Deutung der Zeitgeschichte bei Clemens Sender, Wilhelm Rau, Georg Preu, und Paul Hektor Mair.* Historische Studien, no. 421. Lübeck, 1970.

Kramml, Peter F. *Kaiser Friederich III und die Reichsstadt Konstanz (1440-1493): Die Bodenseemetropole am Ausgang des Mittelalters.* Konstanzer Geschichtsquellen, vol. 29. Sigmaringen, 1985.

Krauss, Samuel. *Die Wiener Geserah von Jahre 1421.* Vienna, 1920.

Krautheimer, Richard. *Mittelalterliche Synagogen.* Frankfurt am Main, 1927.

Kugler, Hartmut. *Die Vorstellung der Stadt in der Literatur des deutschen Mittelalters.* Münchener Texte und Untersuchungen zur deutschen Literatur des Mittelalters, vol. 88. Munich, 1986.

Lasker, Daniel J. *Jewish Philosophical Polemics Against Christianity in the Middle Ages.* New York, 1977.

——. "Major Themes of the Jewish-Christian Debate: God, Humanity, Messiah," in *The Solomon Goldman Lectures,* vol. 7, edited by Dean Phillip Bell (Chicago, 1999): 105–130.

Lau, Franz. "Luther und Balthasar Hubmaier." In *Humanitas, Christianitas: Festschrift fur W. von Lowenich zum 65. Geburtstag,* edited by Karlmann Beyschlag, Gottfried Maron, and Eberhard Wölfel (Witten, 1968): 63–73.

Leff, Gordon. *William of Ockham: The Metamorphosis of Scholastic Discourse.* Manchester, 1975.

Lehmann, Markus. *Rabbi Joselmann von Rosheim: Eine historische Erzählung aus der Zeit der Reformation.* 2 vols. Frankfurt am Main, 1880.

Lesnick, Daniel R. *Preaching in Medieval Florence: The Social World of Franciscan and Dominican Spirituality.* Athens, Georgia, 1989.

Liedl, Eugen. *Gerichtsverfassung und Zivilprozess der freien Reichsstadt Augsburg.* Abhandlungen zur Geschichte der Stadt Augsburg, vol. 12. Augsburg, 1958.

Little, Lester K. *Religious Poverty and the Profit Economy in Medieval Europe.* Ithaca, 1978.

Lorenz, Otto. *Deutschlands Geschichtsquellen im Mittelalter seit der Mitte des 13. Jahrhunderts.* 2 vols. Berlin, 1886–1887.

de Lubac, Henri. *Corpus Mysticum: L'Eucaristie et L'Eglise au Moyen Age.* Paris, 1944.

——. *Exégèse médiévale les Quarte Sens de L'Écriture.* 4 vols. Aubier, 1959–1962.

Marcus, Jacob R., ed. *The Jew in the Medieval World: A Sourcebook: 315-1791.* Jewish History Sourcebooks. Philadelphia, 1938.

Markish, Shimon. *Erasmus and the Jews.* Translated by Anthony Olcott. Chicago, 1986.

Maschke, Erich. "Deutsche Städte am Ausgang des Mittelalters." In *Die Stadt am Ausgang des Mittelalters,* edited by Wilhelm Rausch (Linz/Donau, 1974): 1–44.

——. *Städte und Menschen: Beiträge zur Geschichte der Stadt, der Wirtschaft und Gesellschaft, 1959-1977.* Vierteljahrschrift für Sozial- und Wirtschaftsgeschichte, Beiheften no. 68. Wiesbaden, 1980.

Maschke, Erich, and Jürgen Sydow, eds. *Gesellschaftliche Unterschichten in den südwest-deutschen Städten*. Baden-Württemberg Komission für Geschichte Landeskunde, Veröffentlichen Reihe B, Forschungen, vol. 41. Stuttgart, 1967.

McGrath, Alister. *The Intellectual Origins of the European Reformation*. New York, 1987.

Meinecke, Friederich. *Machiavellism: The Doctrine of Raison d'Etat and its Place in Modern History*. Translated by Douglas Scott. Boulder, 1984. (orig., 1918).

———. *Weltbürgertum und Nationalstaat: Studien zur Genesis der deutschen Nationalstaates*. Munich, 1915. (3rd edition).

Mellinkoff, Ruth. "Cain and the Jews." *Journal of Jewish Art* 6 (1979): 16–38.

———. *The Devil at Isenheim: Reflections of Popular Belief in Grünewald's Altarpiece*. California Studies in the History of Art, Discovery Series, vol. 1. Berkeley, 1988.

———. "Judas's Red Hair and the Jews." *Journal of Jewish Art* 9 (1982): 31–46.

———. *Outcasts: Signs of Otherness in Northern European Art of the Late Middle Ages*. 2 vols. California Studies in the History of Art, vol. 32. Berkeley, 1993.

Mentgen, Gerd. *Studien zur Geschichte der Juden im mittelalterlichen Elsaß*. Forschungen zur Geschichte der Juden, Abteilung A, Abhandlungen, vol. 2. Hanover, 1995.

Metzger, Thérèse, and Mendel Metzger. *La vie Juive au Moyen Age: illustrée par les man-uscrits hébraiques enluminés du xiiie au xviᵉ siècle*. Freiburg im Breisgau, 1982.

Moeller, Bernd. *Imperial Cities and the Reformation: Three Essays*. Edited and translated by H.C. Erik Midelfort and Mark U. Edwards, Jr. Durham, 1982. (orig., 1962).

Mollat, Michel. *The Poor in the Middle Ages: An Essay in Social History*. Translated by Arthur Goldhammer. New Haven, 1986. (orig., 1978).

Montalvo, José Hinojosa. *The Jews of the Kingdom of Valencia: From Persecution to Expulsion, 1391–1492*. Hispania Judaica, vol. 9. Jerusalem, 1993.

Moore, R.I. *The Origins of European Dissent*. Oxford, 1985. (orig., 1977).

Moore, Walter L., Jr. "Catholic Teacher and Anabaptist Pupil: The Relationship Between John Eck and Balthasar Hubmaier." *Archive for Reformation History* 72 (1981): 68–97.

Moorman, John. *A History of the Franciscan Order from Its Origins to the Year 1517*. Oxford, 1968.

Mormando, Franco. *The Preacher's Demons: Bernardino of Siena and the Social Underworld of Early Renaissance Italy*. Chicago, 1999.

Morvay, Karin and Dagmar Grube. *Bibliographie der deutschen Predigt des Mittelalters: Veröffentliche Predigten*. Münchener Texte und Untersuchungen zur deutschen Literatur des Mittelalters, vol. 47. Munich, 1974.

Motis Dolader, Miguel Angel. *The Expulsion of the Jews from Calatayud 1492–1500: Documents and Regesta*. Sources for the History of the Jews in Spain, vol. 2, The Henk Schussheim Memorial Series. Jerusalem, 1990.

Muir, Edward and Guido Ruggiero, eds. *History From Crime*. Translated by Corrada Biazzo Curry, Margaret A. Gallucci, and Mary M. Gallucci. Selections from *Quaderini Storici*. Baltimore, 1994.

———, eds. *Microhistory and the Lost Peoples of Europe*. Selections from *Quaderini Storici*. Translated by Eren Branch. Baltimore, 1991.

Muldoon, James. *Popes, Lawyers, and Infidels: The Church and the Non-Christian World 1250–1550*. Middle Ages Series. Philadelphia, 1979.

Müller, Arndt. *Die Geschichte der Juden in Nürnberg 1146–1945*. Beiträge zur Geschichte und Kultur der Stadt Nürnberg, vol. 12. Nuremberg, 1968.

Müller, Michael. *Die Annalen und Chroniken in Herzogtum Bayern 1250–1314*. Munich, 1983.

Mundy, John H., and Peter Riesenberg. *The Medieval Town*. An Anvil Original, no. 30. U.S.A., 1958.

Nakriss, Bezalel. *Hebrew Illuminated Manuscripts*. New York, 1974.

Narrenfreiheit: Beiträge zur Fastnachtforschung. Edited by Tübinger Vereinigung für Volkskunde. Schriftenreihe zur bayerischen Landesgeschichte, vol. 77. Tübingen, 1980.

Newman, Louis Israel. *Jewish Influences on Christian Reform Movements*. New York, 1925.

Noonan, John T., Jr. *The Scholastic Analysis of Usury*. Cambridge, Massachussets, 1957.

Nübling, Eugen. *Die Judengemeinden des Mittelalters, insbesondere die Judengemeinde der Reichsstadt Ulm: ein Beitrag zur deutsche Städte- und Wirtschaftsgeschichte Ulm*. Ulm, 1896.

Nyhus, Paul L. *The Franciscans in South Germany, 1400–1530: Reform and Revolution*. Transactions of the American Philosophical Society, New Series, vol. 65, pt. 8. Philadelphia, 1975.

Oakley, Francis. *Natural Law, Conciliarism and Consent in the Late Middle Ages: Studies in Ecclesiastical and Intellectual History*. Variorum Reprint, CS 189. London, 1984.

———. *The Western Church in the Later Middle Ages*. Ithaca, 1979.

Oberman, Heiko Augustinus. *The Harvest of Medieval Theology: Gabriel Biel and Late Medieval Nominalism*. Durham, 1983. [Originally publised as vol. 51 of Untersuchungen des Ludwigs-Uhland-Instituts der Universität Tübingen, 1963].

———. *The Roots of Antisemitism in the Age of Renaissance and Reformation*. Translated by James I. Porter. Philadelphia, 1984. (orig., 1981).

Oexle, Otto Gerhard. "Kulturwissenschaftliche Reflexionen über soziale Gruppen in der mittelalterlichen Gesellschaft: Tönnies, Simmel, Durkheim und Max Weber." In *Die Okzidentale Stadt nach Max Weber: Zum Problem der Zugehörigkeit in Antike und Mittelalter*, edited by Christian Meier (Munich, 1994): 115–159.

O'Malley, John W. *Giles of Viterbo on Church and Reform: A Study in Renaissance Thought*. Studies in Medieval and Reformation Thought, vol. 5. Leiden, 1968.

Overdick, Renate. *Die Rechtliche und wirtschaftliche Stellung der Juden in Südwestdeutschland im 15. und 16. Jahrhundert dargestellt an den Reichsstädten Konstanz und Esslingen und an der Markgrafschaft Baden*. Konstanzer Geschichts- und Rechtsquellen, vol. 15. Constance, 1965.

Overfield, James H. *Humanism and Scholasticism in Late Medieval Germany*. Princeton, 1984.

Owen Hughes, Diane, "Distinguishing Signs: Ear-Rings, Jews and Franciscan Rhetoric in the Italian Renaissance." *Past and Present* 112 (1986): 3–59.

Ozment, Steven. *The Age of Reform 1250–1550: An Intellectual and Religious History of Late Medieval and Reformation Europe*. New Haven, 1980.

———, ed. *The Reformation in Medieval Perspective*. Modern Scholarship on European History Series. Chicago, 1971.

Paas, Martha White. *Population Change, Labor Supply and Agriculture in Augsburg 1480–1618: A Study of Early Demographic-Economic Interactions*. Dissertations in European Economic History. New York, 1981.

Packull, Werner O. "Denck's Alleged Baptism by Hubmaier." *Mennonite Quarterly Review* 47 (1973): 327–338.

Pagden, Anthony. *The Fall of Natural Man: The American Indian and the Origins of Comparative Ethnology*. Cambridge Iberian and Latin American Studies Series. Cambridge, 1982.

Parkes, James. *The Conflict of the Church and the Synagogue: A Study in the Origins of Antisemitism*. New York, 1969. (orig., 1934).

———. *The Jew in the Medieval Community: A Study of his Political and Economic Situation*. History of Antisemitism, vol. 2. London, 1938.

Paton, Bernadette. *Preaching Friars and the Civic Ethos: Siena, 1380–1480*. Westfield Publications in Medieval Studies, vol. 7. London, 1992.

Pfeifer, Volker. *Die Geschichtsschreibung der Reichsstadt Ulm von der Reformation bis zum Untergang des Alten Reiches*. Forschungen zur Geschichte der Stadt Ulm, vol. 17. Ulm, 1981.

Pimenta Ferro Tavares, Maria José. "Expulsion or Integration? The Portuguese Jewish Problem." In *Crisis and Creativity in the Sephardic World: 1391–1648*, edited by Benjamin R. Gampel (New York, 1997): 95–103.

Pirenne, Henri. *Medieval Cities: Their Origins and the Revival of Trade.* Translated by Frank D. Halsey. Princeton, 1952. (orig., 1925).

Pocock, J.G.A. "The Concept of Language and the Metier d'Historien: Some Considerations on Practice." In *The Languages of Political Theory in Early-Modern Europe,* edited by Anthony Pagden. Ideas in Context Series (Cambridge, 1987): 19–38.

Poliakov, Léon. *The History of Antisemitism,* Vol. 1. Translated by Richard Howard. London, 1965 (orig., 1955).

Pressel, Friedrich. *Geschichte der Juden in Ulm: Ein Beitrag zur Wirtschafsgeschichte des Mittelalters.* Ulm, 1873.

Preus, James Samuel. *From Shadow to Promise: Old Testament Interpretation from Augustine to the Young Luther.* Cambridge, Massachussets, 1969.

Rabb, Theodore. *The Struggle for Stability in Early Modern Europe.* Oxford, 1975.

Rabinowicz, Harry. "Rabbi Joseph Colon and the Jewish Ban." *Historia Judaica* 22 (1960): 61–70.

Raphael, David, ed. *The Expulsion 1492 Chronicles: An Anthology of Medieval Chronicles Relating to the Expulsion of the Jews from Spain and Portugal.* North Hollywood, California, 1992.

Rauchfuss, Hermann. *Alte Geschichten und neue Sagen auf Thüringen.* Bad Berka, 1924.

Reichel, Jörn. *Der Spruchdichter Hans Rosenplüt: Literatur und Leben im spätmittelalterlichen Nürnberg.* Stuttgart, 1985.

Reuter, Fritz. *Warmaisa: 1000 Jahre Juden in Worms.* Frankfurt am Main, 1984.

Rinn, Hermann, ed. *Augusta 955-1955: Forschungen und Studien zur Kultur- und Wirtschaftsgeschichte Augsburgs.* Munich, 1955.

Roeder, Anke. *Die Gebärde in Drama des Mittelalters: Osterfeiern, Osterspiele.* Münchener Texte und Untersuchungen zur deutsche Literatur des Mittelalters, vol. 49. Munich, 1974.

Rogers, Elizabeth Frances. *Peter Lombard and the Sacramental System.* New York, 1976.

Roller, Hans-Ulrich. *Der Nürnberger Schembartlauf: Studien zum Fest- und Maskenwesen der späten Mittelalters.* Volksleben, vol. 11. Tübingen, 1965.

Roper, Lyndal. "'The Common Man,' 'The Common Good,' 'Common Women': Gender and Meaning in the German Reformation Commune." *Social History* 12, no. 1 (January 1989): 1–21.

———. "Discipline and Respectability: Prostitution and the Reformation in Augsburg." *History Workshop* 19 (Spring 1985): 3–28.

———. *The Holy Household: Women and Morals in Reformation Augsburg.* Oxford Studies in Social History. Oxford, 1989.

Rörig, Fritz. *The Medieval Town.* Translated by Don Bryant. Berkeley, 1967. (orig., 1955).

Rosensweig, Bernard. *Ashkenazic Jewry in Transition.* Waterloo, Ontario, 1975.

———. "Taxation in the Late Middle Ages in Germany and Austria." *Diné Israel: An Annual of Jewish Law, Past and Present* XII (1984–1985): 49–93.

Rosser, Gervase "Communities of Parish and Guild in the Late Middle Ages." In *Parish, Church and People: Local Studies in Lay Religion 1350–1750,* edited by S.J. Wright (London, 1988): 29–55.

Roth, Norman. *Conversos, Inquisition, and the Expulsion of the Jews from Spain.* Madison, 1995.

Rowan, Steven W. "Ulrich Zasius and the Baptism of Jewish Children." *Sixteenth Century Journal* 6 (1975): 3–25.

———. "Urban Communities: Rulers and Ruled." In *Handbook of European History 1400-1600: Late Middle Ages, Renaissance and Reformation,* Vol. 1, edited by Thomas A. Brady, Jr., Heiko A. Oberman, and James D. Tracy (Leiden, 1996): 197–229.

Rubin, Miri. *Corpus Christi: The Eucharist in Late Medieval Culture.* Cambridge, 1991.

———. "Small Groups: Identity and Solidarity in the Late Middle Ages." In *Enterprise and Individuals in Fifteenth-Century England*, edited by Jennifer Kermode (Great Britain, 1991): 132–150.

Rump, Hans-Uwe. *Jüdisches Kulturmuseum Augsburg*. Bayerische Museen, vol. 6. Munich, 1987.

Rupprich, Hans. *Die deutsche Literatur vom späten Mittelalter bis zum Barock, Volume 1: Das ausgehende Mittealter, Humanismus und Renaissance 1370–1520*. Geschichte der deutschen Literatur von den Anfängen bis zur Gegenwart, vol. 4:1. Munich, 1970.

Russell, Frederick H. *The Just War in the Middle Ages*. Cambridge Studies in Medieval Life and Thought, 3rd series, vol. 8. Cambridge, 1975.

Sabean, David. *Power in the Blood: Popular Culture and Village Discourse in Early Modern Germany*. Cambridge, 1988. (orig., 1984).

Sachsse, Carl. *D. Balthasar Hubmaier als Theologe*. Berlin, 1973. (orig., 1914).

Sahlins, Marshall. *Islands of History*. Chicago, 1985.

Said, Edward W. *Orientalism*. New York, 1979. (orig., 1978).

Saperstein, Marc. *Jewish Preaching 1200–1800: An Anthology*. Yale Judaica Series, vol. 26. New Haven, 1989.

Schachar, Isaiah. *The Judensau: A Medieval Anti-Jewish Motif and Its History*. Warburg Institute Survey, vol. 5. London, 1974.

Schatzmiller, Joseph. "Tumultus et Rumor in Sinagoga: An Aspect of Social Life of Provencal Jews in the Middle Ages." *Association for Jewish Studies Review* 2 (1977): 227–255.

Scheid, Elie. "Joselmann de Rosheim," *Revue des Étude Juives* 13 (1886): 62–84 and 248–259.

Scherer, Johann Egid. *Die Rechtsverhältnisse der Juden in den deutsch-österreichischen Ländern, mit einer Einleitung über die Principien der Judengesetzgebung des Mittelalters*. Beiträge zur Geschichte des Judenrechtes im Mittelalter, vol. 1. Leipzig, 1901.

Schilling, Heinz. *Die Stadt in der Frühen Neuzeit*. Enzyklopädie deutscher Geschichte, vol. 42. Munich, 1993.

Schmale, Franz-Josef. *Funktion und Formen Mittelalterlicher Geschichtsschreibung: Eine Einführung*. Geschichtswissenschaft Series. Darmstadt, 1985.

Schmidt, Heinrich. *Die deutschen Städtechroniken als Spiegel des bürgerlichen Selbstverständnisses im Spätmittelalter*. Göttingen, 1958.

Schmidt, Rolf. "Judeneide in Augsburg und Regensburg." *Zeitschrift der Savigny-Stiftung für Rechtsgeschichte* 93 (1976): 322–339.

Schnackenburg, Rudolf. *Baptism in the Thought of Saint Paul: A Study in Pauline Theology*. Oxford, 1964.

Schnith, Karl. "Reichsstädtisches Bewusstsein in der Augsburger Chronistik des Spätmittelalters." In *Festschrift für Andreas Kraus zum 60. Geburtstag*. Edited by Pankraz Fried. Münchener historische Studien, Abteilung bayerische Geschichte, vol. 10 (Kallmunz, 1982): 79–93.

Schubert, Ernst. *Einführung in die deutsche Geschichte im Spätmittelalter*. Grundprobleme der deutschen Geschichte. Darmstadt, 1998 (orig., 1992).

Schwarzfuchs, Simon. *A Concise History of the Rabbinate*. Jewish Society and Culture Series. Oxford, 1993.

Scott, James C. *Weapons of the Weak: Everyday Forms of Peasant Resistance*. New Haven, 1985.

Scott, Tom. "Reformation and Peasants' War in Waldshut and Environs: A Structural Analysis." *Archiv für Reformationsgeschichte* 19 (1978): 82–102; 20 (1979): 140–168.

———. *Regional Identity and Economic Change: The Upper Rhine, 1450–1600*. Oxford, 1997.

Scribner, R.W. "Anticlericalism and the Cities." In *Anticlericalism in Late Medieval and Early Modern Europe*, edited by Peter A. Dykema and Heiko A. Oberman (New York, 1993): 147–166.

——. "Communities and the Nature of Power." In *Germany: A New Social and Economic History, 1450–1630*, edited by R.W. Scribner (London, 1996): 291–325.

——. *For the Sake of Simple Folk: Popular Propaganda for the German Reformation.* Cambridge Studies in Oral and Literate Culture, vol. 2. Cambridge, 1981.

——, ed. *Germany: A New Social and Economic History, 1450–1630.* London, 1996.

Seibt, Ferdinand. "Die Hussitenzeit als Kulturepoche." *Historische Zeitschrift* 195 (1962): 21–62.

Seifert, Arno. *Logik zwischen Scholastik und Humanismus: Das Kommentarwerk Johann Ecks.* Humanistische Bibliothek, Reihe 1, Abhandlung, vol. 31. Munich, 1978.

Sherwin, Byron. *Mystical Theology and Social Dissent: The Life and Works of Judah Loew of Prague.* The Littman Library of Jewish Civilization. New Jersey, 1982.

Shohet, David Menaham. *The Jewish Court in the Middle Ages: Studies in Jewish Jurisprudence according to the Talmud, Geonic, and Medieval German Responsa.* Studies in Jewish Jurisprudence, vol. 3. New York, 1974. (orig., 1931).

Sieh-Burens, Katarina. *Oligarchie, Konfession und Politik im 16. Jahrhundert: Zur Sozialen Verflechtung der Augsburger Burgermeister und Stadtpfleger 1518–1618.* Schriften der Philosophischen Fakultät Universität Augsburg, no. 29. Munich, 1986.

Simonsohn, Shlomo. *The Apostolic See and the Jews: Volume 2, Documents 1394–1464.* Studies and Texts (Pontifical Institute of Medieval Studies), no. 95. Toronto, 1989.

——. *The Apostolic See and the Jews: Volume 3, Documents 1464–1521.* Studies and Texts (Pontifical Institute of Medieval Studies), no. 99. Toronto, 1990.

Skinner, Quentin. *The Foundations of Modern Political Thought.* 2 vols. Cambridge, 1978.

——. "Meaning and Understanding in the History of Ideas." *History and Theory* 8 (1969): 3–53.

Smalley, Beryl. *Historians in the Middle Ages.* Oxford, 1974.

——. *The Study of the Bible of the Middle Ages.* Oxford, 1983. (orig., 1941).

Soloveitchick, Hayim. "Can Halakhic Texts Talk History?" *Association for Jewish Studies Review* 3 (1978): 152–196.

——. "Pawnbroking: A Study in *Ribbit* and of the Halakah in Exile." *Proceedings of the American Academy of Jewish Research* 38/39 (1972): 203–268.

Southern, R.W. "Lanfranc of Bec and Berengar of Tours." In *Studies in Medieval History Presented to F.M. Powicke*, edited by R.W. Hunt, W.A. Pantin, and R.W. Southern (Oxford, 1948): 27–48.

Spitz, Lewis. *The Protestant Reformation, 1517–1559.* New York, 1985.

Spriewald, Ingeborg. *Literatur zwischen Hören und Lesen: Wandel von Funktion und Rezeption im späten Mittelalter. Fallstudien zu Beheim, Folz und Sachs.* Berlin, 1990.

Stallybrass, Peter and Allon White. *The Politics and Poetics of Transgression.* Ithaca, 1986.

Starn, Randolph. "Meaning Levels in the Theme of Historical Decline." *History and Theory: Studies in the Philosophy of History* 14: 1 (1975): 1–31.

Stegmuller, Friedrich. *Repertorium Biblicum Medii Aevi.* 2 vols. Madrid, 1950.

——. *Repertorium Commentariorum in Sententias Petri Lombardi.* 2 vols. Würtzburg, 1947.

Steiman, Sidney. *Custom and Survival: A Study of the Life and Works of Rabbi Jacob Molin Known as Maharil (c. 1360–1427) and his Influence in Establishing the Ashkenazic Minhag.* New York, 1963.

Stein, Isaak. *Die Juden der schwäbischen Reichsstädte im Zeitalter König Sigmunds (1410–1437).* Berlin, 1902.

Stein, Siegfried. "Beiträge zur Geschichte der Juden in Deutschland im 14. Jahrhundert: Unter Besonderer Beruchsichtung der Einschlagigen Responsenliteratur." Ph.D. Dissertation, University of Vienna, 1930.

——. "Interest Taken by Jews from Gentiles: An Evolution of Source Material." *Journal of Semitic Studies* 1 (1956): 141–164.

Steinmetz, David. "The Baptism of John and the Baptism of Jesus in Huldrych Zwingli." In *Continuity and Discontinuity in Church History: Essays Presented to George Huntston*

Williams on the Occasion of his 65th Birthday, edited by F. Forrester Church and Timothy George. Studies in the History of Christian Thought, vol. 19 (Leiden, 1979): 169–181.

———. "Scholasticism and Radical Reform: Nominalist Motifs in the Theology of Balthasar Hubmaier." *Mennonite Quarterly Review* 45 (1971): 123–144.

Steinthal, Fritz Leopold. *Geschichte der Augsburger Juden im Mittelalter*. Berlin, 1911.

Stern, Moritz. "Joselmann von Rosheim und seine Nachkommen," *Zeitschrift für die Geschichte der Juden in Deutschland* 3 (1889): 65–74.

Stern, Selma Stern. *Josel of Rosheim: Commander of Jewry in the Holy Roman Empire of the German Nation*. Translated by Gertrude Hirschler. Philadelphia, 1965. (orig., 1959).

Stobbe, Otto. *Die Juden in Deutschland während des Mittelalters in politischer, sozialer und rechtlicher Beziehung*. Braunschweig, 1866.

Stock, Brian. *The Implications of Literacy: Written Language and Models of Interpretation in the Eleventh and Twelfth Centuries*. Princeton, 1983.

Stow, Kenneth R. *Alienated Minority: The Jews of Medieval Latin Europe*. Cambridge, Massachussets, 1992.

———. "Holy Body, Holy Society: Conflicting Medieval Structural Conceptions." In *Sacred Space: Shrine, City, Land*, edited by Benjamin Z. Kedar and R.J. Zwi Werblowsky (New York, 1998): 151–171.

Strassburger, Ferdinand. "Zur Geschichte der Juden von Ulm nach Responsum 147 des Jacob Weil." In *Festschrift zum 70. Geburtstage des Oberkirchenrats Dr. [Theodor] Kroner*, edited by Association of Württemberg Rabbis (Breslau, 1917): 224–236.

Straus, Raphael. *Die Judengemeinde Regensburg im ausgehenden Mittelalter, auf Grund der Quellen kritisch untersucht und neu dargestellt*. Heidelberger Abhandlungen zur mittleren und neueren Geschichte, no. 61. Heidelberg, 1932.

———. *Regensburg and Augsburg*. Translated by Felix N. Gerson. Jewish Communities Series. Philadelphia, 1939.

Strauss, Gerald. *Law, Resistance, and the State: The Opposition to Roman Law in Reformation Germany*. Princeton, 1986.

———. *Nuremberg in the Sixteenth Century*. New Dimensions in History; Historical Cities Series. New York, 1966.

Strieder, Jakob. *Zur Genesis des modernen Kapitalismus: Forschungen zur Enstehung der grossen bürgerlichen Kapitalvermogen am Ausgänge des Mittelalters und zu Beginn der Neuzeit, zunächst in Augsburg*. Burst Franklin Research and Source Works Series, no. 236. Munich, 1935. (2nd ed.) (orig., 1903).

Taylor, Larissa. *Soldiers of Christ: Preaching in Late Medieval and Reformation France*. Oxford, 1992.

Teich, Shmuel. *The Rishonim: Biographical Sketches of the Prominent Early Rabbinic Sages and Leaders from the Tenth to the Fifteenth Centuries*. Artscroll History Series. New York, 1991.

Thrupp, Sylvia. *Society and History: Essays*. Ann Arbor, 1977.

Tierney, Brian. *Foundations of the Conciliar Theory: The Contribution of the Medieval Canonists from Gratian to the Great Schism*. Cambridge Studies in Medieval Life and Thought, new series, vol. 4. Cambridge, 1955.

Toaff, Ariel. *The Jews in Umbria, Volume 3: 1484–1736*. Studies Post Biblica, vol. 45. Documentary History of the Jews of Italy, vol. 10. Leiden, 1994.

Toch, Michael. "The Jewish Community of Nuremberg in the Year 1489: Social and Demographic Structure." *Zion* 45: 60–72. [Hebrew].

———. *Die Juden im mittelalterlichen Reich*. Enzyklopädie deutscher Geschichte, vol. 44. Munich, 1998.

———. *Die Nürnberger Mittelschichten im 15. Jahrhundert*. Nürnberger Werkstücke zur Stadt- und Landesgeschichte, vol. 26. Nuremberg, 1978.

———. "Siedlungsstruktur der Juden Mitteleuropas im Wandel vom Mittelalter zur

Neuzeit." In *Juden in der christlichen Umwelt während des späten Mittelalters*, edited by Alfred Haverkamp and Franz-Josef Ziwes (Berlin, 1992): 29–39.

———. "Zur wirtschaftlichen Lage und Tätigkeit der Juden im deutschen Sprachraum des Spätmittelalters." In *Judengemeinden in Schwaben im Kontext des Alten Reiches*, edited by Rolf Kießling (Berlin, 1995): 39–50.

Trachtenberg, Joshua. *The Devil and the Jews*. New York, 1961. (orig., 1943).

———. *Jewish Magic and Superstition: A Study in Folk Religion*. New York, 1939.

Trexler, Richard C. *Public Life in Renaissance Florence*. Studies in Social Discontinuity. Ithaca, 1980.

Troeltsch, Ernst. *The Social Teachings of the Christian Churches*. Vol. 2. Translated by Olive Wyon. Chicago, 1981. (orig., 1922).

Van Engen, John. "The Church in the Fifteenth Century." In *Handbook of European History 1400–1600: Late Middle Ages, Renaissance and Reformation*, Vol. 1, edited by Thomas A. Brady, Jr., Hieko A. Oberman, and James D. Tracy (Leiden, 1996): 305–330.

Voltmer, Ernst. "Zur Geschichte der Juden im spätmittelalterlichen Speyer: Die Judengemeinde im Spannungsfeld zwischen König, Bischof und Stadt." In *Zur Geschichte der Juden im Deutschland des späten Mittelalters und der Frühen Neuzeit*, edited by Alfred Haverkamp (Stuttgart, 1981): 94–121.

Weber, Dieter. *Geschichtsschreibung in Augsburg: Hektor Mülich und die Reichsstädte Chronistik des Spätmittelalters*. Abhandlungen zur Geschichte der Stadt Augsburg, vol. 30. Augsburg, 1984.

Weinryb, Bernhard Dov. "Responsa as a Source for History (Methodological Problems)." In *Essays Presented to Rabbi Israel Brodie on the Occasion of his 70th Birthday*, edited by H.J. Zimmels, J. Rabbinowitz, and I. Finestein. London Jews' College Publications, no. 30 (London, 1967): 399–417.

Welt im Umbruch: Augsburg zwischen Renaissance und Barok. 3 vols. Ausstellung der Stadt Augsburg in Zusammenarbeit mit der Evangelisch-Lutherischen Landeskirche anläßlich des 450. Jubiläums der Confessio Augustana. Augsburg, 1980–1981.

Wenninger, Markus J. *Man Bedarf keiner Juden Mehr: Ursachen und Hintergründe ihrer Vertreibung aus den deutschen Reichsstädten im 15. Jahrhundert*. Archiv für Kulturgeschichte, no. 14. Vienna, 1981.

Wenzel, Edith. *"Do worden die Judden alle geschant:" Rolle und Funktion der Juden in spätmittelalterlichen Spielen*. Forschungen zur Geschichte der älteren deutschen Literatur, vol. 14. Munich, 1992.

———. "Zur Judenproblematik bei Hans Folz." *Zeitschrift für deutsche Philologie* 101 (1982): 79–104.

Wiesemann, Falk. *Bibliographie zur Geschichte der Juden in Bayern*. Bibliographien zur deutsch-jüdischen Geschichte, vol. 1. Munich, 1989.

Wilhelm, Johannes. *Augsburger Wandmalerei 1368–1530: Künstler, Handwerker und Zunft*. Abhandlungen zur Geschichte der Stadt Augsburg, vol. 29. Augsburg, 1983.

Williams, George H. *The Radical Reformation*. Philadelphia, 1962.

Windhorst, Christof. *Täuferisches Taufverständnis: Balthasar Hubmaiers Lehre zwischen traditioneller und Reformatorischer Theologie*. Studies in Medieval and Reformation Thought, vol. 16. Leiden, 1976.

Wulf, Christine, ed. *Eine Volksprächige Laienbibel des 15. Jahrhunderts: Untersuchung und Teiledition der Handschrift Nürnberg, Stadtbibliothek, Ms. Solg. 16,2'0*. Münchner Texte und Untersuchungen zur deutschen Literatur des Mittelalters, vol. 98. Munich, 1991.

Würfel, Andreas. *Historische Nachrichten von der Juden-Gemeinde in der Reichstadt Nürnberg*. Nuremberg, 1755.

Yardeni, Myriam. *Anti-Jewish Mentalities in Early Modern Europe*. Studies in Judaism Series. Lanham, Maryland, 1990.

Yerushalmi, Yosef Hayim. "Exile and Expulsion in Jewish History." In *Crisis and Creativity* in the Sephardic World: 1391–1648, edited by Benjamin R. Gampel (New York, 1997): 3–22.

Yoder, John. "Balthasar Hubmaier and the Beginnings of Swiss Anabaptism." *Mennonite Quarterly Review* 33 (1959): 5–17.

Yuval, Israel. "Juden, Hussiten und Deutsche: Nach einer hebräischen Chronik." In *Juden in der christlichen Umwelt während des späten Mittelalters*, edited by Alfred Haverkamp and Franz-Josef Ziwes (Berlin, 1992): 59–102.

———. *Scholars in Their Time: The Religious Leadership of German Jewry in the Late Middle Ages*. Jerusalem, 1988. [Hebrew].

Zanfran, Eric M. "An Alleged Case of Image Desecration by the Jews and its Representation in Art: The Virgin of Cambron." *Journal of Jewish Art* 2 (1975): 62–71.

Zawart, Anscar. *The History of Franciscan Preaching and Franciscan Preachers (1209–1927): A Bio-Bibliographical Study*. Franciscan Studies, no. 7. New York, 1928.

Zika, Charles. "Hosts, Processions and Pilgrimages: Controlling the Sacred in Fifteenth-Century Germany," *Past and Present* 118 (1988): 25–64.

Zimmer, Eric. *Harmony and Discord: An Analysis of the Decline of Jewish Self-Government in Fifteenth-Century Central Europe*. New York, 1970.

Ziwes, Franz-Josef. *Studien zur Geschichte der Juden im mittleren Rheingebiet während des hohen und späten Mittelalters*. Forschungen zur Geschichte der Juden, Abteilung A, Abhandlungen, vol. 1. Hanover, 1995.

Zoepfl, Friedrich. *Das Bistum Augsburg und seine Bischöfe im Reformationsjahrhundert*. 2 vols. Geschichte des Bistums Augsburg und seiner Bischöfe, vol. 2. Augsburg, 1969.

Zorn, Wolfgang. *Augsburg: Geschichte einer deutschen Stadt*. Augsburg, 1972. (orig., 1955).

Index

STUDIES IN CENTRAL EUROPEAN HISTORIES

PUBLISHED